# SAP PRESS e-books

Print or e-book, Kindle or iPad, workplace or airplane: Choose where and how to read your SAP PRESS books! You can now get all our titles as e-books, too:

- ▶ By download and online access
- ▶ For all popular devices
- ▶ And, of course, DRM-free

Convinced? Then go to **www.sap-press.com** and get your e-book today.

# SAP HANA® Certification Guide

 **PRESS**

SAP PRESS is a joint initiative of SAP and Rheinwerk Publishing. The know-how offered by SAP specialists combined with the expertise of the Rheinwerk Publishing house offers the reader expert books in the field. SAP PRESS features first-hand information and expert advice, and provides useful skills for professional decision-making.

SAP PRESS offers a variety of books on technical and business related topics for the SAP user. For further information, please visit our website: *www.sap-press.com*.

Bjarne Berg, Penny Silva
SAP HANA: An Introduction (4th edition)
2016, approx. 610 pages, hardcover and e-book
*www.sap-press.com/4160*

James Wood
Getting Started with SAP HANA Cloud Platform
2015, 519 pages, hardcover and e-book
*www.sap-press.com/3638*

Bilay, Gutsche, Stiehl
SAP HANA Cloud Integration
2016, 420 pages, hardcover and e-book
*www.sap-press.com/3979*

Ankisettipalli, Chen, Wankawala
SAP HANA Advanced Data Modeling
2016, 392 pages, hardcover and e-book
*www.sap-press.com/3863*

Rudi de Louw

# SAP HANA® Certification Guide

Application Associate Exam

Rheinwerk®
Publishing

Bonn • Boston

**Editor** Sarah Frazier
**Acquisitions Editor** Kelly Grace Weaver
**Copyeditor** Melinda Rankin
**Cover Design** Graham Geary
**Image Credit** Shutterstock.com/229432660/© kovadenys
**Layout Design** Vera Brauner
**Production** Graham Geary
**Typesetting** SatzPro, Krefeld (Germany)
**Printed and bound in** the United States of America, on paper from sustainable sources

ISBN 978-1-4932-1230-9
© 2016 by Rheinwerk Publishing, Inc., Boston (MA)
1$^{st}$ edition 2016

**Library of Congress Cataloging-in-Publication Data**
Names: De Louw, Rudi.
Title: SAP HANA certification guide : application associate exam / Rudi de Louw.
Description: 1st edition. | Bonn ; Boston : Rheinwerk Publishing, 2016. | Includes index.
Identifiers: LCCN 2015045017 (print) | LCCN 2016000774 (ebook) | ISBN 9781493212309 (print : alk. paper) | ISBN 9781493212323 (print and ebook : alk. paper) | ISBN 9781493212316 (ebook)
Subjects: LCSH: Relational databases--Examinations--Study guides. | Business enterprises--Computer networks--Examinations--Study guides. | SAP HANA (Electronic resource)--Examinations--Study guides. | Computer programmers--Certification.
Classification: LCC QA76.9.D32 D45 2016 (print) | LCC QA76.9.D32 (ebook) | DDC 005.75/6--dc23
LC record available at http://lccn.loc.gov/2015045017

# Contents at a Glance

1    SAP HANA Certification Track—Overview ............................... 23

2    SAP HANA Training .................................... 35

3    Architecture and Deployment Scenarios ................................. 61

4    Information Modeling Concepts ............................... 101

5    Information Modeling Tools ...................................... 149

6    Information Views ...................................... 181

7    Advanced Information Modeling ............................ 223

8    SQL and SQLScript ....................................... 269

9    Text, Spatial, and Predictive Modeling ..................... 311

10   Optimization of Information Models ........................ 341

11   Administration of Information Models ....................... 367

12   SAP HANA Live ......................................... 403

13   Security .................................... 433

14   Data Provisioning ................................... 467

15   Utilization of Information Models ........................... 513

# Dear Reader,

I write this optimistically. I write this in the hopes that after months of hard work, long nights, and way too many email exchanges initiated by yours truly (sorry Rudi!), that Rudi will finally be able to say: "See, here it is! The fruits of my labor; the sweat from my brow. Take it!"

If this book has taught me anything (besides editors and authors make great teams), it's that SAP HANA is still growing, and sometimes it's a mad dash to keep up. As Rudi can tell you, just when you think a chapter is ready to go, something is updated. However, with a little luck and a whole lot of elbow grease, over the next week this book will slide feet first into the finish line.

But, you don't need me to tell you that the world of SAP HANA is constantly shifting. Like us, you're in the business of staying on top of the latest SAP HANA has to offer. Carefully crafted to prepare test-takers for the exam, this book is your first step in staying one step ahead of the competition and furthering your career. So, as you prepare for the big test, take solace in the fact that you've come to the right place, and, of course, Rudi and I are rooting for you.

What did you think about *SAP HANA Certification Guide: Application Associate Exam*? Your comments and suggestions are the most useful tools to help us make our books the best they can be. Please feel free to contact me and share any praise or criticism you may have.

Thank you for purchasing a book from SAP PRESS!

**Sarah Frazier**
Editor, SAP PRESS

Rheinwerk Publishing
Boston, MA

*sarahf@rheinwerk-publishing.com*
*www.sap-press.com*

# Contents

Acknowledgments ........................................................................... 15
Preface ....................................................................................... 17

## 1  SAP HANA Certification Track—Overview ............................ 23

Who This Book Is For ................................................................... 24
SAP HANA Certifications .............................................................. 25
   Associate-Level Certification ................................................. 27
   Professional-Level Certification .............................................. 28
   Specialist-Level Certification ................................................. 28
SAP HANA Application Associate Certification Exam ...................... 29
   Exam Objective .................................................................. 31
   Exam Structure .................................................................. 31
   Exam Process .................................................................... 33
Summary ................................................................................... 34

## 2  SAP HANA Training ............................................................. 35

SAP Education Training Courses ................................................... 36
   Training Courses for SAP HANA Certifications ......................... 37
   Additional SAP HANA Training Courses .................................. 38
Other Sources of Information ....................................................... 39
   SAP Help ........................................................................... 39
   hana.sap.com and SAP Community Network ........................... 41
   SAP HANA Academy ............................................................ 41
   openSAP and openHPI ........................................................ 44
Hands-On with SAP HANA .......................................................... 46
   Where to Get an SAP HANA System ...................................... 46
   Project Examples ............................................................... 52
   Where to Get Data ............................................................. 54
Exam Questions ......................................................................... 56
   Types of Questions ............................................................. 56
   Elimination Technique ......................................................... 58
   Bookmark Questions ........................................................... 59
General Examination Strategies .................................................... 59
Summary ................................................................................... 60

## 3    Architecture and Deployment Scenarios ................................... 61

Objectives of This Portion of the Test .............................. 62
Key Concepts Refresher ............................................... 63
   In-Memory Technology ........................................... 63
   Architecture and Approach ...................................... 69
   Deployment Scenarios ........................................... 79
Important Terminology ................................................ 89
Practice Questions ................................................... 91
Practice Question Answers and Explanations ........................... 96
Takeaway ............................................................. 99
Summary .............................................................. 99

## 4    Information Modeling Concepts ................................ 101

Objectives of This Portion of the Test .............................. 102
Key Concepts Refresher ............................................... 103
   Tables ......................................................... 103
   Views .......................................................... 103
   Cardinality .................................................... 106
   Joins .......................................................... 107
   Core Data Services Views ....................................... 117
   Cube ........................................................... 119
   Information Views .............................................. 122
   Using Information Views ........................................ 124
   Other Modeling Artifacts ....................................... 127
   Semantics ...................................................... 132
   Hierarchies .................................................... 132
   Best Practices and Modeling Guidelines ......................... 134
Important Terminology ................................................ 135
Practice Questions ................................................... 136
Practice Question Answers and Explanations ........................... 144
Takeaway ............................................................. 147
Summary .............................................................. 148

## 5    Information Modeling Tools ................................. 149

Objectives of This Portion of the Test .............................. 150
Key Concepts Refresher ............................................... 151
   SAP HANA Studio ................................................ 151

SAP HANA Web-Based Development Workbench ................................... 170
Important Terminology ................................................ 174
Practice Questions ................................................ 175
Practice Question Answers and Explanations ................................ 178
Takeaway ................................................ 179
Summary ................................................ 180

## 6 Information Views ................................................ 181

Objectives of This Portion of the Test ................................ 182
Key Concepts Refresher ................................................ 183
Data Sources for Information Views ........................................ 184
Calculation Views: Type Dimension, Type Cube, and Type Cube with
Star Join ................................................ 185
Working with Nodes ................................................ 197
Semantics Node ................................................ 202
Attribute Views and Calculation Views of Type Dimension ....................... 205
Analytic Views and Calculation Views of Type Cube with Star Join ........... 208
Migrating Attribute and Analytic Views ................................ 209
Important Terminology ................................................ 213
Practice Questions ................................................ 214
Practice Question Answers and Explanations ................................ 218
Takeaway ................................................ 220
Summary ................................................ 221

## 7 Advanced Information Modeling ................................ 223

Objectives of this Portion of the Test ................................ 224
Key Concepts Refresher ................................................ 225
Calculated Columns ................................................ 225
Restricted Columns ................................................ 231
Filters ................................................ 236
Variables ................................................ 238
Input Parameters ................................................ 242
Currency ................................................ 246
Decision Tables ................................................ 250
Hierarchies ................................................ 253
Important Terminology ................................................ 258
Practice Questions ................................................ 260
Practice Question Answers and Explanations ................................ 264

Takeaway ............................................................................ 267
Summary ............................................................................ 268

## 8  SQL and SQLScript ............................................................ 269

Objectives of This Portion of the Test ............................ 271
Key Concepts Refresher ................................................ 271
    SQL ........................................................................ 272
    SQLScript ................................................................ 278
    Views, Functions, and Procedures ........................ 293
    Catching Up with SAP HANA SPS 11 ...................... 295
Important Terminology .................................................. 299
Practice Questions ......................................................... 300
Practice Question Answers and Explanations ............... 306
Takeaway ...................................................................... 309
Summary ....................................................................... 309

## 9  Text, Spatial, and Predictive Modeling ............................ 311

Objectives of This Portion of the Test ............................ 313
Key Concepts Refresher ................................................ 313
    Text ......................................................................... 314
    Spatial ..................................................................... 323
    Predictive ................................................................ 327
Important Terminology .................................................. 332
Practice Questions ......................................................... 333
Practice Question Answers and Explanations ............... 337
Takeaway ...................................................................... 338
Summary ....................................................................... 339

## 10 Optimization of Information Models ............................ 341

Objectives of This Portion of the Test ............................ 342
Key Concepts Refresher ................................................ 343
    Architecture and Performance ............................... 343
    Redesigned and Optimized Applications ............... 344
    Information Modeling Techniques ......................... 345
    Optimization Tools ................................................. 346
    Best Practices for Optimization ............................. 358

Important Terminology ............................................................ 359
Practice Questions ................................................................ 360
Practice Question Answers and Explanations ............................. 363
Takeaway .............................................................................. 365
Summary ............................................................................... 366

**11  Administration of Information Models** ...................... **367**

Objectives of This Portion of the Test ...................................... 368
Key Concepts Refresher .......................................................... 369
   Validating and Activating Information Models ....................... 369
   Transporting Information Models ......................................... 374
   Core Data Services ............................................................ 383
   Refactoring Information Models .......................................... 383
   Documenting Information Models ........................................ 387
   Translating Information Models ........................................... 389
Important Terminology ............................................................ 390
Practice Questions ................................................................ 392
Practice Question Answers and Explanations ............................. 397
Takeaway .............................................................................. 400
Summary ............................................................................... 401

**12  SAP HANA Live** ........................................................ **403**

Objectives of This Portion of the Test ...................................... 404
Key Concepts Refresher .......................................................... 405
   Background Information ...................................................... 405
   Architecture ..................................................................... 409
   Virtual Data Model ............................................................ 410
   SAP HANA Live Views ........................................................ 412
   Installation and Administration ........................................... 413
   SAP HANA Live Browser—Browse and Use Views .................. 415
   SAP HANA Live Extension Assistant—Modify Views ............... 422
Important Terminology ............................................................ 424
Practice Questions ................................................................ 425
Practice Question Answers and Explanations ............................. 428
Takeaway .............................................................................. 430
Summary ............................................................................... 430

## 13 Security .......................................................................................... 433

Objectives of This Portion of the Test ........................................ 434
Key Concepts Refresher ............................................................... 435
    Usage and Concepts ................................................................. 435
    Users ......................................................................................... 439
    Roles ......................................................................................... 443
    Privileges .................................................................................. 446
    Testing Security ....................................................................... 458
Important Terminology .................................................................. 459
Practice Questions ......................................................................... 461
Practice Question Answers and Explanations .............................. 463
Takeaway ....................................................................................... 465
Summary ........................................................................................ 465

## 14 Data Provisioning ......................................................................... 467

Objectives of This Portion of the Test ........................................ 468
Key Concepts Refresher ............................................................... 469
    Concepts ................................................................................... 470
    SAP Data Services .................................................................... 476
    SAP LT Replication Server ........................................................ 478
    SAP Replication Server ............................................................. 484
    SAP Direct Extractor Connection ............................................ 485
    SAP HANA Smart Data Access ................................................ 488
    SAP HANA Enterprise Information Management ..................... 495
    SAP HANA Smart Data Streaming ......................................... 497
    Flat Files or Microsoft Excel Datasheets ................................. 500
    Web Services (OData and REST) .............................................. 502
Important Terminology .................................................................. 502
Practice Questions ......................................................................... 505
Practice Question Answers and Explanations .............................. 508
Takeaway ....................................................................................... 510
Summary ........................................................................................ 511

## 15 Utilization of Information Models ............................................. 513

Objectives of this Portion of the Test ......................................... 514
Key Concepts Refresher ............................................................... 515
    Business Intelligence Concepts ............................................... 515

Business Intelligence Tools for Microsoft Office Integration ....................... 522
Business Intelligence Tools for Applications and Dashboards ..................... 527
Business Intelligence Tools for Data Discovery ......................................... 529
Business Intelligence Tools for Reporting .................................................. 532
Choosing the Right Business Intelligence Tool .......................................... 533
Alternative Consumption Methods for SAP HANA ................................... 534
Important Terminology ................................................................................. 538
Practice Questions ......................................................................................... 538
Practice Question Answers and Explanations .............................................. 541
Takeaway ....................................................................................................... 542
Summary ........................................................................................................ 542

The Author ..................................................................................................... 543
Index .............................................................................................................. 545

# Acknowledgments

*"…Write the vision, and make it plain upon tables, that he may run that readeth it."*
– Habakkuk 2:2, King James Bible

SAP PRESS had the *vision* for a book on the SAP HANA certification exam. It was my privilege to *write* it and to make it *plain*. And it is my wish that every reader of this book *run* with the knowledge and understanding gained from it.

In my more than five year journey with SAP HANA, I have met hundreds of people, all passionate about SAP HANA. Thank you to all of you!

Some of these people were SAP colleagues that played a pivotal role in my journey. Thank you to Laura King, Colin Banks, Tim Breitwieser, Markus Schunter, Eva Moreno, Estelle de Beer, the pre-sales team, and Wian Terblanche. Thank you to the SAP HANA team at SAP Education for inviting me to be a part of the team, especially Mathias Montag, Mark Green, and Alain Viguie. Thank you to the SAP HANA certification teams I worked with over the years, especially Katrin Rissberger, Thomas Goettsche, and Sheri Schaaf.

This book presented a unique opportunity for me. Therefore, I'd like to say thank you especially to Sarah Frazier, the editor, for your patience and encouragement. Thank you to the entire team at SAP PRESS for making this book happen. Thank you to Werner Steyn and Thomas Jung for helping clarify the latest changes to SAP HANA, and to all my colleagues who encouraged me each time you saw me.

I'm very thankful to all of you: My family, my friends, my colleagues, and my students.

To my readers: I trust that your journey will be even more amazing!

# Preface

The SAP PRESS Certification Series is designed to provide anyone who is preparing to take an SAP certified exam with all of the review, insight, and practice they need to pass the exam. The series is written in practical, easy-to-follow language that provides targeted content that is focused on what you need to know to successfully take your exam.

This book is specifically written for those preparing to take the SAP Certified Application Associate – SAP HANA C_HANAIMP_11 exam, so if you've purchased this book, you're obviously interested in learning how to successfully pass the certification exam. This book will also be helpful to those of you taking the SPS 09 exam (C_HANAIMP151) and SPS 10 delta exam (D_HANAIMP_10). The SAP Certified Application Associate – SAP HANA exam tests the taker in the areas of data modeling. It focuses on core SAP HANA skills, as opposed to skills that are specific to a particular implementation type (e.g., SAP BW on SAP HANA or SAP Business Suite on SAP HANA). The Application Associate test can be taken by anyone who signs up.

Using this book, you will walk away with a thorough understanding of the exam structure and what to expect in taking it. You will receive a refresher on key concepts covered on the exam, and will be able to test your skills via sample practice questions and answers. The book is closely aligned with the course syllabus and the exam structure, so all of the information provided is relevant and applicable to what you need to know to prepare. We explain the SAP products and features using practical examples and straightforward language, so you can prepare for the exam and improve your skills in your day-to-day work as an SAP HANA data modeler. Each book in the series has been structured and designed to highlight what you really need to know.

## Structure of This Book

Each chapter begins with a clear list of the learning objectives, such as:

### Techniques You'll Master

▶ How to prepare for the exam

▶ Understanding the general exam structure

▶ Practice questions and preparation

From there, you'll dive into the chapter and get right into the test objective coverage.

Throughout the book, we've also provided several elements that will help you access useful information:

▶ Tips call out useful information about related ideas and provide practical suggestions for how to use a particular function.

▶ Notes provide other resources to explore or special tools or services from SAP that will help you with the topic under discussion. The following boxes are examples of these elements:

 **Note**

This certification guide covers all topics you need to successfully pass the exam. It provides sample questions similar to those found on the actual exam.

 **Tip**

This book contains screenshots and diagrams to help your understanding of the many information modeling concepts.

Each chapter that covers an exam topic is organized in a similar fashion so you can become familiar with the structure and easily find the information you need. Here's an example of a typical chapter structure:

▶ **Introductory bullets**
The beginning of each chapter discusses the techniques you must master to be considered proficient in the topic for the certification examination.

▶ **Topic introduction**

This section provides you with a general idea of the topic at hand to frame future sections. It also includes objectives for the exam topic covered.

▶ **Real-world scenario**

This part shows a scenario that provides you with a case where these skills would be beneficial to you or your company.

▶ **Objectives**

This section provides you with the necessary information to successfully pass this portion of the test.

▶ **Key concept refresher**

This section outlines the major concepts of the chapter. It identifies the tasks you will need to be able to understand or perform properly to answer the questions on the certification examination.

▶ **Important terminology**

Just prior to the practice examination questions, we provide a section to review important terminology. This may be followed by definitions of various terms from the chapter.

▶ **Practice questions**

The chapter then provides a series of practice questions related to the topic of the chapter. The questions are structured in a similar way to the actual questions on the certification examination.

▶ **Practice question answers and explanations**

Following the practice exercise are the solutions to the practice exercise questions. As part of the answer, we discuss why an answer is considered correct or incorrect.

▶ **Takeaway**

This section provides a takeaway or reviews the areas you should now understand. The refresher section identifies the key concepts in the chapter. We also provide some tips related to the chapter.

▶ **Summary**

Finally, we conclude with a summary of the chapter.

Now that you have an idea of how the book is structured, the following list will dive into the individual topics covered in each chapter of the exam:

▶ **Chapter 1**, SAP HANA Certification Track—Overview, provides a look at the different certifications for SAP HANA: associate, professional, and specialist. It then looks at the general exam objectives, structure, and scoring.

▶ **Chapter 2**, SAP HANA Training, discusses the available training and training material other there for test takers, so you know where to look for answers beyond the book. We identify the SAP Education training courses available for classroom, virtual, and e-learning, in addition to SAP Learning Hub offerings. We then look into additional resources, including official SAP documentation, SAP HANA Academy video tutorials, and more.

▶ **Chapter 3**, Architecture and Deployment Scenarios, walks through the evolution of SAP HANA's in-memory technology and how it addresses the problems of the past, such as slow disk. From there, you are given an overview of the persistence layer, before looking at the different deployment options including cloud deployments.

▶ **Chapter 4**, Information Modeling Concepts, discusses general modeling concepts such as cubes, fact tables, the difference between attributes and measures, in addition to covering general modeling best practices.

▶ **Chapter 5**, Information Modeling Tools, you'll get to know SAP HANA's primary modeling tools, including SAP HANA studio and the SAP HANA web-based development workbench. In addition, you'll learn how to create new information models, tables, and data.

▶ **Chapter 6**, Information Views, looks in depth at the three primary information views in SAP HANA, as well as the tools for migrating old information views, such as analytic and attribute views, to the new standard.

▶ **Chapter 7**, Advanced Information Modeling, takes what we've learned one step further. In this chapter, you'll learn to enhance information views with calculated columns, filter expressions, and more.

▶ **Chapter 8**, SQL and SQLScript, reviews how to enhance SAP HANA models using SQL and SQLScript to create tables, read and filter data, create calculated columns, implement procedures, use user-defined functions, and more.

- **Chapter 9**, Text, Spatial, and Predictive Modeling, looks at more advanced topics, such as creating a text search index, implementing fuzzy search and text analysis, using the key components of spatial processing, and creating predictive analysis models.

- **Chapter 10**, Optimization of Information Models, reviews how to monitor, investigate, and optimize data models in SAP HANA. We'll look at how optimization effects architecture, performance, and information modeling techniques. We'll then dive into the different tools used for optimization including the Explain Plan, Visualize Plan, Administration console, and the Performance Analysis Mode.

- **Chapter 11**, Administration of Information Models, teaches the finer points of data model administration. In this chapter, you'll learn how to validate information models, the difference between design-time and runtime objects, the transport process, the refactoring process, and much more.

- **Chapter 12**, SAP HANA Live, looks at how to adapt pre-delivered content to your own business solutions using SAP HANA Live. You'll learn about SAP HANA Live's different views, and its two primary tools: SAP HANA Live Browser and the SAP HANA Live Extension Assistant.

- **Chapter 13**, Security, discusses how users, roles, and privileges work together. We'll look at the different types of users, template roles, and privileges that are available in the SAP HANA system.

- **Chapter 14**, Data Provisioning, introduces the concepts, tools, and methods for data provisioning in SAP HANA. From SAP Data Services to SAP HANA smart data streaming (SDS).

- **Chapter 15**, Utilization of Information Models, concludes our book with details on basic business intelligence concepts and technologies. We'll look at business intelligence tools for Microsoft Office integration, applications and dashboards, data discovery, and reporting.

## Practice Questions

We want to give you some background on the test questions before you encounter the first few in the chapters. Just like the exam, each question has a basic structure:

- **Actual question**

  Read the question carefully and be sure to consider all the words used in the question because they can impact the answer.

- **Question hint**

  This is not a formal term, but we call it a hint because it will tell you how many answers are correct. If only one is correct, normally it will tell you to choose the correct answer. If more than one is correct, like the actual certification examination, it will indicate the correct number of answers.

- **Answers**

  The answers to select from depend on the question type. The following question types are possible:

  - Multiple response: More than one correct answer is possible.

  - Multiple choice: Only a single answer is correct.

  - True/false: Only a single answer is correct. These types of questions are not used in the exam, but are used in the book to test your understanding.

## Summary

With this certification guide, you'll learn how to approach the content and key concepts highlighted for each exam topic. In addition, you'll have the opportunity to practice with sample test questions in each chapter. After answering the practice questions, you'll be able to review the explanation of the answer, which dissects the question by explaining why the answers are correct or incorrect. The practice questions give you insight into the types of questions you can expect, what the questions look like, and how the answers relate to the question. Understanding the composition of the questions and seeing how the questions and answers work together is just as important as understanding the content. This book gives you the tools and understanding you need to be successful. Armed with these skills, you'll be well on your way to becoming an SAP Certified Application Associate in SAP HANA.

# SAP HANA Certification Track — Overview

## Techniques You'll Master

▶ Understand the different levels of SAP HANA certifications

▶ Find the correct SAP HANA certification exam for you

▶ Learn the scoring structure of the certification exams

▶ Discover how to book your SAP HANA certification exam

Welcome to the exciting world of SAP HANA! SAP as a company is moving at full speed to update all of its solutions to use SAP HANA. Some solutions have even changed completely to better leverage the capabilities of SAP HANA. In many senses, the future of SAP is tied to the SAP HANA platform.

SAP HANA itself is developing at a fast pace to provide all the features required for innovation. Many of the new areas that we see SAP working in, such as cloud and mobile, are enabled because of SAP HANA's many features. The best-known SAP HANA feature is its fast response times. Both cloud and mobile can suffer from latency issues, and they certainly improve with faster response times.

With the large role that SAP HANA now plays, the demand for experienced professionals with SAP HANA knowledge has grown. By purchasing this book, you've taken the first step toward meeting these demands and advancing your career via knowledge of SAP HANA.

 **Note**

There are six different certifications available for SAP HANA, and each focuses on a different topic. The focus of this book is on the SAP Certified Application Associate—SAP HANA certification, which is the most in demand SAP HANA certification.

In this chapter, we'll discuss the target demographic of this book before diving into a discussion of the various SAP HANA certification exams available. We'll then look at the specific exam this book is based on before examining the structure of that exam.

## Who This Book Is For

This book covers SAP HANA from a modeling and application perspective for the C_HANAIMP_11 exam. As such, this book is meant for quite a large group of people from various backgrounds and interests. In a broad sense, this book talks about how to work with data and information—and more people work with information now than ever before.

This book does not go into the more technical topics (e.g., installations, upgrades, monitoring, updates, backups, and transports) addressed by some of the other SAP HANA certifications.

Let's discuss who can benefit from this book:

- *Information modelers* are a core audience group for this book since the main topic of this book is information modeling. This includes people who come from an enterprise data warehouse (EDW) background.

- *Developers* need to create and use information models—whether for SAP applications using ABAP, cloud applications using Java, web services, mobile apps, or new SAP HANA applications using SAPUI5.

- *Database administrators* (DBAs) must understand how to use the new in-memory and columnar database technologies of SAP HANA.

- *Architects* want to understand SAP HANA concepts, get an overview of what SAP HANA entails, and plan new landscapes and solutions using SAP HANA.

- *Data integration* and *data provisioning specialists* have to get data into SAP HANA in an optimal manner.

- *Report-writing professionals* constantly create, find, and consume information models. Often, the need for these information models arises from the reporting needs of business users. An understanding of how to create these information models in SAP HANA will be of great benefit.

- *Data scientists*, or anyone working with big data and data mining, are always looking for faster, smarter, and more efficient ways to get results that can help businesses innovate. SAP HANA has proven that it can certainly contribute to these areas.

- *Technical performance tuning experts* have to understand the intricacies of the new in-memory and columnar database paradigm to fully utilize and leverage the performance that SAP HANA can provide.

If you fit into one or more of these categories, excellent! You're in the right place. Regardless, if you've bought this book in preparation for the exam, our primary goal is to help you succeed; all exam takers are welcome!

## SAP HANA Certifications

There are currently six certification examinations available for SAP HANA, as listed in Table 1.1.

| Certification | Type of Certification | Keyword | SAP Training Courses | Number of Questions | Time in Minutes |
|---|---|---|---|---|---|
| C_HANAIMP | Associate | Modeling | HA100 HA300 | 80 | 180 |
| C_HANATEC | Associate | Technical | HA100 HA200 HA240 HA250 | 80 | 180 |
| P_HANAIMP | Professional | Modeling | Experience | 80 | 180 |
| E_HANAINS | Specialist | Installation | HA200 Guides | 40 | 90 |
| E_HANAAW | Specialist | ABAP | HA100 HA300 HA400 | 40 | 90 |
| E_HANABW | Specialist | BW | BW362 | 40 | 90 |

**Table 1.1**   SAP HANA Certifications

In Table 1.1, you will see that the certifications have different prefixes. The *C* prefix indicates full, core exams for SAP HANA data modeling, the *E* prefix indicates certification exams for specialists, and the *P* prefix denotes a professional-level certification exam.

Table 1.1 also lists the main SAP training courses available for each certification, how many questions will be asked in each certification exam, and how much time is available when taking the examination.

While not shown here, the exams for all certifications have a unique number at the end of their names (e.g., C_HANATEC_11 is the technical certification exam for SAP HANA SPS 11). We'll discuss these different numbers in Table 1.2.

We can divide these different certifications into three categories: associate, professional, and specialist (as shown in the Type of Certification column in Table 1.1). Let's walk through these different categories.

## Associate-Level Certification

The associate-level certification proves that you understand SAP HANA concepts and can apply them in projects. The associate-level certifications are based in theory and are meant for people who are new to SAP HANA.

The question we ask project members when setting up these certifications is: "What would you want candidates to be able to do and understand when they join your project immediately after passing the certification exam?" Understanding the different concepts in SAP HANA and when to use them is important.

There are two types of SAP HANA certifications that fall under the associate-level: C_HANAIMP (modeling) and C_HANATEC (technical).

### C_HANAIMP Modeling Certification

As previous discussed, the *C* prefix indicates the full, core exams for SAP HANA data modeling. *IMP* refers to the *implementation* of SAP HANA applications. This examination consists of 80 questions, and you are given three hours to complete the exam.

The certification does not have any prerequisites. The main SAP training courses that help you prepare for this certification exam are HA100 and HA300. This book and this certification exam is intended for information modelers, database administrators, architects, developers of SAP HANA applications, ABAP and Java developers, people who perform data integration and reporting, those who are interested in technical performance tuning, SAP BW information modelers, data scientists, and/or anyone who wants to understand basic SAP HANA modeling concepts.

This certification exam tests your knowledge in SAP HANA subjects such as architecture, deployment, information modeling, data provisioning (i.e., how to get data into SAP HANA), using information models (e.g., through reporting), security, optimization, administration, and SAP HANA Live.

### C_HANATEC Technical Certification

The C_HANATEC certification exam is meant for technical people such as system administrators, database administrators, SAP Basis people, technical support personnel, and hardware vendors. This certification does not have any prerequisites. The main training course for this exam is HA200.

This certification exam tests your knowledge of SAP HANA installations, updates, upgrades, migrations, system monitoring, administration, configuration, performance tuning, high availability, troubleshooting, backups, and security.

## Professional-Level Certification

The professional certification (P_HANAIMP) proves that you are truly an SAP HANA expert. For the professional exam, there are no official training materials. This exam is more practical and assumes that you have a wealth of experience working with SAP HANA. SAP recommends that you have worked with SAP HANA and information modeling for at least three years prior to taking this exam. Even though there are no training materials, reading this book and the official documentation at *http://help.sap.com/hana*, going through the materials at the links provided in this book, and helping other people solve problems will certainly help you with this type of certification exam.

The latest version of the professional certification exam is P_HANAIMP142, which came out in the second half of 2014. It focuses on SAP HANA SPS 8 and earlier and is a professional version of P_HANAIMP, so the intended audience is roughly the same as that of this book. This will be retired as of June 30th. The P_HANAIMP exam has not been renewed to the latest releases of SAP HANA, and is getting a bit outdated now.

This certification also does not have any prerequisites, so you don't have to take the associate-level certification exam before you take this one. However, we encourage you to take the associate-level exam first as preparation for the professional-level examination. The areas tested in the professional exam are similar to those tested in the associate-level exam. However, where the associate-level examination bases all the questions and answers on the SAP training course materials, the professional certification is more based on practical and real-life experience.

## Specialist-Level Certification

The specialist exams prove that you can apply SAP HANA concepts in your current specialist area. These are for people who are already certified in other areas outside of SAP HANA and want to gain additional knowledge of SAP HANA and how to apply it to their specialties. Such people might have backgrounds in SAP BW or ABAP, for example.

Each specialist exam includes 40 questions, and you have an hour an a half to complete the exam. They all have prerequisites (i.e., you have to be certified in a specialist area before you are allowed to take these SAP HANA certification exams). There are three specialist exams:

▶ **E_HANAINS Installation Certification**
This exam is for technical people who perform installations of SAP HANA and for hardware vendors. This exam requires that you are certified with C_HANATEC. The main training course for this exam is HA200.

▶ **E_HANAAW ABAP Certification**
This is a specialist exam for ABAP developers. It requires that you are certified with ABAP. The main training course for this exam is HA400, in which you learn how ABAP development is different in SAP HANA systems than in older SAP NetWeaver systems.

▶ **E_HANABW SAP BW on SAP HANA Certification**
This is an exam for people specializing in SAP BW. It requires that you are certified with SAP BW. The main training course for this exam is BW362.

## SAP HANA Application Associate Certification Exam

Now, let's focus on the objective and structure of the C_HANAIMP certification that this book targets and look at the latest C_HANAIMP certification exam.

SAP is evolving fast and is constantly being updated. There is a new major SPS update of SAP HANA released twice a year. Therefore, every six months, SAP Education has to update all training materials and certification exams. All SAP certifications remain valid for the last two versions. This means that your SAP HANA certification, depending on when you received it, will be valid from somewhere between about six months and about a year and a half. This is regrettably a much shorter timeframe than for most other SAP certifications, some of which can remain valid for many years. In a sense, this is the cost of working in such a fast-moving environment.

As previously mentioned, the SAP HANA Application Associate Certification exam is named C_HANAIMP.

Table 1.2 lists the exam names for the SAP Certified Application Associate—SAP HANA certification through the years. The exam names are linked to the different SPS release numbers, though originally referred to the year.

| SAP HANA Application Certification Exam | SAP HANA SPS | Year |
|---|---|---|
| C_HANAIMP_1 | First few releases | 2012 |
| C_HANAIMP131 | SPS 05 | 2013 |
| C_HANAIMP141 | SPS 07 | 2014 |
| C_HANAIMP142 | SPS 08 | 2014 |
| C_HANAIMP151 | SPS 09 | 2015 |
| D_HANAIMP_10 | SPS 10 | 2015 |
| C_HANAIMP_11 | SPS 11 | 2016 |

**Table 1.2**  SAP Certified Application Associate—SAP HANA Exam Names

 **Note**

This book deals specifically with the latest C_HANAIMP_11 certification exam.

You will notice in Table 1.2 that the C_HANAIMP_1 certification exam included _1 at the end of the name, showing that it was the first certification exam. Over time, SAP started including the year in the certification exam name—for example, C_HANAIMP151. The first two numbers of *151* refer to the year, 2015, and the last number, *1*, refers to the first half of the year. In this case, this combination corresponds to SPS 09.

Recently, the naming convention was updated to refer directly to the SAP HANA SPS number. That is, the exam is now called C_HANAIMP_11 instead of C_HANAIMP161. The *_11* suffix indicates *SPS 11*.

SAP Education now also has started delivering delta exams for SAP HANA. This will make it easier to extend the life of your SAP HANA certification. The *D* prefix in Table 1.2 indicates a delta certification exam. You need to have passed the C_HANAIMP151 certification exam before you can take the D_HANAIMP_10 delta exam.

Now that we've introduced the SAP Certified Application Associate–SAP HANA certification, the next section will look at the exam as whole: its objective, structure, and general process.

## Exam Objective

In Figure 1.1, in large letters, you can see the official name of the certification examination. On the left, you can see that the LEVEL is ASSOCIATE.

On the right side, you can see that the exam has 80 questions. The CUT SCORE in this example page is 59%, which means that you need to get 59% in this certification examination in order to pass. The DURATION of the exam is 180 minutes. The exam is available in English, Japanese, and Chinese.

Note that there is a PDF link for sample questions. In this case, there are 10 sample questions you can look at to get an idea of what the actual examination questions look like. We normally recommend that you keep the sample questions in reserve for later; don't dive in right away. You can use the sample questions to judge whether or not you're ready for the certification examination.

 **Tip**

I always joke with my students that if you say "Huh?" when you look at the sample questions, then you're not ready for the exam.

The examination itself is focused on certain tasks.

## Exam Structure

When you scroll down through the web page shown in Figure 1.1, you will see how the exam is structured and scored. Each of the topic areas are mentioned there, as well as the percentage that each area contributes towards your final score in the certification exam.

The first area is MODELING FUNCTIONS. When you expand this area, you can see that the HA300 training course is available. More than 12% of the questions fall into the MODELING FUNCTIONS, which means that there are roughly 15 questions in the certification exam on this topic.

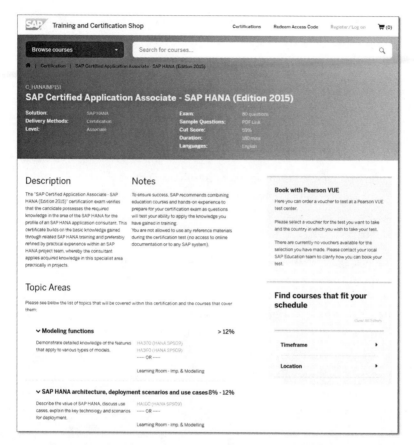

**Figure 1.1**    An Example C_HANAIMP Certification Exam Information Page

The SAP HANA ARCHITECTURE, DEPLOYMENT SCENARIOS AND USE CASES topic is roughly 10% (between 8% and 12%) of the exam, meaning that it covers about eight questions. The HA100 training course is available for more information on this topic. Other portions of the exam follow this same percentage determination and provide short descriptions.

As you can see, SAP recommends two training courses: HA100 and HA300. As of SPS 10, the HA300 training course has been expanded from three to five days and now includes the relevant topics previously found only in HA360 and HA900.

Table 1.3 lists the different topic areas you need to study for the C_HANAIMP_11 certification exam, the weighted percentage for each section, the estimated number of questions, and the chapters that correspond to these topics from the book.

| Topic | Percent of Exam | Estimated Number of Questions | Corresponding Chapters |
|---|---|---|---|
| SAP HANA architecture and deployment scenarios | 8%–12% | 8 | 3 |
| Information views | 8%–12% | 8 | 4, 5, 6 |
| Modeling functions | 12% – 18% | 12 | 7 |
| SQL and SQLScript | 8%–12% | 8 | 8 |
| Text, spatial, and predictive modeling | 8%–12% | 8 | 9 |
| Optimization of models | < 8% | 4 | 10 |
| Management and administration of models | 8%–12% | 8 | 11 |
| SAP HANA Live | 8%–12% | 8 | 12 |
| Security in SAP HANA modeling | < 8% | 4 | 13 |
| Overview of SAP HANA Data Provisioning | 8%–12% | 8 | 14 |
| Consumption of SAP HANA models | < 8% | 4 | 15 |

**Table 1.3**   C_HANAIMP_11 Exam Scoring Structure

## Exam Process

You can book the certification exam you want to take at *https://training.sap.com/ shop/sap-search/certifications?q=C_HANAIMP_11*.

On the SAP training website, choose the country you live in or the country that you wish to take the exam in. The price of the certification exam and available dates will appear in the right column on the web page. Currently, all SAP HANA certification exams are administered in examination centers even though the exam is an online exam.

> **Note**
>
> In the future, all certification exams will be administered in the cloud. Cloud certifications use remote proctoring, in which an exam proctor watches you (the test taker) remotely via your computer's webcam. You have to show the proctor the entire room before the exam begins by moving your webcam or your computer around. These test proctors have been trained to identify possible cheating.

When you arrive at the examination center, you will need a form of identification. During your certification exam, you will not have access to online materials, books, your mobile phone, or the Internet.

As you mark answer options, the answers are immediately stored on a server to ensure you do not lose any work. When you finish all your certification exam questions and submit the entire exam, you receive the results immediately. If you do not pass the certification exam, you can take it up to two more times. This retake option hopefully will not be important to any of the readers of this book!

Normally, you will receive the printed certificate about a week later at your examination center, or you can receive it by mail.

You can also see your certificate in the SAP Credentials Manager. You can find more information on how to register yourself at *https://training.sap.com/shop/content/Credential-Manager*. You can display your certification status here, and allow potential customers or employers to verify your certifications.

At the same link, you can find the SAP Consultants Registry, which you can use to promote your services with your certification credentials. Using this portal, companies can search for SAP professionals who are certified in a specific topic like SAP HANA.

## Summary

You should now understand the various SAP HANA certification examinations and be able to identify which exam is right for you. You know about the scoring structure of C_HANAIMP_11, and can focus your study time and energy accordingly.

As you work through this book, we will guide you through the questions and content that can be expected.

Best wishes on your exam!

# SAP HANA Training

## Techniques You'll Master

- ▶ Identify SAP Education training courses for SAP HANA
- ▶ Find related SAP courses
- ▶ Discover other sources of information and courses on the Internet
- ▶ Develop strategies for taking your SAP certification exam

In this chapter, we will provide an overview of options for available resources and training courses to prepare for your certification exam. We will look into SAP Education, which makes SAP HANA training courses available for each certification and provides related courses that can enhance your skills and understanding. We also will discuss various sources on the Internet that provide SAP HANA documentation, video tutorials, how to get hands-on expirience, and free online courses. Finally, we will review some techniques for taking the certification exam.

## SAP Education Training Courses

You can attend SAP official training courses in a couple of different ways. These training course options provide flexibility for learning and access to relevant materials, so you can customize your studies to your lifestyle.

These different types of training courses include:

▶ **Classroom training**
The first and most obvious option is *classroom training*, in which you attend SAP HANA courses in a classroom with a trainer for a few days. Classroom training courses provide a printed manual and a system through which you can practice and perform exercises. At the end of the week, you will walk away with a better understanding of what is described in that training material.

Classroom training is a popular option that allows individuals to focus on learning in an environment in which they can ask questions, perform exercises, discuss information with other students, and get away from their offices and emails.

▶ **Virtual classrooms**
You can also attend SAP courses via *virtual classrooms*. The virtual approach is similar to training in real-life classrooms, but you do not sit in a physical classroom with a trainer. Instead, your trainer teaches you via the Internet in a virtual classroom. You still have the ability to ask questions, chat online with other students, and perform exercises.

▶ **E-learning**
You can participate in the same training courses via *e-learning* as well. In this case, you are provided with a training manual and an audio recording of

course presentations. However, you don't have an instructor to ask questions of, and there is no interaction with others who are learning the same topic. Given that this type of training normally happens after hours, it requires some discipline.

▶ **SAP Learning Hub**
The last training course option is to use the SAP Learning Hub, a service you subscribe to yearly. Your subscription grants you access to the entire SAP portfolio of e-learning courses across every topic in the cloud, training materials, some vouchers for taking certification exams, learning rooms, hands-on training systems, and forums for asking questions. You can find further details about the SAP Learning Hub at *https://training.sap.com/shop/learninghub* and *www.sap.com/ training-education/learning-software-svc/learn/solutions/hub/index.html*.

In the next two subsections, we'll discuss SAP HANA training courses specific to the certification exams and additional courses related to SAP HANA that may prove useful in your learning.

## Training Courses for SAP HANA Certifications

Table 2.1 lists the SAP HANA training courses for the latest C_HANAIMP certification exams, the length of each course, and each course's prerequisites, if any.

| Certification | SAP Training Course | Length | Prerequisites |
|---|---|---|---|
| **C_HANAIMP151** (SPS 10 courses) | HA100, collection 10 | 2 days | N/A |
| | HA300, collection 10 | 5 days | HA100 |
| **D_HANAIMP_10** | Delta materials provided | Self-determined | C_HANAIMP151 |
| **C_HANAIMP_11** | HA100 collection 11 | 2 days | N/A |
| | HA300 collection 11 | 5 days | HA100 |

**Table 2.1** SAP Training Courses for C_HANAIMP Certification Exams

The HA100 training course is the two-day introductory course that everyone must take, regardless of which direction you want to go with SAP HANA. HA100 provides a quick introduction to SAP HANA architecture, the different concepts of in-memory computing, modeling, data provisioning (how to get data into SAP HANA), and how to use SAP HANA information models in reports.

The HA300 training course goes into more detail on the SAP HANA modeling concepts and the security aspects of SAP HANA.

As of SPS 10, the HA300 training course has been expanded from three to five days and now includes related topics previously found only in the HA360 and HA900 courses. Now, you only need to take the HA100 and HA300 courses to prepare for the certification exam.

 **Tip**

All the answers to the associate-level SAP HANA certification exams are guaranteed to be (somewhere) in the official SAP training material.

## Additional SAP HANA Training Courses

The following SAP training courses related to SAP HANA modeling can complement your skills and knowledge of SAP HANA:

▶ **HA450**
This three-day course merges SAP HANA modeling with the native application development that you can perform from SAP HANA's application server. It teaches you how you can take an SAP HANA information model, expose it as an OData or REST web service, and consume it in the JavaScript framework called SAPUI5.

▶ **SAPX05**
This course complements the HA450 training course. It focuses on SAPUI5 development.

▶ **HA215**
If you want to learn about SAP HANA performance tuning, the two-day HA215 course will complement the HA100 and HA300 courses.

▶ **BW362**
If you come from a SAP BW background, BW362 is a related course that might help you. This course shows you how you can build information models with SAP BW on SAP HANA.

▶ **HA400**
If you come from an ABAP background, you should think about attending the HA400 training course. It takes the knowledge that you gained in HA100 and

HA300 and shows you how to apply that knowledge in your ABAP development environment. You'll learn that the ways in which you access the SAP HANA information models and interface with the SAP HANA database are completely different than ways to perform similar tasks in all the other databases you've used through the years.

SAP Education offers a wide variety of courses to enhance your skills and further your career. However, it's important to know what resources are available outside the classroom as well. In the next section, we will look at additional resources for continued learning.

## Other Sources of Information

You will find that there is no shortage of information about SAP HANA. In fact, there is so much information available that it's almost impossible to get through it all! To help focus your search, let's look at some of the most popular sources of information.

### SAP Help

SAP Help (*http://help.sap.com*) is a valuable resource for your SAP and SAP HANA education. There is a lot of great documentation provided on this website. At *http://help.sap.com/hana_platform*, you will see all available documentation provided in PDF format (see Figure 2.1).

Useful PDF files include the following:

▶ **What's New in the SAP HANA Platform (Release Notes)**
This document lists the new features in the SPSs of SAP HANA since SPS 5.

▶ **SAP HANA Modeling Guide**
We highly recommend this modeling guide, which provides the foundation for working with and building SAP HANA information models.

▶ **SAP HANA Interactive Education (SHINE)**
This guide is a demo package that you can install into your own SAP HANA system. It provides a lot of data and models, with examples of how to create good information models. In the training course, you can gain access to a SAP HANA system. You can also gain access using Amazon or Microsoft Azure Cloud (see the Hands-On with Your SAP HANA Server section of this chapter).

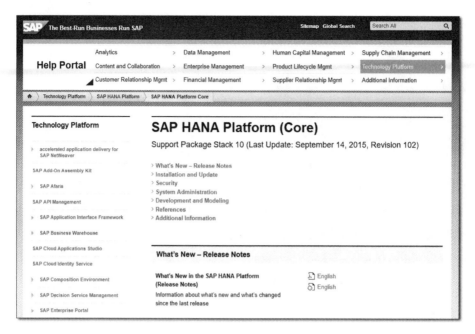

**Figure 2.1**  SAP HANA Documentation on SAP Help

One whatever system you use, you can install the SHINE content. You can then use the data, information models, and applications provided to enhance your learning. The example screens in this book make use of the SHINE package.

▶ **SAP HANA Security Guide**
This guide tells you everything you need to know about security in more detail. We will discuss what you need to know about security for the exam in Chapter 14.

▶ **SAP HANA Troubleshooting and Performance Analysis Guide**
Learn how to properly troubleshoot your SAP HANA database and enhance overall performance with this guide.

▶ **SAP HANA reference guides**
There is an entire section of reference guides that provide more specific and focused discussions of particular SAP HANA topics:

   ▶ SAP HANA SQLScript Reference

   ▶ SAP HANA XS JavaScript Reference

- ▸ SAP HANA XS JavaScript API Reference

- ▸ SAP HANA XSUnit JavaScript API Reference

- ▸ SAP HANA XS DB Utilities JavaScript API Reference

- ▸ SAP HANA Business Function Library (BFL)

- ▸ SAP HANA Predictive Analysis Library (PAL) Reference

- ▸ **SAP HANA Developer Quick Start Guide**
  This specific developer's guide is presented as a set of tutorials.

- ▸ **SAP HANA Developer Guide**
  We recommend reviewing this guide, especially because development and information modeling are closely linked in SAP HANA. This guide teaches you how to build applications in SAP HANA, write procedures, and more.

- ▸ **SAPUI5 Developer Guide for SAP HANA**
  This guide provides insight into building SAPUI5 applications on SAP HANA.

For some of these documents, it might be helpful to have an actual system to play with, because some guides provide step-by-step instructions for certain actions. We discuss how to access a system in the Hands-On with SAP HANA section.

## hana.sap.com and SAP Community Network

The main website for SAP HANA is *http://hana.sap.com/*, which offers the latest news about SAP HANA and its different use cases. Startup companies that wish to develop solutions on the SAP HANA platform can join the SAP HANA Startup Forum here.

SAP Community Network (SCN) provides a central location for members of different SAP communities and solution users. At *http://scn.sap.com/community/hana-in-memory*, you can ask questions about your own SAP HANA system. Many SAP employees will answer questions posted on this website.

## SAP HANA Academy

From *http://hana.sap.com/*, you can find a link to the SAP HANA ACADEMY; clicking it takes you directly to YouTube. The SAP HANA Academy area of YouTube provides hundreds of free video tutorials on all topic areas of SAP HANA. You can also access it directly via *www.youtube.com/user/saphanaacademy/playlists? view=1&flow=grid&sort=lad*. Figure 2.2 shows the main screen for SAP HANA Academy.

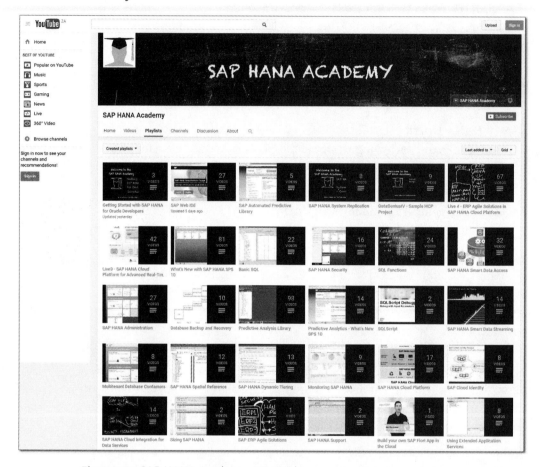

**Figure 2.2**   SAP HANA Academy at YouTube

SAP employees who perform actual tasks on an SAP HANA system make these videos. If you've never made a backup of an SAP HANA system, for example, you can search for a video on how to do just that, with step-by-step instructions.

Because there are so many video clips available, we recommend that you select the PLAYLISTS option from the YouTube menu. In the dropdown, just below this menu, select CREATED PLAYLISTS. Then, from the dropdown menu on the right side, select LAST ADDED TO. Alternately, go to the URL provided previously to see the latest video clips at the top. This is useful when a new SAP HANA SPS is released, for example, and you want to find out about the new features it brings to SAP HANA.

With each new SAP HANA release, new videos are added to the SAP HANA Academy YouTube channel—so if you're really bored this weekend and you don't know what to do with all your time, you can watch a few hours of SAP HANA video clips!

You can also find videos on SAP HANA Academy for building solutions. On the PLAYLISTS page, when you scroll down, you will see a section called BUILDING SOLUTIONS. This is shown in Figure 2.3.

**Figure 2.3**   Playlists for Building Solutions

You will now see about nine different series for building a solution. In Figure 2.4, we have selected the LIVE2 series, which helps you to build a social network solution with SAP HANA.

Some of these series will be using older support packs of SAP HANA. You can always adapt the learning to the latest techniques discussed in this book. For example, instead of using analytic views, you will use calculation views of type cube with star join.

As noted earlier, the *http://help.sap.com* website provides all the PDFs for you to read, which is great if you like reading and you want the PDFs on your tablet or phone, for example. On the other hand, the SAP HANA Academy YouTube channel is good if you prefer visual learning, and it may be more practical.

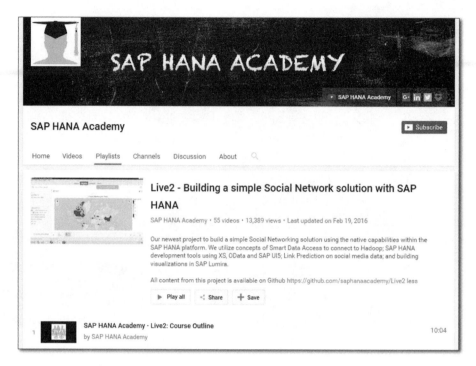

**Figure 2.4**   Guided Learning on SAP HANA Academy

## openSAP and openHPI

The next websites for you to explore are *https://open.sap.com/* (openSAP; see Figure 2.5) and *https://open.hpi.de/* (openHPI). The openHPI website provides a good training course on SAP HANA by Hasso Plattner, and the openSAP website provides many free training courses on a large variety of SAP topics.

These websites frequently add new online training courses, of which some focus on SAP HANA. When new training courses become available, you can enroll in them. Every week, you will receive a few video clips. These courses are normally four to six weeks long, and every week you will take a test. All the tests together are worth 50% of your total score. In the last week, you take an exam, which is worth the other 50% of your score. At the end of the course, you receive a certificate of attendance, and if you performed well, the certificate will show your score. If appropriate, the certificate will also show that you were in the top 10% or top 20% of your class.

**Note**

These openSAP certificates do not hold the same weight as the official SAP Education certifications!

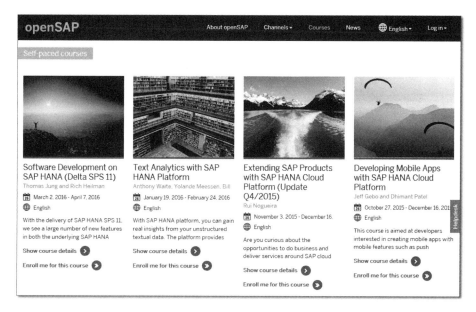

**Figure 2.5**   openSAP Website

After you complete one of these free online courses, you cannot retake the tests or exams, but you can still access all of the other course materials. You can always download the video clips, the PowerPoint slides, and the transcripts for your records.

**Tip**

We recommend a series of SAP HANA development courses presented by Thomas Jung, including a new course available specifically for SAP HANA SPS 11. You can find the Software Development on SAP HANA (Delta SPS 11) course at *https://open.sap.com/courses/hana4*. Many of the courses on openSAP focus on SAP HANA. While these courses do not focus on modeling, some of them are excellent complementary training. At *https://open.sap.com/courses* you can see a list of available courses.

## Hands-On with SAP HANA

Everyone learns differently. Some people like visuals, others learn by listening, and still others learn by doing. In this section, we look at how to gain some hands-on experience with practice systems, projects, and data. We'll begin with the different ways you can personally access an SAP HANA system.

### Where to Get an SAP HANA System

On the SAP HANA Developer Center site (*http://go.sap.com/developer/hana.html*) you can get a free SAP HANA server for 30 days or create your own server in the cloud (see Figure 2.6).

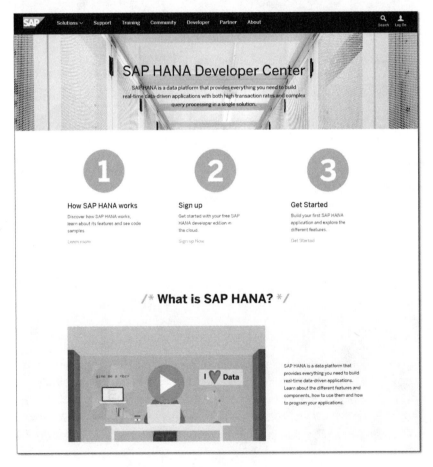

**Figure 2.6**   SAP HANA Developer Center Website

When you scroll down through this page, you will find links to sign up for SAP HANA CLOUD PLATFORM, MICROSOFT AZURE CLOUD, and AMAZON WEB SERVICES (see Figure 2.7).

**Figure 2.7**   SAP HANA Trial and Sign-Up Options

You can view a tutorial on how to SAP HANA developer edition in the cloud at *http://go.sap.com/developer/tutorials/hana-setup-cloud.html*.

Both the Amazon Web Services (AWS) and the Microsoft Azure Cloud offerings are ideal for learning more about SAP HANA in a practical manner. They're both quite inexpensive, so long as you remember to switch things off when you're finished—that is, essentially pressing a pause button on your SAP HANA system. Otherwise, the cloud providers will continue charging you for the CPU, the memory, the network, and the disk space being used. You can also put a limit on your finances to ensure you don't go over your budget.

In this section, we'll look at these options in greater detail, whether you're using a free trial, paying a cloud provider for the hardware, or using your own server.

### SAP HANA Cloud Platform—Free Trial

We can start with the cheapest and easiest way to get your own SAP HANA system.

Figure 2.8 shows *https://account.hanatrial.ondemand.com/*, where you can get an SAP HANA system for free on SAP HANA Cloud Platform (SAP HCP). After a quick registration process, you will gain access to SAP HCP.

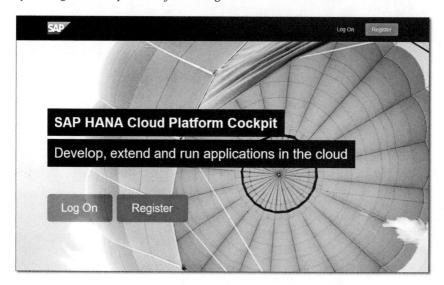

**Figure 2.8**   SAP HCP Registration

To learn how to set up your own SAP HANA system in SAP HCP, you can read the SAP HANA GETTING STARTED information, as shown in Figure 2.9, on *https://help.hana.ondemand.com/help/frameset.htm*.

The free account on the SAP HCP has some restrictions. You do not get a lot of memory for loading large datasets. The cloud platform is shared with many other users. User restrictions can prevent you from easily loading packages like SHINE. You can load SHINE on SAP HCP, but it is not as straightforward and easy as on other options.

SAP HCP is however an excellent choice to get going quickly, and does not cost you anything.

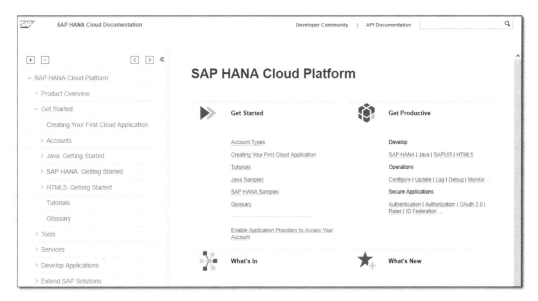

**Figure 2.9** SAP HCP Help Documentation

### Developer Edition on Amazon Web Services and Microsoft Azure Cloud

The next option is to get your own SAP HANA system on the AWS cloud or the Microsoft Azure Cloud. While the developer license for SAP HANA is free from SAP, you still need to pay for the hosted solution on AWS or Microsoft. You can, however, bring down the costs by pausing your SAP HANA system when you are not using it.

The easiest way to create your own SAP HANA system on AWS or Microsoft Azure Cloud is by using the SAP Cloud Appliance Library. You can find this at *https://cal.sap.com/*. Figure 2.10 shows you what the home screen looks like. Registration is also for free on this website.

Once you are registered you can select the SAP HANA system you want to create. Figure 2.11 shows the SOLUTIONS tab. Here you can filter the solution by typing "HANA Dev" in the text field on the top right of the screen.

On the next screen, you will be shown a list of possible solutions. In Figure 2.11, you can see the SAP HANA DEVELOPER EDITION 1.0 SPS 10 solution.

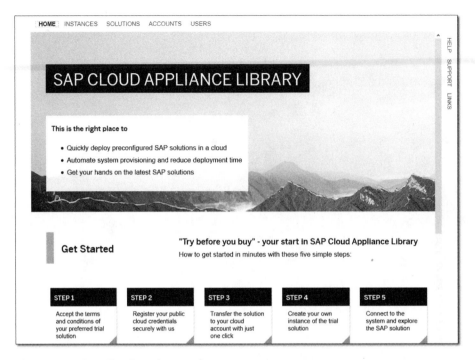

**Figure 2.10**   SAP Cloud Appliance Library

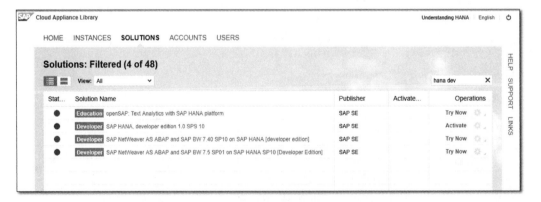

**Figure 2.11**   SAP HANA Development System on SAP Cloud Applicance Library

Once you select this, you can select the size of the SAP HANA server you require. You can play around with the various options. Based on the options you select, the cost per hour and the total monthly costs will be displayed.

The SAP Cloud Appliance Library will also allow you to automatically switch your SAP HANA system on and off at predefined times. The savings are also automatically reflected in the monthly cost calculations.

Once you are satisfied with your choices, you can ask the SAP Cloud Appliance Library to automatically create your SAP HANA system for you on AWS or Microsoft Azure Cloud.

The steps to create your own SAP HANA system on AWS or Microsoft Azure are found at *http://scn.sap.com/docs/DOC-58418*.

If you are a Microsoft MSDN subscriber, you get a certain amount of credit each month for Microsoft Azure Cloud. We found some people use that credit to pay for their SAP HANA systems.

 **Note**

You can find more free trial offerings for the SAP Cloud Appliance Library at *http://scn.sap.com/docs/DOC-47930*. If you want to work with an SAP BW on SAP HANA system, or an SAP S/4HANA system, you will find links on this page to the various offerings.

You can also find a list of frequently asked questions on the SAP Cloud Appliance Library FAQ page at *http://scn.sap.com/docs/DOC-33673*.

### Building Your Own SAP HANA System

You can also build your own server with SAP HANA. You will need some hardware, an operating system, and the SAP HANA software.

The requirements for the hardware, and how to install the SAP HANA software, can be found at *http://help.sap.com/hana_platform/*.

 **Note**

It is recommended that you use a machine with a minimum of 24GB or 32GB of memory. SAP HANA will not start on a machine with less than 16GB of memory.

The certified operating systems for SAP HANA are SUSE Linux Enterprise Server for SAP Applications and Red Hat Enterprise Linux for SAP HANA. You can find the SUSE Linux Enterprise Server for SAP Applications at *https://www.suse.com/ products/sles-for-sap/*. Or, you can get a copy of Red Hat Enterprise Linux for SAP HANA from *https://www.redhat.com/en/resources/red-hat-enterprise-linux-sap-hana*.

**Tip**

If you plan to use your own desktop or laptop, the SAP HANA software will warn you about using non-certified hardware. However, if you install SAP HANA in a VMware virtual machine, you will not get such a warning as this is seen as certified "hardware."

The VMware Workstation 12 Player is free for personal use and can be downloaded at *https://www.vmware.com/go/downloadplayer/*.

You will also need to download a copy of the SAP HANA software. You can download this from *https://support.sap.com/software/installations/a-z-index.html*.

In the alphabetical list of products, select H, and then choose SAP HANA PLATFORM EDITION.

Please note that you will need a registered S-user name and password before you can download the software. If you are an existing SAP customer or SAP partner you can ask your system administrator for a logon user.

**Install SAP HANA Studio**

Whether you get an SAP HANA system on the cloud somewhere, or build your own SAP HANA server, you can easily connect to your SAP HANA system using the SAP HANA web-based development workbench. You just need a HTML5-compatible browser.

If you want to use SAP HANA studio, you will have to install a copy on your laptop (or desktop) computer. You can find instructions on how to install SAP HANA studio at *https://tools.hana.ondemand.com/#hanatools*.

## Project Examples

Once you have your own SAP HANA system, the next step will be to start using it. In this section, we will discuss how to start working on SAP HANA projects, and how you can use the SHINE demo package or create your own project.

### Using the SHINE Demo Package

One option to get some practice in SAP HANA is to explore the content available in the SHINE demo package. We will use the SHINE demo throughout this book. It is fully documented, and is used by SAP as an example for how to develop SAP HANA applications.

The SHINE documentation can be found at *http://help.sap.com/hana_platform/*.

You can download the SHINE package from *https://store.sap.com/*. In Figure 2.12, you can see the SAP Store. Type "SHINE" in the search bar to locate the package.

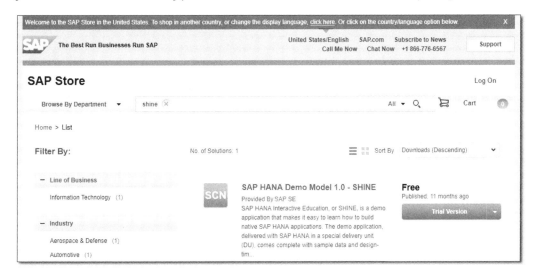

**Figure 2.12**   SHINE Package on the SAP Store

Alternatively, you can download the SHINE package from *https://support.sap.com/ patches* or from *https://github.com/SAP/hana-shine*.

You install SHINE like any other delivery unit (see Chapter 11 for more information). In the FILE menu of SAP HANA studio, select IMPORT • SAP HANA CONTENT • DELIVERY UNIT.

### Creating Your Own Project

You can also think up your own projects. You can start very simply by just learning to work with individual topics discussed in the book. Examples can include things like fuzzy text search, currency conversion, input parameters, hierarchies, and spatial joins. You can also add some security on top of this, for example, to limit the data for a single user to just one year.

The next step is to think about creating a report that can analyze the performance of a particular dataset. This is a good exercise, as you will have to take end user requirements and learn how to translate them into the required SAP HANA information models. Then, you will design and create these models.

Finally, you can expand these information models into an application.

You can also look at incorporating something like SAP Lumira to easily create attractive storyboards. You can download a free copy of SAP Lumira from *http:// saplumira.com/*.

## Where to Get Data

SAP HANA can process large amounts of data. To get hands-on practice in the SAP HANA system, you'll want some sort of data to play with. There are a couple of places where you can access data to play with:

▶ **SHINE demo package**
The SHINE demo package is a great place to get large datasets. To do this, in the SHINE package, use the GENERATE DATA option.

▶ **Datahub**
Datahub is website and free open data management system that can be used to get, use, and share data. At *https://datahub.io/en/dataset* (Figure 2.13) you can find many free datasets.

▶ **United States Department of Transportation database**
If you want a larger dataset to play with, you can use the United States Department of Transportation database on flights in the United States. It has more than 50 million records, with about 20 years of data.

You can find this at *http://www.transtats.bts.gov/* (see Figure 2.14).

You can download this data from *http://apps.bts.gov/xml/ontimesummarysta-tistics/src/index.xml*.

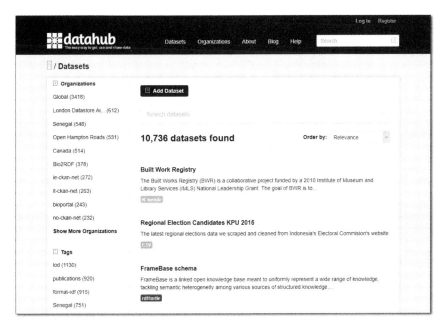

**Figure 2.13**    Datahub

**Figure 2.14**    Flight Data from the United States Department of Transportation Website

## Exam Questions

Now, we'll change gears a bit and look at the SAP certification exams and how to approach them. Let's look at the examination question types and some tips and hints about how to complete the certification exam.

### Types of Questions

An international team sets up the SAP HANA certification exams. All the questions are written in English, and all the communication is in English. Because the exam teams are international, a lot of attention is focused on making sure that everybody will understand what is meant by each question, avoiding possible double meanings or ambiguities.

Figure 2.15 shows three types of questions that you will find in the certification exam.

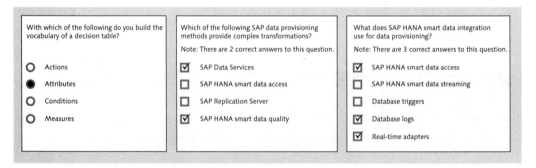

**Figure 2.15**  Three Types of Certification Exam Questions

The first question is *multiple choice*. The radio buttons indicate that you can only choose one of the four options. There always will be only four different options, with only one correct answer.

The other two questions are called *multiple response questions*. There are two types of multiple response questions:

▶ With the first type of multiple response question, there are *four possible answers*, and there will always be two correct answers and two incorrect answers. In the exam, this will be indicated by the words, "Note: There are two correct answers to this question."

▶ The other type of multiple response question has *five possible answers*, of which three will always be correct and two will be incorrect; you must select three correct answers. Above the answers, you will see the words, "Note: There are three correct answers to this question."

Both types of multiple response questions use checkboxes, and you must select however many answers are correct.

All three types of questions have exactly the same weight. You either get a question right or you get it wrong. It's a binary system: 0 or 1.

For a multiple response question with two correct and two incorrect answers, you must select two answers. If you select three answers or one answer, you do not receive any points. If you select two answers and they are the correct two answers, then you earn a point.

 **Tip**

Select as many answers as are required! If you are certain that an option is correct, then select it. If you are doubtful about an answer, at least select one option. If you don't select anything, you will not earn any points. Even if you plan to come back to the question later, we still recommend that you select the exact number of answers required.

Multiple choice questions normally make up the majority of the questions for the associate-level core exams. More than half of the questions will have only one correct answer and three incorrect answers. There are no true or false questions in the certification exam. However, we will use true or false questions in this book, but only for training purposes.

 **Note**

In the certification exam, there are no fill-in-the-blank questions.

The questions and the answers themselves appear randomly. In other words, two people could be taking the same exam, sitting next to each other, and the order in which the questions appear for each person would be different. Also, for similar questions, the order of a, b, c, and d (the answer options) is different for different people.

Because answer options are randomized, you will never find any questions that list "All of the above" or "None of the above" as a possible answer.

The questions in the SAP certification exams tend to be very short and to the point. All extra words and descriptions have been cut away, ensuring that you will have enough time to complete the exams. We've never heard anyone complain about the time limits in the SAP HANA certification exams. Because the questions are to the point, every word counts. Every word is there for a reason and has a purpose, so don't ignore any word—especially words like *always*, *only*, and *must*.

*Always* indicates on every occasion. *Only* means that no other options are allowed. *Must* indicates something that is mandatory. In the answer options, you could see some optional actions that would be valid actions in normal circumstances, but if they are not mandatory, they are incorrect answers for questions asking what you *must* do. Therefore, for questions using the word *must*, pay attention to optional steps versus mandatory steps.

The certification exams use a minimum of *negative words*, which are only used for troubleshooting questions. All negative words in a question are written in capital letters—for example, "You did something and it is NOT working. What is the reason?"

Now that we've looked at the general structure of SAP certification exam questions, let's look at the strategy of elimination in the exam.

### Elimination Technique

Experience has shown that the *elimination technique* can be useful for answering exam questions. In this technique, you start by finding the wrong answers instead of finding the right answers.

When creating exams, it is fairly easy to set up questions, but it's hard to think up wrong answers that still sound credible. Because it is so difficult to write credible wrong answers, it's normally easier to eliminate the wrong answers first. As Sherlock Holmes would say: Whatever remains, however improbable, must be the truth.

To show how efficient this technique can be, look at the multiple response question with five different options (Figure 2.15, right). There are three correct and two incorrect answers, so it saves you time to find the two incorrect ones, rather than trying to find the three correct answers.

## Bookmark Questions

In the certification exam, you can always *bookmark* questions and return to them later. If you are not confident about a question, mark it. We still recommend that you complete the right number of answer options: If two answers are required, fill in two options. If three are required, select three options. Then, mark the question so that you can review it later.

 **Tip**

Watch out when you do the review; your initial choice tends to be the correct one. Remember, don't overanalyze the question.

Now, let's turn our attention to some general exam strategies. Implementing test-taking strategies will help you to succeed on the exam.

## General Examination Strategies

The following are some good tips, tricks, and strategies to help you during an exam:

- If you have the SAP training manuals, pay attention to pages with lots of bullet points; that means there are normally lots of options, and these are likely good sources for questions.

- For the associate-level certification exams, in this book, read the entire chapters and answer all the questions. If you do not get the answers right, or do not understand the question, re-read that section. This is the equivalent of reading the SAP training materials twice.

- Make sure you get a good night's rest before the exam.

- Make sure that you've answered all the questions and that you've selected the correct number of answer options. If the question says that three answers are correct, then make sure that you've marked three—not four or two.

- ▶ Occasionally, you will find answer options that are opposites—for example, X is true, and X is NOT true. In that case, make sure you select one of the pair.

- ▶ In our experience with SAP HANA certification exams, the answers from one question do not always provide answers to another question. SAP Education is careful to make sure that this doesn't happen in its exams.

- ▶ Watch out for certain trigger words. Alarm bells should go off when you see words like *only*, *must*, and *always*.

- ▶ Look out for impossible combinations. For example, if a question is about measures, then the answer cannot be something to do with dimension (attribute) views, because you cannot find measures for such views.

- ▶ Some words can be different in different countries. For example, some people talk about a right-click menu, but in other places in the world this same feature is known as a context menu. This is the menu that pops up in a specific context, and you access this menu by right-clicking.

## Summary

You should now know which SAP Education training courses you can attend for your certification examination and which related SAP courses will complement your knowledge and skills, and where to get hands-on experience. In addition, we introduced many free sources of information on the Internet, training videos on YouTube, and online courses at openSAP.

You can now form a winning strategy for taking your SAP certification exam. In the next chapter, we will begin looking at exam questions and concepts, focusing first on the architecture and deployment scenarios of SAP HANA.

# Architecture and Deployment Scenarios

3

## Techniques You'll Master

- ▶ Understand in-memory technologies and how SAP HANA uses them

- ▶ Get to know the internal architecture of SAP HANA

- ▶ Describe the SAP HANA persistence layer

- ▶ Learn the different ways that SAP HANA can be deployed

- ▶ Know when to use different deployment methods

In this chapter, you'll become familiar with the various deployment scenarios for SAP HANA and evaluate appropriate system configurations, including cloud deployments. We'll provide an introduction to the new in-memory paradigm and the thinking behind how SAP HANA uses in-memory technologies. By the end, you'll better understand how SAP HANA functions in all the types of solutions you might require.

### Real-World Scenario

You start a new project. The business users describe what they want and expect you to suggest an appropriate architecture for how to deploy SAP HANA. You have to decide between building something new in SAP HANA or migrating the current SAP system to use SAP HANA. You also have to decide if you should use SAP HANA in the cloud and, if so, which type of service you will need.

When you understand the internal architecture of SAP HANA, it can lead to unexpected benefits for the company. You can use the fact that SAP HANA uses compression in memory combined with an understanding of how SAP HANA uses disks and backups to provide a customer with an excellent business case for moving their business solution to SAP HANA; this can lead to dramatically lower operational costs and reduced risk.

## Objectives of This Portion of the Test

The objective of this portion of the SAP HANA certification test is to evaluate your basic understanding of the various SAP HANA deployment scenarios and the corresponding system configurations. The certification exam expects SAP HANA modelers to have a good understanding of the following topics:

▶ How SAP HANA uses in-memory technology, including elements such as columns, tables, and compression

▶ The persistence layer in SAP HANA

▶ The various ways that SAP HANA can be deployed

▶ How SAP HANA can be deployed in the cloud

**Note**

This portion contributes up to 10% of the total certification exam score.

# Key Concepts Refresher

We'll start with something that most people know very well: Moore's Law. Even if you have never heard of it, you have seen its effects on the technology around you. Put simply, this means that the overall processing power for computers doubles about every two years. Therefore, you can buy a computer for roughly the same price as about two years ago, and it will be twice as fast as the older one.

Moore's Law is useful for understanding system performance and response times. If you have a report that is running slow, let's say an hour long, you can fix this by buying faster hardware. You can easily get the processing time of your slow report from 1 hour to 30 minutes to 15 minutes by just waiting a while and then buying faster computers. However, a few years ago that simple recipe stopped working. Our easy upgrade path was no longer available, and we had to approach the performance issues in new and innovate ways. Data volumes also keep growing, adding to the problem. SAP realized these problems early, and worked on the solution we now know as SAP HANA.

In this chapter, we will discuss SAP HANA's in-memory technology and how it addresses the aforementioned issues. We'll then look at SAP HANA's architecture and new approaches. Finally, we'll walk through the various deployment options available, including cloud options.

## In-Memory Technology

SAP HANA uses in-memory technology. But, just what is in-memory technology?

In-memory technology is an approach to querying data residing in RAM, as opposed to physical disks. The results of doing so lead to shortened response times. This enables enhanced analytics for business intelligence/analytic applications.

In this section, we'll walk through the process that lead us to use in-memory technology, which will illustrate the importance in new technology.

## Multicore CPU

When CPU speed reached about 3 GHz, we seemed to hit a wall. It became difficult to make a single CPU faster while keeping it cool enough. Therefore, chip manufacturers moved from a single CPU per chip to multiple CPU cores per chip.

Instead of increasingly fast machines, machines now stay at roughly the same speed but have more cores. If a specific report only runs on a single core, that report will not run any faster thanks to more CPU cores. We can run multiple reports simultaneously, but all of them will run for an hour. To speed up reports, we need to rewrite software to take full advantage of new multicore CPU technology, a problem that has been faced by most software companies.

SAP addressed this problem in SAP HANA by making sure that all operations are making full use of all available CPU cores.

## Slow Disk

When talking about poor system performance, you can place a lot of blame on slow hard disks. Table 3.1 shows how slow a disk can be compared to memory.

| Operation | Latency (In Nanoseconds) | Relative to Memory |
| --- | --- | --- |
| Read from level 1 (L1) cache | 0.5 ns | 200 x faster |
| Read from level 2 (L2) cache | 7 ns | 14 x faster |
| Read from level 3 (L3) cache | 15 ns | 6.7 x faster |
| Read from memory | 100 ns | – |
| Send 1 KB over 1 Gbps network | 10,000 ns | 100 x slower |
| Read from solid state disk (SSD) | 150,000 ns | 1,500 x slower |
| Read from disk | 10,000,000 ns | 100,000 x slower |
| Send network packet from the US West Coast to Europe and back | 150,000,000 ns | 1,500,000 x slower |

**Table 3.1**  Latency of Hardware Components and Performance of Components Shown Relative to RAM Memory

To give you an idea of how slow a disk really is, think about this: If reading data from RAM memory takes one minute, it will take more than two months to read the same data from disk! In reality, there is less of a difference when we start reading and streaming data sequentially from disks, but this example prompts the idea that there must be better ways of writing systems.

The classic problem is that alternatives like RAM memory have been prohibitively expensive, and there has not been enough RAM memory available to replace disks.

Therefore, the way we have designed and built software systems for the last 30 or more years has been heavily influenced by the fact that disks are slow. This affects the way everyone from technical architects to developers to auditors thinks about system and application design. For example:

▶ SAP NetWeaver architecture uses one database server and multiple application servers (Figure 3.1). Because the database stores data on disk and disks are slow, the database becomes the bottleneck in the system. In any system, you always try to minimize the impact of the bottlenecks and the load on it. Therefore, we move the data into multiple application servers to work with it there, using the database server as little as possible. In SAP systems, we use it so little that we can be database independent. SAP systems even have their own independent ABAP data dictionaries.

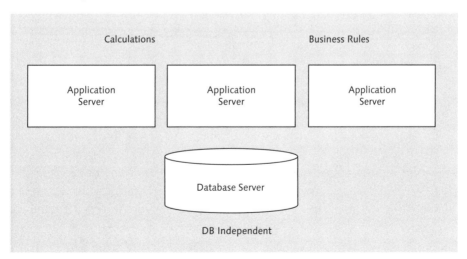

**Figure 3.1**  SAP NetWeaver Architecture: One Database Server, Many Application Servers

In the application servers, we run all the code, perform all the calculations, and execute the business rules. We use memory buffers to store a working set of data. In many SAP systems, 99.5% of all database reads come from these memory buffers, thus minimizing the effects of the slow disk. SAP system architecture was heavily influenced by the fact that disk is slow.

▶ Inside financial systems, we store data such as year-to-date data, month-to-date data, balances, and aggregates. For reporting, we have cubes, dimensions, and more aggregates. These values are all updated and stored in financial systems to improve performance.

Take the case of the year-to-date figure. We do not really need to store this information, because we can calculate it from the data. The problem is that to calculate the year-to-date figure, we need to read millions of records from the database, which the database reads from the slow disk. Therefore, we could calculate the current year-to-date figure, but doing so would be too slow. Because disk storage is cheap and plentiful, we just add this value into the database in another table. With every new transaction, we simply add the new value to the current year-to-date value and update the database. Now reports can run a lot faster on disk.

If the disk was fast, we would not need to store these values. Can you imagine a financial system without these values? Ask accountants to imagine a financial system without balances! Why store balances when you can calculate them? When you see the reaction on their faces, you will understand how even their thinking has been influenced by the effects of slow disks.

We will return to this example in the next section.

▶ One of the many reasons we have data warehouses is that we need fast and flexible reporting. We build large cubes with precalculated, stored aggregates that we can use for reporting and to slice and dice the data. Building these cubes takes time and processing power. Reading the masses of data from disk for the reports can be slow. If we keep these cubes inside, for example, our financial system, then a single user running a large report from these cubes can pull the system's performance down. That one user affects thousands of users.

Therefore, SAP created separate data warehouses to reduce the impact of reporting on operational and transactional systems. Those reporting users can now run their heavy, slow reports away from the operational and transactional systems. The database world now is split into two parts: The online transactional processing (OLTP) databases for the financial, transaction, and operations systems, and the online analytical processing (OLAP) data warehouses (see Figure 3.2).

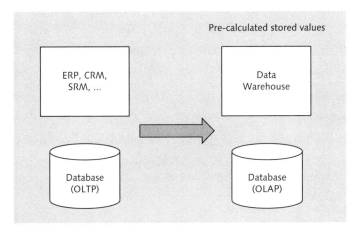

**Figure 3.2** OLTP vs. OLAP: Operational Reporting Seperate from Operational Systems for Performance Reasons

If disks were fast and we could create aggregates fast enough, we would be able to perform most of our operational reporting directly in the operational system, where the users expect and need it. We would not have separate OLTP and OLAP systems. Again, slow disks influenced architectural design principles.

These three examples prove that slow disks have influenced SAP system design, architecture, and thinking for many years now. If we could eliminate the slow disk bottleneck from our systems, we could then change our minds about how to design and implement systems. Hence, SAP HANA represents a paradigm shift.

**Loading Data into Memory**

In the first of the three examples in the previous section, you saw that we have used memory where possible to speed things up with memory caching. Nevertheless, until a few years ago, memory was still very expensive. Then, memory prices started coming down fast, and we asked, "Can we load all data into memory instead of just storing it on disk?"

Customer databases for business systems can easily be 10 TB (10,000 GB) in size. The largest available hardware when SAP HANA was developed had only 512 GB to 1 TB of memory, presenting a problem. SAP obviously needed to compress data to fit it into the available memory. We're not talking here about ZIP or RAR compression, which needs to be decompressed again before it is usable, but *dictionary compression*. Dictionary compression involves mapping distinct values to consecutive numbers.

### Column-Oriented Database

For years, it was common to store data in rows. Row-based databases work well with spinning disks to read single records faster. However, when we start storing data in memory, there is no longer a valid reason to use row-based storage. At that point, we have to decide to use row-based or column-based storage.

Why would we use columns instead of rows? If we start looking at compressing data, then row-oriented data does not work particularly well. This is because we mix different types of data—like cities with salaries and employee numbers—in every record. The average compression we get is about two times (that is, data is stored in about 50% of the original space).

When we store the same data in columns, we now group similar data together. By using dictionary compression, we can achieve excellent compression, and thus column-based storage starts making more sense for in-memory databases.

Another way in which we can save space is via indices. If we look inside an SAP system, we find that about half the data volume is taken up by indices. An index is a sorted column; if we store the data in columns in memory, do we really need indices? We can save that space. With such column-oriented database advantages, we end up with 5 to 20 times compression.

Back to our original problem: 10 TB databases, but machines with only 1 TB of memory. By using column-based storage, compression, and no indices, we can fit a 10 TB database into the 1 TB of available memory. Even though we focused on the column-oriented concept here, note that SAP HANA can handle both row- and column-based tables.

### Removing Bottlenecks

When we manage to load the database entirely into memory, exciting things start happening. We break free from the slow disk bottleneck that had a stranglehold on system performance for many years. The architecture is designed to work around this problem.

As always, even if our systems become thousands of times faster, at some stage we will reach new constraints. These constraints will determine what the new architecture will look like. The way we provide new business solutions will depend on the characteristics of this new architecture.

## Architecture and Approach

The new in-memory computing paradigm has changed the way we approach solutions. Different architectures and deployment options are now possible with SAP HANA.

### Changing from a Database to a Platform

The biggest change in approach is how and where we work with the data. Disks were always slow, causing the database to become a bottleneck. Thus, we moved the processing of data to the application servers to minimize the pressure on this disk bottleneck.

Now, data storage has moved from disk to memory, which is much faster. Therefore, we needed to reexamine our assumptions about the database being the bottleneck. In this new in-memory architecture, it makes no sense to move data from the memory of the database server to the memory of the application servers via a relatively slow network. In that case, the network will become the bottleneck, and we will duplicate functionality.

New bottlenecks require new architectures. Our new bottleneck arises because we have many CPU cores that need to be fed as quickly as possible from memory. Therefore, we put the CPUs close to the memory (i.e., the data). In doing so, the first point that we realize is that SAP HANA can be sold as an appliance. As shown in Figure 3.3, it doesn't make sense to copy data from the memory of the database server to the memory of the application server as we have always done (left arrow). We instead now move the code to execute within the SAP HANA server (right arrow).

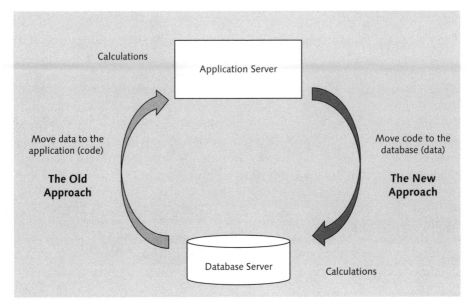

**Figure 3.3**  Moving Data In-Memory

Our solution approach also needed to change. Instead of moving data away from the database to the application servers, as we have done for many years, we now want to keep it in the database. Many database administrators have done this for years via *stored procedures*. Instead of stored procedures, in SAP HANA we use *graphical data models*, as we will discuss in Chapter 4. You can also use stored procedures and table functions if you need to do so. We will look at this process in Chapter 8.

 **Note**

Instead of moving data to the code, we now move the code to the data. We can implement this process by way of SAP HANA graphical modeling techniques.

When you start running code inside the database, it is only a matter of time before it changes from a database into a platform. When people tell you that SAP HANA is "just another database," ask them which other database incorporates more than five programming languages, a web server, an application server, an HTML5 framework, a development environment, replication and cleaning of data, integration with most other databases, predictive analytics, and multi-tenancy; the reactions can be interesting.

### Parallelism in SAP HANA

In the Slow Disk section, we provided three examples of the wide-ranging effects of slow disks on performance. In the second example, we looked at calculating the year-to-date value. We do not really need to store a year-to-date value because we can calculate it from the data. With slow disks, the problem is that to calculate this value we need to read millions of records from the database, which the database reads from the slow disk. Because disk storage is cheap and plentiful, we just added this aggregate into the database *in another table*.

When we have millions of records in memory and many CPU cores available, we can calculate the year-to-date value faster than an old system can read it from the new table from a slow disk. Look at Figure 3.4: Even though we require a single year-to-date value, we use memory and all the available CPU cores *in parallel* to calculate it. We just divide the memory containing the millions of records into several ranges and ask each available CPU core to calculate the value for its memory range. Finally, we add all the answers from each of the CPU cores to get the final value. Even a single sum is run in parallel inside SAP HANA.

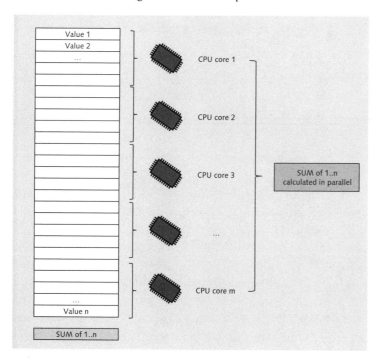

**Figure 3.4**   Single Year-to-Date Value Calculated in Parallel Using All Available CPU Cores

Although it's relatively easy to understand this example, don't overlook the important consequences of this process: If we can calculate the value quickly, we do not need to store it in another table. By applying this new approach, we start to get rid of many tables in the system. This then leads to simpler systems. We also have to write less code, because we do not need to maintain a particular table, insert or update the data in that table, and so on. Our backups become smaller and faster because we do not store unnecessary data. That is exactly what has happened with SAP S/4HANA: Functional areas that had 37 tables, for example, now have two or three tables remaining.

To get an idea of the compound effect that SAP HANA has on the system, Figure 3.5 shows how a system shrinks when you start applying this new approach.

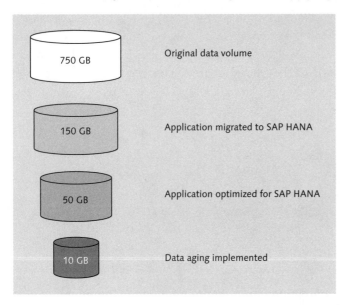

**Figure 3.5**   Database Shrinks with SAP HANA In-Memory Techniques

Say that we start with an original database of 750 GB. Because of column-based storage, compression, and the elimination of indices, the database size easily comes down to 150 GB. When we then apply the techniques we just discussed for calculating aggregates instead of storing them in separate tables, the database goes down to about 50 GB. When we finally apply data aging, the database shrinks to an impressive 10 GB. In addition, we are left with less code, faster reporting response times, and smaller backups.

### Delta Buffer and Delta Merge

Before we start sounding like overeager sales people, let's look at something that column-based databases are *not* good at.

Row-based databases are good at reading, inserting, and updating single records. Row-based databases are not efficient when we have to add new columns (fields).

When we look at column-based databases, we find that these two sentences are reversed. This is because data stored in columns instead of in rows is effectively "rotated" by 90 degrees. Adding new columns in a column-based database is easy and straightforward, but adding new records can be a problem. In short, column-based databases tend to be very good at *reading data*, whereas row-based databases are better at *writing data*.

Fortunately, SAP took a pragmatic rather than a purist approach and implemented both column-based and row-based storage in SAP HANA. This allows users to have the best of both worlds: Column storage for compressed data and fast reading and row storage for fast writing of data. Because reading data happens more often than writing, the column-based store is obviously preferred.

Figure 3.6 shows how this is implemented in SAP HANA table data storage. The main table area is using the column store as we just discussed. The data in here is optimized for fast reading.

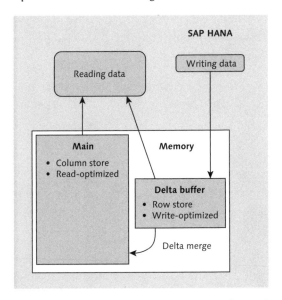

**Figure 3.6** Column and Row Storage Used to Achieve Fast Reading and Writing of Data

Next to the main table area, we also have an area called the *delta buffer*, sometimes called the *delta store*. When SAP HANA needs to insert new records, it inserts them into this area. This is based on the row store and is optimized for fast data writing. Records are appended at the end of the delta buffer. The data in this delta buffer is therefore unsorted.

Some people believe the read queries are slowed down when the system has to read both areas (for old and newly inserted data) to answer a query. Remember that everything in SAP HANA runs in parallel and uses all available CPU cores. For the query shown in Figure 3.6, 100 CPU cores can read the main table area and another 20 CPU cores can read the buffer area. The cores then combine all the data read to produce the result set.

We have looked at cases in which new data is inserted — but what about cases in which data needs to be updated? Column-based databases can also be relatively slow during updates. Therefore, in such a case, SAP HANA marks the old record in the main storage as "updated at date and time" and inserts the new values of the records in the delta buffer. The SAP HANA system effectively changes an update into a flag and insert. This is called the *insert-only* technique.

When the delta buffer becomes too full or when you trigger it, the *delta merge* process takes the values of the delta buffer and merges them into the main table area. SAP HANA then starts with a clean delta buffer.

Column-based databases also do not handle SELECT * SQL statements well. We will look at this in more detail in Chapter 10. For now, we encourage you to avoid such statements in column-based databases.

In the next section, we will look at how the SAP HANA in-memory database persists its data, even when we switch off the machine.

### Persistence Layer

The most frequently asked question people hear about SAP HANA and its in-memory concept is as follows: "Memory is volatile. That is, it loses its contents when you switch off its power source. So, what happens to SAP HANA's data when you lose power or switch off the machine?"

The short answer is that SAP HANA still uses disks. However, whereas other databases are disk-based and optionally load data into memory, SAP HANA is in-memory and merely uses disks to back up the data for when the power is switched off. The focus is totally different.

The disk storage and the storing of data happens in the *persistence layer*, and storing data on disk is called *persistence*.

Let's look at how SAP HANA uses disks and the persistence layer in the following subsections.

### SAP HANA as a Distributed Database

Just like many newer databases, SAP HANA can be deployed as a distributed database. One of the advantages that SAP HANA has due to its in-memory architecture is that it is an *ACID-compliant* database. ACID (atomicity, consistency, isolation, and durability) ensures that database transactions are reliably processed. Most other distributed databases are disk-based, with the associated performance limitations, and most of them—most notably NoSQL databases—are not ACID-compliant. NoSQL databases use *eventual consistency*, meaning that they cannot guarantee consistent answers to database queries. They might come back with different answers to the same query on the same data. SAP HANA will always give consistent answers to database queries. This detail is vital for financial and business systems.

Figure 3.7 shows an instance in which SAP HANA is running on three servers. A fourth server can be added to facilitate *high availability*. Should any one of the three active servers fail, the fourth standby server will instantly take over the functions of the failed server.

SAP HANA can *partition* tables across active servers. This means that we can take a table and split it to run on all three servers. This way, we don't only use multiple CPU cores of one server with SAP HANA to execute queries in parallel, but also use multiple servers. We can partition data in various ways—for example, people whose surnames start with the letters A–M can be in one partition N–Z in another.

In the case of SAP HANA as a distributed database, we use shared disk storage to facilitate high availability. This configuration of SAP HANA is called the *scale-out* solution.

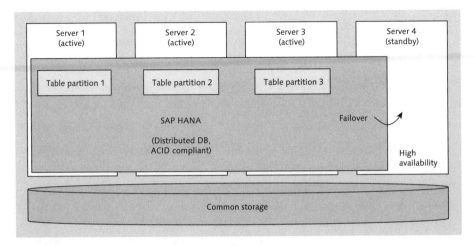

**Figure 3.7**   SAP HANA as a Distributed Database

### Data Volume and Data Backups

Figure 3.8 shows the various ways that SAP HANA uses disks. At the top left, you can see that the SAP HANA database is in memory. If it is not in memory, it is not a database. The primary storage for transactions is the memory. The disk is used for secondary storage—to help when starting up after a power down or hardware failure, with backups, and with disaster recovery.

Data is stored as *blocks* (also sometimes called *pages*) in memory. Every 10 minutes, a process called a *savepoint* runs that synchronizes these memory blocks to disks in the *data volume*. Only the blocks that contain data that have changed in the last 10 minutes are written to the data volume. This process is controlled by the *page manager*. The savepoint process runs asynchronously in the background.

Data backups are made from the disks in the data volume. When you request a backup, SAP HANA first runs a savepoint and ensures that the data in the data volume is consistent, then starts the backup process.

 **Note**

The backup reads the data from the disks in the data volume. This does not affect the database operations, because the SAP HANA database continues working from memory. Therefore, you do not have to wait for an after-hours time window to start a backup.

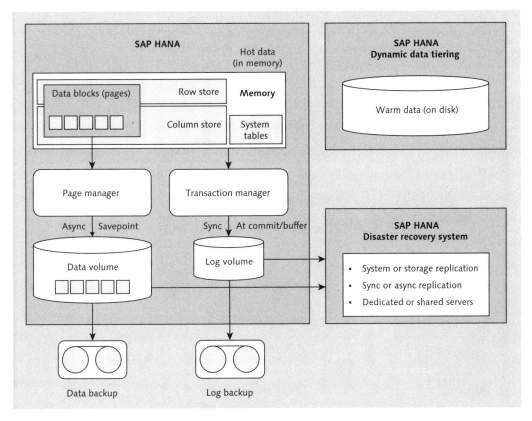

**Figure 3.8**  Persistence of Data with SAP HANA

SAP HANA can unload (drop) data blocks from memory when it needs more memory for certain operations. This unloading of data from memory is not a problem, because SAP HANA knows that all the data is also safely stored in the data volume. It will unload the least-used portions of the data. It does not unload the least-used table, but only the columns or even portions of a column that were not used recently. In a scale-out solution, it can unload parts of a table partition.

### Log Volume and Log Backups

In the middle section of Figure 3.8, you can see the *transaction manager* writing to the *log volume*. The page manager and transaction manager are subprocesses of the SAP HANA *index server* process. This is the main SAP HANA process. Should this process stop, then SAP HANA stops.

When you edit data in SAP HANA, the transaction manager manages these changes. All changes are stored in a *log buffer* in memory. When you COMMIT the transaction, the transaction manager does not commit the transaction to memory unless it is also committed to the disks in the log volume, so this is a synchronous operation. Because the system has to wait for a reply from a disk in this case, fast SSD disks are used in the log volume. This synchronous writing operation also is triggered if the log buffer becomes full.

The log files in the log volume are backed up regularly, using scheduled log backups.

**Note**

SAP HANA does not lose transactions, even if a power failure should occur, because it does not commit a transaction to the in-memory database unless it is also written to the disks in the log volume.

### Startup

The data in the data volume is not a "database." Instead, think of it as a *memory dump*—an organized and controlled one. If it was a database on disk, it would have to convert the disk-based database format to an in-memory format each time it started up. Now, it can just reload the memory dump from disk back into memory as quickly as possible.

When you start up an SAP HANA system, it performs what is called a *lazy load*. It first loads the system tables into memory and then the row store. Finally, it loads any column tables that you have specified. Because the data volumes are only updated by the savepoint every 10 minutes, some transactions might not be in the data volume; SAP HANA loads those transactions from the log volume. Any transaction that was committed stays committed, and any transaction that was not committed is rolled back. This ensures a consistent database.

SAP HANA then reports that it is ready for work. This ensures that SAP HANA systems can start up quickly. Any other data that is required for queries gets loaded in the background. Again, SAP HANA does not have to load an entire table into memory; it can load only certain columns or part of a column into memory. In a scale-out system, it will load only the required partitions.

Disks are therefore useful for getting the data back into memory after system maintenance or (potential) hardware failures.

### Disaster Recovery

At the bottom right of Figure 3.8, you can see that the data volume and logs also are used to facilitate *disaster recovery*. In disaster recovery, you make a copy of the SAP HANA system in another data center. Should your data center be flooded or damaged in an earthquake, your business can continue working from the disaster recovery copy.

The initial large copy of the system can be performed by replicating the data volume. Once the initial copy is made, only the changes are replicated as they are written to the log volume. (In the older versions of SAP HANA, the changes are continuously replicated in both the data and the log volumes.)

This replication can be performed by the SAP HANA system itself, or by the storage vendor of the disks in the data and log volumes. The replication can happen either *synchronously* or *asynchronously*. You can also choose whether to use *dedicated hardware* for the disaster recovery copy, or *shared hardware* for development and quality assurance purposes.

Disaster recovery is covered in more detail in the HA200 course, and in the SAP HANA administration guide on *http://help.sap.com/hana_platform*.

### Data Aging

The final piece of the persistence layer is found at the top right of Figure 3.8. This is where disks are used for data aging.

SAP HANA has a feature called *dynamic data tiering*. You can specify data aging rules inside SAP HANA to take, for example, all data older than five year and write it to this area. All queries to the data still work perfectly, but are just slower as they are read from disk instead of memory.

The data in the in-memory portion of SAP HANA is often referred to as the *hot data*, while the data stored in the dynamic data tiering portion is referred to as *warm data*. We can later expand this to include *cold data*, by using SAP HANA smart data access (SDA) with Hadoop. We discuss this in Chapter 14.

## Deployment Scenarios

People sometimes get confused about SAP HANA when it is only defined with a single concept, such as *SAP HANA is a database*. After a while, they hear seemingly conflicting information that does not fit into that simple description. In this section, we'll look at the various ways that SAP HANA can be used and deployed: as a database, as an accelerator, as a platform, or in the cloud.

When looking at SAP HANA's in-memory technology, and especially the fact that we should ideally move code away from the application servers to the database server, it seems that SAP systems need to be rewritten completely. Because SAP HANA does not need to store values like year-to-date, aggregates, or balances, we should ideally remove them from the database. By doing so, we can get rid of a significant percentage of the tables in, for example, a financial system. However, that implies that we should also trim the code that calculated those aggregates and inserted them into the tables we removed. In this way, we can also remove a significant percentage of our application code.

Next, the slow parts of the remaining code that manipulates data should be moved into graphical calculation views in SAP HANA, removing even more code from our application. If we follow this logic, we obviously have to completely rewrite our systems. This is not easy for SAP, which has millions of lines of code in every system and an established client base. This approach can be very disruptive. Disruptive innovation is great when you are disrupting other companies' markets, but not so much when you disrupt your own markets. Ask an existing SAP customer if he wants this new technology, and he probably will say, "Yes, but not if it means a reimplementation that will require lots of time, money, people, and effort." Completely rewriting the system would lead to customers replacing their systems with the new solution; that also means that customers with the older systems would not benefit at all from this innovation.

If you look at the new SAP S/4HANA systems, you will see that they follow the more disruptive approach we just described. However, there are other ways in which we can implement this disruptive new technology in a nondisruptive way—and this is how SAP approached the process when implementing SAP HANA a few years ago. The following sections walk through the deployment scenarios for implementation.

### SAP HANA as a Sidecar Solution

The first SAP HANA deployment scenario is a standalone, native, or "sidecar" solution. Think of a motorcycle with a passenger on the side in their own little car seat; that seat is the sidecar. Figure 3.9 illustrates SAP HANA as a sidecar solution.

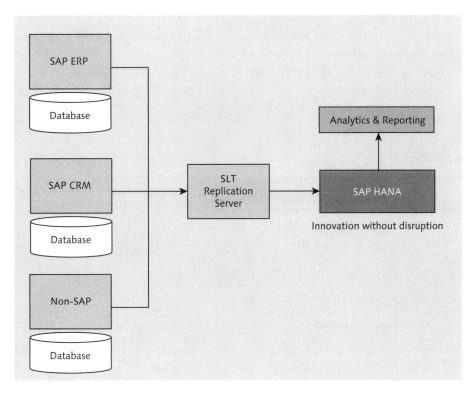

**Figure 3.9**   SAP HANA Deployed as Nondisruptive Sidecar Solution

In this deployment scenario, the source systems stay as they are. No changes are required. We add SAP HANA on the side to accelerate any transactions or reports that have performance issues in the source systems and duplicate the relevant data from the source system to SAP HANA. This duplication is normally performed by the SAP LT Replication Server (SLT). (We'll discuss SLT in more detail in Chapter 14.) The copied data in SAP HANA is then used for analysis or reporting.

The advantages of this deployment option include the following:

▶ Because we just copy data, we do not change the source system at all. Therefore, everyone can use this innovation, but without the disruption (even those who have very old SAP systems, such as SAP R/3 4.6C).

▶ We can use this option for all types of systems, not just the latest SAP systems. In fact, a large percentage of the systems that use SAP HANA are non-SAP systems.

▶  We don't have to copy the data for an entire system. If a report already runs in three seconds, that's good enough; it doesn't have to run in three milliseconds. If a report runs for two hours, but runs only once a year and is scheduled to run overnight, that's fine too. We only take the data into SAP HANA that we need to accelerate.

▶  We can replicate data from a source system in real time. The reports running on SAP HANA are always fully up-to-date.

Even though we make a copy of data, remember that SAP HANA compresses this data and that we do not copy all the data. Therefore, the SAP HANA system is always much smaller than the source system(s) in this deployment scenario.

However, the SAP HANA system in this scenario is blank. You will have to load the data into SAP HANA, build your own information models, link them to your reports and programs, and look after the security. Much of what we will discuss in this book is focused on this type of work.

### SAP HANA as a Database

When SAP released the sidecar solution, many people thought that it would replace their data warehouses. However, this worry was alleviated when SAP announced that SAP HANA would be used as the database under SAP Business Warehouse (SAP BW). Figure 3.10 illustrates a typical (older) SAP landscape.

SAP HANA can now be used to replace the databases under SAP BW, SAP CRM, and SAP ERP (which are part of the SAP Business Suite). There are well-established database migration procedures to replace a current database with SAP HANA. In each case, SAP HANA replaces the database only. The SAP systems still use the SAP application servers as they did previously, and end users still access the SAP systems as they always did, via the SAP application servers. All reports, security, and transports are performed as before. Only the system and database administrators have to learn SAP HANA and log into the SAP HANA systems.

Figure 3.11 looks very similar to Figure 3.10, except that the various databases were replaced by SAP HANA.

By only replacing the database, SAP again managed to provide most of the benefit of this new in-memory technology to businesses, but without the cost, time, and effort of disruptive system replacements. The applications' code was not forked to produce different code for SAP BW on SAP HANA versus SAP BW on older databases.

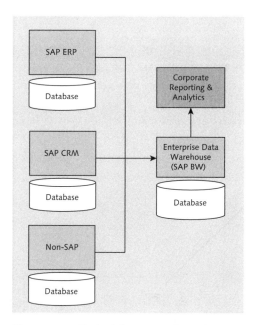

**Figure 3.10**   Typical Current SAP Landscape Example

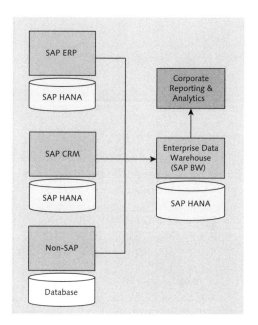

**Figure 3.11**   SAP HANA as Database Can Change Current Landscape

### SAP HANA as an Accelerator

Using SAP HANA in the sidecar deployment can be a lot of work because it is a "blank" system. SAP quickly realized that special use cases occurred at a majority of their customers where some common processes were slow; one of these processes is profitability analysis. Profitability is something that any company needs to focus on, but profitably analysis reports are slow running due to the large amounts of data they have to process. By loading profitability data into SAP HANA, the response times of these reports go from hours to mere seconds (see Figure 3.12).

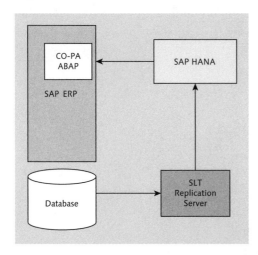

**Figure 3.12**   SAP HANA Used as an Accelerator for a Current SAP Solution

For these accelerators, SAP provides prebuilt models in SAP HANA. SAP also slightly modified the ABAP code for SAP CO-PA to read the data from SAP HANA instead of the original database. SLT replicates just the required profitability data across from the SAP ERP system to the SAP HANA system.

The installation and configuration process is performed at a customer site over a few days, instead of weeks and months. The only thing that changes for the end users is that they have to get used to the increased processing speed, and no one has a problem with that!

### SAP HANA as a Platform

The next way we can deploy SAP HANA is by using it as a full development platform. SAP HANA is more than just an in-memory database.

Which other database has several different programming languages included and has version control, code repositories, and a full application server built in?

SAP HANA has all of these. This makes SAP HANA not just a database, but a platform. You can program in SQL, SQLScript (an SAP HANA-only enhancement that we'll look at in Chapter 8), R, and JavaScript.

However, the main feature we use inside SAP HANA when deploying SAP HANA as a platform is the application server, called the *SAP HANA extended application services* (SAP HANA XS) *engine*, which is used via web services (see Figure 3.13).

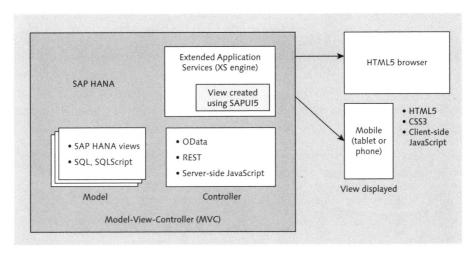

**Figure 3.13**  SAP HANA as a Development Platform

The SAP HANA XS engine is a full web and application server built into SAP HANA and is capable of serving and consuming web pages and web services.

When we deploy SAP HANA as a platform, we only need an HTML5 browser and the SAP HANA XS engine. In this case, we still develop data models as we discussed previously with the sidecar and accelerator deployments, but we also develop a full application in SAP HANA, using JavaScript and an HTML framework called SAPUI5. All this functionality is built-in to SAP HANA.

The development paradigm that most frameworks use is called *Model-View-Controller* (MVC). *Model* in this case refers to the information models that we will build in SAP HANA and is the focus of this book. We expose these information models in the *controller* by exposing them as OData or REST web services. This functionality is available in SAP HANA and is easy to use. You can enhance these web services using *server-side JavaScript*. This means that SAP HANA runs JavaScript as a programming language inside the server.

The last piece is the *view*, which is created using the SAPUI5 framework. The screens are the same as the SAP Fiori screens seen in the new SAP S/4HANA systems, which are HTML5 screens. What is popularly referred to as HTML5 actually consists of HTML5, Cascading Style Sheets (CSS3), and *client-side JavaScript*. In this case, the JavaScript runs in the browser of the end-user.

By using JavaScript for both the view and the controller, SAP HANA XS developers only have to learn one programming language to create powerful web applications and solutions that leverage the power and performance of SAP HANA.

We can even create native mobile applications for Apple iOS, Android, and other mobile platforms. Some free applications such as Cordova take the SAP HANA XS applications and compile them into native mobile applications, which can then be distributed via mobile application stores. As a result, you can use SAP HANA's power directly from your mobile phone.

**Multitenant Database Containers**

*Multitenant Database Containers* (MDC) is a new deployment option that became available as of SAP HANA SPS 09. We can now have multiple isolated databases inside a single SAP HANA system, as shown in Figure 3.14. Each of these isolated databases is referred to as a *tenant*.

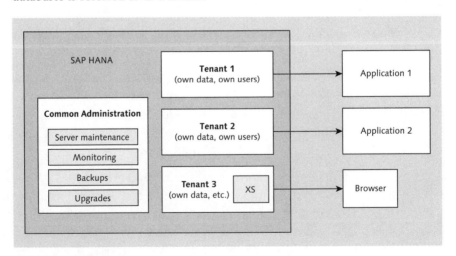

**Figure 3.14**  Multitenancy with SAP HANA Multitenant Database Containers

Think of tenants occupying an apartment building: Each tenant has his or her own front door key and own furniture inside his or her apartment. Other tenants cannot get into another tenant's apartment without permission. However, the maintenance of the entire apartment building is performed by a single team. If the building needs repairs to the water pipes, all tenants will be without water for a few minutes.

In the same way, tenants in MDC have their own unique business systems, data, and business users. In Figure 3.14, you can see that each of the three tenants has his own unique application installed and connected to their own tenant database inside SAP HANA.

Each tenant can make its own backups if the user wishes. Tenants can also collaborate, so one tenant can use the SAP HANA models of another tenant if they has been given the right security access.

However, all the tenants share the same technical server infrastructure and maintenance. The system administration team can make a backup for all the tenants. (Any tenant can be restored individually, though.) SAP HANA upgrades and maintenance schedules happen at the same time for all the tenants.

### Cloud Deployments

We've now discussed various ways to deploy SAP HANA. Most of the time, we think of these deployments as running on-premise on a local server, but all of these scenarios can also be deployed in the cloud. In cloud deployments, virtualizations manage applications like SAP HANA. VMware vSphere virtual machine deployments of SAP HANA are fully supported, both for development and production instances.

With cloud deployments, you'll be introduced to various new terms:

▶ **Infrastructure as a Service (IaaS)**
An infrastructure includes things like network, memory, CPU, and storage. IaaS provides infrastructure in the cloud to support your deployments.

▶ **Platform as a Service (PaaS)**
PaaS uses solutions such as SAP HANA Cloud Platform (HCP). In this scenario, you use not only the same infrastructure as IaaS, but also a platform—for example, a Java application service or the SAP HANA platform.

▸ **Software as a Service (SaaS)**

A cloud offering that provides certain software, such as SAP SuccessFactors or SAP Hybris.

▸ **Managed Cloud as a Service (MCaaS)**

In MCaaS, SAP manages the entire environment for you, including backups, disaster recovery, high availability, patches, and upgrades. An example of this is the SAP HANA Enterprise Cloud (SAP HEC).

### Public, Private, and Hybrid Cloud

Your cloud scenario could be a public, private, or hybrid cloud scenario. Let's look at what each of those terms means and when each scenario would apply.

The easiest and cheapest way for you to get an instance of SAP HANA for use with this book is probably via Amazon Web Services (AWS). You can simply go to *http://aws.amazon.com* and look for an SAP HANA development environment. By using your Amazon account, you can have a 28 GB or larger SAP HANA system up and running in minutes. This is available to everyone—the public—so therefore this is a *public cloud*. In this example, AWS provides IaaS.

The reason this is called a public cloud is that the infrastructure is shared by members of the public. You do not get your own dedicated machine at Amazon or any other public cloud provider.

If you host SAP HANA in your own data center or in a hosted environment specifically for you only, then it is a *private* or *hybrid* cloud. A private cloud offers the same features that you would find in a public cloud, but is dictated by different forms of access. With a private cloud, the servers in the cloud provider's data center are dedicated for your company only. No other companies' programs or data are allowed on these servers.

A hybrid cloud involves either combining a public and private cloud offering, or running a private and public cloud together. With a hybrid cloud, you connect your private cloud's server back to your own data center via a secure network connection. In that case, the servers in the cloud act as if they are part of your data center, even though they are actually in the cloud provider's data center. An example of a hybrid cloud would be if we used Amazon EC2 and operated another private cloud together.

SAP HANA works great as a cloud enabler because it accelerates applications, providing users with fast response times—which we all expect from such environments.

### SAP HANA Enterprise Cloud

SAP HEC offers SAP applications as cloud offerings. You can choose to run SAP HANA, SAP BW, SAP ERP, SAP CRM, SAP Business Suite, and many others as a full service offering in the cloud. All the systems that you would normally run on-premise are available in SAP HEC.

SAP provides the hardware, infrastructure, and all system administration services to manage the solutions for the customer. The customer only has to provide the license keys for these systems. This is referred to as *bring your own license*.

SAP HEC is seen as an MCaaS solution and a private cloud, but it can be deployed in a hybrid cloud offering.

### SAP HANA Cloud Platform

SAP HANA Cloud Platform (SAP HCP) is a PaaS that allows you to build, extend, and run applications in the cloud. This includes SAPUI5, HTML5, SAP HANA XS, Java applications, and more.

The SAP HCP Cockpit is at the core of this technology where you can manage and create all of your applications.

 **Additional Resources**

For more information on cloud deployments, including details on SAP HEC and SAP HCP, check out the book *Operating SAP in the Cloud: Landscapes and Infrastructures* (SAP PRESS, 2016) at *https://www.sap-press.com/3841*.

## Important Terminology

The following important terminology was covered in this chapter:

▸ **In-memory technology**
In-memory technology is an approach to querying data residing in RAM, as opposed to physical disks. The results of doing so lead to shortened response

times. This enables enhanced analytics for business intelligence/analytic applications.

▶ **SAP HANA Architecture**
No longer constrained by disks, solutions like column-based storage, compression, no indices, delta merges, scale-out, partitioning, and parallelism were added.

With the paradigm shift to in-memory technologies, various programming languages and application development processes were added to SAP HANA.

SAP HANA still uses disks, but purely as secondary (backup) storage because memory is volatile. With the data and log volumes, SAP HANA ensures that no data ever gets lost. The data and log volumes are also used for backups, when starting up the SAP HANA system, and for disaster recovery.

▶ **Persistence layer**
The disk storage and the storing of data happens in the persistence layer, and storing data on disk is called persistence.

▶ **SAP HANA as a sidecar**
Source systems stay as they are, and SAP HANA is added on the side to accelerate any transactions or reports that have performance issues in the source systems. The relevant data is duplicated from the source system to SAP HANA. This duplication is normally performed by the SLT. The copied data in SAP HANA is then used for analysis or reporting.

▶ **SAP HANA as a database**
Used to replace the databases under SAP BW, SAP CRM, and SAP ERP (which are part of the SAP Business Suite). There are well-established database migration procedures to replace the current database with SAP HANA. In each case, SAP HANA replaces the database only.

▶ **SAP HANA as an accelerator**
SAP provides prebuilt models in SAP HANA to accelerator processes such as profitability data. SLT replicates just the required profitability data across from the SAP ERP system to the SAP HANA system.

▶ **SAP HANA as a platform**
SAP HANA is a development platform. By combining the SAP HANA information models with development in the SAP HANA XS application server, we can build powerful custom web applications.

▶ **Public cloud**
A public cloud is available to anyone, offering any type of cloud service. The infrastructure is shared by members of the public. You do not get your own dedicated machine at Amazon or any other public cloud provider.

▶ **Private cloud**
Offers the same features that you would find in a public cloud, but is dictated by different forms of access. With a private cloud, the servers in the cloud provider's data center are dedicated for your company only. No other companies' programs or data are allowed on these servers.

▶ **Hybrid cloud**
Involves either combining a public and private cloud offering, or running a private and public cloud together. With a hybrid cloud, you connect your private cloud's server back to your own data center via a secure network connection. In that case, the servers in the cloud act as if they are part of your data center, even though they are actually in the cloud provider's data center.

▶ **SAP HANA Enterprise Cloud (SAP HEC)**
Offers all the SAP applications as cloud offerings. You can choose to run SAP HANA, SAP BW, SAP ERP, SAP CRM, SAP Business Suite, and many others as a full service offering in the cloud. All the systems that you would normally run on-premise are available in the SAP HEC.

▶ **SAP HANA Cloud Platform (SAP HCP)**
A PaaS that allows you to build, extend, and run applications in the cloud. This includes SAPUI5, HTML5, SAP HANA XS, Java applications, and more.

## Practice Questions

These practice questions will help you evaluate your understanding of the topics covered in this chapter. The questions shown are similar in nature to those found on the certification examination. Although none of these questions will be found on the exam itself, they will allow you to review your knowledge of the subject. Select the correct answers and then check the completeness of your answers in the Practice Question Answers and Explanations section. Remember that on the exam you must select all correct answers and only correct answers to receive credit for the question.

1.  Which technologies does SAP HANA use to load more data into memory? (There are 3 correct answers.)

☐  **A.** Eliminate indices

☐  **B.** Use RAR compression

☐  **C.** Use dictionary compression

☐  **D.** Store data in column tables

☐  **E.** Use multicore CPU parallelism

2.  True or False: With SAP HANA, you can run OLAP and OLTP together in one system with good performance.

☐  **A.** True

☐  **B.** False

3.  True or False: SAP HANA contains both row and column tables.

☐  **A.** True

☐  **B.** False

4.  How do you move code to SAP HANA? (There are 2 correct answers.)

☐  **A.** Delete the application server

☐  **B.** Use stored procedures in SAP HANA

☐  **C.** Use graphical data models in SAP HANA

☐  **D.** Use row tables in SAP HANA

5.  In which SAP HANA solution do you eliminate stored data, like year-to-date figures?

☐  **A.** SAP BW on SAP HANA

☐  **B.** SAP CRM on SAP HANA

☐  **C.** SAP S/4HANA

☐  **D.** SAP HANA Enterprise Cloud

6. Which deployment scenario can you use to accelerate reporting from an old SAP R/3 4.6C system?

☐ **A.** SAP HANA as a database

☐ **B.** SAP HANA as a platform

☐ **C.** SAP HANA as a sidecar solution

☐ **D.** SAP HANA multitenant database containers

7. In which deployment scenarios does security stay in the application server, and end users do not log into the SAP HANA system? (There are 2 correct answers.)

☐ **A.** SAP HANA as a platform with an SAP HANA XS application

☐ **B.** SAP HANA as a database

☐ **C.** SAP HANA as a sidecar solution

☐ **D.** SAP HANA as an accelerator

8. For which deployment scenario does SAP deliver prebuilt data models?

☐ **A.** SAP HANA as a platform

☐ **B.** SAP HANA as a sidecar solution

☐ **C.** SAP HANA as an accelerator

☐ **D.** SAP HANA on the cloud

9. True or False: SAP HANA is just a database.

☐ **A.** True

☐ **B.** False

10. What is normally used to build SAP HANA XS applications inside SAP HANA? (There are 2 correct answers.)

☐ **A.** Java

☐ **B.** JavaScript

☐ **C.** SAPUI5

☐ **D.** ABAP

11. Which type of cloud solution is SAP HANA Enterprise Cloud (HEC) an example of?

☐   **A.** Platform as a Service (PaaS)

☐   **B.** Infrastructure as a Service (IaaS)

☐   **C.** Software as a Service (SaaS)

☐   **D.** Managed Cloud as a Service (MCaaS)

12. Which type of cloud solution is Amazon Web Services (AWS) an example of?

☐   **A.** Hybrid cloud

☐   **B.** Public cloud

☐   **C.** Private cloud

☐   **D.** Community cloud

13. True or False: VMware vSphere virtual machines are fully supported for productive SAP HANA instances.

☐   **A.** True

☐   **B.** False

14. You use parallelism to calculate a year-to-date value quickly, and you eliminate a table from the database. What are some of the implications of this action? (There are 3 correct answers)

☐   **A.** Smaller database backups

☐   **B.** Less code

☐   **C.** Better user interfaces

☐   **D.** Faster response times

☐   **E.** Faster inserts into the database

15. What enables the delta buffer technique to speed up both reads and inserts in SAP HANA?

☐   **A.** Using column-based tables only

☐   **B.** Using row-based tables only

☐   **C.** Using both row-based and column-based tables

☐   **D.** Using only the insert-only technique

16. What technique is used to convert record updates into insert statements in the delta buffer?

☐ **A.** Unsorted inserts
☐ **B.** Insert-only
☐ **C.** Sorted inserts
☐ **D.** Parallelism

17. What phrase describes the main table area in the delta merge scenario?

☐ **A.** Read-optimized
☐ **B.** Write-optimized
☐ **C.** Unsorted inserts
☐ **D.** Row store

18. What does the C in ACID-compliant stand for?

☐ **A.** Complexity
☐ **B.** Consistency
☐ **C.** Complete
☐ **D.** Constant

19. Which of the following are results of deploying SAP HANA as a distributed (scale-out) solution? (There are 3 correct answers.)

☐ **A.** Partitioning
☐ **B.** Disaster recovery
☐ **C.** High availability
☐ **D.** Failover
☐ **E.** Backups

20. Which words are associated with the log volume? (There are 2 correct answers.)

☐ **A.** Synchronous
☐ **B.** Transaction manager
☐ **C.** Page manager
☐ **D.** Savepoint

21. Of which SAP HANA process are the transaction manager and page manager a part?

□   **A.** SAP HANA XS server

□   **B.** Statistics server

□   **C.** Index server

□   **D.** Name server

22. What type of load does SAP HANA perform when starting up?

□   **A.** Lazy load

□   **B.** Complete load

□   **C.** Fast load

□   **D.** Log load

23. What does SAP HANA load when starting up and before indicating that it is ready? (There are 3 correct answers.)

□   **A.** All row tables

□   **B.** All system tables

□   **C.** All partitions

□   **D.** Some column tables

□   **E.** Some row tables

## Practice Question Answers and Explanations

1. Correct answers: **A, C, D**

   SAP HANA uses column tables, dictionary compression, and eliminating indices to load more data into memory. However, it does not use RAR compression, because RAR-compressed files would have to be uncompressed before we can use the data.

   Multicore CPU parallelism helps with the performance, but does not directly address the data volume issue. It contributes indirectly, because by using it we can eliminate things like year-to-date tables as in SAP S/4HANA.

2. Correct answer: **A**

   Yes, with SAP HANA we can run OLAP and OLTP together in one system with good performance. This is normally not possible in the traditional database system. Please note that there are no True-False questions in the actual certification exam, but we use them here to help you check if you understood this chapter.

3. Correct answer: **A**

   Yes, SAP HANA contains both row and column tables.

4. Correct answers: **B, C**

   Use stored procedures and graphical data models to execute the code in SAP HANA. Deleting the application server will not help with running the code in SAP HANA, unless we develop all that same functionality in the SAP HANA XS server. Using row tables in SAP HANA has nothing to do with executing code.

5. Correct answer: **C**

   In SAP S/4HANA, many aggregate tables are removed and the solution is simplified.

6. Correct answer: **C**

   SAP HANA as a sidecar solution does not change the source systems.

7. Correct answers: **B, D**

   With SAP HANA as a sidecar and platform, users have to log in to SAP HANA. With SAP HANA as a database and accelerator, users log in via the application server.

8. Correct answer: **C**

   SAP delivers prebuilt data models for the accelerators.

9. Correct answer: **B**

   SAP HANA can also be used as a platform. Databases do not normally have application servers, version control, code repositories, and various programming languages built in.

10. Correct answers: **B, C**

    SAP HANA XS applications in SAP HANA are built using JavaScript and SAPUI5. Java and ABAP are not part of SAP HANA. SAP HANA SPS 11 includes a new SAP HANA XS advanced server, in which it is now possible to run other programming languages, like Java and C++.

11. Correct answer: **D**

    SAP HANA Enterprise Cloud is a Managed Cloud as a Service.

12. Correct answer: **B**

    Amazon Web Services is a public cloud.

13. Correct answer: **A**

    Productive SAP HANA is supported on VMware vSphere.

14. Correct answers: **A, B, D**

    The implications of eliminating such tables from the database are smaller database backups, less code, and faster response times. Doing so will not necessarily improve user interfaces. It actually eliminates extra inserts into the database, but does not make the current data inserts any faster. Techniques such as removing indices will achieve that.

15. Correct answer: **C**

    The delta buffer technique speeds up both reads and inserts in SAP HANA because it uses both row-based and column-based tables. Using column-based tables only speeds up reads, but not inserts. Using row-based tables only speeds up inserts, but not reads. Using only the insert-only technique is useless without having both row-based and column-based tables. Watch out for the word "only."

16. Correct answer: **B**

    The insert-only technique is used to convert record updates into insert statements in the delta buffer. Unsorted inserts are used in the delta buffer, but it does not convert updates to insert statements. Sorted inserts are not used in the delta buffer. Parallelism is not relevant in this case.

17. Correct answer: **A**

    The main table area in the delta merge scenario is read-optimized. The delta store is write-optimized, uses unsorted inserts, and is based on the row store.

18. Correct answer: **B**

    ACID stands for Atomicity, Consistency, Isolation, and Durability.

19. Correct answers: **A, C, D**

    Did you see the hidden hint here? The answers almost spell out ACID! Deploying SAP HANA as a distributed (scale-out) solution results in partitioning, high availability, and failover capability. Disaster recovery and backups work whether the SAP HANA system is distributed or on a single server.

20. Correct answers: **A, B**

    Synchronous and transaction manager are associated with the log volume. Page manager and savepoint are associated with the data volume.

21. Correct answer: **C**

    The transaction manager and page manager are part of the index server. The other three services are also part of SAP HANA, but are not discussed in this book.

22. Correct answer: **A**

    SAP HANA performs a lazy load when starting up.

23. Correct answers: **A, B, D**

    During the lazy load, SAP HANA loads all row tables, all system tables, and some column tables.

## Takeaway

You should now understand in-memory technologies such as column-based storage, compression, no indices, delta merges, scale-out, partitioning, and parallelism. You also know how SAP HANA uses disks for its persistence storage.

You can now describe the various SAP HANA deployment scenarios, how SAP HANA uses in-memory technologies like columns, tables, and compression, and the various ways that SAP HANA can be deployed. We looked at the different advantages of each deployment method to help you decide which one fits your requirements best. Finally, we looked at how SAP HANA can also be deployed in the cloud and for multiple tenants.

## Summary

You have learned the various ways you can deploy SAP HANA. With this knowledge, you can make recommendations to business users for an appropriate system architecture and landscape.

In the next chapter, we will discuss important information modeling concepts.

# Information Modeling Concepts

## Techniques You'll Master

- Understand general data modeling concepts like views, cubes, fact tables, and hierarchies

- Know when to use the different types of joins in SAP HANA

- Examine the differences between attributes and measures

- Learn about the different types of information views that SAP HANA uses

- Get to know projections, aggregations, and unions used in SAP HANA information views

- Describe Core Data Services (CDS) in SAP HANA

- Get a glimpse of best practices and general guidelines for data modeling in SAP HANA

Before moving onto the more advanced modeling concepts, it's important to understand the basics. In this chapter, we'll discuss the general concepts of information modeling in SAP HANA. We'll start off by reviewing views, join types, cubes, fact tables, hierarchies, the differences between attributes and measures, the different types of information views that SAP HANA offers, and CDS views. From there, we'll take a deeper dive into SAP HANA's information views, as well as concepts like calculated columns, how to perform currency conversions, input parameters, decision tables, and so on.

## Real-World Scenario

You start a new project. Many of the project team members have some knowledge of traditional data modeling concepts and describe what they need in those terms. You need to know how to take those terms and ideas, translate them into SAP HANA modeling concepts, and implement them in SAP HANA in an optimal way.

Some of the new concepts in SAP HANA are quite different than what you're used to—for example, not storing the values of a cube, instead calculating it when required. If you understand these modeling concepts, you can quickly understand and create real-time applications and reports in SAP HANA.

## Objectives of This Portion of the Test

The objective of this portion of the SAP HANA certification is to test your understanding of basic SAP HANA modeling artifacts.

For the certification exam, SAP HANA modelers must have a good understanding of the following topics:

▶ The different types of joins available in SAP HANA and when to use each one

▶ How the SAP HANA information views correspond to traditional modeling artifacts

▶ The different types of SAP HANA views and when to use them

▶ The purpose of Core Data Services (CDS) in SAP HANA

> **Note**
>
> This portion contributes up to 5% of the total certification exam score.

# Key Concepts Refresher

This section looks at some of the core data modeling concepts used when working with SAP HANA and that will be covered on the exam. Let's start from where the data is stored in SAP HANA by looking at tables.

## Tables

*Tables* allow you to store information in *rows* and *columns*. Inside SAP HANA, there are different ways of storing data. We can either store it in a table as *row-oriented* or *column-oriented*. In a normal disk-based database, we use row-oriented storage because it works faster with transactions in which we are reading and updating single records. However, because SAP HANA works in memory, we prefer the column-oriented method of storing data in the tables, with which we can make use of compression in memory, remove the storage overhead of indexes, save a lot of space, and optimize for performance by loading compressed data into computer processors.

Once we have our tables, we can begin combining them in SAP HANA information models.

## Views

The first step in building information models is building *views*. A *view* is a database entity that is not persistent and is defined as the projection of other entities, like tables.

For a view, we take two or more tables, link these different tables together on matching columns, and select certain output fields. Figure 4.1 illustrates this process.

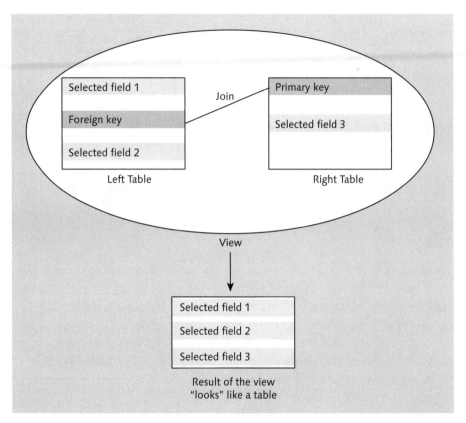

**Figure 4.1**    Database View

There are four steps when creating database views:

1. **Select the tables**
   Select two or more tables that have related information—for example, two tables listing the groceries you bought. One table contains the shop where you bought each item, the date, the total amount, and how you paid for your groceries. The other table contains the various grocery items you bought.

2. **Link the tables**
   Next, link the selected tables on matching columns. In our example, perhaps our two tables both have shopping spree numbers, should ideally a unique number for every shopping trip you took. We call this a *key field*.
   We can link the tables together with *joins* or *unions*.

3. **Select the output fields**

   We want to show a certain number of columns that are of interest to us—for example, to use in our grocery analytics. Normally, you don't want all the available columns as part of the output.

4. **Save the view**

   Finally, save your view, and it's created in the database. These views are sometimes called *SQL views*. We can even add some filters on our data in the view—for example, to show only the shopping trips in 2015 or all the shopping trips in which we bought apples.

When we call this view, the database gathers the data. The database view pulls the tables out, links them together, chooses the selected output fields, reads the data in the combined fields, and returns the result set. After this, the view "disappears" until we call it again. Then, the database deletes all of the output from the view. It does not store this data from the view inside the database storage.

 **Tip**

It's important to realize that database views don't store the result data. Each time you call a view, it performs the full process again.

You might have also heard about *materialized views*, in which people store the output created by a view in another table. However, in our definition of *views*, we stated that a view is a database entity that *is not persistent*; that is the way we use the term *view* in SAP HANA.

The data stays in the database tables. When we call the view, the database gathers the subset of data, showing us only the data that we asked for. If we ask a database view for that same data a few minutes later, the database will regather and recalculate the data again.

This concept is quite important going forward, because you make extensive use of views in SAP HANA. SAP HANA creates a cube-like view, for example, sends the results back to us, and "disappears" again. SAP HANA performs this process fast, and we avoid consuming a lot of extra memory by not storing static results. What really makes this concept important is the way it enables us to perform *real-time reporting*.

In the few minutes between running the same view twice, our data in the table might have changed. If we use the same output from the view every time, we will not get the benefit of seeing the effect of the updated data. Extensive caching of result sets does not help when we want real-time reporting.

> **Note**
>
> Real-time reporting requires recalculating results, because the data can keep changing. Views are designed to handle this requirement elegantly.

We have discussed the basic type of database views here, but SAP HANA takes the concept of views to an entirely new level!

Before we get there, we'll look at a few more concepts that we will need for our information modeling journey.

## Cardinality

When we join tables together, we need to define how much data we expect to get from the various joined tables. This part of the relationship is called the *cardinality*.

There are four basic cardinalities that you will typically work with. The cardinality is expressed in terms of how many records on the left side join to how many records on the right side.

▶ **One-to-one**
Each record on the left side matches with one record on the right side. For example, say that you have a lookup table of country codes and country names. In your left table, you have a country code called ZA. In the right table (the lookup table), this matches with exactly one record, showing that the country name of South Africa is associated with ZA.

▶ **One-to-many**
In this case, each record on the left side matches with many records on the right side. For example, say you have a list of publishers in the left table. For one publisher—such as SAP PRESS—we find many published books.

- ▶ **Many-to-one**

  This is the inverse of one-to-many. For example, this case may apply when we have many people in a small village all buying items at the local corner shop.

- ▶ **Many-to-many**

  For example, this case may apply when many people read many web pages.

## Joins

Before we look at the different types of joins, let's quickly discuss the idea of "left" and "right" tables. Sometimes, it does not make much of difference which table is on the left of the join and which table is on the right, because some join types are symmetrical. However, with a few join types it does make a difference.

We recommend putting the most important table, seen as the *main table*, on the left of the join. An easy way to remember which table should be the table on the right side of the join is to determine which table can be used for a lookup or for a dropdown list in an application (see Figure 4.2).

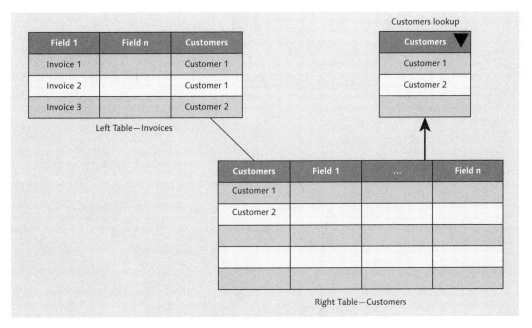

**Figure 4.2**  Table Used for Dropdown List on Right-Hand Side of a Join

This does not always mean that this table has to be physically positioned on the left of the screen in our graphical modeling tools. When we create a join in SAP HANA, the table we start the join from (by dragging and dropping) becomes the "left table" of the join.

Databases are highly optimized to work with joins; they are much better at it than you can hope to be in your application server or reporting tool. SAP HANA takes this to the next level with its new in-memory and parallelization techniques.

In SAP HANA, there are a number of different types of joins. Some of these are the same as what you would find in traditional databases, but others are unique to SAP HANA. Let's start by looking at the basic join types.

### Basic Join Types

The first basic join types that you will find in most databases are inner joins, left outer joins, right outer joins, and full outer joins. We will discuss SQL in more detail in Chapter 8.

The easiest way to visualize these join types is to use circles, as shown in Figure 4.3. This is a simplified illustration of what these join types do. (The assumption is that the tables illustrated here contain unique rows; that is, we join the tables via primary and foreign keys, as illustrated in Figure 4.1. If the tables contain duplicate records, this visualization does not hold.)

The left circle represents the table on the left side of the join. In Figure 4.3, the left table contains the two values A and B. The right circle represents the table on the right side of the join and contains the values B and C.

### *Inner Join*

The *inner join* is the most widely used join type in most databases. When in doubt and working with a non-SAP HANA database, try an inner join first.

The inner join returns the results from the area where the two circles overlap. In effect, this means that a value is shown only if it is found to be present in both the left and the right tables. In our case, in Figure 4.3, you can see that the value B is found in both tables.

Because we are only working with the "overlap" area, it does not matter for this join type which table is on the left or on the right side of the join.

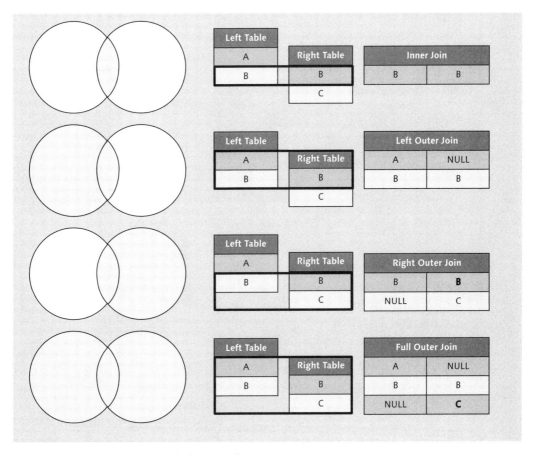

**Figure 4.3** Basic Join Types and Their Result Sets

### Left Outer Join

When using an inner join you may find that you're not getting all the data back that you require. To retrieve the data that was *left out*, you would use a *left outer* join. You will only use this join type when this need arises.

With a left outer join, everything in the table on the left side is shown (first table). If there are matching values in the right table, these are shown. If there are any "missing" values in the right hand table, these are shown with a NULL value.

For this join type, it is important to know which tables are on the left and the right side of the join.

### Right Outer Join

The inverse of the left outer join is the right outer join, This shows everything from the right table (second table). If there are matching values in the left table, these are shown. If there are any "missing" values in the left hand table, these are shown with a `NULL` value.

### Full Outer Join

As of SAP HANA SPS 11, we now have the full outer join. Many other databases also have this join type, so it is still regarded as one of the four basic join types.

This join type combines the results sets of both the left outer join and right outer join into a single result set.

### Self-Joins

There isn't really a join type called a *self-join*; the term refers to special cases in which a table is joined to itself. The same table is both the left table and the right table in the join relationship. The actual join type would still be something like an inner join.

This configuration is used mostly in recursive tables—that is, tables that refer back to themselves, such as in HR organizational structures. All employee team members have a manager, but managers are also employees of their companies and have someone else as their manager. In this case, team members and managers are all employees of the same company and are stored in the same table. Other examples include cost and profit center hierarchies or bills of materials (BOMs).

We return to this concept when we look at the Hierarchies section later in this chapter.

### SAP HANA Join Types

The join types on the right side of Figure 4.4 are unique to SAP HANA: referential join, text join, and temporal join.

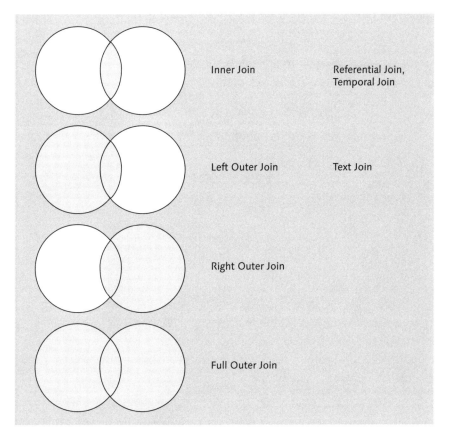

**Figure 4.4**   Basic Join Types and Some SAP HANA-Specific Join Types

### Referential Join

The referential join type normally returns exactly the same results as an inner join. So, what's the difference? There are many areas SAP HANA tries to optimize the performance of queries and result sets. In this case, even though a referential join gives the same results as an inner join, it provides a performance optimization under certain circumstances.

The referential join uses *referential integrity* between the tables in the join. Referential integrity is used in a business system to ensure that data in the left and right tables match. For example, we can't have an invoice that isn't linked to a customer, and the customer must be inserted into the database before we are allowed to create an invoice for that customer. Note that you do not need a value on both sides of the join: You may have a customer without an invoice, but you may not have an invoice without a customer.

If we can prove that the data in our tables has referential integrity, which most data in financial business systems has, then we can use a referential join. In this case, if we're not reading any data from the right table, then SAP HANA can quite happily ignore the entire right table and the join itself, and it doesn't have to do any checking, which speeds up the whole process.

> **Tip**
>
> A referential join is the optimal join type in SAP HANA.

### Text Join

Another SAP HANA-specific joint type is a text join. The name gives a clue as to when we will use this type of join.

The right-hand table, as shown in Figure 4.5, would be something like a text lookup table—for example, a list of country names. On one side, we would have a country code such as US or DE, and in the text lookup table we would have the same country code and would link it with the key, and also would have the actual name of the country (e.g., United States or Germany).

SAP sells software in many countries, and SAP business systems are available in multiple languages, and the name of the country and be translated into different languages. The fourth column in the text lookup table, called the language code, indicates into which language the country name has been translated. For example, for the country called DE and a language code of EN, the name of the country is in English and thus would be Germany. If the language code was DE (for German), the name of the country would be Deutschland, and if the language code was ES (for Español, indicating Spanish) then the name of the country would be Alemania.

Therefore, the same country can have totally different names depending on what language you speak.

In such a case, SAP HANA does something clever: By looking at the browser, the application server, or the machine that you are working on, it determines the language that you are logged on in. If you are logged in using English, it knows to use the name Germany. If you are logged on using German, it provides the German country name Deutschland for you.

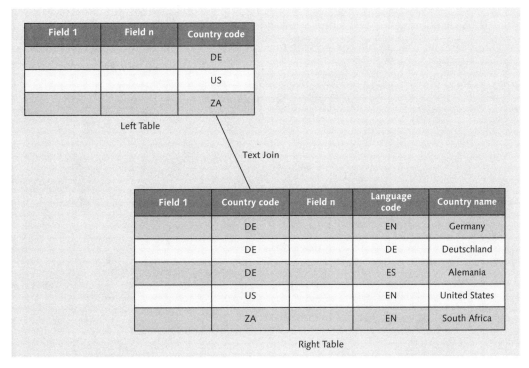

**Figure 4.5** Text Join

The text join behaves like a left outer join but always has a cardinality of one-to-one (1:1). In other words, it only returns a single country name based on the language you're logged on with. Even if you're logged in via mobile phone, your mobile phone has a certain language setting.

### Temporal Join

We use the temporal join when we've got FROM and TO date and time fields, or integers.

For example, say that you're storing the fuel price for gasoline in a specific table. From the beginning of this month to the end of this month, gasoline sells for a certain price. Next month, the price differs, and maybe two weeks later, it's adjusted again. Later, you'll have a list of all the different gasoline prices over time.

As a car owner, you now want to perform calculations for how much you've paid for your gasoline each time you filled up your tank. However, you just have the number of gallons and the dates of when you filled up.

You can say, "OK, on this date, I filled up the tank." You then have to look up which date range your filling-up date falls within and find the price for that specific date. You can then calculate what you paid to fill your tank for each of your dates. Figure 4.6 illustrates this example.

| Field 1 | Field n | Date |
|---|---|---|
| | | 27 February |
| | | 14 April |
| | | 13 May |

Left Table

Temporal Join

| Field 1 | From | To | Gas Price |
|---|---|---|---|
| | 1 January | 28 February | 12.22 |
| | 1 March | 1 April | 11.45 |
| | 2 April | 25 April | 11.50 |
| | 26 April | 10 May | 12.77 |
| | 11 May | 25 May | 11.33 |

Right Table—Pricelist

**Figure 4.6**   Temporal Join for Gasoline Prices

This date range lookup can be a little more complicated in a database. Sometimes, programmers read the data into an application server and then loop through the different records. In this case, a temporal join makes it easy, because SAP HANA will perform the date lookups in the FROM and the TO fields automatically for you, compare it to the date you've supplied, and get you the right fuel price at that specific date. It will perform all the calculations automatically for you—a great time and effort saver.

A temporal join uses either  a referential join; or an inner join to do the work. A temporal join requires valid to and from dates (in the gasoline price table) and a valid date-time column (in your car log book table).

### Spatial Join

Spatial joins became available in SAP HANA SPS 09. SAP HANA provides spatial data types, which we can use, for example, with maps. These all have the prefix *ST_*. A location on a map, with longitude and latitude, would be an ST_POINT data type. (We will discuss spatial data and analytics further in Chapter 9.)

We can use special spatial joins between tables in SAP HANA (see Figure 4.7). Say that you have a map location stored in a ST_POINT data type in one table. In the other table, you have a list of suburbs described in a ST_POLYGON data type. You can now join these two tables with a spatial join and define the spatial join to use the ST_CONTAINS method. This will calculate for each of the locations (ST_POINT) in which suburb (ST_POLYGON) they are located (ST_CONTAINS).

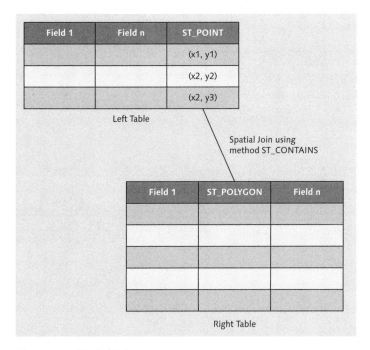

**Figure 4.7** Spatial Join

There are about a dozen methods like ST_CONTAINS available for spatial joins. For example, you can test if a road crosses a river, if one area overlaps another (e.g., mobile phone tower reception areas), or how close certain objects are to each other.

We have only mentioned the two-dimensional aspects in relation to maps, but many of these spatial functions can be used in three dimensions.

### Dynamic Joins

A dynamic join is not really a join type; it's a join property. It is also a performance enhancement available for SAP HANA. Once you have defined a join, you can mark it as a dynamic join. For this to work, you have to join the tables on multiple columns.

Let's assume you define a static (normal) join on columns A, B, and C between two tables, as shown in Figure 4.8. In this case, the join criteria on all three columns will be evaluated every time the view is called in a query.

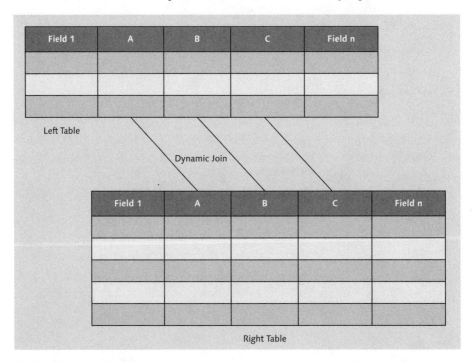

**Figure 4.8**  Dynamic Join on Multiple Columns

If you now mark the join as *dynamic*, the join criteria will only be evaluated on the columns involved in the query to the view. If you only ask for column A in your query of the view, then only column A's join criteria will be evaluated. The join criteria on columns B and C will not be evaluated, and your system performance improves.

 **Tip**

If your query does not request any of the join columns in the dynamic join, it will produce a runtime error.

## Core Data Services Views

CDS is a modeling concept that is becoming more important with every new release of SAP HANA. To understand why we need CDS, it is important to remember the wider context of how SAP HANA systems are deployed.

While learning SAP HANA, you work with a single system, but productive environments normally include development, quality assurance, and production systems. You perform development in the development environment, in which you have special modeling and development privileges. Your models and code then enter the quality assurance system for testing. When everyone is satisfied with the results, the models and code move to the production system. You do not have any modeling and development privileges in the quality assurance and production systems; you need a way to create views and other database objects in the production system, ideally without giving people special privileges.

An SAP HANA system can be deployed as the database for an SAP business system. In such a case, ABAP developers do not have any modeling and development privileges, even in the development system. We need a way to allow ABAP developers to create views and other database objects in the production system without these special privileges.

With that in mind, let's look at why CDS is a good idea with the following example:

You need to create a new schema in your SAP HANA database. It's easy to use a short SQL statement to do this, but remember the wider context. Someone will need the same create privileges in the production system! We want to avoid this, because giving anyone too much authorization in a production system can weaken security and encourage hackers.

CDS allows for a better way to create such a schema: Specify the schema creation statement once by creating a CDS (text) file with the `schema_name="DEMO";`

instruction. When we take this CDS file to the production system, the SAP HANA system automatically creates the schema for us. In the background, SAP HANA automatically converts the CDS file into the equivalent schema creation SQL statement and executes this statement.

The system administrators do not get privileges to create any schemas in the production system. They have rights to import CDS files, but they have no control over the contents of the CDS files; that's decided by the business. CDS thus gives us a nice way to separate what the business needs from what database administration can do.

There's much more to CDS. You can specify table structures (metadata) and associations (relationships) between tables with CDS, and taking this CDS file to production creates a new table. Even more impressive, if you want to modify the table structure later, SAP HANA does not delete the existing tables and recreate them; it automatically generates and executes the correct SQL statements to modify only the minimal changes to the existing table structures—for example, adding only a new column. CDS does not replace SQL statements, because it ultimately translates back into SQL statements. CDS adds the awareness to use a table creation SQL statement the first time it's run but a table modification SQL statement the second time it's run.

We can also create views using CDS. These CDS views can be used as data sources in our SAP HANA information views. Please note that these CDS views do not replace the more powerful information views we can create in SAP HANA.

ABAP developers can also use CDS inside ABAP. When a CDS view is sent to the SAP HANA system, it creates the necessary SAP HANA database objects without the ABAP developer having to log into the SAP HANA database. Because ABAP is database-independent, the same CDS file sent to another database will create the database objects relevant to that database. Because of this database independence, the versions of CDS for ABAP and for SAP HANA have slight differences.

The example screens in this book make use of the SHINE demo package described in Chapter 2. SHINE is a good example of CDS in action. You do not have to create a schema, create tables, or import data into these tables. When SHINE is imported into your SAP HANA system, it automatically creates all that content for you by using CDS statements.

Now, let's take our knowledge of these concepts to the next "dimension."

## Cube

One of the most important modeling concepts we will cover is the *cube*. We'll expand on this concept when we discuss the information views available in SAP HANA. In this section, we'll use a very simplistic approach to describing cubes to give you an understanding of the important concepts.

When you look at a cube the first time, it looks like multiple tables that are joined together—and at a database level, that might be true. What makes a cube a cube are the "rules" for joining these tables together.

The tables you join together contain two types of data: transactional data and master data. As shown in Figure 4.9, we have a main table in the middle called a *fact table*. This is where our transactional data is stored. The transactional data stored in the fact table is referred to as either *key figures* or *measures*. In SAP HANA, we just use the term *measures*.

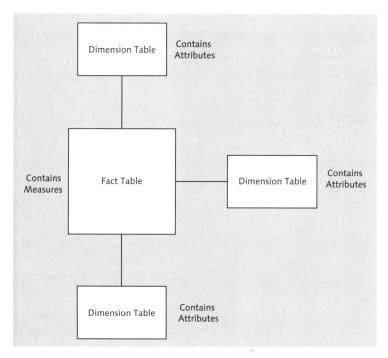

**Figure 4.9**   Cube Features

The side tables are called *dimension tables*, and this is where our master data is stored. The master data that is stored in the dimension table are referred to as *characteristics* or *attributes*, or sometimes even *facets*. In SAP HANA, we just use the term *attributes*.

To clear up these statements, let's walk through an example. Our cube example will be simplified to communicate the most basic principles.

In our example, we'll work with the sentence "Laura buys 10 apples." You will agree that this sentence describes a financial transaction: Laura went to the shop to buy some apples, she paid for them, and the shop owner made some profit.

Where will we will store this transaction's data in the cube? There are a couple of "rules" that we have to follow. The simplest rule is that you store the data with which you can perform calculations on in the fact table, and you store everything else that you can't perform calculations on in the dimension tables.

In our transaction of "Laura buys 10 apples," we first look at *Laura*. Can we perform a calculation on Laura? No, we can't. Therefore, we should put her name into one of the dimension tables. We put her name in the top dimension table in Figure 4.10. Laura is not the only customer of that shop; her name is stored with those of many other people in this dimension table. We will call this table the Customer dimension table.

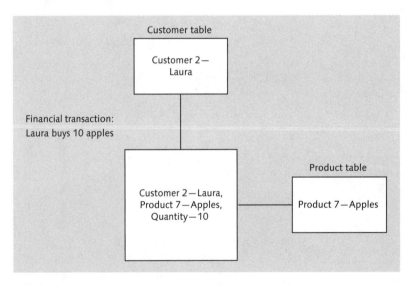

**Figure 4.10**  Financial Transaction Data Stored in a Cube

Next, let's look at the apples. Can we perform calculations on apples? No, we can't, so again this data goes into a dimension table. The shop doesn't sell only apples; it also sells a lots of other products. The second dimension table is therefore called the Product dimension table.

In an enterprise data warehouse, we would normally limit the number of dimension tables that we link to the fact table for performance reasons. Typically, in an SAP BW system, we limit the number of dimension tables to a maximum of 16 or 18.

Finally, let's look at the number of apples, 10. Can we perform a calculation on that? Yes, because it's a number. We therefore store that number in the fact table.

To complete the picture, if Laura buys more apples, then she is a top customer; let's say she's customer number 2. Apples are something the store keeps in stock, so apples are product number 7.

If we store a link (join) to customer 2 and another link (join) to product 7 and the number 10 (number of apples), we would say that that constitutes a complete transaction. We can abbreviate the transaction "Laura buys ten apples" to 2, 10, and 7 in our specific cube.

Laura and apples are part of our master data. The transaction itself is stored in the fact table. We've now put a real-life transaction into the cube.

Hopefully, this gives you a better idea of what a cube is, and how to use it. Let's complete this short tour of cubes by clarifying a few terms ahead.

**Attributes and Measures**

As previously shown in Figure 4.9, attributes are stored in dimension tables, and measures are stored in fact tables. Let's define attributes and measures:

▸ **Attributes**
Attributes describe a transaction, like the customer Laura or the product apples. This is also referred to as master data. We cannot perform calculations on attributes.

▸ **Measures**
Measures are something we can *measure* and perform calculations on. Measurable (transactional) information goes into the fact table.

### Fact Tables in the Data Foundation

Figure 4.10 showed only a single fact table, but sometimes we have more complex cubes that include multiple fact tables. In SAP HANA, we call a group of fact tables (or the single fact table) the *data foundation*.

When we join the data foundation (fact tables) to the dimension tables, we always put the data foundation on the left side of the join.

### Star Joins

The join between the data foundation and the dimension tables is normally a referential join in SAP HANA. We refer to this as a *star join*, which indicates that this is not just a normal referential join between low-level tables, but a join between a data foundation and dimension tables. This is seen as a join at a higher level.

Originally, we called these *logical joins* in SAP HANA, however they were renamed star joins as of SAP HANA SPS 10.

With all the building blocks in place, let's start examining SAP HANA information views.

## Information Views

Let's start our introduction to SAP HANA information views by looking back at what we learned when we discussed cubes.

### Dimension Views

The first thing we need to build cubes is the master data. Master data is stored in dimension tables. Sometimes, these dimension tables are created for the cubes. In SAP HANA, we do not create dimension tables as separate tables; instead we build them as views.

We join all the low-level database tables that contain the specific master data we are interested in into a view. For example, we might join two tables in a view to build a new Products dimension in SAP HANA, and maybe another three tables to build a new Customers dimension.

In this book, we will refer to these type of views simply as *dimension views*. In SAP HANA, there are currently two types of dimension views available:

▶ **Attribute views**
  The older version of dimension views are called *attribute views*. This name refers to the data, called *attributes*, stored in dimension tables. Attribute views are still used in exceptional cases in SAP HANA SPS 11.

▶ **Calculation views of type dimension (dimension calculation views)**
  As of SAP HANA SPS 10, we now use *calculation views of type dimension*, also called *dimension calculation views*. In SAP HANA SPS 11, a new migration tool is available to help migrate your old attribute views to the new dimension calculation views.

Just as the same master data is used in many cubes, so will we reuse dimension views in many of the other SAP HANA information views. You can even build your own "library" of dimension views.

**Star Join Views**

In the same way, instead of storing data in cubes, we can create another type of view in SAP HANA that produces the same results as a traditional cube. There are currently two types of SAP HANA views that produce the same results as an old-fashioned, traditional cube:

▶ **Analytic views**
  We still have an older version of these SAP HANA views called *analytic views*. This name refers to the fact that we use cubes for analytics. Analytic views are still used in some cases in SAP HANA SPS 11.

▶ **Calculation views of type cube with star join**
  As of SAP HANA SPS 10, we now use *calculation views of type cube with star join*. In SAP HANA SPS 11, a new migration tool is available to help you to migrate your old analytic views to the new calculation views of type cube with star join.

**Terminology**

In this book, we will simply refer to these types of views as *star join views*, not as *cube views*, which would lead to confusion. This is because the third type of SAP HANA views is called *calculation view of type cube*.

The results created by the star join views in SAP HANA are the same as that of a cube in an enterprise data warehouse, except that in a data warehouse, the data is stored in a cube. With SAP HANA, the data is not stored in a cube, but is calculated when required.

### Calculation Views of Type Cube

This view type, provides even more powerful capabilities. For example, you can combine multiple star join views ("cubes") to produce a combined result set. In SAP Business Warehouse (BW), we call this combined result set a *MultiProvider*.

In SAP HANA, we call these *calculation views of type cube*. Use cases for this type of view include:

▶ In your holding company, you want to combine the financial data from multiple subsidiary companies.

▶ You want to compare your actual expenses for 2015 with your planned budget for 2015.

▶ You have archived data in an archive database that you want to combine with current data in SAP HANA's memory to compare sales periods over a number of years.

## Using Information Views

Let's examine how to use the different types of SAP HANA information views together in information modeling. Figure 4.11 provides an overview of everything you've learned in this chapter and how each topic fits together.

On the top left-hand side, you can see our source systems: an SAP source system and a non-SAP source system. SAP HANA doesn't care from which system the data comes. In many projects, we have more non-SAP systems that we get data from than SAP systems. We extract the data from these systems using various data provisioning tools, which we'll look at in Chapter 14.

The data is stored in row tables in these source systems. When we use our data provisioning methods and tools, the data is put into column tables in the SAP HANA database. This is illustrated in the bottom-left corner of Figure 4.11.

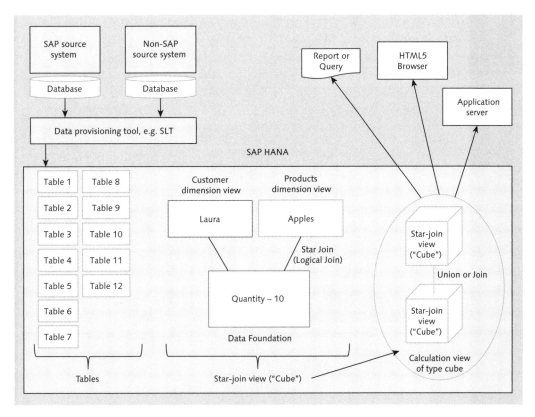

**Figure 4.11**   Different SAP HANA Information Views Working Together

## Building the Information Model

Now, let's start building our information models on top of these tables.

If we want to build something like a cube for our analytics or reporting, we use SAP HANA information views. First, we need the equivalent of a dimension table, such as our Product or Customer dimension table. How would we build this?

We will build a dimension view (a calculation view of type dimension, or an attribute view). This is indicated in Figure 4.11 by Laura and Apples, which represent the Customer and Product dimension views. We create these dimension views the same way we create any other view: Take two tables, join them together, select certain output fields, and save it.

Once we have our dimension views, we build a data foundation for the cube. The data foundation is for all our transactional data. The data foundation stores measures, like the number *10* for the 10 apples that Laura bought. We build a data foundation in a similar fashion to building a dimension view: We take multiple tables or a single table. If using multiple tables, we join them together, select the output fields, and build our data foundation.

To complete the cube, we have to link our data foundation (fact tables) to the dimensions with a star join. Finally, to complete our star join view, we also select the output fields for our cube. The created star join view will produce the same result as a cube, but in this case no data is stored and it performs much better.

In the next step, we can create calculation view of type cube, in which we combine two star join views (cubes). We can combine the star join views using a join or a union. We recommend a union in this case, because it leads to better performance than a join.

Finally, we can build reports, analytics, or applications on our calculation view. This is shown in the top right of Figure 4.11.

**Using the Information Model**

In the previous section, we looked at how to build an information model from the bottom up. Let's now think about the process from the other side and look at what happens when we call our report or application that built on the calculation view. This is the top-down view of Figure 4.11.

The calculation view does not store the data: It has to gather and calculate all the data required by the report. SAP HANA looks at the calculation view's description and says, "Oh, I've got to build two star join views and union them together. How do I build these star join views?"

SAP HANA then goes down one level and says, "OK, how do I build the first star join view? I need a data foundation, and I need two dimension views, and I join them together with a star join."

Then, it goes down another level: "How do I build the dimension view? I'll read two different tables, join them together, and select the output fields." SAP HANA then builds the two dimension views.

Going back up one level, SAP HANA needs to combine these two dimension tables with a data foundation. It creates the data foundation and joins it with the two dimension tables. It also builds the second star join view in the same way. Going up to the level of the calculation view, it combines the two star join views with a union. Finally, SAP HANA sends the result set out to the report, and then cleans out the memory again. (It does not store this data!) If someone else asks for the exact same data five minutes later, SAP HANA happily performs the same calculations all over again.

At first, this can seem very wasteful. Often we're asked "Why don't you use some kind of caching?" However, *caching* means that we store data in memory. In SAP HANA the entire database is already in memory. We don't need caching because everything is in memory already.

The reason people ask this question is that in their traditional data warehouses, data normally doesn't change until the next evening when the data is refreshed. Inside SAP HANA, the data can be updated continuously, and we always want to use the latest data in our applications, reports, and analytics. That means we have to recalculate the values each time; caching static result sets will not work.

In summary, to use real-time data, you have to continuously recalculate.

## Other Modeling Artifacts

We will now discuss some of the other modeling concepts we will use when building our information views.

The power of calculation views of type cube is that you can build them up in many layers. In the bottom layer, you can perhaps have a union of two star join views (cubes), as shown in Figure 4.12. In the next (higher) layer, we sum up all the values from the union. In the level above that, we rank the summed results to show the top 10 most profitable customers.

### Projection

A *projection* is used to change an output result set. For example, we can get a result set from a star join view (cube) and find that it has too many output fields for what we need in the next layers. Therefore, we use a projection as an additional in-between layer to create a subset of the results.

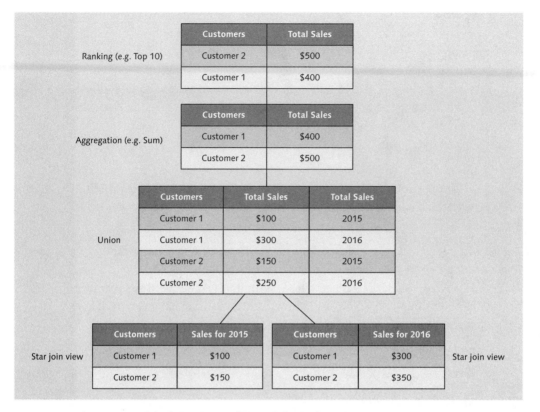

**Figure 4.12**   Calculation View of Type Cube Built in Various Layers

We can also use the projection to calculate additional fields—for example, sales tax—or we can rename fields to give them more meaningful names for our analytics and reporting users.

### Ranking

As illustrated in the top node of Figure 4.12, we can use *ranking* to create useful top-N or bottom-N reports and analytics. This normally returns a filtered list (e.g., only the top 10 companies) and is sorted in the order we specify.

## Aggregation

The word *aggregation* means a collection of things. In SQL, we use aggregations to calculate values such as the sum of a list of values. Aggregations in databases provide the following functions:

▶ **Sum**
Adds up all the values in the list

▶ **Count**
Counts how many values (records) there are in the list

▶ **Minimum**
Finds the smallest value in the list

▶ **Maximum**
Finds the largest value in the list

▶ **Average**
Calculates the arithmetical mean of all the values in the list

▶ **Standard deviation**
Calculates the standard deviation of all the values in the list

▶ **Variance**
Calculates the variance of all the values in the list

Normally, we would only calculate aggregations of measures. (Remember that measures are values we can perform calculations on, which usually means our transactional data.) For example, we could calculate the total number of apples a shop sold in 2015. However, in the latest versions of SAP HANA, we can also create aggregations of attributes, essentially creating a list of unique values.

## Union

A *union* combines two result sets. Figure 4.12 illustrates this by combining the results of two star join views.

In SAP HANA graphical calculation views, we're not restricted to combining two result sets; we can combine multiple result sets. SAP HANA merges these multiple result sets into a single result set.

Let's say we have four result sets—A, B, C, and D—that we union together. Although we union multiple result sets, that doesn't mean the performance will be bad. If SAP HANA detects that you are not asking for data from A and D, it will not even generate the result sets for A and D; it will only work with B and C.

> **Note**
>
> The union expects the two result sets to have the same number of columns, in the same order, and the matching columns from each result set must have similar data types.

You can have variations in unions, such as the following:

▶ **Union all**
Will merge the result sets and return all records

▶ **Union**
Will merge the results and only give you the unique results back

▶ **Union with constant values**
Lets you "pivot" your merged results to help get the data ready for reporting output

Figure 4.13 compares the output generated by a union to that of a union with constant values.

| Customers | Total Sales | Total Sales |
|---|---|---|
| Customer 1 | $100 | 2015 |
| Customer 1 | $300 | 2016 |
| Customer 2 | $150 | 2015 |
| Customer 2 | $250 | 2016 |

**Standard Union**

| Customers | Sales for 2015 | Sales for 2016 |
|---|---|---|
| Customer 1 | $100 | $300 |
| Customer 2 | $150 | $350 |

**Union with constant values**

| Customers | Sales for 2015 |
|---|---|
| Customer 1 | $100 |
| Customer 2 | $150 |

| Customers | Sales for 2016 |
|---|---|
| Customer 1 | $300 |
| Customer 2 | $350 |

**Figure 4.13**  Standard Union Compared to Union with Constant Values

Often, we want a report that looks like the top right of the figure. If we're given the output from the standard union, it takes more work to create a report with sales for 2015 and 2016 in separate columns. With the output from the union with constant values, writing the report is easy.

In Figure 4.11, we showed that you should use a union rather than a join for performance reasons—but what happens if the two star join views that you want to union together do not have the same outputs? In that case, the union will return an error. How do we solve this problem?

Figure 4.14 illustrates an example. On top, we have the ideal case in which both star join views have matching columns. In the middle, we have a case in which only column B matches. Normally, we would use a join, as shown.

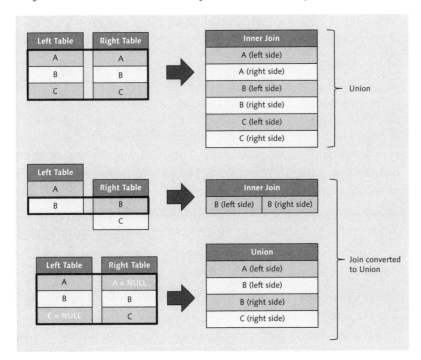

**Figure 4.14** Standard Union, Join, and Join Converted to Union

We solve this problem by creating a projection for each of the two star join views. We add the missing columns and assign a NULL value to those columns. We then perform the union on the two projections, because they now have matching columns.

## Semantics

An important step that many modelers skip is to add more meaning to the output of their information models. *Semantics*, as a general term, is the study of meaning. We can use semantics in SAP HANA to, for example, rename fields in a system so they are more clear. Some database fields have really horrible names. Using semantics, you can change the name of these fields to be more meaningful for your end users. This is especially useful when they create reports. If you have a reporting background, you will know that a reporting universe can fulfill a similar function.

We can also show that certain fields are related to each other—for example, a customer number and a customer name field.

One example that is used often is that of building a hierarchy. By using a hierarchy, you can see how fields are related to each other with regards to "drilling down" for reports.

## Hierarchies

*Hierarchies* are used in reporting to enable intelligent drilldown. Figure 4.15 illustrates two examples: Users can start with a list of sales for all the different countries; they can then drill down to the sales of the provinces (or states) of a specific country, and finally down to the sales of a city.

End users can see the sales figures for just the country, state, or province or for a specific city. Even though countries and cities are two different fields, they're related to each other by use of a hierarchy. This extra relationship enhances the data and gives it more meaning (semantic value).

There are two different types of hierarchies: *level hierarchies* and *parent–child hierarchies*. The hierarchy we just described is the level hierarchy; level 1 is the country, level 2 is the state or province, and level 3 is the city or town.

Another example of a level hierarchy is a *time-based hierarchy* that goes from a year to a month to a day. You can even keep going deeper, down to seconds. This is illustrated on the right side of Figure 4.15.

HR employee organizational charts or a cost center structures are examples of parent–child hierarchy, as illustrated in Figure 4.16. In this case, we join a table to itself, as described in the Self-Joins section.

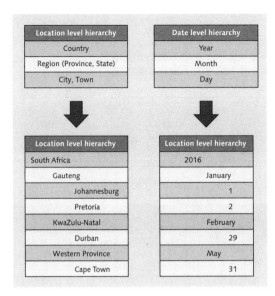

**Figure 4.15**   Examples of Level Hierarchies

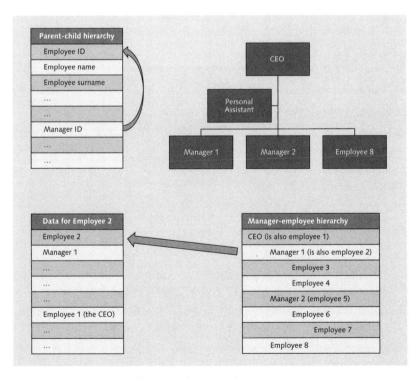

**Figure 4.16**   Parent–Child Hierarchy Example

Table 4.1 provides a quick summary of the differences between the two types of hierarchies and when you should use which one.

| Level Hierarchies | Parent–Child Hierarchies |
| --- | --- |
| Fixed (rigid) number of levels in the hierarchy. | Variable hierarchy depth. |
| Different data fields on every level of the hierarchy (e.g., country, state, city). | The same (two) fields used on every level of the hierarchy. |
| The fields on each level of the hierarchy can be different data types (e.g., country can be text, while zip/postal code can be numeric). | The parent and child fields have the same data type. |

**Table 4.1**  Comparing Level Hierarchies and Parent–Child Hierarchies

## Best Practices and Modeling Guidelines

Let's end our tour of modeling concepts with a summary of best practices for modeling views in SAP HANA. Many of the basic modeling guidelines that we find in traditional data modeling and reporting environments are still applicable in SAP HANA. We can summarize the basic principles as follows:

▶ **Limit (filter) the data as early as possible**
It's wasteful to send millions of data records across a slow network to a reporting tool when the report only uses a few of these data records. It makes a lot more sense to send only the data records that the report requires, so we want to filter the data before it hits the network.

In the same way, we don't want to send data to a star join view when we can filter it in the earlier dimension view. Hence, the rule to filter as early as possible.

▶ **Perform calculations as late as possible**
Assume you have column A and column B in a table. The table contains billions of records. We can use the values of column A and column B in a formula for every data record, which means the server performs billions of calculations, and finally add up the sum total of the calculated fields.

It would be much faster to add up the sum total for column A and the sum total for column B and then calculate the formula. In that case, we perform the calculation once instead of billions of times. We delay the calculation as long as possible for performance reasons.

## Important Terminology

In this chapter, we focused on various modeling concepts and how they're used in SAP HANA. We introduced the following important terms:

▶ **Views**
We started at by looking at *views* and realized that we can leverage the fact that SAP HANA already has all the data in memory, that the servers have lots of CPU cores available, and that SAP HANA runs everything in parallel. We therefore do not need to store the information in cubes and dimension tables, but can use views to generate the information when we need it. This also gives us the advantage of real-time results.

▶ **Joins**
We have both normal database join types, like inner and left outer joins, and SAP HANA-specific types, like referential, text, temporal, and spatial joins. In the process, we also looked at the special case of self-joins and at dynamic joins as an optimization technique.

▶ **Core Data Services (CDS)**
CDS provides a way to separate business semantics and intent from database operations.

▶ **Cubes**
A cube consists of a data foundation with fact tables that contain the transactional data, linked to dimension tables that contain master data. The data foundation is linked to the dimension tables with star joins.

▶ **Attributes and measures**
Attributes describe elements involved in a transaction. Transactional data that we can perform calculations on is called a measure and stored in the fact tables.

▶ **Information views**
In SAP HANA, we take the concept of views to higher levels. We can create

dimension tables and cubes as dimension views and star join views. Dimension views are attribute views and calculation views of type dimension. Star join views are analytic views and calculation views of type cube with star join. The final type of information view is the calculation view of type cube, which we can use to perform even more powerful processes.

▶ **Modeling artifacts**
Inside our views, we can use unions, projections, aggregations, and ranking. Unions are quite flexible and can be used for a direct merge of result sets, or we can use a union with constant values to create report-ready result sets.

## 🔏 Practice Questions

These practice questions will help you evaluate your understanding of the topics covered in this chapter. The questions shown are similar in nature to those found on the certification examination. Although none of these questions will be found on the exam itself, they will allow you to review your knowledge of the subject. Select the correct answers and then check the completeness of your answers in the Practice Question Answers and Explanations section. Remember that on the exam you must select all correct answers and only correct answers to receive credit for the question.

In this section, we have a few questions with graphics attached. In the certification exam, you might also see a few questions that include graphics.

1.  In which SAP HANA views will you find measures? (There are 2 correct answers.)

☐    **A.** Attribute views

☐    **B.** Calculation view of type cube with star join

☐    **C.** Calculation view of type cube

☐    **D.** Database views

2.  True or False: A database view stores data in the database.

☐    **A.** True

☐    **B.** False

3.  A traditional cube is represented by which SAP HANA view type? (There are 2 correct answers.)

☐  **A.** Attribute view

☐  **B.** Analytic view

☐  **C.** Calculation view of type cube with star join

☐  **D.** Calculation view of type dimension

4.  A referential join gives the same results as which other join type?

☐  **A.** Inner join

☐  **B.** Left outer join

☐  **C.** Spatial join

☐  **D.** Star join

5.  Which join type makes use of date ranges?

☐  **A.** Spatial join

☐  **B.** Text join

☐  **C.** Temporal join

☐  **D.** Inner join

6.  If we change the transaction "Laura buys 10 apples" to "Laura buys 10 green apples," how would we store the color *green*?

☐  **A.** Store *green* as an attribute

☐  **B.** Store *green* as a measure

☐  **C.** Store *green* as a spatial data type

☐  **D.** Store *green* as a CDS view

7.  True or False: A view always shows all the available columns of the underlying tables.

☐  **A.** True

☐  **B.** False

8.  You have a view with two tables, joined by a left outer join. If you redesign the view and accidently swap the two tables around, what should you do to the join?

☐   **A.** Keep the left outer join.

☐   **B.** Change the join to a text join.

☐   **C.** Change the join to a right outer join.

☐   **D.** Change the join to a referential join.

9.  What do you call the data displayed in the data foundation of an SAP HANA information view?

☐   **A.** Facets

☐   **B.** Measures

☐   **C.** Characteristics

☐   **D.** Key figures

10. You are writing a mobile application for the World Series. You have details about all the baseball players and the baseball scores for all the previous matches. How do you use the data of the player information and the scores?

☐   **A.** Both the player information and the scores are used as master data.

☐   **B.** Both the player information and the scores are used as transactional data.

☐   **C.** The player information is used as master data, and the scores are used as transactional data.

☐   **D.** The player information is used as transactional data, and the scores are used as master data.

11. Look at Figure 4.17. You are selling books that have been translated into various languages. What join type should you use?

☐   **A.** Left outer join

☐   **B.** Text join

☐   **C.** Temporal join

☐   **D.** Referential join

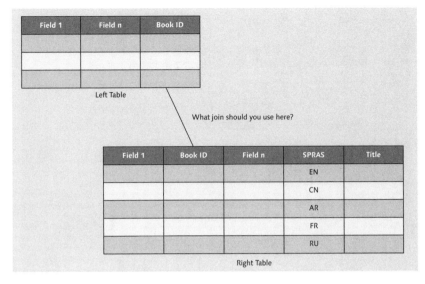

**Figure 4.17**   What Type of Join Should You Use?

12. Which of the following are reasons you should use Core Data Services (CDS) to create a schema? (There are 2 correct answers.)

☐   **A.** The database administrator might type the name wrong.

☐   **B.** The database administrator should not get those privileges in the production system.

☐   **C.** The focus is on the business requirements.

☐   **D.** The focus is on the database administration requirements.

13. Look at Figure 4.18. A company sends out a lot of quotes. Some customers accept the quotes, and they're invoiced. The company asks you to find a list of the customers that did NOT accept the quotes. How do you find the customers that received quotes but did NOT receive invoices?

☐   **A.**
   ▸ Use a right outer join.
   ▸ Filter to show only the NULL values on the right table.

☐   **B.**
   ▸ Use a left outer join.
   ▸ Filter to show only customers on the right table.

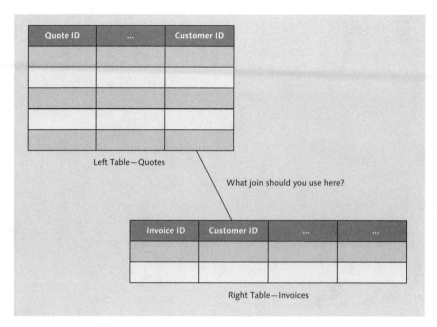

**Figure 4.18**   Find the Customers That Received Quotes but Not Invoices

☐   **C.**

   ▸ Use a left outer join.

   ▸ Filter to show only the `NULL` values on the right table.

☐   **D.**

   ▸ Use a right outer join.

   ▸ Filter to show only customers on the left table.

14. True or False: When you use a parent–child hierarchy, the depth in your hierarchy levels can vary.

☐   **A.** True

☐   **B.** False

15. Look at Figure 4.19. What type of join should you use? (*Hint:* Watch out for distractors.)

☐   **A.** Temporal join

☐   **B.** Text join

☐ **C.** Referential join

☐ **D.** Inner join

| Field 1 | Field n | Person |
|---|---|---|
| | | Sarah |
| | | Katrin |
| | | Amanda |

Left Table—Persons

What join should you use here?

| Field 1 | From airport | To airport | Language code |
|---|---|---|---|
| Amanda | Johannesburg | Frankfurt | EN |
| Katrin | Frankfurt | JFK | DE |
| Sarah | JFK | Madrid | ES |
| Sarah | Madrid | London | EN |
| Amanda | London | Cape Town | EN |

Right Table—Flights

**Figure 4.19** What Type of Join Should You Use?

16. You have a list of map locations for clinics. The government wants to build a new clinic, but wants to build it where there is the greatest need. You need to find the largest distance between any two clinics. With your current knowledge, how do you do this?

☐ **A.**

- Use a temporal join to find the distance between clinics.
- Use a union with constant values to "pivot" the values.

☐ **B.**

- Use a spatial join to find the distance between clinics.
- Use a level hierarchy for drilldown.

    ☐   **C.**

        ▶ Use a dynamic join to find the longest distance between clinics.

        ▶ Use a ranking to find the top 10 values.

    ☐   **D.**

        ▶ Use a spatial join to find the distance between clinics.

        ▶ Use an aggregation with the maximum option.

17. Look at Figure 4.20. What are the values for X, Y, and Z? (*Note:* You will not see a question like this on the certification exam; it's only added here to test your understanding.)

    ☐   **A.** X = Customer 2, Y = 400, Z = 800.

    ☐   **B.** X = Customer 1, Y = 400, Z = 400.

    ☐   **C.** X = Customer 1, Y = 800, Z = 800.

    ☐   **D.** X = Customer 2, Y = 200, Z = 400.

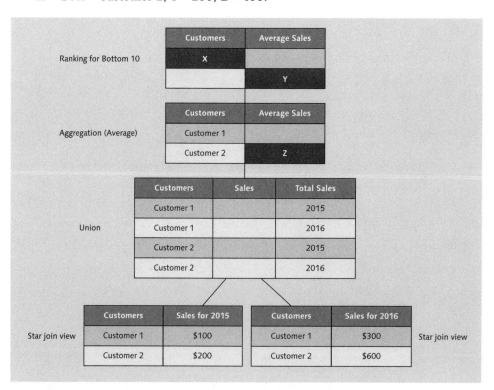

**Figure 4.20**   Find Values for X, Y, and Z

18. You have to build a parent–child hierarchy. What type of join do you expect to use?

☐   **A.** Relational join

☐   **B.** Temporal join

☐   **C.** Dynamic join

☐   **D.** Self-join

19. Look at Figure 4.21. What join type should you use to see all the suppliers?

☐   **A.** Left outer join

☐   **B.** Right outer join

☐   **C.** Inner join

☐   **D.** Referential join

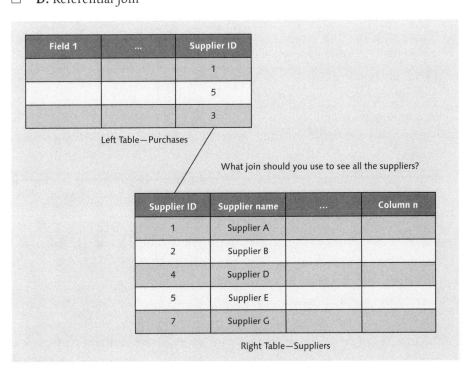

**Figure 4.21**   What Join Should You Use to See All Suppliers?

## Practice Question Answers and Explanations

1. Correct answers: **B, C**

   You find measures in analytic views, calculation views of type cube with star join (the new type of analytic view), and calculation views of type cube. Attribute views do not contain measures—only attributes!

2. Correct answer: **B**

   False. A database view does not store data in the database.

3. Correct answers: **B, C**

   A traditional cube is represented by an analytic view or a calculation view of type cube with star join. Both are different from a cube in that they do not store any data like a cube does. An attribute view and a calculation view of type dimension are similar to a dimension table.

4. Correct answer: **A**

   A referential join gives the same results as an inner join but speeds up the calculations in some cases by assuming referential integrity of the data. It is the optimal join type in SAP HANA.

5. Correct answer: **C**

   A temporal join requires `FROM` and `TO` fields in the table on the right side of the join and a date-time column in the table on the left side of the join.

6. Correct answer: **A**

   We cannot "measure" or perform calculations on the color green. Green is not a spatial data type. CDS views are not relevant in this context.

7. Correct answer: **B**

   False. A view does NOT *always* show all the available columns of the underlying tables. You have to select the output fields of a view. The word *always* in the statement is what makes it false.

8. Correct answer: **C**

   A right outer join is the inverse of the left outer join. Therefore, if you reverse the order of the tables, you can "reverse" the join type. It is important to note that this does not work for a text join. A text join is only equivalent to a left outer join. For a text join, you have to be careful about the order of the tables.

9.  Correct answer: **B**

    The data displayed in the data foundation of an SAP HANA information view is called measures. In SAP HANA, we talk about *attributes* and *measures*. The other names might be used in other data modeling environments, but not in SAP HANA.

10. Correct answer: **C**

    The player information is used as master data, and the scores are used as transactional data. You cannot perform calculations on the players. Therefore, this data is used in the dimensions and is seen as master data. You definitely perform calculations on the scores, so these are used in the fact tables, which means they are transactional data.

11. Correct answer: **B**

    Figure 4.17 shows the SPRAS column and shows a list of languages. The need for a translation is also hinted at in the question, meaning this should be a text join. There is not enough information to select any of the other answer options.

12. Correct answers: **B, C**

    You should use CDS to create a schema because the database administrator should not get those privileges in the production system and the focus should be on the business requirements.

13. Correct answer: **C**

    Look carefully at Figure 4.18. The question asks you to find all the customers that received quotes but did NOT receive invoices.

    The answer only gives us left outer or right outer as options. Because the question states they want *all* customers from the quotes tables, you might try a left outer join first.

    Now look at Figure 4.3 to see the difference between the left and right outer joins. Look especially at the where the NULL values are shown. With a left outer join, the NULL values are found in the right table. With a right outer join, the NULL values are found in the left table.

    We want to find the customers that did not get invoices. With a left outer join, the NULL values are found on the right side: That group is the one we are looking for. Therefore, filter for the NULL values on the right table.

> **Note**
>
> Any time that a negative phrase or word is used in the certification exam, it is shown in capital letters to bring attention to the fact that it is a negative word.

14. Correct answer: **A**

    True. Yes, the depth of your hierarchy levels can vary when you use a parent–child hierarchy.

15. Correct answer: **C**

    You should use a referential join.

    There are two distractors to try and throw you off track:

    ▶ A temporal join uses FROM and TO fields, but only for date-time fields. This example is for airports.

    ▶ The second distractor was to try to get you to select the text join: The language code has nothing to do with translations, but has to do with the airline's primary language.

    Choose a referential join because you can see the same people traveling in both tables, so it seems that these two tables have referential integrity.

    If the tables did not have referential integrity, you would have chosen an inner join.

16. Correct answer: **D**

    A spatial join can give the distance between different points on a map.

    There are two ways you can find the largest distance between any two clinics:

    ▶ Use a ranking to find the top 10 values.

    ▶ Use an aggregation with the maximum option.

17. Correct answer: **B**

    See the full solution in Figure 4.22.

    X = Customer 1, Y = 400, Z = 400.

    Note that we are using average in the aggregation node, not sum.

    In the ranking node, we are asking for the bottom 10, not the top 10.

18. Correct answer: **D**

    You expect to use a self-join when you build a parent–child hierarchy. See Figure 4.16 for an illustration.

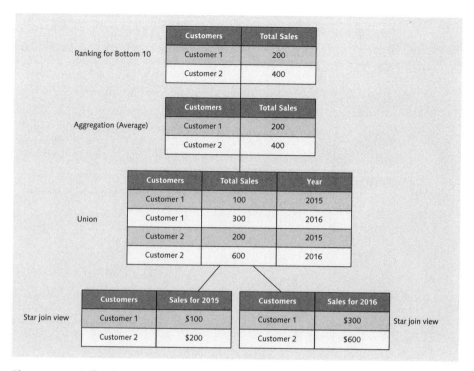

**Figure 4.22**  Full Solution: X = Customer 1, Y = 400, Z = 400

19. Correct answer: **B**

   To see everything on the right table, use a right outer join.

   Note that these tables do not have referential integrity. If we had asked the question a little differently, this could have been important.

# Takeaway

You should now have a general understanding of information modeling concepts: views, joins, cubes, star joins, data foundations, dimension tables, and so on. In this chapter, you learned about the differences between attributes and measures and the value of CDS in the development cycle. You have seen the various types of views that SAP HANA uses, how to use them together, and what options you have available for your information modeling. Finally, we examined a few best practices and guidelines for modeling in SAP HANA in general.

## Summary

You have learned about many modeling concepts and how they are applied and implemented in SAP HANA.

You're now ready to go into the practical details of learning how to use all the SAP HANA information views and how to enhance these views with the various modeling artifacts that we have available to us in each of these different views.

# Information Modeling Tools

## Techniques You'll Master

- Get to know the SAP HANA modeling tools in more detail
- Identify the different working areas in SAP HANA studio
- Learn how to work with tables and data
- Know how to create new information models
- Understand the developer perspective
- Get a working knowledge of best practices and guidelines for modeling with the SAP HANA modeling tools

There are two development environments used for SAP HANA modeling. The first is *SAP HANA studio*, a Java-based development environment for laptops and desktops. The second, more recent development environment is a web-based development environment that you run from your browser: the *SAP HANA web-based development workbench*.

We will look at both of these environments and how you can use them to create your information models. Because SAP HANA studio is the most complete tool and has been around the longest, we'll look at it in greater detail. We'll then show you the web-based development environment, how to use it, and how it differs from SAP HANA studio.

## Real-World Scenario

You're working on a project that requires you to create calculation views. To do so, you use SAP HANA studio to create and edit these views graphically.

Sometimes you reach for the other tool in your toolkit, the SAP HANA web-based development workbench, because you can use this tool from anywhere, even using your tablet.

When working on a project with SAP HANA, you will use modeling tools all the time. You have to be familiar with the SAP HANA modeling tools, know when to use which one, and be able to find your way around the various screens. SAP HANA has grown over the last few years, and the modeling tools now have a wide variety of tasks you can accomplish with them. The features have also grown to provide rich functionality. It therefore takes some time to learn how to find your way around the various menus, options, and screens.

## Objectives of This Portion of the Test

The purpose of this portion of the SAP HANA certification exam is to test your general knowledge of the SAP HANA modeling tools.

The certification exam expects you to have a good understanding of the following topics:

- Overview of SAP HANA studio

- Differences between the catalog and the content areas

- Table definitions and runtime information

- Preview result sets, with all the preview options

- The development perspective and how to create SAP HANA development objects

- Overview of the SAP HANA web-based development workbench

> **Note**
>
> This portion contributes up to 3% of the total certification exam score.

## Key Concepts Refresher

As noted, there are two modeling tools available in SAP HANA. We will now look at both tools and how you can use them to create your SAP HANA information models.

We will start by looking at SAP HANA studio.

### SAP HANA Studio

SAP HANA studio is built in a development environment based on *Eclipse*, an open-source framework by IBM. (For more information about Eclipse, visit *http://www.eclipse.org*.) This development environment is written in Java, so it only runs on your desktop or laptop.

Eclipse originally started out as a Java development environment, but was later adapted into other programming languages, such as JavaScript, PHP, HTML, Cascading Style Sheets (CSS), Ruby, and many others.

That IBM called the product Eclipse proves that IBM has a good sense of humor. During the time of the Eclipse release, IBM was in competition with Sun over their respective Java Virtual Machines. We all know what happens to the sun during an eclipse!

Figure 5.1 shows an overview screen of SAP HANA studio in an Eclipse environment, with the different work areas indicated.

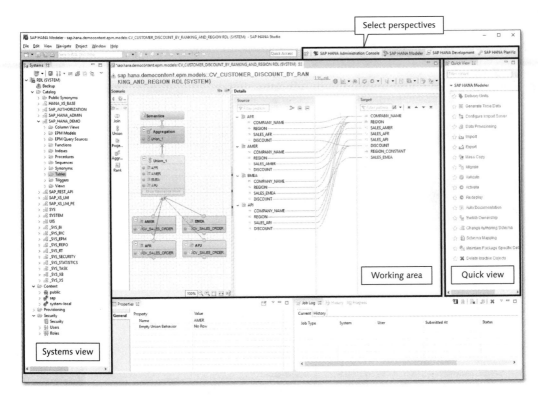

**Figure 5.1**  SAP HANA Studio

On the top right is an area called *perspectives*. On the left of the screen is an area in which you can see the different SAP HANA systems you work with, and the components for each system. In the middle is the main working area. On the right-hand side, you'll see a tab called QUICK VIEW, which is specifically used in the modeler perspective.

In this section, we will look at the different working areas of SAP HANA studio, including the SAP HANA studio perspectives, main workspace, system views, two primary consoles (the SQL Console and Administration Console), and the application function modeler (AFM). Finally, we'll discuss the steps to set up the session client.

### Perspectives

The Eclipse environment uses different perspectives to give you different layouts for different development tasks. In SAP HANA studio, there are perspectives for information modeling, administrators, plan visualization, and SAP HANA development. When you select another perspective, it changes the screen layout, menu options, and so on. In Eclipse, you can even create your own perspectives or change the available perspectives to suit your requirements.

To select or change to another perspective, simply click the name of that perspective in the top right-hand side of the SAP HANA studio screen, as shown in Figure 5.1. If you want to select a perspective that is not on that list, click the ⊞ button to the left side of these names. This will open a menu from which you can select the perspective that you want to use.

To get a better idea of how these perspectives vary in look and available options, Figure 5.2 shows the differences between the modeler and development perspectives.

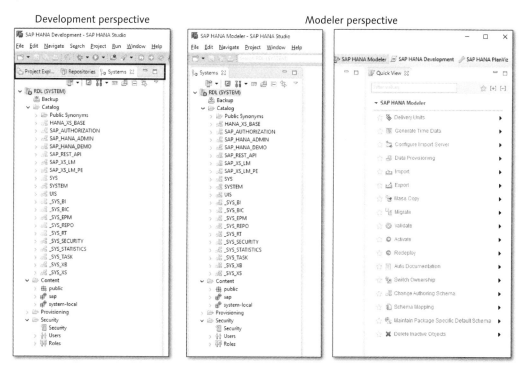

**Figure 5.2**   Development vs. Modeler Perspective

The left-hand side of Figure 5.2 shows the development perspective. In this perspective, three different tabs appear: SYSTEMS, REPOSITORIES, and PROJECT EXPLORER.

When you select the modeler perspective (right-hand side), you only have one tab: SYSTEMS. This means that you cannot access the repositories or projects from the modeler perspective.

 **Tip**

In SAP HANA, we prefer the development perspective, even when performing modeling tasks, because it has a lot more features than the modeler perspective.

The only thing that the modeler perspective has that the development perspective does not is the QUICK VIEW tab shown on the right-hand side. We will discuss the functionality available in the QUICK VIEW tab throughout this book.

### Main Workspace

In the middle of Figure 5.1, the main workspace is displayed. In this case, you can see a calculation view with a union. You can see the mapping of the different fields in the union.

When you open table definitions, stored procedures, or different views, or just preview the output of an information model, you will see the results in this main workspace. Each of the SAP HANA objects that you open will be displayed inside its own tab.

### Systems View

You can see the systems view on the left side of Figure 5.1. Figure 5.3 provides a more detailed look.

All your different SAP HANA systems are shown this area. From SAP HANA studio, you can work with multiple SAP HANA systems—for example, with both a development and production system.

Within each SAP HANA system, you will find different areas shown as folders in the systems view. The following areas are found in the systems view:

▶ BACKUP folder
The BACKUP folder is used by administrators to manage the backups and recovery of SAP HANA databases. Depending on your security settings, you might not even see this folder, because it is meant for administrators only. We will not discuss this folder in this book.

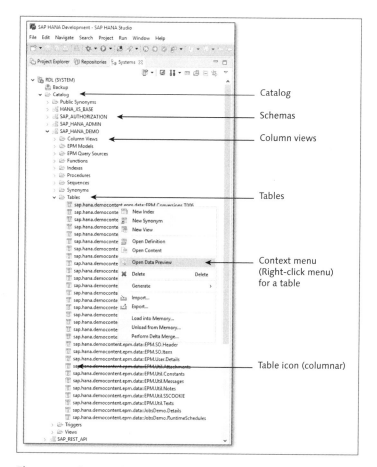

**Figure 5.3**   Systems View

▶ CATALOG area
The CATALOG area is used, for example, for schemas and tables. You can see your tables, their definitions, and data in the CATALOG area.

▶ CONTENT area
The CONTENT area is used for information modeling. This is where all your SAP HANA models are created and stored.

▶ PROVISIONING area
The PROVISIONING area is used by SAP HANA smart data access (SDA; discussed in Chapter 14). This area is used for creating virtual tables, to get data from other databases into SAP HANA.

▶ SECURITY folder

The SECURITY folder, which we will discuss in more detail in Chapter 13, is where you can create SAP HANA users and assign them privileges to work with your information models.

In this chapter, we will focus on the CATALOG and CONTENT areas.

### Catalog Area

The CATALOG area houses most of the artifacts for the SAP HANA database. It is divided into *schemas*. SAP HANA schemas are groupings of tables and other artifacts. The main database objects we find here are tables. Inside SAP HANA, we can also find items such as column views, functions, indexes, procedures, synonyms, and triggers.

If you have an SAP BW on SAP HANA system or an SAP ERP on SAP HANA system, you will find a schema inside the CATALOG area of the SAP HANA database that corresponds to the *system identity* (SID) of the SAP system. For example, if the SID of your SAP BW system is *BW1*, you will find a schema inside the SAP HANA database called *BW1* that contains all the SAP BW system's tables.

When you open the tree structure—for example, down to the tables—you'll find a list of all the tables inside that schema. Check the icon in front of each table to determine if it's a column or a row table. The 🖽 icon indicates that this table is a row-based table, the 🎛 icon indicates a column-based table, and the 🖽 icon indicates a virtual table. In SAP HANA, column-based tables are the preferred table type. They compress much better than row-based tables and do not need indexes.

When you right-click on a table, a *context menu* appears (sometimes referred to as a *right-click menu*) for that table. Through that menu, you can look at the table definition, table contents, or open a data preview for that specific table. In the CATALOG area, you can also delete tables, import more tables, and export tables.

Let's look more closely at table definitions and the data preview:

▶ **Table definitions**

Figure 5.4 shows the definition of a table. On the top right-hand side of the screen, you can see the table TYPE—whether it is COLUMN STORE or ROW STORE.

Table definition

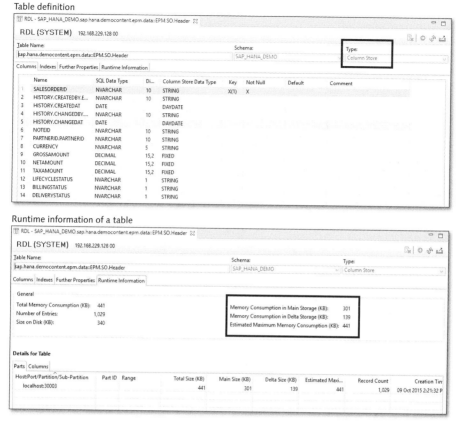

**Figure 5.4**   Definition of a Column Table

When you click the RUNTIME INFORMATION tab, as shown at the bottom in Figure 5.4, you can see the memory consumption of a specific table and whether it is loaded into memory. From the table context menu, you can load the table into memory or unload it from memory.

▶ **Data preview**

When you run a data preview of a table, you'll see three different tabs with quite a lot of functionality:

  ▷ RAW DATA

  The RAW DATA tab (Figure 5.5) displays the table contents. You will notice in the top right-hand corner that there is a SORT option available. You can either sort and display the top records of the entire dataset, or sort the current dataset, which by default would be the top 200 records. You can also export that dataset. This data preview is available not only for tables, but also for SAP HANA models. You can view the output from any of the information models and export the output of these information models.

**Data Preview: Sorting and Export**

The sorting and data export features were introduced in SAP HANA SPS 10. You can change the default of 200 records shown in the top-right field (Max Rows), and you select what sorting behavior you want from the dropdown menu (see Figure 5.5). There are two options here:

▸ Sort Entire Data Set
This sorts all the records in the table, view or information model, even if there are, for example, 5 million records. It then gives you the top 200 records from that large sorted list.

▸ Sort Current Data Set
This only shows the sorted result set of the first 200 records that are returned.

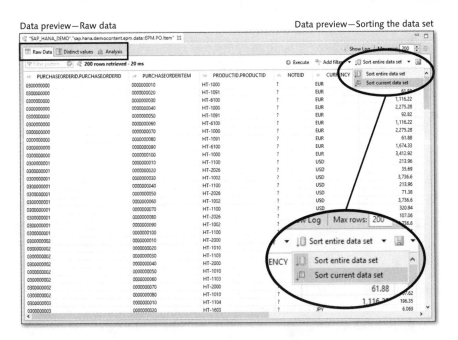

**Figure 5.5**  Raw Data in Data Preview in SAP HANA Studio

► DISTINCT VALUES

In the DISTINCT VALUES tab (Figure 5.6), you can see the quantities sold for every product. It graphically shows the number of unique values for your selection of fields.

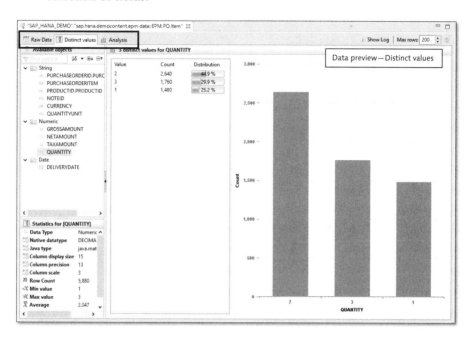

**Figure 5.6**   Uniques Values in Data Preview in SAP HANA Studio

► ANALYSIS

In the ANALYSIS tab (Figure 5.7), you can perform a full analysis of table outputs or information model outputs. This works the same as a Microsoft Excel pivot table. You can show the data using many different types of graphs—for example, the tree map graph shown in Figure 5.5.

### Content Area

The CONTENT area is where you perform all your SAP HANA modeling. This area is divided into *packages*, which can again be divided into *subpackages*, up to as many levels as you want. These packages and subpackages are then used to transport your information models from the development system to testing and production systems. (We discuss this in Chapter 12.)

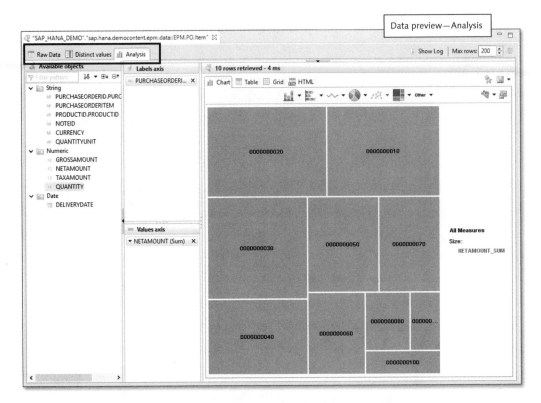

**Figure 5.7**   Data Analysis in Data Preview in SAP HANA Studio

As an example, let's say you're working on a project, and you create a main package for your project. In this package, you create three subpackages: one for financial modeling, one for HR modeling, and one for logistics modeling. You will assign your financial modelers to work in the financial subpackage, HR modelers to work in the HR subpackage, and logistics modelers to work in the logistics subpackage. Your project lead will have access to the main package, including the three subpackages. You can then take the main project package and transport all of your project's models from the development system to the production system with just a few clicks.

Figure 5.8 shows an example of SAP HANA models created inside a subpackage. Here, you can see attribute views, analytic views, and calculation views. This example is from the SHINE package of SAP HANA SPS 09. (The newer versions of SHINE do not have any attribute views and analytic views.) We discussed SHINE in Chapter 2.

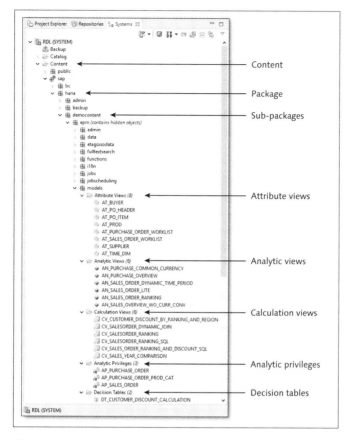

**Figure 5.8**   Content Area

**SHINE Package**

When possible, we will use examples from the SHINE package in this book. This package is freely available, and you can easily use it in your own SAP HANA system.

When you right-click on a package or a subpackage, you will see a context menu, as illustrated in Figure 5.9.

At the top of the menu, click NEW to display all the SAP HANA model types that you can create. You can create another subpackage, attribute views, analytic views, calculation views, analytic privileges, procedures, and decision tables via this option.

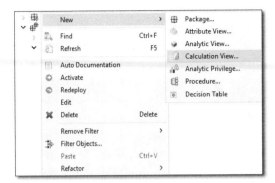

**Figure 5.9**   Context Menu to Create New Modeling Objects

Now that we've looked at the available system views, in the next two sections we will discuss the two primary consoles in SAP HANA studio.

**SQL Console**

As with any other database, you can use SQL statements when working with the SAP HANA database. Figure 5.10 shows the different ways to open the SQL Console: You can either use the context menu of a schema, or click the SQL button  in the top menu of the SYSTEMS view. This will open the SQL Console in your main work space. You can now enter different SQL statements to perform tasks such as creating tables, inserting data, maintaining data, creating a schema, assigning authorizations, and more.

Enabling line numbers in your editor is helpful if, for example, you're troubleshooting and an error message tells you that the error is in line 35. With line numbers enabled, you can see where line 35 is instead of having to count down 35 lines.

To enable this functionality, go to the WINDOW menu at the top of the screen, and then to PREFERENCES. Go to GENERAL • EDITORS • TEXT EDITORS, and then enable SHOW LINE NUMBERS.

There's another method to view line numbers, too. Something not everyone knows is that when you right-click on the little gray line to the left of the SQL statements, a menu appears from which you can select SHOW LINE NUMBERS.

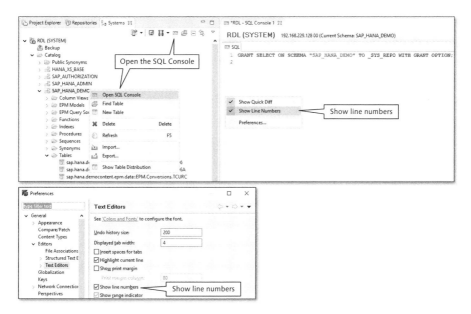

**Figure 5.10**   SQL Console

 **Tip**

Pressing ⌨Ctrl + ⌨Spacebar in SAP HANA studio automatically completes your typing for you. This autocomplete feature saves you time and minimizes typing errors.

We recommend that you only use the SQL Console for one-off SQL statements. If you want to create functions or procedures, instead use the steps we discuss in the Development Perspective section.

We will look at SQL and stored procedures in more detail in Chapter 8.

### Administration Console

The Administration Console is used primarily by data administrators (see Figure 5.11). From here, admins can get a good view of all the technical aspects of an SAP HANA system.

As an information modeler, there are two subtabs that might be helpful to you: the PERFORMANCE tab and the DIAGNOSIS FILES tab. These tabs will help you with troubleshooting, which we will look at in more detail in Chapter 10.

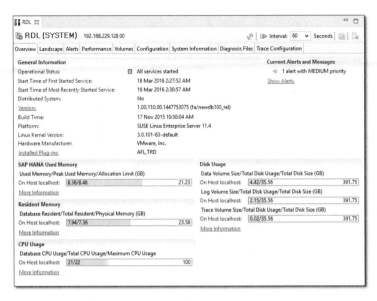

**Figure 5.11**  Administration Console

In Figure 5.11, you can see that this SAP HANA system seems to be healthy as everything is shown in green. The bars are only partly filled, which means this system has plenty of spare capacity. You can also see information such as the current status, when the system was started, what version number is installed, what operating system is used, and what is happening with the memory and CPU inside the system. This is all shown on the OVERVIEW screen of the Administration Console.

Next, we will look at the developer perspective and how to create your own repository for SAP HANA modeling work.

## Development Perspective

We mentioned earlier that we prefer the development perspective, even when modeling in SAP HANA. This perspective has a lot more functionality available than the modeler perspective. In this perspective, you can create repositories as well as projects and SAP HANA development objects that simply are not available in the modeler perspective.

Let's look at one of these objects—namely, a *flowgraph* model. Flowgraph models are used in a number of places in SAP HANA. We will quickly go through the steps to build a flowgraph model and then look at where it is used.

### Creating a Repository

Before you can create any SAP HANA development objects, you first have to create a *repository*, also called a *repository workspace* or a *workspace*. This is an area in which your objects will be stored. Figure 5.12 illustrates the three steps of creating a repository workspace in SAP HANA studio:

1. First, select the REPOSITORIES tab, and click on the REPOSITORY icon ![icon]. Note that the system shows that no repository has been created yet via the ![icon] icon.

2. The CREATE NEW REPOSITORY WORKSPACE window will open. Here, specify the SAP HANA system, whether this is the default workspace, and the WORKSPACE ROOT. When you're done, click FINISH.

3. Once you have created the repository workspace, the system now shows the ![icon] icon, indicating that a repository exists. You only have to do this once. You can now use the workspace.

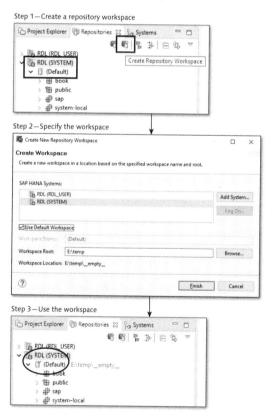

**Figure 5.12**   Creating a New Repository Workspace in SAP HANA Studio

### Creating a Project

Next, you have to create an *SAP HANA XS project*. You can think of an SAP HANA XS project as a folder in which your development objects will be created. The three steps to create the project are illustrated in Figure 5.13:

1. Start by right-clicking in the PROJECT EXPLORER tab, and select NEW • OTHER.

2. In the NEW window, under the APPLICATION DEVELOPMENT folder, select XS PROJECT.

3. In the NEW XS PROJECT window, enter the PROJECT NAME, LOCATION, and so on. Upon completion, click FINISH.

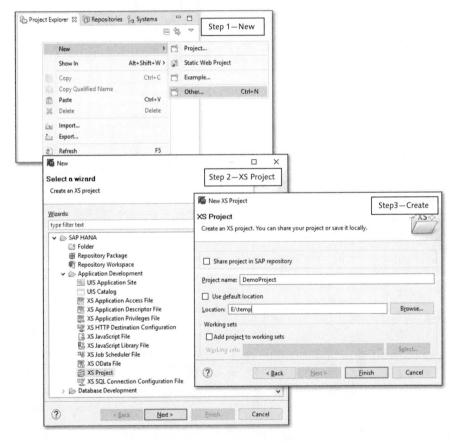

**Figure 5.13**   Creating a New Project in SAP HANA Studio

You only have to create the SAP HANA XS project once. You can now create your SAP HANA development objects in this project.

### Creating an SAP HANA Development Object

Finally, create the SAP HANA development object (flowgraph model) via the following steps:

1. In the PROJECT EXPLORER tab, right-click your project, as shown in Figure 5.14. Select the NEW menu option from the context menu, and then select OTHER.

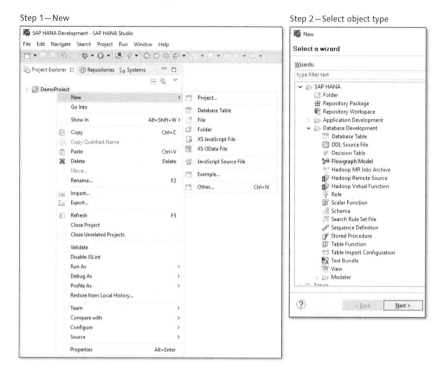

**Figure 5.14**   Creating a New SAP HANA Development Object

2. In the next dialog box, choose which type of SAP HANA development object you want to create. There are two main subareas to choose from: An APPLICATION DEVELOPMENT area, as shown in step two of Figure 5.13, and a DATABASE DEVELOPMENT area, as shown in step two of Figure 5.14. For this example, select the FLOWGRAPH MODEL object type.

3. As shown in Figure 5.15, the NEW FLOWGRAPH MODEL window appears, providing options for naming and selecting the type of flowgraph model that you require. Click FINISH after you've selected the correct settings.

At this point, SAP HANA studio will place you into the editor for creating and editing the appropriate type of SAP HANA development object you've created.

For a flowgraph model, you are placed in the *SAP HANA AFM*. Note that a file with the extension .HDBFLOWGRAPH was created (see the top tab of the right-side screen in Figure 5.15). In the AFM graphical editor, you can create several nodes with inputs and outputs. You can, for example, connect a table to the input of a node, and then connect the output to another node.

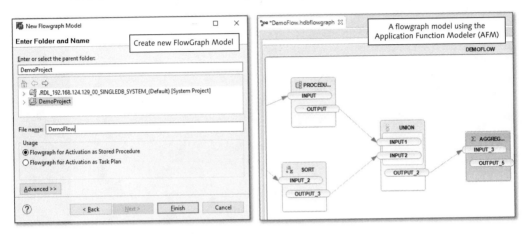

**Figure 5.15**  Creating and Editing a New Flowgraph in the AFM

There are a few places where we will use the AFM in the course of this text:

▶ In Chapter 9, we use the AFM for modeling predictive analytics using an SAP HANA predictive library called Predictive Analysis Library (PAL).

▶ In Chapter 14, we use AFM for SAP HANA smart data integration (SDI) to help ensure data quality in SAP HANA and also for SAP HANA smart data streaming (SDS) to model streaming projects.

### Session Client

In SAP systems, we work with the concept of different *clients*. This use of *client* does not have the same meaning as the word *client* used to mean *customer* or as in *client server*. In this case, we are talking about an SAP system database being subdivided into different so-called clients. When you log in to an SAP system, it asks not only for your user name and password but also for a client number. You then are logged into the corresponding client. You can only see the data in that client—not everything inside the SAP database. You can think of a client in SAP systems as a "filter" that prevents you from seeing all the data.

Because SAP HANA is used as the database for many different SAP systems, SAP HANA must also allow for this concept of limiting data to a specific client. By setting the session client, you can say what the default client number is for your SAP HANA studio.

There are several ways to set the session client. One option in SAP HANA studio is to go to the WINDOW menu at the top of the screen, and go to PREFERENCES. Figure 5.16 shows you what the PREFERENCES screen looks like. By drilling down into SAP HANA and then MODELER, you will reach a screen called DEFAULT MODEL PARAMETERS where you can set the default client.

Where it now says SESSION CLIENT on the screen, you just type the client number—for example, 100.

**Figure 5.16**   Session Client Settings in SAP HANA Studio

In this section, we looked at the different aspects of SAP HANA studio as a modeling tool. In the next section, we will look at the other tool available in SAP HANA for modeling.

## SAP HANA Web-Based Development Workbench

The second main modeling tool for SAP HANA is a web-based development environment. Today, SAP is focusing more on cloud and mobile technologies. Tablets can't run desktop Java and therefore can't use SAP HANA studio. In addition, some people don't like to use desktop Java Virtual Machines due to various security issues.

To address these issues, SAP introduced the SAP HANA web-based development workbench, which runs from inside SAP HANA and only requires the use of a browser.

**HTML5 Browser**

You have to use an HTML5 browser for the development workbench to work properly. All newer browsers, including all mobile browsers, are acceptable: Just avoid Internet Explorer 8 and earlier.

Based on the current trends at SAP, this modeling environment is getting a lot of attention and development effort. Already, you can do almost everything in this web-based environment that you can currently do in SAP HANA studio.

Figure 5.17 shows how to open the SAP HANA web-based development workbench in your browser. The URL you use looks like *http://server:8000/sap/hana/ide/*.

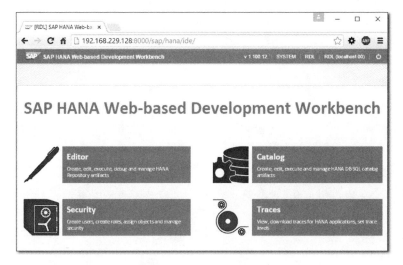

**Figure 5.17**   SAP HANA Web-Based Development Workbench

You start with the server's host name or IP address, a colon, and then a port number. This port number is 8000 plus whatever the instance number is of your specific system. For example, if your system is using instance number 10, then the port number should be 8010. You then type in "/sap/hana/ide/" as a web server path.

You can see a part of this path in Figure 5.8, looking at the subpackages. You will notice that there is an SAP subpackage with a HANA subpackage underneath. This means you can actually see the code used for this development environment in your SAP HANA system.

Once you have logged on, you will see the main screen (as shown in Figure 5.17), which has four different areas:

▶ EDITOR
  The EDITOR area corresponds to the CONTENT area in SAP HANA studio.

▶ CATALOG
  This is the same as the CATALOG area in SAP HANA studio.

▶ SECURITY
  The SECURITY area allows you to manage security settings, create users and roles, and assign objects.

▶ TRACES
  In this area, you can download traces and set trace levels for SAP HANA applications.

Clicking on any of these four blocks will open another tab in your browser and allow you to work in the selected area.

In this chapter, we will look primarily at the CATALOG area and the EDITOR area as security and traces are discussed in Chapter 13.

## Catalog Area

In the CATALOG area, your browser-based screen will look fairly similar to the same functionality we saw in SAP HANA studio (see Figure 5.18).

The layout of the screen is similar as well. For example, you will find that you can right-click to access menus with the same options, such as to open the definition of a table, to run a data preview, or to view the content of a table's data.

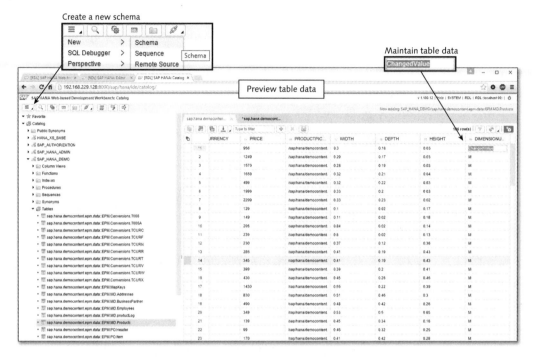

**Figure 5.18**  Catalog Area, with Table Preview

Figure 5.18 shows a table and the data contents being previewed. In this case, you will notice something that you can do in the web-based development environment that you cannot do in SAP HANA studio. By clicking on the menu, you have the option of creating a schema. In SAP HANA studio, there is no such menu option. You can only create a schema there using a SQL command.

**Maintain Table Data**

As of SAP HANA SPS 10, you can maintain table data when you view the table data in the SAP HANA web-based development workbench. You can insert data and update data while you preview the table contents, as illustrated in Figure 5.18. This obviously can be dangerous in a production system: It can be prevented through security settings.

**Editor Area**

Compare Figure 5.19 to Figure 5.1 at the start of this chapter and you'll notice that the screen layout and functionality are similar. Both figures present a graphical calculation view with a union mapping.

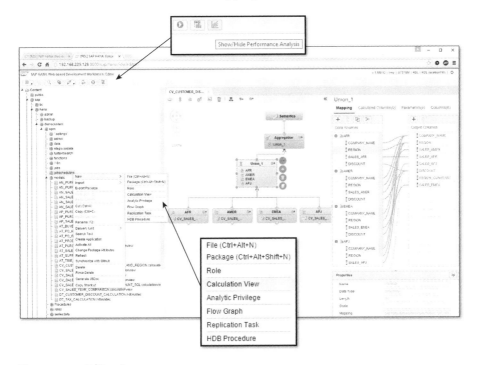

**Figure 5.19**   Editor Area

However, there is one big difference between SAP HANA studio and the SAP HANA web-based development workbench: In SAP HANA studio, you can graphically create and edit attribute views and analytic views. When you look at the context menu (right-click menu) in Figure 5.19, you will notice that you can only create and edit calculation views graphically in the SAP HANA web-based development workbench.

 **Tip**

> Modeling in SAP HANA is geared towards doing everything with graphical calculation views. Attribute views and analytic views are fading quickly and are not even available in the newer SAP HANA web-based development workbench. We will discuss this in more detail in Chapter 6.

When you try to edit existing attribute views and analytic views that you previously created in SAP HANA studio in the SAP HANA web-based development workbench, the workbench only shows them as XML files (see Figure 5.20).

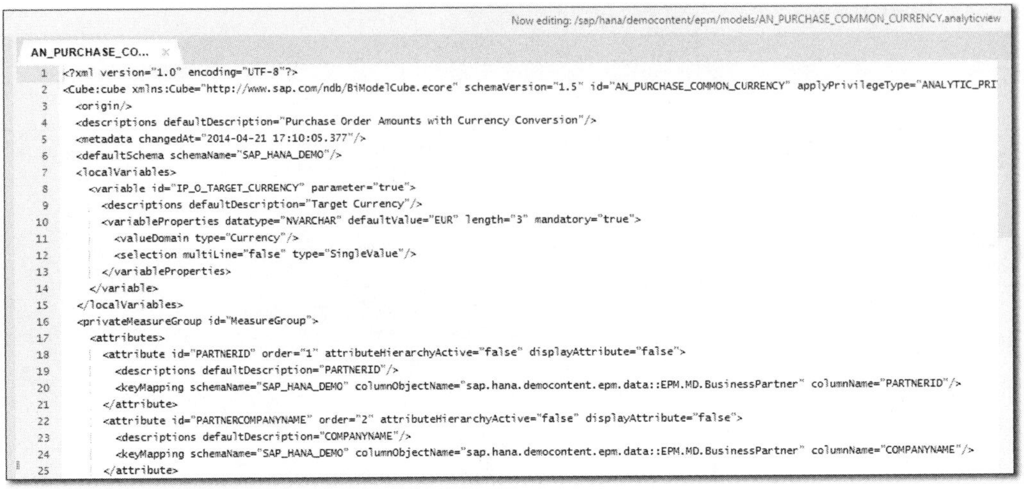

**Figure 5.20**  Analytic Views Not Shown Graphically in SAP HANA Web-Based Development Workbench

As of SAP HANA SPS 10, the web-based development environment can also use the new PERFORMANCE ANALYSIS MODE option for graphical calculation views. In this mode, SAP HANA suggests ways that you can improve your model.

Please note that this mode is only available for graphical calculation views. When you select a graphical calculation view, the ![icon] icon will appear in the menu at the top, as illustrated in Figure 5.19.

## Important Terminology

It's important to understand the differences between the two SAP HANA modeling tools. Table 5.1 provides a quick summary of the differences between SAP HANA studio and the SAP HANA web-based development workbench.

| SAP HANA Studio | SAP HANA Web-Based Development Workbench |
|---|---|
| Java-based. | Web-based, using an HTML5 browser. |
| Attribute views, analytic views, and graphical calculation views are created and edited graphically. | Only graphical calculation views are created and edited graphically. |
| Can only create a schema via SQL or Core Data Services (CDS). | Can create a schema via SQL, Core Data Services (CDS), or via a context menu. |
| Security roles are created as runtime (nontransportable) objects. | Security roles are created as design-time (transportable) objects. |

**Table 5.1**   Key Differences between SAP HANA Modeling Tools

# Practice Questions

These practice questions will help you evaluate your understanding of the topics covered in this chapter. The questions shown are similar in nature to those found on the certification examination. Although none of these questions will be found on the exam itself, they will allow you to review your knowledge of the subject. Select the correct answers and then check the completeness of your answers in the Practice Question Answers and Explanations section. Remember that on the exam you must select all correct answers, and only correct answers, to receive credit for the question.

1. Which development tools are available for creating SAP HANA information models? (There are 2 correct answers)

☐   **A.** Java-based Eclipse tool

☐   **B.** Web-based development tool

☐   **C.** iPad app for development

☐   **D.** Java applet in the browser

2.  In which SAP HANA studio perspective do you find the QUICK VIEW tab options?

☐   **A.** Administration perspective

☐   **B.** Developer perspective

☐   **C.** Modeler perspective

☐   **D.** Plan visualizer perspective

3.  In which subarea (folder) in the SYSTEMS view of SAP HANA studio can you find the SAP HANA database schemas?

☐   **A.** SECURITY area

☐   **B.** CONTENT area

☐   **C.** CATALOG area

☐   **D.** PROVISIONING area

4.  Where in SAP HANA studio can you unload a table's data from memory?

☐   **A.** The context menu of the table

☐   **B.** The list of export destinations

☐   **C.** The data preview of the table

☐   **D.** The table definition

5.  Where in SAP HANA studio can you see if a table is row-based or column-based? (There are 2 correct answers.)

☐   **A.** The tooltip that appears on mouse hover over the table title

☐   **B.** The table definition

☐   **C.** The context menu of a table

☐   **D.** The table's icon

6.  What can you do in the RAW tab of the data preview in SAP HANA studio? (There are 2 correct answers.)

☐   **A.** Sort the entire data result set and show the top 200 records.

☐   **B.** Show all distinct values in the entire data result set.

☐   **C.** Create a graph while analyzing the entire data result set.

☐   **D.** Export the entire data result set to your local machine.

7.   Where in the SYSTEMS view of SAP HANA studio can you create new SAP HANA models?

☐   **A.** In the schemas of the CATALOG area

☐   **B.** In the packages of the CATALOG area

☐   **C.** In the packages of the CONTENT area

☐   **D.** In the schemas of the CONTENT area

8.   Which modeling objects can you create in a package in SAP HANA studio? (There are 2 correct answers.)

☐   **A.** Calculation views

☐   **B.** Procedures

☐   **C.** Triggers

☐   **D.** Schemas

9.   Which modeling views are fading out and are not available in the SAP HANA web-based development workbench? (There are 2 correct answers.)

☐   **A.** Analytic views

☐   **B.** Scripted calculation views

☐   **C.** Graphical calculation views

☐   **D.** Attribute views

10.   Which steps do you have to perform once before you can create SAP HANA development objects? (There are 2 correct answers.)

☐   **A.** Create a dataflow model in the AFM.

☐   **B.** Create a predictive model using PAL.

☐   **C.** Create a repository workspace

☐   **D.** Create an SAP HANA XS project.

11. True or False: The performance analysis mode is available for graphical calculation views in the SAP HANA web-based development workbench.

☐   **A.** True

☐   **B.** False

## Practice Question Answers and Explanations

1. Correct answers: **A, B**

   We have SAP HANA studio, which is a Java-based Eclipse tool, and the SAP HANA web-based development workbench. There are no Java applets or iPad apps for modeling.

2. Correct answer: **C**

   The QUICK VIEW tab is located in the modeler perspective (see Figure 5.2).

3. Correct answer: **C**

   The SAP HANA database schemas are housed in the CATALOG area of SAP HANA studio (see Figure 5.3).

4. Correct answer: **A**

   You can unload a table's data from memory in the context menu of the table (see Figure 5.3).

5. Correct answers: **B, D**

   The table definition (see Figure 5.4) and the table icon in the CATALOG area both show if a table is row-based or column-based.

6. Correct answers: **A, D**

   Although all of the options are possible in the data preview, you can only 1) sort all the data result sets and show the top 200 records and then 2) export that data result set to your local machine from the RAW tab of the data preview. The other two actions are available in the other tabs.

7. Correct answer: **C**

   You can only create models in the CONTENT area, so any reference to the CATALOG area is invalid. There are no schemas in the CONTENT area. Schemas are only found in the CATALOG area. (See Figure 5.9.)

8. Correct answers: **A, B**

   Calculation views and procedures are created in the CONTENT area. Triggers and schemas are created in the CATALOG area. (See Figure 5.9.)

9. Correct answers: **A, D**

   Attribute and analytic views are fading out. We recommend using graphical calculation views going forward.

10. Correct answers: **C, D**

    You have to create a repository workspace an SAP HANA XS project once. A flowgraph model (in AFM) is an SAP HANA development object, and you create it many times once you have performed the correct setup. A predictive model using PAL is an example of a flowgraph model. Answers A and B are therefore basically the same.

11. Correct answer: **A**

    As of SAP HANA SPS 10, the web-based development environment can use the PERFORMANCE ANALYSIS MODE option for graphical calculation views. Please note that there are no true–false questions in the actual certification exam.

## Takeaway

You should now understand the two main SAP HANA modeling tools in more detail. They have many similarities, and a few subtle differences. After reading this chapter, you should be able to identify the different workspaces in SAP HANA studio, know how to work with tables and data, and know how to create new information models. You also learned how to set up and use the (preferred) development perspective for SAP HANA modeling.

In addition, you now should have a working knowledge of best practices and guidelines for modeling with the SAP HANA modeling tools in general.

## Summary

In this chapter, we discussed the SAP HANA modeling tools: SAP HANA studio and the SAP HANA web-based development workbench. You know how they work, their similarities, and their differences, and you have learned how to use them.

We will now use this knowledge for the modeling chapters ahead. The next chapter will teach you how to create and work with SAP HANA views using these modeling tools.

# Information Views

## Techniques You'll Master

- ▶ Learn to create SAP HANA information views
- ▶ Identify which type of SAP HANA information view to use
- ▶ Explore the various types of calculation views
- ▶ Know how to select the correct joins and nodes
- ▶ Know when you should still use attribute and analytic views
- ▶ Learn to migrate older types of SAP HANA information views

In the last two chapters, we discussed the modeling concepts and tools required for building SAP HANA information views. In this chapter and the next, we will build on that foundation. We'll focus on how to create information views in the SAP HANA system and how to enhance these views with additional functionality.

In this chapter, you'll learn to create the different types of calculation views, select the correct nodes for what you want to achieve, and use the semantics node to add additional value for business users.

We'll also discuss the older attribute and analytic views, when you would still use them in SAP HANA SPS 11, and how to migrate them to the equivalent calculation views.

**Real-World Scenario**

You start a new project in which a business wants to expand the range of services it offers its customers. You're responsible for building the information models in SAP HANA.

You have to build about fifty new SAP HANA information views. As you plan your information views, you notice several master data tables that you will use. By creating a few well-designed dimension views, you cater not only for the needs of this project, but also for future requirements. You see this as a "library" of reusable dimension views.

While you're busy designing these dimension views, you also gather some analytics and reporting requirements. Most of the analytic requirements are addressed by building star join views and calculation views of type cube. You address some of the reporting requirements by delivering semantically enhanced information models that are easier for your colleagues and the end users to work with.

## Objectives of This Portion of the Test

The purpose of this portion of the SAP HANA certification exam is to test your knowledge of modeling SAP HANA information views.

The certification exam expects you to have a good understanding of the following topics:

▶ How to create SAP HANA information views

▶ Calculation views of type dimension

▶ Calculation views of type cube with star join

▶ Calculation views of type cube

▶ Selecting the correct joins and nodes to produce accurate results

▶ Choosing the correct type of SAP HANA information view

▶ Understanding the older attribute and analytic views

▶ Migration of the older information views

> **Note**
>
> This portion contributes up to 10% of the total certification exam score.

# Key Concepts Refresher

In Chapter 4, we looked at modeling concepts, and in Chapter 5, we examined SAP HANA modeling tools. Now, it's time to put them together, implementing the modeling concepts with the tools to create SAP HANA information views.

There are three types of SAP HANA information views, which we briefly covered in Chapter 4. First are dimension views, the master data in the system. Second, star join views let you build cube-like information models. Third, calculation views of type cube let you build enhanced multidimensional data structures and information models.

> **Reminder!**
>
> We refer to *calculation views of type dimension* as dimension views and to *calculation views of type cube with star join* as star join views. The last category is called *calculation views of type cube*.
>
> The older SAP HANA systems had *attribute views* (for dimension views), *analytic views* (for star join views), and *calculation views*.
>
> The last category can cause some confusion, because many people and web pages still refer to the last category simply as *calculation views*.

In this book, we use the latest official name—*calculation views of type cube*—because that's what they're referred to in the SAP HANA SPS 11 certification exam. We use the name *calculation views* to refer to all three types of calculation views.

In this chapter, we start by briefly reviewing the different types of data sources that can be used be information views. We then dive into the creation process for the different calculation views before discussing the various types of nodes you'll encounter, including the semantic node. We then review and compare attribute views and calculation views of type dimension and analytic views and calculation views of type cube with star join. We round out the section by walking through the migration tools available in SAP HANA SPS 11 for attribute and analytic views.

## Data Sources for Information Views

SAP HANA information views can use data from a wide variety of sources. We will discuss some of the *data sources* in later chapters, so don't worry if you don't yet know what all of them are. The main data sources are as follows:

▶ Tables in the SAP HANA system; both row-based and column-based tables are supported. The different types of column tables—for example, history column tables and temporary tables—are all supported.

▶ SAP HANA information views in the SAP HANA system. We can build new information views on top of other existing views.

▶ Decision tables.

▶ SQL views.

▶ Table functions.

▶ Virtual tables with data from other databases.

▶ Core Data Services (CDS) data sources—for example, CDS views. You can use these source to deploy table definitions together with the information view to the production system.

▶ Data sources from another tenant in the SAP HANA system, if SAP HANA is set up as a multitenant database container (MDC) system. These can include tables, SQL views, and calculation views from another tenant, provided that the proper authorizations are in place.

## Calculation Views: Type Dimension, Type Cube, and Type Cube with Star Join

As of SAP HANA SPS 10, you'll mostly create calculation views. Attribute and analytic views are only used in a few exceptional cases for functionality that is not yet available in the calculation views.

Existing attribute and analytic views will still work as they always did, but it is not recommended to use them in any new SAP HANA modeling work. As you've seen, the SAP HANA web-based development workbench only supports graphical editing of calculation views.

The aim is to do as much modeling work as possible with graphical calculation views. As SAP HANA has matured, there has been less emphasis on writing code when creating information models. The new focus typically is on keeping the entire modeling process graphical.

As previous discussed in Chapter 4, there are now three different types of calculation views:

- **Calculation view of type dimension (dimension calculation views)**
  As of SAP HANA SPS 10, attribute views and calculation views of type dimension are both types of dimension views. In SAP HANA SPS 11, a new migration tool is available to help migrate your old attribute views to the new dimension calculation views. We'll discuss the migration tool in the Migrating Attribute and Analytic Views section.

- **Calculation view of type cube with star join**
  As of SAP HANA SPS 10, analytic views and calculation views of type cube with star join are star join views. In SAP HANA SPS 11, a new migration tool is available to help you to migrate your old analytic views to the new calculation views of type cube with star join. Again, refer to the Migrating Attribute and Analytic Views section for instructions on migration.

- **Calculation view of type cube**
  This view type provides even more powerful capabilities. For example, you can combine multiple star join views ("cubes") to produce a composite result set.

In this section, we will walk through the steps for creating these calculation views.

## Creating Calculation Views

You create calculation views in the CONTENT area of the SYSTEMS tab in SAP HANA studio. Select the package or subpackage in which you want to create the calculation view and right-click it. You'll see a context menu like the one shown in Figure 6.1.

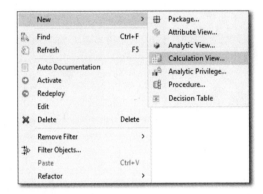

**Figure 6.1**   Context Menu for Creating SAP HANA Calculation View

Click NEW and select CALCULATION VIEW.

 **Note**

You can create attribute views and analytic views via the same context menu if needed.

The options for creating different types of calculation views appear in the popup dialog box, as shown in Figure 6.2.

At the top of the dialog box, give the calculation view a NAME and a LABEL (description). You can choose to make a copy of another calculation view with the COPY FROM selection.

From SAP HANA SPS 10 on, always select the GRAPHICAL option in the TYPE dropdown list. The SQLSCRIPT option is no longer used, and in SAP HANA SPS 11 any existing SQLScript calculation views can be migrated to table functions, as will be discussed in Chapter 8.

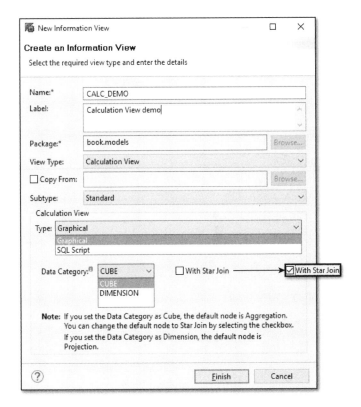

**Figure 6.2** Creating Calculation View in SAP HANA Studio

 **Script-based vs. Graphical Calculation Views**

Script-based calculation views are used to create views using SQLScript. Graphical calculation views avoid the need for code by creating views graphically.

Use the DATA CATEGORY dropdown list and the WITH STAR JOIN checkbox to create the different types of calculation views. (Note the information below these dropdown selection lists, which indicates the default view node for each type of calculation view. We'll discuss default nodes shortly.)

The following instructions explain how to create each type of calculation view:

▶ **Calculation view of type dimension**
Select the DIMENSION option in the DATA CATEGORY dropdown list. The default view node will be a PROJECTION node. These views do not support

multidimensional reporting and data analysis. You can use these information views as data sources for other calculation views.

▶  **Calculation view of type cube with star join**
Select the CUBE option in the DATA CATEGORY dropdown list, and select the WITH STAR JOIN checkbox. The default view node will be a STAR JOIN node. These views can be used for multidimensional reporting and data analysis purposes.

▶  **Calculation view of type cube**
Select the CUBE option in the DATA CATEGORY dropdown list. The default view node will be an AGGREGATION node. These views can be used for multidimensional reporting and data analysis purposes.

If you select the BLANK option in the DATA CATEGORY dropdown list, you will create a dimension view. This type of calculation view can only be used internally in SAP HANA. An external client tool—for example, a reporting tool—will not be able to see this calculation view.

Click the FINISH button to create the calculation view.

**Creating Time Dimensions**

You can also change the SUBTYPE of the calculation view (in the middle of the dialog screen) to create a time-based calculation view. When you set the SUBTYPE to TIME, the dialog screen changes as shown in Figure 6.3.

The time-based calculation view adds a *time dimension* to information views. Remember that dimensions contain attributes that describe a transaction. If we add a time and date when the transaction happens, we have added another (time) attribute. These time attributes are stored in a time dimension.

You can set the calendar to the standard GREGORIAN calendar or to the FISCAL (financial) calendar. You can also set the GRANULARITY to YEAR, MONTH, and all the way down to SECOND.

If you use this option, you will need to generate time data in SAP HANA. You can do this from the QUICK VIEW menu in the MODELER perspective.

If you have tables T009 and T009B from your SAP ERP system available in SAP HANA, you can use these tables to define the FISCAL calendar.

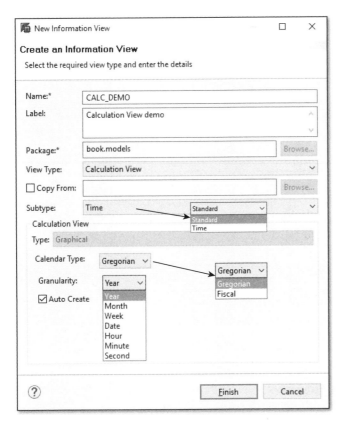

**Figure 6.3** Creating Time-Based Calculation Views in SAP HANA Studio

## Working with a Calculation View

A calculation view includes different working areas. A calculation view of type dimension is shown in Figure 6.4 in SAP HANA studio. Work from left to right in this layout.

In the left work area, called the SCENARIO area, you'll see different nodes. The top node is always the SEMANTICS node. In the semantics node, you can rename fields to give them more meaning (i.e., semantics). You can also create hierarchies in the semantic node. (In Chapter 7, we'll discuss adding hierarchies to SAP HANA views.)

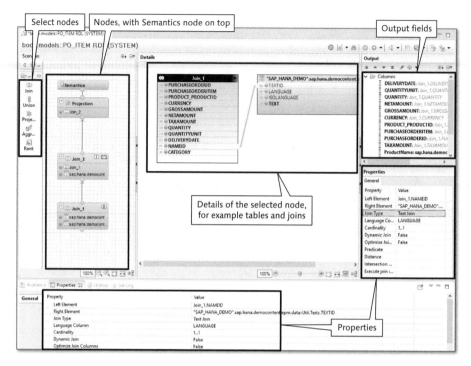

**Figure 6.4**   Working with Calculation Views

The node below the semantics node is called the default view node. The default node is the top-most node used for modeling in the view. Figure 6.5 illustrates the default nodes for the different types of calculation views. You can add other types of nodes below the default node; for example, Figure 6.4 shows two join nodes below the default PROJECTION node of the dimension view.

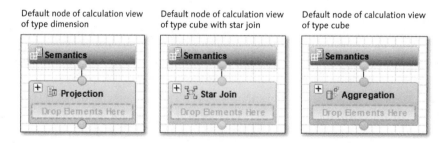

**Figure 6.5**   Default View Nodes for Different Types of Calculation Views

> **Tip**
>
> Always work bottom-up when building SAP HANA information views: Start at the nodes at the bottom and work your way up to the default node. The output of each node becomes the input of the node above it. The final output of the view, which is the output of the default node, is shown in the semantics node.

When you select a node in the SCENARIO section, the information for the selected node is shown in the DETAILS area in the middle. In Figure 6.4, we selected the second join node. In the DETAILS area, you can see the tables in this join node and how they are joined together.

On the right-hand side of the screen in Figure 6.4, you can see all the selected OUTPUT fields, and directly below that, the PROPERTIES of whatever field or join you have currently selected from the DETAILS or OUTPUT area. You can also see the properties in the bottom working area, in the PROPERTIES tab.

### Adding Nodes

You can add new nodes to the SAP HANA information view by selecting a node type from the PALETTE on the left side and dropping it onto the SCENARIO work area. Drag the node around on the work area to align it with other nodes. When the node lines up with another node, an orange line indicates that the node is aligned (see Figure 6.6). Link the nodes by dragging from the circle on top of the node block to the circle at the bottom of the node above it.

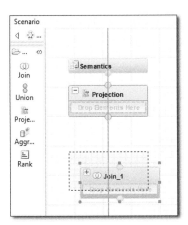

**Figure 6.6** Adding and Aligning Join Node to the Dimension View

## Adding Data Sources

Once you've added a node to the work area, you can add data sources to it. There are two ways of adding data sources:

1. Hover the mouse cursor over the node. A popup overlay menu with a green plus sign ✚ and a tooltip (ADD OBJECTS) will appear. Click on the plus sign. A dialog box will appear and ask you which data source(s) you want to add to the data foundation. Type a few characters of the table's name to search for any data sources in the entire SAP HANA system that match those characters. Then, select the data source(s), and click on OK to add them to the node.

2. Drag and drop tables from the SYSTEMS tab. Open the TABLES folder in the schema in the CATALOG area, then simply drag and drop the name of the table or data source onto the node.

Both methods are shown in Figure 6.7.

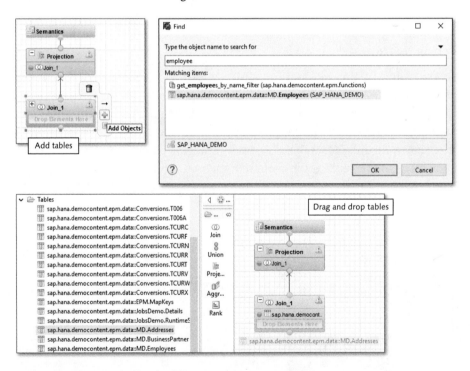

**Figure 6.7**  Two Methods of Adding Data Sources to Nodes

## Creating Joins

After you've added the data sources to the data foundation, you'll want to join the data sources together. Create a join by taking the field from one table and dropping it onto a related field of another table. Figure 6.8 shows what this looks like in SAP HANA studio.

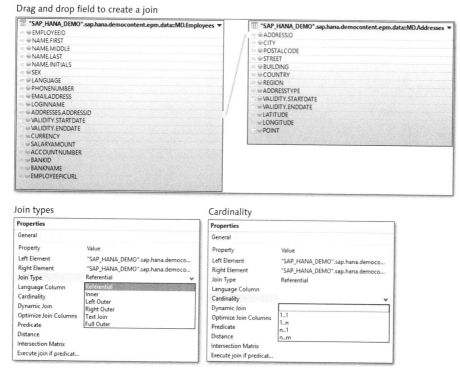

**Figure 6.8**   Creating a Join in SAP HANA Studio and Setting Its Properties

Go to the Properties area to select the Join Type from the dropdown, and set the Cardinality. Make sure you have the join (the line between the tables) selected as illustrated; otherwise, the properties will not show the correct information.

**Tip**

When you create a join, get into the habit of always dropping the field from the main table onto the related field of the (smaller) lookup table.

For some join types, it makes no difference in which direction you do the drag and drop. With a text join, however, it matters.

The join types that are available in calculation views are as follows:

▶ Referential join

▶ Inner join

▶ Left outer join

▶ Right outer join

▶ Full outer join

▶ Text join

▶ Dynamic join

▶ Spatial join

Referential joins and full outer joins are available in join nodes as of SAP HANA SPS 11. Previously, referential joins were only available in star join nodes.

### Selecting Output Fields

The next step is to select output fields. There are two ways to do this:

1. In the context menu of a field name in the table, select the ADD TO OUTPUT option.

2. A quicker way is clicking the round dot next to the field name. The dot will turn orange when the field appears as an output column.

Both methods are shown in Figure 6.9.

Figure 6.10 shows what a list of output fields looks like in SAP HANA studio.

When you select one of the fields in the output columns, you can see the properties of that field in the PROPERTIES tab underneath the OUTPUT area. (See the overview screen in Figure 6.4.) You can see the name of the column in Figure 6.11. You can change column names to make them more meaningful for end users. The MAPPING property ensures that SAP HANA knows what the original field is.

You can also change the data type and specify whether the attribute is a key attribute or if the field should be hidden or not.

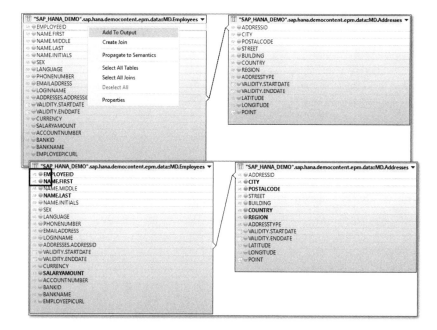

**Figure 6.9**   Selecting Fields for Node Output

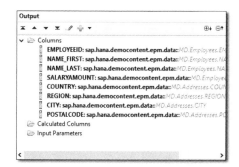

**Figure 6.10**   List of Output Fields for Selected Node

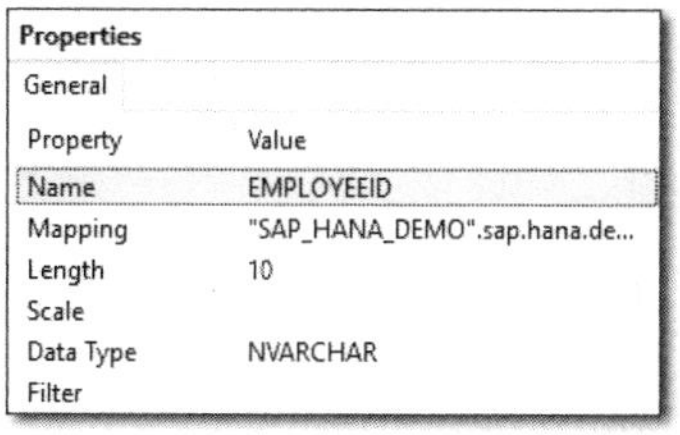

**Figure 6.11**   Properties of Output Field

**Tip**

Even though you can set the different properties in the PROPERTY area in the node, we find it easier to set many of these in the SEMANTICS node. Changing the name or the label, setting a key attribute, and setting an attribute as hidden are much easier to do in the SEMANTICS node. We will discuss the SEMANTICS node later in the chapter.

Often, you'll want to select all the fields coming from a lower node as the output fields of the node. In this case, right-click the top bar of the data source and select the ADD ALL TO OUTPUT, as shown in Figure 6.12.

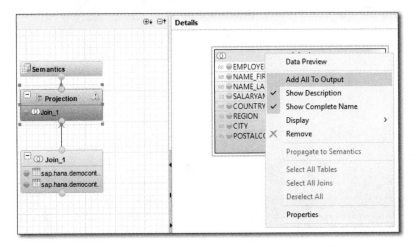

**Figure 6.12**   Selecting All Fields from Lower Node as Output Fields

**Finalizing the Calculation View**

In Chapter 4, we discussed how to build SAP HANA information views in layers, with each node building on the previous ones.

Once you've finished building the calculation view, there are two final steps to follow:

1. Click the SAVE AND ACTIVATE ⬡ button on the toolbar above the OUTPUT area (see Figure 6.13). We'll discuss the activation process in Chapter 11, but for now, just think of it as a step you need to take before you can run your calculation view.

2. Preview your data by clicking the ⬚ button on the toolbar. We discussed the preview functionality in Chapter 5.

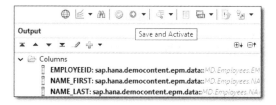

**Figure 6.13**   Save and Activate the Information View

Congratulations! You now know how to create calculation views in SAP HANA.

## Working with Nodes

In Chapter 4, we looked at the modeling concepts of joins, star joins, projection, ranking, aggregation, and union.

All of these options are available in calculation views as nodes. You can add these nodes from the PALETTE on the left of the SCENARIO work area, as shown in Figure 6.6. These are the basic building blocks to use in the different layers of calculation views.

Let's take a quick look at the available nodes, working in alphabetical order.

### Aggregation Node

The *aggregation node* in calculation views can calculate single summary values from a large list of values; for example, you can create a sum (single summary value) of all the values in a table column. These summary values are useful for high-level reporting, dashboards, and analytics. (The functionality is similar to the GROUP BY statement in SQL.) The aggregation node in calculation views also supports all the usual functions: sum, count, minimum, maximum, average, standard deviation, and variance.

The last three functions (average, standard deviation, and variance) are new as of SAP HANA SPS 11. For performance reasons, we recommend not using these three functions when you have very large stacked calculation views.

You normally calculate aggregates of measures, but in the latest versions of SAP HANA you also can create aggregates of attributes, which basically creates a list of unique values.

### Join Node

The earlier examples shown in Figure 6.4 and Figure 6.12 used a join node. *Join nodes* are used at the bottom layers to get data sources in to the view. Join nodes have only two inputs, so if you want to add five tables in the calculation view, you'll need four join nodes. Because of this, joins tend to be highly stacked. (You can see an example in Figure 6.21.)

### Projection Node

*Projection nodes* can be used to remove some fields from a calculation view. If you do not send all the input fields to the output area, the fields that are not in the output area will not appear to client tools.

You can also use projection nodes to rename fields, filter data, and add new calculated columns to a calculation view. (We'll discuss filter expressions and calculated columns in Chapter 7.)

### Rank Node

We can use *rank nodes* to create top N or bottom N lists of values to sort results. In the DETAILS area of a rank node, you can access extra properties to specify the rank node behavior.

Figure 6.14 shows the RANK NODE area. The SORT DIRECTION field specifies if you want a top N or bottom N list. The ORDER BY field specifies what you want to sort the list by.

The THRESHOLD field specifies how many entries you want in the list. If you specify a FIXED value of 10, you'll produce a top 10 or bottom 10 list. You can also choose to set this value from an INPUT PARAMETER, which means that the calculation view will ask for a value each time it's run. (We'll discuss input parameters in Chapter 7.)

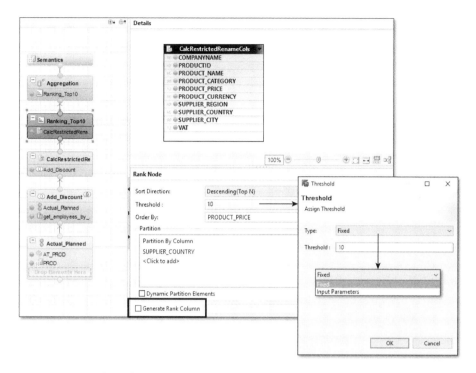

**Figure 6.14**   Rank Node

You can tell the rank node to create an additional generated field with the rank values. By setting the GENERATE RANK COLUMN flag, the additional field is generated with the name provided in the field. You can use this generated field to sort the results in ranking order—for example, in a reporting tool. The generated field is created with a `BIGINT` data type.

### Star Join Node

The *star join node* is used only to join a data foundation with fact tables to dimension views. The join types available in the star join node are the same as the normal joins in a join node. It's *what* they're joining that differs.

Figure 6.15 shows a star join node. The left data source in the DETAILS area is the data foundation, which comes from a join node with two fact tables. The right data source is a calculation view of type dimension.

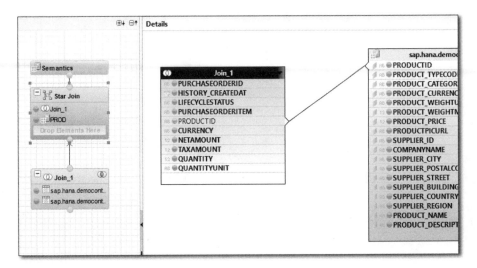

**Figure 6.15**  Star Join Node

  **Note**

Only calculation views of type dimension are supported as the dimension data sources in the star join node of a calculation view.

The star join node is the default node of calculation views of type cube with star join. Use join nodes, as shown in Figure 6.15, to join all the transactional tables together. The upper-most join node contains all the measures. The output from this last join node becomes the data foundation for the star join node. Figure 6.15 only has one join node for the data foundation.

Then, drag and drop the required dimension views (which have to be calculation views of type dimension) into the star join node and join them to the data foundation.

### Union Node

In Chapter 4, we explained the difference between a *standard union* and a *union with constant values*. Figure 6.16 shows a standard union with two data sources in the SOURCE area. These sources are combined into a list of output fields on the right side.

**Tip**

Union nodes in SAP HANA can have more than two data sources.

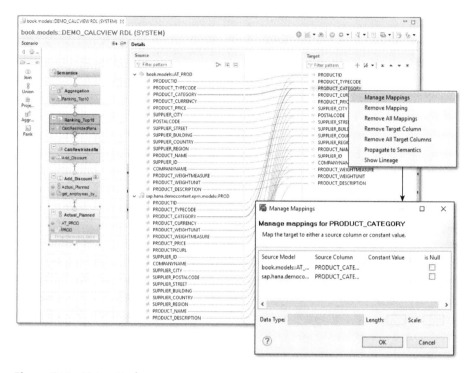

**Figure 6.16**   Union Node

From the context menu of a field in the list of TARGET fields on the right, you can select the MANAGE MAPPINGS option to open the MANAGE MAPPINGS dialog screen, where you can edit the current mappings. You can also set up a CONSTANT VALUE for one of the data sources. In this case, we'll change the standard union to a union with constant values.

SAP HANA SPS 11 includes some performance enhancements for the union node. You can make unions run even faster by using a *pruning configuration table*. In this table, you can specify pruning conditions (like filters) to be applied to some columns. For example, a pruning condition can specify that the year must be 2016 or later. This filters the data and complies with our first modeling guideline: Limit (filter) the data as early as possible. You can specify the PRUNING

CONFIGURATION TABLE in the ADVANCED area of the SEMANTICS node. (An example is shown in Figure 6.19.)

## Semantics Node

*Semantics* is the study of meaning. In the semantics node, you can give more meaning to the data itself. One basic example is renaming fields: Some database fields have really horrible names—but in the semantics node, you can change the names of these fields to make them more meaningful for end users. This is especially useful when users have to create reports. If you have a reporting background, you'll know that a reporting universe can fulfill a similar function.

The semantics node includes four different tabs, as shown in Figure 6.17. We'll only discuss the first two tabs in this chapter; the other two tabs will be discussed in Chapter 7.

**Figure 6.17**    Tabs in Semantics Node

### Columns Tab

The first tab in the semantics node is the COLUMNS tab (see Figure 6.18).

| Type | Key | Name | Label | Aggregation | Variable | Semantic Type | Label Column | Hidden | Value Help Column | Conversion Functions |
|---|---|---|---|---|---|---|---|---|---|---|
| | ☑ | EMPLOYEEID | EMPLOYEEID | | | | | ☐ | | |
| | ☐ | NAME_FIRST | NAME_FIRST | | | | | ☐ | | |
| | ☐ | NAME_LAST | NAME_LAST | | | | | ☐ | | |
| | ☐ | SALARYAMOUNT | SALARYAMOUNT | | | | | ☐ | | |
| | ☐ | COUNTRY | COUNTRY | | | | | ☐ | | |
| | ☐ | REGION | REGION | | | | | ☐ | | |
| | ☐ | CITY | CITY | | | | | ☐ | | |
| | ☐ | POSTALCODE | POSTALCODE | | | | | ☐ | | |

**Figure 6.18**    Columns Tab in Semantics Node

Renaming fields is easy. In the COLUMNS tab, click the NAME of the field and type the new name. The same rule applies for the LABEL. The label is used, for example, when creating SAP HANA XS (HTML5) applications, or in some reporting tools. Next to the name of the field, you'll see a checkbox indicating whether this is a KEY field or not.

You might want to hide fields if you don't want to show the original field to the end user. Even if a field is hidden, it can be still used in a formula or a calculation; the field will still be available internally in SAP HANA for the calculation view, but will not be shown to the end users.

### View Properties Tab

The next tab in the semantic node is the VIEW PROPERTIES tab. Here, as shown in Figure 6.19, you can change the properties of the entire calculation view.

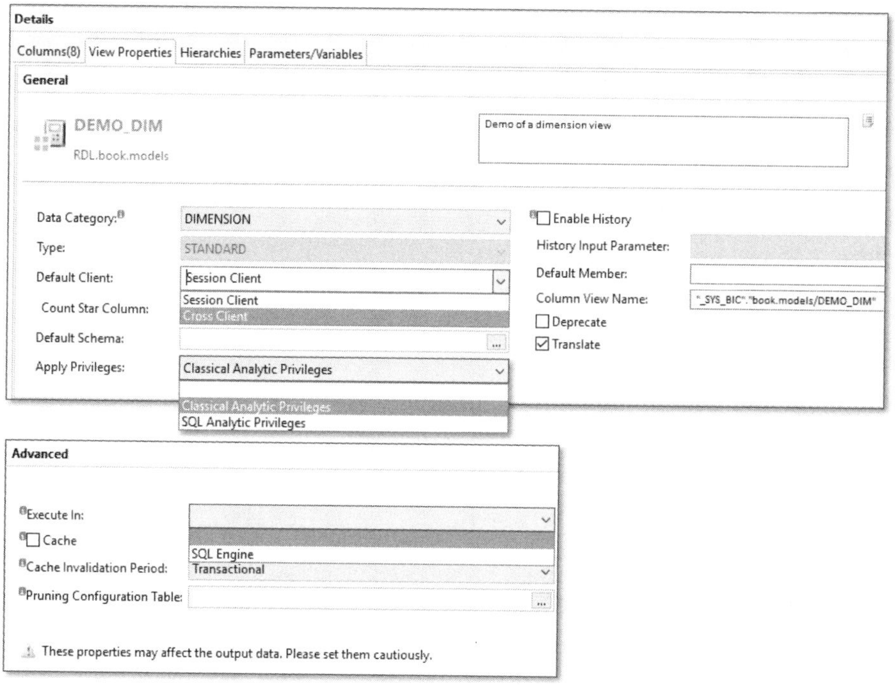

**Figure 6.19** View Properties Tab in Semantics Node

You've seen that when working with SAP data you sometimes have to set the default client. In Chapter 5, we explained how to set the default client for SAP HANA studio. You can also specify a default client for this calculation view, as shown in the DEFAULT CLIENT dropdown list in Figure 6.19. If you select the CROSS CLIENT option, data from all the SAP clients will be shown; it will not filter the data to a specific client. The SESSION CLIENT option will filter the data to display only data from a specific SAP client. Instead of using one of these two options, you can also enter the SAP client number that you want to display data for—for example, "800". This setting takes precedence over the SAP HANA studio preferences.

Many of the features in the VIEW PROPERTIES tab are new as of SAP HANA SPS 10, including new security options, the DEPRECATE checkbox, the TRANSLATE checkbox, and the ability to add comments. The PRUNING CONFIGURATION TABLE field is new as of SAP HANA SPS 11. (We discussed this feature in the Union Node section.)

For the security settings, you can choose between CLASSICAL ANALYTIC PRIVILEGES or SQL ANALYTIC PRIVILEGES. (We'll discuss these options in more detail in Chapter 13 when discussing security.) We recommend always using SQL ANALYTIC PRIVILEGES. In SAP HANA SPS 11, there is a migration tool that migrates older classical analytic privileges to SQL analytic privileges.

Setting the DEPRECATE checkbox doesn't mean that the calculation view will not work any longer; it will merely warn people that this calculation view has now been succeeded by a newer version somewhere in the system and that they should use the newer version, because this one will disappear someday in the future. When you add this calculation view in another data model, you'll see a warning in SAP HANA studio that says, THIS MODEL IS DEPRECATED. The calculation view will still work as usual, however.

When you select the new TRANSLATE checkbox, more functionality opens up in the tab's work area. You can translate field names and labels into different languages. This is useful if you need to create an SAP HANA HTML5 (XS) application for users in different countries.

Finally, take note of the COMMENTS feature. By clicking on any of the COMMENTS icons ▤ scattered throughout the calculation view, you can create comments about the calculation view. Use this functionality for internal notes to yourself, for notes to your modeling team members, or to remind yourself why you changed something.

In the ADVANCED section, you can set the EXECUTION IN to SQL ENGINE. You'll only set this preference when developing SAP HANA Live calculation views. More information on SAP HANA Live calculation views can be found in Chapter 12.

## Attribute Views and Calculation Views of Type Dimension

Currently, you can access two types of dimension views in SAP HANA. The older dimension views are called attribute views, and the newer dimension views are calculation views of type dimension. SAP HANA SPS 11 provides a migration tool to convert attribute views to calculation views of type dimension. You can use these information views as data sources for other calculation views.

In Figure 6.20, you can compare the same information model created as an attribute view (left) to the equivalent calculation view of type dimension (right).

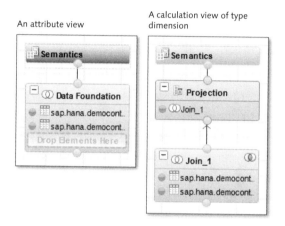

**Figure 6.20**   Comparing an Attribute View with the Equivalent Calculation View of Type Dimension

The attribute view always contains only one node (except for the semantics node). The data foundation node is always the bottom node. You can join multiple tables in the data foundation.

The calculation view of type dimension has a default projection node at the top (below the semantics node). However, you have the flexibility to add any of the calculation view nodes below it. In this case, we used a join node with the same tables to achieve the equivalent of the "data foundation."

The disadvantage of a join node is that it accepts only two inputs. The impact of this is illustrated in Figure 6.21, in which you can see the highly stacked model on the right.

An attribute view                 A calculation view of type dimension

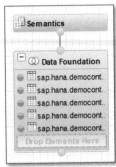
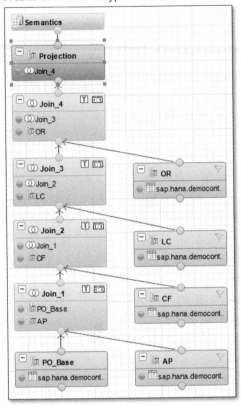

**Figure 6.21**   Disadvantage of a Join Node

 **Tip**

Attribute views have a single data foundation node because dimension views only work with attributes. Even numeric values will be treated as attributes. You also do not use fact tables with attribute views, so you don't need an additional star join node.

Calculation views of type dimension have many advantages over attribute views—for example:

▶ A flexible layout in which you can use any node. You're not restricted to the single data foundation node. For example, you can use union nodes, which are not available in attribute views.

▶ Attribute views do not have full outer and spatial joins.

▶ Time-dependent hierarchies. (For more information, see Chapter 7.)

There are some reasons to use attribute views, however, such as the following:

▶ Attribute views can use fuzzy text search directly in the view. (See Chapter 9 for more information.) Currently, these are the only views for which this is true. When this functionality has been incorporated into calculation views of type dimension, we can get rid of attribute views.

▶ Derived attribute views.

Let's look a little closer at the concept of derived attribute views. Think about shortcuts on your Windows or Mac desktop, or even the icons on the home screen of your phone or tablet. These shortcuts point to a program somewhere else on your computer or mobile device. When you tap the shortcut, the machine knows how to access the actual program. You can even rename the shortcut to something more meaningful for you; the program that it points to stays the same.

*Derived attribute views* are like shortcuts to attribute views. You create a derived attribute view when you want to reuse the same attribute view multiple times in an analytic view, but each time for slightly different purposes.

For example, think about business partners in a contact management system. In our company, we have two groups of people with contact details: customers and suppliers. All these people are in a certain city, are in a certain country, and have a specific zip or postal code. It doesn't make sense to store these addresses and contact details in two separate attribute views, so the contact details are in one attribute view called Contact Details.

We can now create two derived attribute views. Both will behave like shortcuts to the original Contact Details attribute view. We'll name one derived attribute view Customer Contact Details and the other Supplier Contact Details.

In our data model, we can then use the (derived) Customer Contact Details attribute view when we work with customers and the (derived) Supplier Contact Details attribute view when we work with suppliers.

Just as with shortcuts on your desktop computer or mobile device, the derived attributed views are dependent on the existence of the attribute view they are based on: If you delete a program, the shortcuts to that program become useless. In the same way, derived attribute views need the base attribute view to function properly. When you update the base attribute view, the derived attribute views point to the updated version and also provide the updated functionality.

Calculation views of type dimension do not yet have this functionality.

## Analytic Views and Calculation Views of Type Cube with Star Join

There are two types of star join views in SAP HANA: the older star join views, called analytic views, and the newer calculation views of type cube with star join. SAP HANA SPS 11 provides a tool to migrate analytic views to calculation views of type cube with star join.

Similar to the attribute view example, in Figure 6.22 you can compare the same information model created as an analytic view (left) to the equivalent calculation view of type cube with star join (right).

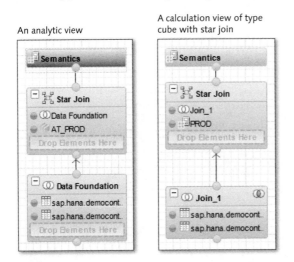

**Figure 6.22**   Comparing an Analytic View with the Equivalent Calculation View of Type Cube with Star Join

Analytic views always have two nodes (excluding the semantics node). The data foundation node is always the bottom node, and the star join node is the top node. Analytic views are built in the same bottom-up approach that you use for calculation views: First join multiple transactional tables (with measures) in the data foundation, then, in the star join node, join the data foundation to several attribute views.

The calculation view of type cube with star join has a default star join node at the top (below the semantics node). Again, you have the flexibility to add any of the calculation view nodes below it. In Figure 6.22, we used a join node with the same tables to achieve the equivalent of the data foundation.

Calculation views of type cube with star join have many advantages over analytic views—for example:

▸ You can use any nodes, have a flexible layout, and build up layers as you require. You're not restricted to two fixed nodes.

▸ Analytic views cannot use full outer and spatial joins.

▸ You can't create any hierarchies in analytic views; analytic views can only show the hierarchies they inherit from included attribute views. Because attribute views don't have time-dependent hierarchies, analytic views don't have them either.

▸ A star join in an analytic view can't point to multiple physical tables used in a single attribute view. For example, say an attribute view uses tables A and B. When you join the fact table in the analytic view to the attribute view and create a join to one field from table A and another field from table B, the analytic view will produce an activation error.

There is only one reason to still use analytic views: Analytic views are the only type of SAP HANA information view that can use temporal joins. (The temporal joins in analytic views are only available in the star join node, and only when you use inner or referential joins.)

## Migrating Attribute and Analytic Views

In SAP HANA SPS 11, you can migrate attribute and analytic views to calculation views. As you've seen, calculation views offer far more flexibility and functionality than these older types of views. There are still two cases for which attribute and analytic views cannot be migrated yet, because calculation views do not have certain functionality yet: attribute views with fuzzy text search and analytic views with temporal joins.

To migrate your old attribute and analytic views to calculation views of type dimension and calculation views of type cube with star join, follow these steps:

1. Start the migration tool from the QUICK VIEW menu in the MODELER perspective, as shown in Figure 6.23. Select the MIGRATE option. In the dialog box, select the option to migrate ATTRIBUTE VIEWS AND ANALYTIC VIEWS TO CALCULATION VIEWS.

2. Next, select the attribute and analytic views you want to convert to calculation views (see Figure 6.24).

3. Hidden columns have to be made visible during migration; otherwise, the migration tool will not include these fields as outputs in the calculation view that it will create. Therefore, enable the MAKE HIDDEN COLUMNS VISIBLE option.

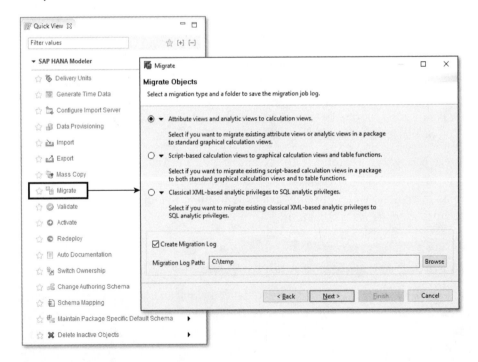

**Figure 6.23**  Selecting Migration Options

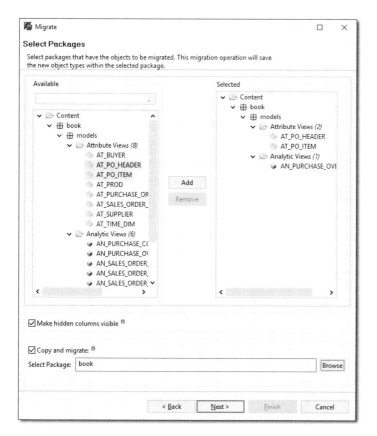

**Figure 6.24**  Selecting Attribute and Analytic Views to Migrate

4. You can simulate the migration by enabling the COPY AND MIGRATE option. The migration tool will not adjust or modify the original attribute and analytic views and will generate the calculation views in a package that you specify for the simulation. This is useful in order to understand the impact of the migration before you proceed with the actual migration.

5. Next, an overview screen displays a list of the views that will be impacted (Figure 6.25). Confirm the list of impacted objects by clicking FINISH.

6. When you start the migration, it runs as a background job. When the migration has finished, you can check the log file in the JOB LOG VIEW or in the folder specified in the MIGRATION LOG PATH (as shown in Figure 6.23).

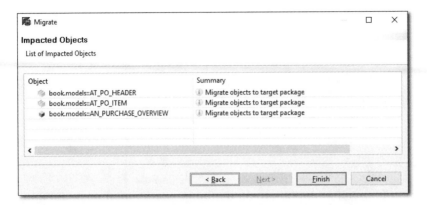

**Figure 6.25**  Selected Attribute and Analytic Views

There are three points to note about the migration of attribute and analytic views to equivalent calculation views:

▶ Filters are handled differently in SAP HANA SPS 11. You now use projection nodes with filter expressions. Column filters in the attribute and analytic views will be converted to additional projection nodes with filter expressions. (We'll discuss filter expressions in Chapter 7.)

▶ Calculation views do not currently have derived attribute view functionality. The migration tools will migrate each of the derived attribute views as a fully independent copy of the base attribute view. There is no dependency to a base (attribute) view once the derived attribute views have been migrated. If you only choose to migrate the derived attribute view, the base attribute view is not migrated, because the new migrated view is now fully independent and does not need the base attribute view any longer.

▶ Analytic views just need a single analytic privilege for the analytic views and any joined attribute views. After the migration, the calculation view of type cube with star join and any joined calculation views of type dimension will each need an analytic privilege. (We'll discuss analytic privileges in Chapter 13.)

# Important Terminology

In this chapter, the following terminology was used:

▶ **Data sources**
SAP HANA information views can use data from a wide variety of sources. The main data sources are as follows:

  ▶ Row-based and column-based tables

  ▶ SAP HANA information views in the SAP HANA system

  ▶ Decision tables

  ▶ SQL views

  ▶ Table functions

  ▶ Virtual tables with data from other databases

  ▶ CDS

  ▶ Data sources from another tenant in the SAP HANA system, if SAP HANA is set up as a multitenant database container (MDC) system

▶ **Aggregation node**
Used to calculate single summary values from a large list of values; supports sum, count, minimum, maximum, average, standard deviation, and variance.

▶ **Join node**
Used to get data sources into information views.

▶ **Projection node**
Used to remove some fields from a calculation view, rename fields, filter data, and add new calculated columns to a calculation view.

▶ **Rank node**
We can use rank nodes to create top N or bottom N lists of values to sort results.

▶ **Star join node**
Used to join a data foundation with fact tables to dimension views. The join types available in the star join node are the same as the normal joins in a join node. It's what they're joining that differs.

▶ **Union node**
   Used to combine multiple data sources. You can make unions run even faster
   by using a pruning configuration table.

▶ **Semantics node**
   Used to give meaning to the data in information views.

▶ **Calculation view of type dimension/attribute views**
   You can use these information views for master data.

▶ **Calculation view of type cube with star join/analytic view**
   These views can be used for multidimensional reporting and data analysis
   purposes.

▶ **Calculation view of type cube**
   These views can be used for more powerful multidimensional reporting and
   data analysis purposes.

## Practice Questions

These practice questions will help you evaluate your understanding of the topics
covered in this chapter. The questions shown are similar in nature to those found on
the certification examination. Although none of these questions will be found on the
exam itself, they will allow you to review your knowledge of the subject. Select the
correct answers and then check the completeness of your answers in the Practice
Question Answers and Explanations section. Remember that on the exam you must
select all correct answers and only correct answers to receive credit for the question.

1.  For what type of data are SAP HANA calculation views of type dimension
    used?

    ☐  **A.** Transactional data

    ☐  **B.** Master data

    ☐  **C.** Materialized cube data

    ☐  **D.** Calculated data

2. Which of the following node types can you use to build an analytic view? (There are 3 correct answers.)

☐  **A.** Star join node

☐  **B.** Aggregation node

☐  **C.** Data foundation node

☐  **D.** Semantics node

☐  **E.** Union node

3. Which types of calculation views can you create? (There are 2 correct answers.)

☐  **A.** Standard

☐  **B.** Derived

☐  **C.** Materialized

☐  **D.** Time-based

4. In which direction do you build calculation views when including the source tables in join nodes?

☐  **A.** From the join nodes up to the semantic node

☐  **B.** From the semantic node up to the default node

☐  **C.** From the join node down to the default node

☐  **D.** From the semantic node down to the join nodes

5. You rename a field in the semantics node to add clarity for end users. What does SAP HANA use to keep track of what the original field name is?

☐  **A.** The label column property

☐  **B.** The mapping property

☐  **C.** The label property

☐  **D.** The name property

6. You want to use a field in a formula but do not want to expose the values of the original field to the end users. What do you do?

☐  **A.** Make the field a key column

☐  **B.** Change the data type of the field

☐    **C.** Rename the field

☐    **D.** Mark the field as hidden

7.    Where can you set the default value for the SAP client for the entire calculation view?

☐    **A.** In the join node of the calculation view

☐    **B.** In the semantic layer of the calculation view

☐    **C.** In the default node of the calculation view

☐    **D.** In the WINDOW menu of SAP HANA studio

8.    True or False: When you mark a calculation view as deprecated, that view no longer works.

☐    **A.** True

☐    **B.** False

9.    What node can you use to generate a column for use in sorting results?

☐    **A.** Aggregation node

☐    **B.** Projection node

☐    **C.** Rank node

☐    **D.** Union node

10.    For what SQL keyword is the aggregation node the equivalent?

☐    **A.** ORDER BY

☐    **B.** GROUP BY

☐    **C.** DISTINCT

☐    **D.** UNIQUE

11.    What is the default node for a calculation view of type cube?

☐    **A.** Aggregation node

☐    **B.** Projection node

☐    **C.** Star join node

☐    **D.** Join node

12. What node is used to link dimension views to a data foundation (fact tables)?

- ☐ **A.** Join node
- ☐ **B.** Projection node
- ☐ **C.** Union node
- ☐ **D.** Star join node

13. What data source is available for join nodes in calculation views?

- ☐ **A.** All procedures in the current SAP HANA system
- ☐ **B.** Scalar functions from all SAP HANA systems
- ☐ **C.** Calculation views from other tenants in an MDC system
- ☐ **D.** Web services from the Internet

14. What feature is similar between an attribute view and a calculation view of type dimension?

- ☐ **A.** Full outer join
- ☐ **B.** Fuzzy text search attributes
- ☐ **C.** Derived views
- ☐ **D.** Left outer join

15. Which join types are available in a join node of a calculation view? (There are 2 correct answers.)

- ☐ **A.** Referential joins
- ☐ **B.** Spatial joins
- ☐ **C.** Cross joins
- ☐ **D.** Temporal joins

16. What issue do you have to address after you have migrated your old views to calculation views?

- ☐ **A.** Change filters on table columns to filter expressions
- ☐ **B.** Unhide the hidden fields in the semantics node
- ☐ **C.** Manually migrate the base view for derived views
- ☐ **D.** Check the analytic privileges for star join situations

17. What node uses a special configuration table to optimize performance?

☐  **A.** Union node

☐  **B.** Aggregation node

☐  **C.** Join node

☐  **D.** Projection node

18. Which features are similar between an analytic view and a calculation view of type cube with star join? (There are 3 correct answers.)

☐  **A.** Fact tables

☐  **B.** Spatial joins

☐  **C.** Temporal joins

☐  **D.** Referential joins

☐  **E.** Star join nodes

## Practice Question Answers and Explanations

1. Correct answer: **B**

   You use SAP HANA calculation views of type dimension for master data.

   Transactional data needs a calculation view marked as CUBE. SAP HANA does not store or use materialized cube data. You cannot calculate data when you only work with attributes; you need measures to do that.

2. Correct answers: **A, C, D**

   You use a data foundation, a star join node, and a semantics node to build an analytic view. Aggregation nodes and union nodes are not available in analytic views.

3. Correct answers: **A, D**

   You can create standard and time-based calculation views. Derived views are only available for attribute views. SAP HANA does not use materialized views.

4. Correct answer: **A**

   You build calculation views (when including the source tables in join nodes) from the join nodes up to the semantic node. The semantic node is above the default node, which is above the join nodes. You always start from the bottom and work upwards.

5. Correct answer: **B**

   SAP HANA uses the mapping property to keep track of what the original field name is when you rename a field in the semantic node.

6. Correct answer: **D**

   Mark a field as hidden when you want to use a field in a formula, but don't want to expose the values of the original field to end users.

7. Correct answer: **B**

   You set the default value for the SAP client for the entire calculation view in the semantic layer of the calculation view. You cannot set properties for the entire view in the join or default nodes of the calculation view. The WINDOW menu of SAP HANA studio is used for user-specific system-wide settings, not for a specific calculation view.

8. Correct answer: **B**

   False. When you mark a calculation view as deprecated, that view will still work.

9. Correct answer: **C**

   You use a rank node to generate a rank column for use in sorting results. Aggregation and projection nodes have calculated columns (which we'll discuss in Chapter 7), but not generated columns.

10. Correct answer: **B**

    Aggregation nodes are equivalent to the GROUP BY keyword.

11. Correct answer: **A**

    The default node for a calculation view of type cube is an aggregation node. A projection node is the default node of a calculation view of type dimension. A star join node is the default node of a calculation view of type cube with star join.

12. Correct answer: **D**

    A star join node is used to link dimension views to a data foundation (fact tables).

13. Correct answer: **C**

    Calculation views from other tenants in an MDC system are available as data sources for join nodes in calculation views.

    Scalar functions do not return table result sets, and procedures do not have to generate any result sets. (For more information, see Chapter 8.)

14. Correct answer: **D**

    An attribute view and a calculation view of type dimension both have left outer joins. Only calculation views of type dimension have full outer joins. Only attribute views have fuzzy text search attributes and derived views.

15. Correct answers: **A, B**

    Referential joins and spatial joins are available in a join node of a calculation view. Temporal joins are only available in analytic views.

16. Correct answer: **D**

    After you have migrated your old views to calculation views, you have to check the analytic privileges for star join situations. Revealing the hidden fields is done during the migration, not afterwards. The migration automatically changes filters on table columns to filter expressions. You do not have to manually migrate the base view of derived views.

17. Correct answer: **A**

    Union nodes can use a special configuration table to optimize performance for union pruning.

18. Correct answers: **A, D, E**

    An analytic view and a calculation view of type cube with star join both use fact tables, referential joins, and star join nodes. Only calculation views of type cube with star join have spatial joins. Only analytic views have temporal joins.

## Takeaway

You should now know how to create SAP HANA information views and when to create each type of calculation view based on your business requirements. You have learned how to add data sources, create joins, add nodes, and select output fields.

In Table 6.1, we define our different information views and provide a list of their individual features.

| Calculation Views of Type Dimension | Calculation View of Type Cube with Star Join | Calculation View of Type Cube |
|---|---|---|
| **Purpose:** Create a dimension for our analytic modeling needs | **Purpose:** Create a cube for our analytic requirements | **Purpose:** Create more advanced information models |
| ▸ Replacing attribute views<br>▸ Treats all data as attributes<br>▸ Uses mostly joins | ▸ Replacing analytic views<br>▸ Combines fact tables with dimensions | ▸ Adds extra functionality like aggregations, joins, projections, ranking, and unions. |

**Table 6.1**  Information View Features

## Summary

You learned how to create calculation views, and add data sources, joins, nodes, and output columns. You added meaning to the output columns in the semantics node and set the properties for the view.

We explained when to use attribute and analytic views and how to migrate existing attribute and analytic views to equivalent calculation views.

In the next chapter, we'll discuss how to further enhance our information views with additional functionality, like filter expressions, calculated columns, currency conversions, and hierarchies.

# Advanced Information Modeling

## Techniques You'll Master

- ▶ Learn how to define calculated and restricted columns
- ▶ Examine filter operations and filter expressions
- ▶ Identify when to create variables and input parameters
- ▶ Understand currency and currency conversions
- ▶ Describe decision tables
- ▶ Know how to create hierarchies

In previous chapter we learned how to build SAP HANA information views. In this chapter, we will see how to enhance calculation views with additional functionality, including adding output fields, methods for filtering data, how to convert currencies, how to add business rules, and how to implement hierarchies.

## Real-World Scenario

You are working on an SAP HANA modeling project, and are asked to help with publishing the company's financial results for the year.

You copy some of the calculations views that you have created before, and start adding additional features to them. First, you filter the data to the last financial year, and to the required company code. You then implement currency conversions on all the financial transactions, so that the results can be published in a single currency.

The board members aren't sure if they want the results in US dollars, or in euros, so they ask you to give them a choice when they run their queries on the SAP HANA information views. They also ask you to create a dashboard for them, where they can drill down into the results. They want to see where there might be any missing data or issues.

In addition, the CFO wants to use this opportunity to run some what-if analysis scenarios on the data to see where he can improve the company's bottom-line for the new financial year.

Finally, you create an overview report for them, showing the last few years of financial results side-by-side.

## Objectives of this Portion of the Test

The purpose of this portion of the SAP HANA certification exam is to test your knowledge of SAP HANA modeling and information views, and how to enhance and refine these views with additional functionality.

The certification exam expects you to have a good understanding of the following topics:

▶  Calculated columns

▶  Restricted columns

- ▸ Filter operations

- ▸ Variables

- ▸ Input parameters

- ▸ Currency and currency conversions

- ▸ Decision tables

- ▸ Hierarchies

 **Note**

This portion contributes up to 15% of the total certification exam score. This is larger than any other portion of the certification exam.

# Key Concepts Refresher

In the previous chapter, we saw how a generated rank column can be added to the list of output fields in a calculation view. In this chapter, we will learn about four more such additional output fields. We will see how to add calculated columns, restricted columns, counters, and currency conversion columns to the list of output fields in our calculation views.

In our discussions on these topics, see if you can identity which feature solves each problem described in the real-world scenario described above.

Let's start with the first of our eight topics on how to enhance our SAP HANA information views.

## Calculated Columns

Up to this point, we have created information views using available data sources. However, quite often, we'll want SAP HANA to do some calculations for us on that data to, for example, calculate the sales tax on a transaction.

In the past, this was usually done using reporting tools. Now, SAP HANA has all the data available, and can do the calculations without having to send all the data to the reporting tool. It does the calculations faster than reporting tools, and sends only the results to reporting tools, saving calculation time, bandwidth, and network time.

Figure 7.1 illustrates how calculated columns work. When we create *calculated columns* in SAP HANA, it adds additional output columns to our information views. The calculated results are displayed in these calculated columns.

| | | | | Calculated columns | |
| | | | | 5% discount, but 10% if more than 100 items | 15% Sales Tax (VAT) |
| Table | | | | | |
| Item | Quantity | Price | Total | Discount | Sales Tax (VAT) |
| Device | 2 | $200 | $400 | $380 | $57 |
| Plug | 500 | $5 | $2500 | $2250 | $338 |
| Cable | 200 | $10 | $2000 | $1800 | $270 |
| Connector | 7 | $20 | $140 | $133 | $20 |
| Adapter | 3 | $50 | $150 | $143 | $21 |

**Figure 7.1**   Calculated Columns Added as Additional Output

On the left side of Figure 7.1 is our source data from a table. We added two calculated columns on the right. The first calculated column calculates discounts and the second one calculates the sales tax.

**Note**

The calculated columns are part of the information view. The results are not stored anywhere, but are calculated and displayed each time the view is called.

Calculated columns are available in the join, star join, projection, and aggregation nodes. They are not available in the rank and union nodes.

### Creating Calculated Columns

In the SAP HANA studio, we create CALCULATED COLUMNS in the OUTPUT area. In the context menu of the CALCULATED COLUMNS, we select the NEW option, as shown in Figure 7.2.

In the CREATE A CALCULATED COLUMN dialog screen, shown in Figure 7.3, we first specify the name and data type of the calculated column.

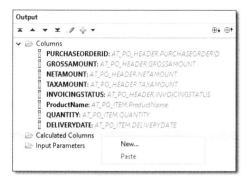

**Figure 7.2**   Create a New Calculated Column in the Output Area

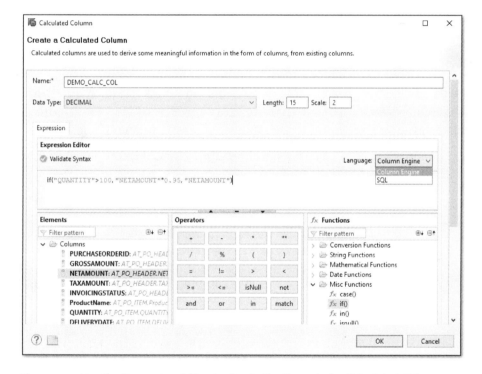

**Figure 7.3**   Use the Expression Editor to Create the Formula for Calculated Columns

The EXPRESSION EDITOR takes up the rest of the space in the dialog screen. The focus is the formula (called the expression) in the middle.

The three areas at the bottom help us to create the expression:

▶ ELEMENTS

The ELEMENTS area contains all available columns, previously created calculated columns, and input parameters (see the Input Parameters section). We can build our new calculated column on previous calculations, to build up more complex calculations.

▶ OPERATORS

The OPERATORS area contains operators, for example, for adding, multiplying, comparing, or combining columns.

▶ FUNCTIONS

The FUNCTIONS area contain various useful functions, like converting data types, working with strings, doing the basic mathematical calculations, and working with dates. We also have some extra functions, for example the `if()` function for if-then-else calculations.

All the examples here were using measures. However, we can also create calculated columns for attributes as well. The functions allow us to work with strings and dates as well, so we can create expressions using attributes.

The LANGUAGE selection allows us to either use a normal expression, which SAP HANA will translate to SQL for us, or directly use SQL syntax.

 **Tip**

We recommend that you use the mouse to click on the various components. You can type the expression directly in the text area, but we found that many people either mistype a column name, or forget that SAP HANA column names can be case-sensitive. By using the mouse, SAP HANA studio assists you with the typing.

The Expression Editor also helps us with on-the-fly syntax checking. In Figure 7.4, we see an example of this. In the top example, the Expression Editor highlights the error, even with a tooltip. When we inserted the missing ">" sign, the Expression Editor displays the formula in green text to show that it contains no errors.

With most, if not all, of the enhanced features we discuss in this chapter, we have the ability to add comments. In Figure 7.4 we commented what the formula meant. This will remind us later what we did, or inform our team members why we wrote the expression the way we did.

**Figure 7.4** On-the-Fly Syntax Checking in the Expression Editor

### Calculate before Aggregation in Analytic Views

In analytic views we have an additional flag (tick box) in the Expression Editor called CALCULATE BEFORE AGGREGATION, as shown in Figure 7.5. The CALCULATE BEFORE AGGREGATION flag is only applicable for measures, and by default this is switched off.

As you know, one of our main modeling rules is "Calculate as late as possible." With addition and subtraction we can delay the calculations to as late as possible. There are cases, for example, with multiplication and division, where we have to do calculations earlier than normal. An example would be when we want to aggregate totals for quantities and price per unit. If we add all the prices first, and all the prices per unit, and then multiply these two sums, we will get totally inaccurate results. In this case we have to do the quantity multiplied by price per unit calculations first for each record, and then we can add up the total costs. To do this, we need to manually enable the CALCULATE BEFORE AGGREGATION flag under the CLIENT AGGREGATION field (see Figure 7.5).

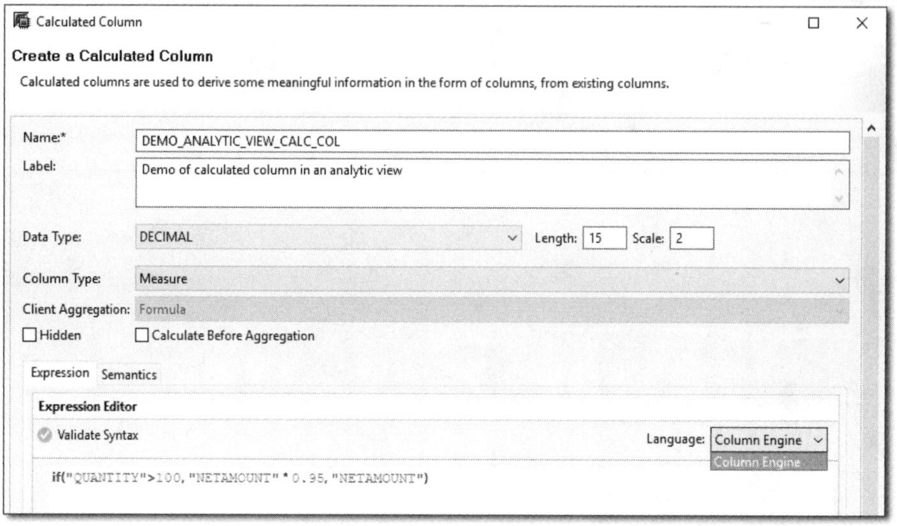

**Figure 7.5**   Calculate Before Aggregation Flag

The CALCULATE BEFORE AGGREGATION flag is only in the Expression Editor for analytic views. In calculation views, SAP HANA knows when to do the calculations earlier for accuracy, and does not require us to set a flag.

### Counters

In aggregation and star join nodes we sometimes want to know how many times in the result set a certain item occurs for an attribute. For example, we might want to know how many unique items were sold in each shop to find the shops with the largest variety. We do this using *counters*.

The NEW COUNTER option is found in the calculated column's context menu in the OUTPUT area of aggregation and star join nodes (see Figure 7.6). In our example, we will put the counter on items sold.

We can also use multiple columns to expand our example to add item categories, for example, to show which shop had the largest variety of items for meats, the largest variety of items for the bakery section, etc.

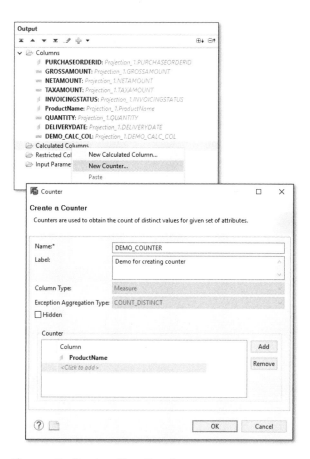

**Figure 7.6**   Create a New Counter

## Restricted Columns

The easiest way to explain *restricted columns* is to think of a reporting requirement that you frequently encounter. For example, let's say we have a website
where we work with the data of who visited the website. We use a view like the
one shown in Figure 7.7. Our data from the source table is in the two columns
on the left. We can see how many users connected with which type of device,
organized per row.

We would like our report to be like the bottom right of the screen in Figure 7.7,
where we have a column for each device, with the total number of users for each

device. You might know this as a pivot table. We already saw in Chapter 4 that we could use a union with constant values to achieve a similar result.

We can also achieve this by creating a restricted column for each device. This adds a new additional output column to our view. When we create a restricted column for the mobile phones, we *restrict* our column to only show mobile phone data. Everything else in that column is NULL. When we now aggregate the restricted column, we get the total number of users visiting the website on mobile phones. We create a restricted field for each device to create our report.

Because we need aggregation for this to work properly, restricted columns are only available in the aggregation and star join nodes.

| Table | | Restricted columns | | | |
|---|---|---|---|---|---|
| Device | Number of users | Mobile phone | Tablet | Laptop | Desktop |
| Mobile phone | 20 | 20 | | | |
| Tablet | 10 | | 10 | | |
| Desktop | 10 | | | | 10 |
| Mobile phone | 10 | 10 | | | |
| Mobile phone | 40 | 40 | | | |
| Laptop | 20 | | | 20 | |
| Tablet | 20 | | 20 | | |
| Laptop | 30 | | | 30 | |
| Mobile phone | 50 | 50 | | | |
| Mobile phone | 40 | 40 | | | |
| Laptop | 20 | | | 20 | |
| Desktop | 20 | | | | 20 |

| Aggregated results | | | |
|---|---|---|---|
| Mobile phone | Tablet | Laptop | Desktop |
| 160 | 30 | 70 | 30 |

**Figure 7.7**   Creating Four Restricted Columns and Aggregating the Result Sets

**Note**

We create restricted columns on attributes. For example, it doesn't make sense to create a REPORTING column with a heading of '25' (measure). However, a MOBILE PHONE column (attribute) provides more useful information.

## Creating Restricted Columns

Creating a restricted column is similar to creating a calculated column. In the context menu, as shown in Figure 7.8, we choose the NEW option.

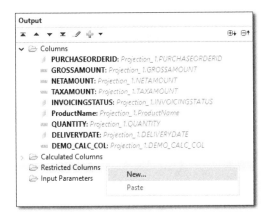

**Figure 7.8**   Create a Restricted Column

In the dialog screen for creating the restricted column, we specify the name of the restricted column and what data we want to display in the column.

In the RESTRICTIONS area, we can add one or more restrictions, for example, the year has to be 2016, the device has to be a mobile phone, or, as shown in Figure 7.9, if we only want to see the financial information for invoices.

If we add multiple restrictions, SAP HANA automatically creates the relevant AND and OR operators. For example if we have two restriction for the year 2015 and 2016, the Expression Editor will use year = 2015 OR year = 2016.

When we enter a value, like 2016 for the year, we can ask the Expression Editor to give us a list of existing values currently stored in the system. In Figure 7.10 we asked for a list of invoice statuses. In the list, we see I for Invoices, and D for Delivery notes. This popup list is called the *value help* list. You will find these value help lists in all the modeling screens.

In the restricted column creation dialog, in the RESTRICTIONS area, we can choose to use an EXPRESSION rather than specify individual COLUMN values. We can then use the Expression Editor to generate the relevant portion of the SQL WHERE statement directly.

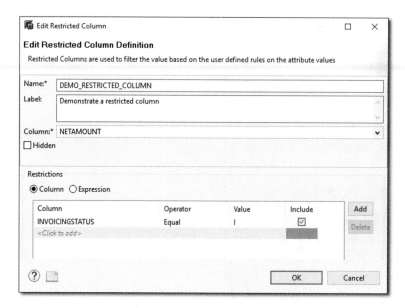

**Figure 7.9**   Create a Restricted Column for the Net Amount of Invoices

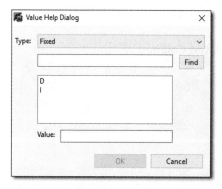

**Figure 7.10**   Choosing a Restriction Value from a Predefined List of Values

If you first filled in the values in the COLUMN view, and then change to the EXPRESSION view, the Expression Editor automatically convert this for you, as shown in Figure 7.11.

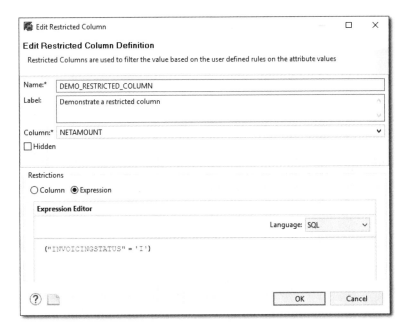

**Figure 7.11**   Use the Expression Editor to Create Restrictions on Restricted Columns

## Creating Restricted Columns Using Calculated Columns

You can also create a restricted column using a calculated column. Just use the expression if("Device"='Mobile phone', "Number of users", NULL). The if() function in the Expression Editor works similarly as the IF function in Microsoft Excel. If the condition (first part with the equal sign) is true, then show the second part, otherwise show the last part.

Just like with a calculated column, a restricted column does not store data. Each time an information view is used, the restricted column is created and aggregated.

 **Tip**

A restricted column differs from a filter or a SQL WHERE condition.

If you filter on the year 2016, all the data in the view will be trimmed to only show the data for 2016. When you create a restricted column for the year 2016, only the data in that column is trimmed for 2016.

## Filters

Sometimes we do not want to show all the data from a specific table. For example, we might only want to show data for the year 2016. In this case, we can apply a *filter*. Filters restrict the data for the entire data source.

When we apply filters, SAP HANA can work a lot faster because it doesn't have to work with/sift through all the data. In the SCENARIO area, select the projection node of your view. Then, in the DETAILS area, select the data source, select the field, and right-click for the context menu. From the context menu, select APPLY FILTER, as shown in Figure 7.12.

In the popup dialog box, we can select the OPERATOR from the dropdown. Normally, it would be EQUAL, but there is a whole list of other operators available in the dropdown list. We then add the filter value by either selecting it from the dropdown or typing it in.

When the filter has been applied, you will see a FILTER icon ▽ next to the field name in the table.

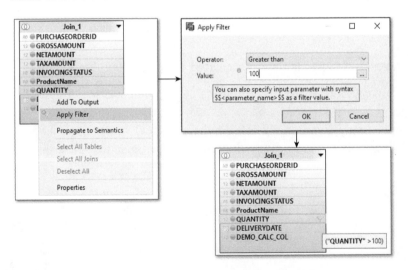

**Figure 7.12**  Apply a Filter to a Field in the Projection Node

## Filter Expressions

In the OUTPUT area, we also see a FILTER icon ⅋ next to the output field, as shown in Figure 7.13. At the bottom of the OUTPUT area we find the filter EXPRESSION option.

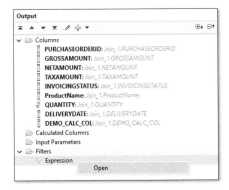

**Figure 7.13**   Open Filter Expression Dialog from the Output Area

When we open the filter expression, we see the dialog screen shown in Figure 7.14. Just as with the Expression Editor for calculated and restricted columns, we can set the value for the columns, or use the SQL syntax.

Filters and filter expressions are only available in projection nodes.

**Figure 7.14**   Edit a Filter Expression.

### Filtering for SAP Clients

Filtering of data can be implemented more widely than the examples we have just seen. In Chapter 5, of the Session Client section, we already discussed how to set the SAP HANA studio preferences to only show data coming from an SAP ERP system for a specific SAP client. In Chapter 6, of the Semantics Node section, we saw how to set an option for filtering to an SAP client in the semantics node. Chapter 8 and Chapter 13 also provide further details on filtering for an SAP client.

### Domain Fix Values

SAP ERP uses the ABAP programming language, which has some powerful data dictionary features. In ABAP, we can define re-usable data elements (like data types). We can use these data elements in our table definitions.

Sometime we want these data elements to only allow a range of values. We define a domain with the range of values, and use this domain with the data element. In all the tables where that specific data element is used, the users can now only enter values that are in the specified range.

Instead of a range, we can also specify fixed values for the domain. This is known as the *domain fix values*. These are values that will not change, and the users can only choose from the available list when they enter data into the fields.

Let's look at some examples: Maybe the users need to enter a gender. The domain values are fixed to *male* and *female*. This is very similar to the value help shown in Figure 7.10. Another example could be the possible statuses of a sales order. The sales order statuses could be *quoted*, *sold*, *delivered*, *invoiced*, and *paid*.

The lists of fixed values are stored in the DD07L and DD07T tables in the SAP ERP system. Because these tables are so valuable for business systems, many times we replicate (or import) these tables to SAP HANA. We can then use these values in SAP HANA for the value help dialog screens, similar to Figure 7.10.

These domain fixed values can now also be used to filter business data, for example we can filter the sales data to the domain fixed value of *paid* to see only the sales that are already paid.

### Variables

In the previous section, we looked at filtering. These filters were all static, in the sense that we could not change them once we specified them. Each time you query the view, the same filters are used.

Frequently, however, we'll want the system to ask us at runtime what we would like to filter on. Instead of always filtering the view on the year 2016, we can specify which year's data we want to see. If we query the view from a reporting tool, we even expect the reporting tool to pop up a dialog box and ask us what we would like to filter on.

This dynamic type of filtering is done with *variables*.

We define variables in the SEMANTICS node of a calculation view. In Chapter 6, we discussed the first two tabs available in the SEMANTICS node. Now we will look at one of the remaining two tabs, called PARAMETERS/VARIABLES.

In Figure 7.15 we see the SEMANTICS node. In the PARAMETERS/VARIABLES tab, we select the CREATE VARIABLE option by clicking the plus icon ✚ to reveal the drop-down menu.

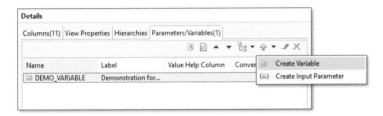

**Figure 7.15**   Create a Variable in the Semantics Node

In the CREATE A VARIABLE dialog screen (Figure 7.16) we start by specifying the NAME of the variable.

We have to specify the ATTRIBUTE on which we want to create our variable. This is the field on which we want to implement our "dynamic filter."

In the SELECTION TYPE we can choose what type of variable we want to create. There are three types of variables:

▶ SINGLE VALUE
The variable only asks one (single) value, for example, the year is 2016.

▶ INTERVAL
The variable asks for from and to values, for example, the years from 2012 to 2015.

▶ RANGE
The variable asks a single value, but combines it with another operator, for example, the year is greater and equal to 2012.

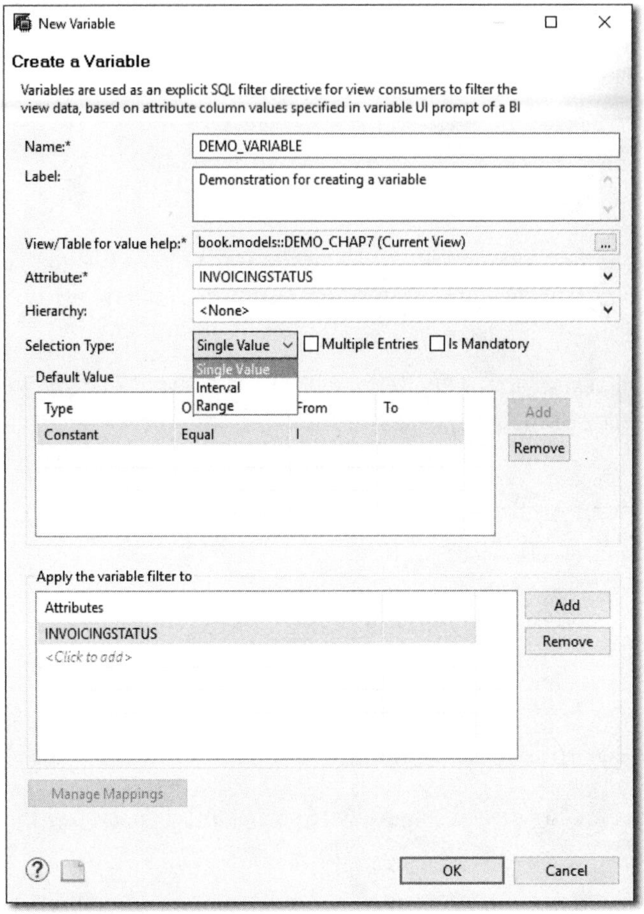

**Figure 7.16**  Create a Variable

We can specify a DEFAULT VALUE. If the user selects CANCEL or presses Esc in the VALUE HELP DIALOG, like the one in Figure 7.18, the variable will then use this default value.

When the MULTIPLE ENTRIES flag is enabled, we can use the Ctrl key when selecting (multiple) entries. We can select, for example, the years 2011, 2014, and 2015 from the value help dialog.

By default the variable uses the view or table that it is based on to display a list of available values in the value help dialog. Changing the VIEW/TABLE FOR VALUE HELP option allows us to specify a different view or table for the list of available values in the value help dialog.

Ideally, the data source we specify should be in sync with the view we are using the variable on, else the users might choose a value from value help dialog which is not available in the current view, and therefore will not be shown any information. The reason we do this is to ensure we have consistent value help lists for all our different views by specifying the same value help data source for all the views. Sometimes this can also help to speed up the display of the value help.

With the HIERARCHY option we can link a hierarchy to our variable. Users can then drill down using this hierarchy when they want to select a value from the value help dialog. We will learn to set up hierarchies later in this chapter.

Once we have created the variable, it will show up in the COLUMNS tab of the SEMANTICS node, next to the name of the attribute we selected. You can see an example in Figure 7.17.

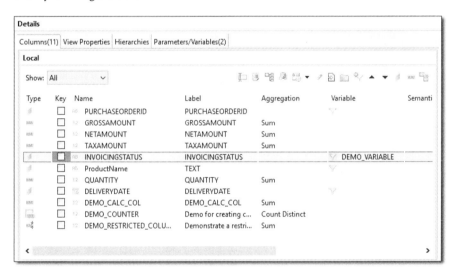

**Figure 7.17**  Variable Shown in the Columns Tab of the Semantics Node

When we preview our calculation view, a VARIABLE/INPUT PARAMETERS VALUES dialog screen will appear in the SAP HANA studio. We have to supply these values before SAP will run our view, and return the results.

When we select the ellipsis (…) menu button, the VALUE HELP DIALOG will appear with a list of available values that we can choose from (see Figure 7.18).

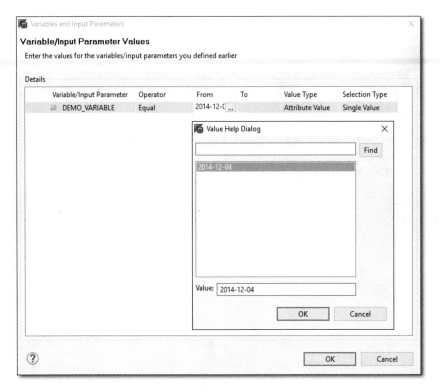

**Figure 7.18**   Variable Value Help Dialog

## Input Parameters

*Input parameters* are very similar to variables. However, while variables are specifically created for "dynamic filtering," input parameters are more generic. For example, we can use them in formulas or expressions.

Let's look at an example: An outstanding payments report asks you for how many months outstanding you want to see the results. This time period can then be used in a calculated column's expression to calculate the results we asked for. The same report can be used by the debt collecting department for payments outstanding longer than two months, while the legal department will ask for payments outstanding longer than six months.

Input parameters are created in the semantics node (see Figure 7.19). We can also create input parameters in all the nodes types, except in a union node.

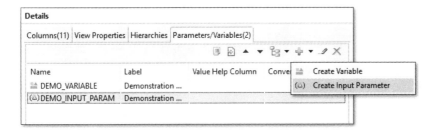

**Figure 7.19** Create an Input Parameter

The CREATE AN INPUT PARAMETER dialog screen is shown in Figure 7.20. The various dropdown menu options are shown on the right side of the screen.

We start with the NAME of the input parameter. The PARAMETER TYPE specifies what type of data we expect to use this input parameter for.

There are five types of input parameters we can create:

▶ DIRECT
The end users directly type in the value. We can specify the DATA TYPE of the expected value. There are three data types we can use for DIRECT, namely CURRENCY, UNIT OF MEASURE, and DATE.

▶ COLUMN
The end users can choose a value from all the possible values in a specified column in the current view.

▶ DERIVED FROM TABLE
The end users can choose a value from data in another table.

▶ STATIC LIST
The end users can choose a value from a pre-defined (static) list of values.

▶ DERIVED FROM PROCEDURE/SCALAR FUNCTION
The end users can choose a value from a list of values generated by a scalar function or a procedure.

The DEFAULT VALUE can be typed in as a single value, or it can be an expression. Similar to variables, if the user selects CANCEL or presses ⎡Esc⎤ in the value help dialog, the input parameter will use this default value.

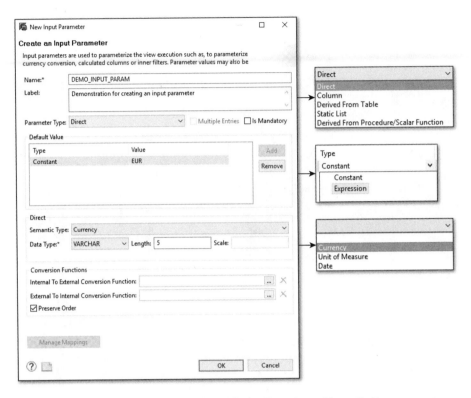

**Figure 7.20**   Create an Input Parameter with the Dropdown Menu Options

In Figure 7.20, we created an input parameter called `DEMO_INPUT_PARAM`. We can now use this input parameter, for example, in a calculated column. When we use the input parameter in an expression, we add a `$$` at the start and end of the name of the input parameter. This makes it very clear that we are referring to an input parameter. The name of our input parameter will become `$$DEMO_INPUT_PARAM$$`.

In Figure 7.21 we use the input parameter in an expression. The expression,

```
daysbetween("DELIVERYDATE", $$DEMO_INPUT_PARAM$$)
```

calculates the number of days between the date that the end user supplies and the delivery date.

In this case, the input parameter has a PARAMETER TYPE of DIRECT, and a DATA TYPE of DATE.

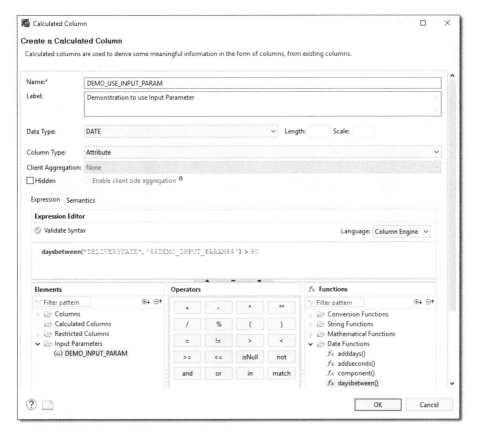

**Figure 7.21**   Use an Input Parameter in an Expression for a Calculated Column

 **Tip**

We have `$$CLIENT$$` and `$$LANGUAGE$$` built into SAP HANA. These do not ask for values at runtime, but instead give the SAP client number filter currently in use, and the log-on language of the end user.

When we preview the calculation view in SAP HANA studio, and the input parameter has a DATA TYPE of DATE, a calendar is displayed where you can choose the date you want (see Figure 7.22).

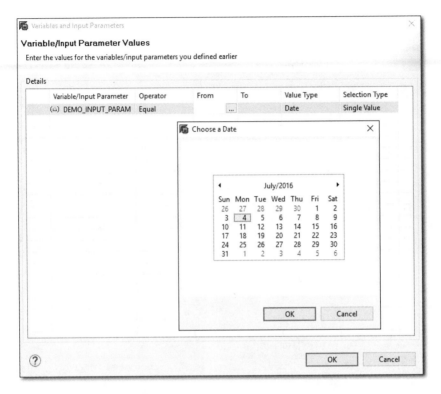

**Figure 7.22**   Date Input Parameter

## Currency

SAP is well-known for its business systems. An important part of financial and business information models is their ability to work with *currencies*.

In Figure 7.23 we can see the OUTPUT area of a calculation view. We have a few output fields that are currency fields, for example, GROSSAMOUNT, NETA-MOUNT, and TAXAMOUNT.

When we look at the PROPERTIES of these fields, they are treated as numeric fields (measures). We can improve on that by changing the SEMANTIC TYPE property to AMOUNT WITH CURRENCY CODE.

When we change the SEMANTIC TYPE of a field to currency, an ASSIGN SEMANTICS dialog screen like Figure 7.24 appears.

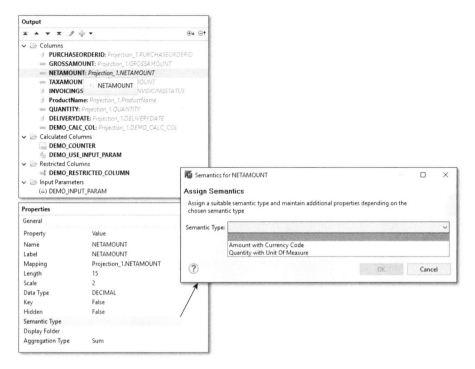

**Figure 7.23** Assign an Output Field to the Semantic Type "Amount with Currency Code"

Most of this dialog screen is focused on *currency conversion*. Via the Internet, even small companies can do business internationally. Or a company can buy parts from different suppliers world-wide. Their taxes and financial reporting however happen in their home country.

When converting from one currency to another, we have a *source currency* and a *target currency*. Something else as equally important is the date, because exchange rates fluctuate all the time

But what date do we use? Do we use the date of the quote, the date of the invoice, the date of the delivery, the date the customer paid, the end of that month, or the financial year-end? All of the mentioned dates are valid. It depends on the business requirements.

In SAP systems, the exchange rate data gets stored in some tables prefixed with the TCUR name. There are many programs from banks and other financial institutions that help update the TCUR tables in SAP systems. These TCUR tables are used by the SAP business systems for currency conversions. SAP HANA also knows how to use the TCUR tables. You can easily get a copy of these tables by installing the SHINE package. It will create these TCUR tables for you to demonstrate currency conversions in its information models.

By default, most of the options in the ASSIGN SEMANTICS dialog screen of Figure 7.24 are unavailable. Enabling the CONVERSION flag opens up the entire dialog screen.

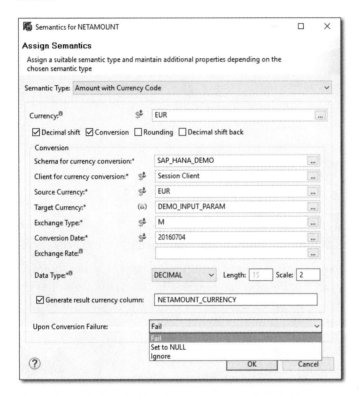

**Figure 7.24**  Output Field Setup for Currency Conversion

Let's go through some of the options in this dialog screen to learn more about currency fields and currency conversions in SAP HANA:

▶ CURRENCY
We can specify in what currency the current field is.

▶ DECIMAL SHIFT
Some currencies require more than two decimal places. This is indicated with this flag.

- DECIMAL SHIFT BACK

  ABAP programs automatically do a decimal shift. When these ABAP programs work with SAP HANA information views, they might receive currency data from SAP HANA that has already been shifted, and a double decimal shift occurs. In those cases, we need to set this flag to "undo" the extra DECIMAL SHIFT.

Some of the currency conversion-specific options in the dialog screen include:

- SCHEMA FOR CURRENCY CONVERSION

  You have to specify in which schema the SAP HANA system can find the TCUR tables. SHINE automatically installs these tables in the SAP_HANA_DEMO schema.

- SOURCE CURRENCY and TARGET CURRENCY

  We can specify the specific currencies codes, for example, EUR for euros and USD for United States dollars, directly in these fields. There are two other options as well:

  - COLUMN: If we are storing multiple currencies in the same column, we will have another column that specifies what currency each record is in. We can tell SAP HANA to read the currency codes from that column, and automatically convert each of the individual records.

  - INPUT PARAMETERS: We can choose the currency code to use for the currency conversion at runtime using an input parameter. We can get a financial report to ask an end user if they want the report in euros or dollars, or pick any currency from the list of available currency codes in the value help dialog.

    We have to specify the input parameter as a VARCHAR data type with a length of 5 (see Figure 7.20 for an example).

- CONVERSION DATE

  The date of the conversion is used to read the exchange rate information for that date from the TCUR tables.

- GENERATE RESULT CURRENCY COLUMN

  The converted currency value is shown in a new additional output column with the specified name.

Some of the remaining options specify what type of currency conversion you want to retrieve from the TCUR tables, for example, are you using the buying rate or the selling rate.

## Decision Tables

*Decision tables* enable us to easily implement business rules in SAP HANA.

The top table in Figure 7.25 shows what a typical business rule might look like: If the region is EMEA, and one of the following four conditions are true, for example, more than 100 orders are placed, then the discount is 5%.

The traditional way to implement business rules in business systems has been to hard-code the business rules into the application. This is very laborious, and has some disadvantages, including the following:

▶ Business users cannot update the business rules themselves. They have to always find a developer, and explain the new business rules.

The developer then codes lots of IF statements into the application.

▶ New rules get tested in the development and quality assurance systems, and after a week or two finally gets deployed into the production system.

▶ Business users cannot do what-if analysis on production data because the process is very lengthy.

Decision tables in SAP HANA simplify and speed up the entire process. The process then becomes as follows:

1. Business users see a table with the business rules, as in Figure 7.25. They can update this table using Microsoft Excel.

2. In the background, SAP HANA converts the decision table to a procedure, with all the necessary IF statements.

3. The decision table can be used directly in a graphical calculation view. The users can immediately preview the data, and do a what-if analysis. They can tweak the business rules, using different values, and see the results very quickly in SAP HANA.

4. Once they are satisfied, they can deploy the final values for the decision table to the production system. They will need the correct authorizations in the SAP HANA system to allow them to update values in the decision table.

The entire process becomes business-driven, rather than slowed down by the need for a developer and a database administrator. Payroll users can, for example, simulate the effects of changes in the tax rules for a new tax year in a few minutes.

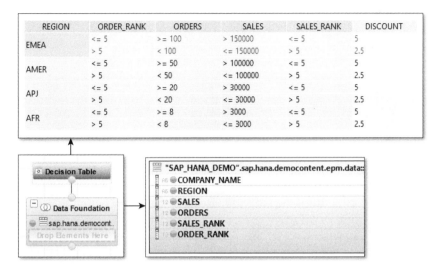

| REGION | ORDER_RANK | ORDERS | SALES | SALES_RANK | DISCOUNT |
|--------|-----------|--------|-------|-----------|----------|
| EMEA | <= 5 | >= 100 | > 150000 | <= 5 | 5 |
|  | > 5 | < 100 | <= 150000 | > 5 | 2.5 |
| AMER | <= 5 | >= 50 | > 100000 | <= 5 | 5 |
|  | > 5 | < 50 | <= 100000 | > 5 | 2.5 |
| APJ | <= 5 | >= 20 | > 30000 | <= 5 | 5 |
|  | > 5 | < 20 | <= 30000 | > 5 | 2.5 |
| AFR | <= 5 | >= 8 | > 3000 | <= 5 | 5 |
|  | > 5 | < 8 | <= 3000 | > 5 | 2.5 |

Decision Table

Data Foundation

sap.hana.democont..

Drop Elements Here

"SAP_HANA_DEMO".sap.hana.democontent.epm.data::
- COMPANY_NAME
- REGION
- SALES
- ORDERS
- SALES_RANK
- ORDER_RANK

**Figure 7.25**   Create a Decision Table

We create decision tables in the same context menu where we create calculation views. From the context menu of a package, choose NEW, and select the DECISION TABLE option.

A new decision table information view is created. In the SCENARIO area, we will see two nodes—a DATA FOUNDATION node and a DECISION TABLE node. This is shown at the bottom left of Figure 7.25.

As always, we start working from the bottom up. In the data foundation we add any data sources that we need (the bottom right of Figure 7.25). These data sources are normally tables, but can also be calculation views, virtual tables, table functions, or table types.

The ability to use table functions or table types gives us great flexibility. We could have, for example, stores in the company that sell different products. These stores would have their own product inventory tables. Because the product tables have a similar structure, we can decide to re-use the same decision table on all the various product inventory tables. The same discount rules will thus apply to all our stores. At runtime, using the table function or table type, we can decide which of the store's tables to send to the decision table.

Another example could be that we have moved our older 2012 data to an external database like SAP IQ. Using a virtual table, we can use the 2012 data from SAP IQ. At runtime, using the table function or table type, we can decide whether we want to use the latest data from SAP HANA, or the older data from SAP IQ. The table structures for the tables in SAP HANA and SAP IQ are the same, so we can re-use the decision table.

In the DECISION TABLE node, we build the decision table as shown in the top part of Figure 7.25. We build this table in the OUTPUT area of the DECISION TABLE node.

In the DATA FOUNDATION node we have selected our data sources and our output fields. These fields are available in our DECISION TABLE node as VOCABULARY ATTRIBUTES. These are the five columns on the left in our example in Figure 7.25.

We want to use these attributes to decide what the discount should be for our customers. We have to create the discount column as a VOCABULARY PARAMETER.

We can use the VOCABULARY, which consists of the attributes and the parameters, to build CONDITIONS and ACTIONS.

From the context menu, as shown in Figure 7.26, we can choose to add the attributes as conditions and the parameter as an action.

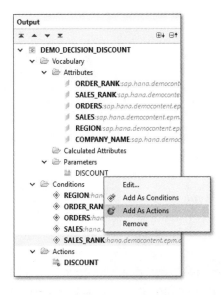

**Figure 7.26**   Decision Table Node Output Fields

Once our output area is built, SAP HANA can generate a Microsoft Excel file for us. This spreadsheet will have exactly the same layout and column headings as the decision table shown in Figure 7.25. Business users can then fill in the

Microsoft Excel spreadsheet, and upload it back into the SAP HANA system. When we activate the decision table, SAP HANA will automatically create a procedure for us.

We can use the decision table in a graphical calculation view, for example, in a join node, to add the discount field with all our business rules to our information view.

We can also call the generated procedure directly in SQLScript. We will look at SQLScript and procedures in Chapter 8. We pass all the conditions to the procedure using the SQLScript procedure's input parameters.

 **Note**

Unfortunately, the phrase *input parameters* have two meanings in SAP HANA. The first meaning is for the input parameters we discussed in this chapter. The second meaning is that SQLScript procedures and functions can have input parameters and output parameters. In the above paragraph we specified the second meaning when consuming the decision table via SQLScript.

## Hierarchies

*Hierarchies* are important modeling artifacts that are often used in reporting to enable intelligent drilldown. In Figure 7.27, we can see an example in Microsoft Excel. Users can start with a list of sales for different countries. They can then drill down to the sales of the provinces (regions or states) of a specific country, and finally down to the sales of a city.

| | A | B | C |
|---|---|---|---|
| 1 | | | |
| 2 | | | |
| 3 | Row Labels | Sum of Sales | |
| 4 | ⊞ Germany | 2500000 | |
| 5 | ⊟ South Africa | 2400000 | |
| 6 | ⊟ Gauteng | 1400000 | |
| 7 | Johannesburg | 800000 | |
| 8 | Pretoria | 600000 | |
| 9 | ⊟ KwaZulu-Natal | 400000 | |
| 10 | Durban | 400000 | |
| 11 | ⊟ Western Cape | 600000 | |
| 12 | Cape Town | 600000 | |
| 13 | ⊞ United States | 3900000 | |
| 14 | Grand Total | 8800000 | |
| 15 | | | |

**Figure 7.27**  Hierarchy of Sales Data from SAP HANA in Microsoft Excel

We have discussed the concepts of hierarchies in Chapter 4 already. We saw that we have two types of hierarchies, namely *level hierarchies* and *parent-child hierarchies*. We saw when we should use each type of hierarchy, and what the differences are between these two types of hierarchies.

You can use multidimensional expression (MDX) queries to use these hierarchies. Just like SQL has become a standard for querying relational databases, MDX is a standard for querying OLAP data. SAP uses BICS instead of MDX when communicating between SAP systems. BICS is a proprietary connection, so SAP can only use it for SAP systems. We use it because it is a lot faster than MDX.

### Creating a Hierarchy

We create a hierarchy in the third tab of the SEMANTICS node in a calculation view, as shown in Figure 7.28. Select the plus icon ➕ in the top-right menu on the HIERARCHIES tab. A CREATE NEW HIERARCHY dialog box will appear.

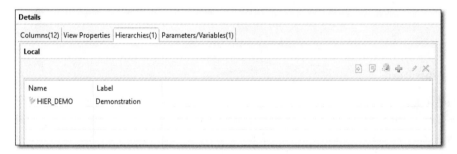

**Figure 7.28**    Create a Hierarchy

After specifying the NAME of the hierarchy, you can choose the HIERARCHY TYPE. We have level hierarchies and parent-child hierarchies available (see Figure 7.29).

To create a level hierarchy in SAP HANA, you specify the HIERARCHY TYPE as LEVEL HIERARCHY, and then you add the different levels. On each level you select a specific field name in the dropdown. Each level uses a different column in a level hierarchy. You can also specify the sorting order, and on which column it has to sort.

In Figure 7.30, we can see an example of a level hierarchy, using geographic attributes. Level 1 is the country, level 2 is the state or province, and level 3 is the city or town.

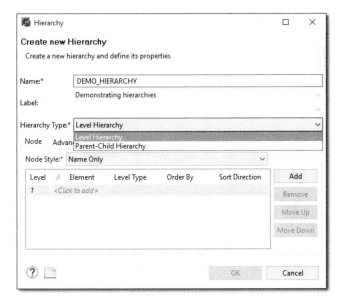

**Figure 7.29** Hierarchy Type

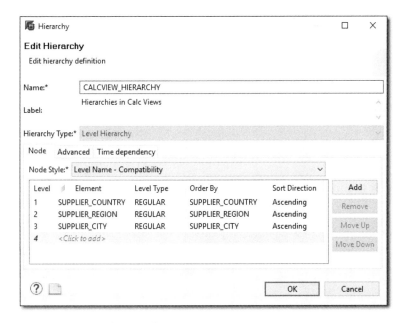

**Figure 7.30** Level Hierarchy

In Figure 7.31 you can see an example of a parent-child hierarchy. We have an HR organizational structure, with managers and employees. In this case, the manager has the "parent" role, and the employee has the "child" role.

We can also use parent-child hierarchies for cost and profit centers, or for a bill of materials (BOM).

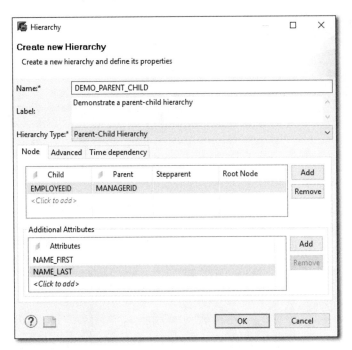

**Figure 7.31**  Parent-Child Hierarchy

### Time-Dependent Hierarchies

As of SAP HANA SPS 10, we can now create *time-dependent hierarchies* in calculation views. In the CREATE NEW HIERARCHY dialog box we have another tab available for TIME DEPENDENCY, as shown in Figure 7.32.

The fields in the tab are grayed out, until we enable the ENABLE TIME DEPENDENCY option. Once the rest of the fields become available, we supply the required VALID FROM and VALID TO columns for the time periods.

**Figure 7.32**   Time-Dependency for Parent-Child Hierarchies

 **Note**

Time-dependent hierarchies are only available for parent-child hierarchies. With level hierarchies, the ENABLE TIME DEPENDENCY option is grayed out.

### Hierarchies in Value Help

As shown in Figure 7.16, we can use hierarchies in variables to drilldown into the list of available values in a value help dialog. In this case, the variable has to be created on the deepest level of the hierarchy, for example, in Figure 7.30 the variable has to be created at the city level.

Value help hierarchies can also be time-dependent hierarchies.

## Important Terminology

In this chapter we touched on different ways to enhance our SAP HANA information views, and enrich our information models. The following list describes the important terms covered in this chapter:

▶ **Calculated columns**
Adds additional output columns to our calculation views, and allows us to calculate new values.

▶ **Counters**
Used to understand how many times something has occurred within a result set.

▶ **Restricted columns**
Restricts the data shown in a particular column or field and outputs the restricted values in an additional output field.

▶ **Filters**
Used if we do not want to show all the data from a specific table or to only show specific data. Can use both static and dynamic filtering.

▶ **Domain fix values**
These are values that will not change, and the users can only choose from the available list when they enter data into the fields.

▶ **Variables**
There are three types of variables:

  ▶ SINGLE VALUE: The variable only asks one (single) value, for example, the year is 2016.

  ▶ INTERVAL: The variable asks for from and to values, for example, the years from 2012 to 2015.

  ▶ RANGE: The variable asks a single value, but combines it with another operator, for example, the year is greater and equal to 2012.

▶ **Input parameters**
There are five types of input parameters we can create:

  ▶ DIRECT: Directly type in the value. We can specify the DATA TYPE of the expected value. There are three data types we can use for DIRECT, namely CURRENCY, UNIT OF MEASURE, and DATE.

- ▸ Column: Choose a value from all the possible values in a specified column in the current view.

- ▸ Derived From Table: Choose a value from data in another table.

- ▸ Static List: Choose a value from a pre-defined (static) list of values.

- ▸ Derived From Procedure/Scalar Function: Choose a value from a list of values generated by a scalar function or procedure.

▸ **Currency conversion**
Used when converting from source currency to target currency. A date for the conversion also has to be supplied.

▸ **Decision tables**
Enable you to implement business rules in SAP HANA.

▸ **Hierarchies**
Used in reporting to enable intelligent drilldown.

▸ **Time-dependent hierarchies**
Hierarchies that change over time, for example, before and after a restructuring of the HR organizational structure, and is dependent on the time period of your query.

Table 7.1 shows in which node each feature is available. For example, filter expressions are only in projection nodes.

| Node Type | Calculated Columns | Columns | Restricted Columns | Input Parameters | Filter Expressions | Generated Rank Columns |
|---|---|---|---|---|---|---|
| Join | Yes | – | – | Yes | – | – |
| Star Join | Yes | Yes | Yes | Yes | – | – |
| Projection | Yes | – | – | Yes | Yes | – |
| Aggregation | Yes | Yes | Yes | Yes | – | – |
| Rank | – | – | – | Yes | - | Yes |
| Union | – | – | – | – | – | – |

**Table 7.1**  Features per Node

## Practice Questions

These practice questions will help you evaluate your understanding of the topics covered in this chapter. The questions shown are similar in nature to those found on the certification examination. Although none of these questions will be found on the exam itself, they will allow you to review your knowledge of the subject. Select the correct answers and then check the completeness of your answers in the Practice Question Answers and Explanations section. Remember that on the exam you must select all correct answers and only correct answers to receive credit for the question.

1.  In which type of node can you create calculated columns? (There are 2 correct answers.)

☐  **A.** Rank node

☐  **B.** Union node

☐  **C.** Join node

☐  **D.** Projection node

2.  You want to build a hierarchy on a time-based data structure. What type of hierarchy do you use?

☐  **A.** Parent-child hierarchy

☐  **B.** Level hierarchy

☐  **C.** Ragged hierarchy

☐  **D.** Unbalanced hierarchy

3.  Which are features of a calculated column? (There are 2 correct answers.)

☐  **A.** It is a column in the result set

☐  **B.** Its calculations are persisted

☐  **C.** It is created in the output area

☐  **D.** It is created in the semantics node

4.  You want to show a male and female option to users. What feature do you use? (There are 3 correct answers.)

☐  **A.** Domain fix values

☐  **B.** Value help

☐ **C.** Variables

☐ **D.** Expressions

☐ **E.** Input parameters

5. You are creating a currency conversion. What options do you have for the TARGET CURRENCY field? (There are 3 correct answers.)

☐ **A.** Select a fixed currency

☐ **B.** Select a column

☐ **C.** Use the DERIVED FROM TABLE option

☐ **D.** Use an input parameter

☐ **E.** Select a table type

6. What can you use as data sources for a decision table? (There are 2 correct answers.)

☐ **A.** Table types

☐ **B.** Scalar functions

☐ **C.** CDS views

☐ **D.** Calculation views

7. Where do you create a variable?

☐ **A.** In the context menu of a package

☐ **B.** In the semantics node

☐ **C.** In the output area of a join node

☐ **D.** In the scenario area of an aggregate node

8. You have logs from a website. How do you show the total number of website visitors that used a mobile phone? (There are 2 correct answers.)

☐ **A.** Create a restricted column

☐ **B.** Create an action

☐ **C.** Create a filter expression

☐ **D.** Create a rank column

9.  Which can a level hierarchy do?

☐   **A.** Have time-dependency

☐   **B.** Be used for a bill of materials structure

☐   **C.** Enable drill-down in a value help list

☐   **D.** Show variable deepness in the data

10.  What can a variable be used for?

☐   **A.** Currency conversion

☐   **B.** Calculated column expression

☐   **C.** Call decision table in SQLScript

☐   **D.** Filtering

11.  You are working with a currency measure. What is decimal shift used for?

☐   **A.** Increase the accuracy of the currency conversion

☐   **B.** To undo the decimal adjustment for ABAP

☐   **C.** For currencies with more than two decimal places

☐   **D.** Avoid rounding errors during the conversion

12.  What variable type do you use if you want to allow the user to choose dates from 2011 to 2014?

☐   **A.** Single value

☐   **B.** Interval

☐   **C.** Range

☐   **D.** Multiple entries

13.  What do you create to find the number of unique items sold per shop?

☐   **A.** A calculation view with a restricted column in an aggregation node

☐   **B.** A calculation view with a counter in a projection node

☐   **C.** A calculation view with a counter in an aggregation node

☐   **D.** An analytic view with a calculated column in an star join node

14. What artifacts do you use in the output area of a decision table node? (There are 2 correct answers.)

☐  **A.** Input parameters
☐  **B.** Restrictions
☐  **C.** Actions
☐  **D.** Conditions

15. What can you use to limit the number of records produced by a calculation view? (There are 3 correct answers.)

☐  **A.** SAP client restrictions
☐  **B.** Domain fix values
☐  **C.** Filter expressions
☐  **D.** Restricted columns
☐  **E.** Generated columns

16. You created a calculated column in an analytic view for a table containing the number of units ordered, the price per unit, and the number of units in stock. You get the wrong results in your results. What could be the problem?

☐  **A.** You mistyped the calculated column expression
☐  **B.** You chose the SQL expression syntax
☐  **C.** You did NOT enable calculate before aggregation
☐  **D.** You did NOT enable the currency conversion

17. Where can you create a filter expression?

☐  **A.** In an aggregation node
☐  **B.** In a data foundation node
☐  **C.** In a projection node
☐  **D.** In the semantics node

18. The company's board members want to run simulations on the year-end financial data. What do you use to build this for them?

☐  **A.** A parent-child hierarchy
☐  **B.** A variable

☐   **C.** An expression

☐   **D.** A decision table

19. Which tables do you need for currency conversion?

☐   **A.** DD07*

☐   **B.** TCUR*

☐   **C.** BICS*

☐   **D.** SHINE*

20. You build a financial report for the company's board members that allows them to choose if they want the report to be in euros or dollars. What do you use?

☐   **A.** An input parameter from an aggregation node

☐   **B.** A variable from the semantics node

☐   **C.** A variable from a projection node

☐   **D.** An input parameter from the semantics node

21. What type of input parameters do you use to choose the data from a field in the current table?

☐   **A.** Direct

☐   **B.** Derived from table

☐   **C.** Value help

☐   **D.** Column

## Practice Question Answers and Explanations

1. Correct answers: **C, D**

   You can create calculated columns in a join node and a projection node.

2. Correct answer: **B**

   You use a level hierarchy to build a hierarchy on a time-based data structure. Time-based means you have year on level 1, months on level 2, days on level 3, and hours on level 4. A parent-child hierarchy can be time-dependent. (The words are confusing, so watch out.)

Ragged and unbalanced hierarchies are not mentioned in SAP HANA.

3. Correct answers: **A, C**

    Features of a calculated column:

    ▶ It is a column in the result set.

    ▶ It is created in the output area.

    ▶ Its calculations are NOT persisted! It is NOT created in the semantics nodes.

4. Correct answers: **B, C, E**

    You can show a male and female option to users with either variables or input parameters, and then opening the value help.

    Domain fix values can be used for filtering. Male and female got mentioned in this section, but the context was completely different.

5. Correct answers: **A, B, D**

    The options you have for the target currency field in a currency conversion are:

    ▶ Select a fixed currency

    ▶ Select a column

    ▶ Use an input parameter

6. Correct answers: **A, D**

    You can use table types and calculation views as data sources for a decision table. Scalar functions do not return table-type data. More information will be available in the next chapter.

7. Correct answer: **B**

    You create a variable in the semantics node.

8. Correct answers: **A, C**

    You show the total number of website visitors that used a mobile phone by creating either a restricted column or a filter expression. An action is part of decision tables. A rank column will rank then by numbers, not show the total number. (You could perhaps rank all the data, rank the data, and then search for the total number in the rankings. So technically it is possible, but requires that you still manually search the correct output.)

9.  Correct answer: **C**

    A level hierarchy can enable drill-down in a value help list. Only parent-child hierarchies have time-dependency, variable deepness in the data, and can be used for a bill of materials structure.

10. Correct answer: **D**

    A variable can be used for filtering. You will use input parameters for currency conversion, and in calculated column expression. The input parameters when calling a decision table in SQLScript is different from the input parameters discussed in this chapter.

11. Correct answer: **C**

    Decimal shift is used for currencies with more than two decimal places. Decimal shift back is used to undo the decimal adjustment for ABAP.

12. Correct answer: **B**

    You use an interval variable type if you want to allow the user to choose dates from 2011 to 2014. Range would allow for year > 2011. Do not confuse the range type with the interval type.

13. Correct answer: **C**

    You create a calculation view with a counter in an aggregation node to find the number of unique items sold per shop. You need a counter for this, so two answers are eliminated. A calculation view with a counter in a projection node is not valid because a counter cannot be created in a projection node.

14. Correct answers: **C, D**

    You use actions and conditions in the output area of a decision table node. Input parameters are not the same as vocabulary parameters.

15. Correct answers: **A, B, C**

    You can use SAP client restrictions, domain fix values, and filter expressions to limit the number of records produced by a calculation view. Restricted columns do not restrict the number of records.

16. Correct answer: **C**

    If you get errors in a calculated column in an analytic view, you must enable the CALCULATE BEFORE AGGREGATION flag.

17. Correct answer: **C**

    You can only create a filter expression in a projection node.

18. Correct answer: **D**

    You use a decision table to run simulations on the year-end financial data.

19. Correct answer: **B**

    You need the TCUR* tables for currency conversion. You need the DD07* tables for domain fix values.

20. Correct answer: **D**

    You use an input parameter from the semantics node (that is where it gets created) to build a financial report for the company's board members that allows them to choose if they want the report to be in euros or dollars. You just reference the already created input parameter in the currency conversion.

21. Correct answer: **D**

    You use a COLUMN type of input parameter to choose the data from a field in the current table. The DIRECT type is used to directly type in values. The DERIVED FROM TABLE type is used to get data from another table.

## Takeaway

You should now know how to enhance SAP HANA information views with the eight different modeling features we've discussed in this chapter.

You have learned how to create calculated and restricted columns to add additional output fields to your information views. You have looked at filters and filter expressions, and learned how to limit the data early in your modeling process.

You can now identify when to create variables and input parameters to allow business users to specify what outputs they want to see in the result sets of your information views at runtime.

Working with currency, you now understand how to add currency conversions to your financial reports. You can now describe decision tables, how to create them, use them, and what value they can add to your business users.

Finally, your now know how to create hierarchies to provide powerful drilldown capabilities for your end users.

## Summary

We learned how to work with calculated columns, restricted columns, and filters in our information views. We added variables and input parameters to add a new level of dynamic interaction to our modeling by allowing the end users to specify what they are looking for in each query of the SAP HANA information views. We also saw how to enrich our information models with currency conversions, decision tables, and hierarchies.

In the next chapter, we will discuss how to use SQL and SQLScript to provide the advanced features that you (occasionally) might not be able to do with the graphical calculation views we discussed in previous chapters.

# SQL and SQLScript

## Techniques You'll Master

▶ Get a basic understanding of SQL and how to use it with your SAP HANA information models

▶ Learn SQLScript in SAP HANA and find out how it extends and complements SQL

▶ Understand how the SAP HANA modeling environment with SQL and SQLScript has changed over the last few years

▶ Create and use table and scalar functions with your graphical SAP HANA information views

▶ Develop procedures in SAP HANA using SQL and SQLScript

In many large SAP HANA projects, you'll reach a point at which you need to do something more than what is offered by the graphical information views. Information modeling using SQL and SQLScript offer more powerful options. You lose the productivity and simplicity of working graphically with information views, but you gain flexibility and control.

As SAP HANA has matured, the graphical modeling tools have grown such that the requirements for SQL and SQLScript have been reduced. In the past, once you started working with SQL and SQLScript, you had to continue in that environment (or choose to create any subsequent layers in your information models there as well). This issue has been addressed in the latest versions of SAP HANA.

You can now work graphically with your SAP HANA information views, address the occasional constraint with SQL and SQLScript, and bring this development back into the graphical SAP HANA modeling environment. You can then continue building the remaining layers of your information models using the graphical information views. The focus has therefore dramatically shifted towards the graphical modeling environment.

 **Note**

> There is definitely less focus now on SQL and SQLScript in the average modeling workflow than there was in the past.
>
> To enable this shift, many of the SAP HANA modeling constructs and objects have changed. If you haven't looked at SQL and SQLScript in SAP HANA in the last two years, you will probably find that everything you knew has changed!

In this chapter, we will get you up to speed quickly on the new SAP HANA information views, how to convert the old information views, and how to integrate all SQL/SQLScript back into the graphical modeling environment.

## Real-World Scenario

You have been working on a large SAP HANA project for a few months when you get a request from business users: They love working with the decision tables and updating the values via a Microsoft Excel spreadsheet, but many of their decision tables use exactly the same rules and are based on similar tables. They want to know if there is a way to reuse the same decision table rules and dynamically change the tables used. A few months ago, you would probably have said this was impossible, but you now know that you can base the decision tables on table types, and so you can help these business users.

Soon after, another group of business users asks you if you can help to make security access more powerful and sync it to automatically use their hierarchal organizational structures. You base the analytic privileges on a procedure that easily exploits these structures.

The company is quickly moving into the area of mobile business services. They plan to deliver some new, real-time business dashboards to executives and managers. SAP HANA is an obvious choice, and your modeling and development skills are required to build the link to the mobile screens.

## Objectives of This Portion of the Test

The purpose of this portion of the SAP HANA certification exam is to test your knowledge of modeling using SQL and SQLScript.

The certification exam expects you to have a good understanding of the following topics:

▶  Standard SQL and how it relates to SAP HANA

▶  SQLScript in SAP HANA

▶  How to create and use user-defined functions, especially table functions

▶  Procedures in SAP HANA using SQL and SQLScript

**Note**

This portion contributes up to 10% of the total certification exam score.

## Key Concepts Refresher

*Structured Query Language* (SQL) is a widely used database programming language standardized by the American National Standards Institute (ANSI) and the International Organization for Standardization (ISO). The standard is often referred to as ANSI SQL.

Despite the existence of these standards, most SQL vendors extend ANSI SQL to provide enhanced capabilities for their individual database products. Microsoft uses an extended version called Transact-SQL (T-SQL), and Oracle uses PL/SQL.

SAP HANA provides *SQLScript*, which is an extension of ANSI SQL, to provide extra capabilities for the unique in-memory components that SAP deliver. We have already seen many of these features—for example, column tables, parameterized information views, delta buffers, working with multiple result sets in parallel, and built-in currency conversions. The ANSI SQL standard does not provide these features. However, SAP HANA supports ANSI SQL statements.

In this chapter, we provide only a short introduction to SQL and SQLScript, and we do assume some knowledge of SQL.

You can find the full SAP HANA SQL and SQLScript reference guides at *http:// help.sap.com/hana_platform*.

## SQL

SQL uses a *set-oriented* approach for working with data.

**Tip**

Rather than working with individual records, you should focus on working with the entire result set that consists of many data records.

You specify what should happen to all the data records in the result set at once. This allows databases to be efficient when processing data, because they can parallelize the processing of these records. Databases are faster at processing data than application servers, becacause SQL is a set-oriented declarative language, whereas application servers typically use procedural or object-oriented languages that process records one at a time.

### SQL Language

SQL is used to define, manipulate, and control database objects. These actions are specified by various subsets of the language:

▶ **Data Definition Language (DDL)**

This is used, for example, to CREATE, ALTER (modify), RENAME, or DROP (delete) table definitions.

▶ **Data Manipulation Language (DML)**

This is used to manipulate data—for example, insert new data into a table or update the data in a table. Examples in SQL include INSERT, UPDATE, and DELETE.

▶ **Data Query Language (DQL)**

This is used to SELECT (access) data. It does not modify any data.

▶ **Data Control Language (DCL)**

This is used for data security—for example, to GRANT privileges to a database user.

▶ **Transaction Control Language (TCL)**

This is used to control database transactions—for example, to COMMIT or ROLLBACK database transactions.

SQL is also subdivided into several language elements, as listed in Table 8.1.

| Element | Short Description |
| --- | --- |
| Identifiers | Names of database objects—for example, a table called BOOKS. |
| Data types | Specify the characteristics of the data stored in the database; for example, a string can be stored as a NVARCHAR data type. |
| Operators | Use to assign, compare, or calculate values—for example, =, >=, + (add), * (multiply), AND, and UNION ALL. |
| Expressions | Clauses that produce result sets consisting of either scalar values or tables consisting of columns and rows of data. Examples include aggregations like SUM, or IF...THEN...ELSE logic using CASE. |
| Predicates | Specify conditions that can be evaluated to TRUE, FALSE, or UNKNOWN. Can be used to filter statement and query results or to change program flow. Typically used in the WHERE conditions of the SELECT statement—for example, A >= 100. |

**Table 8.1** Elements of SQL Language

| Element | Short Description |
|---|---|
| Queries | Retrieve data from the database based on specific criteria. Use the `SELECT` statement—for example, `SELECT * from BOOKS`. |
| Statements | Commands to create persistent effects on schemas or data and control transactions, program flow, connections, and sessions. |
| Functions | Provide methods to evaluate expressions. Can be used anywhere an expression is allowed. Various functions are built into SQL—for example, `LENGTH(BOOKNAME)`. |

**Table 8.1**   Elements of SQL Language (Cont.)

There are a few important points to remember about SQL when working with SAP HANA:

▸ Identifiers can be *delimited* or *undelimited*, meaning the names of database objects are enclosed in double quotes or not. If you do not enclose identifiers with quotes, they are treated as uppercase. Therefore, `BOOKS`, `Books`, and `books` all reference the same table name.

   Delimited identifiers are treated as case-sensitive and can include characters in the name that would be forbidden by undelimited identifiers. SAP HANA uses Unicode, so the range of characters in a name can be wide. In this case, table `"BOOKS"` and table `"books"` are treated as two separate tables.

▸ `NULL` is a special indicator used by SQL to show that there is no value.

▸ The `LIKE` predicate can be used for SQL searches. `SELECT author FROM books WHERE title LIKE '%HANA%';` will search for all books with the word *HANA* in the title. We will look at this in more detail in Chapter 10.

▸ Statements in SQL include the semicolon (;) statement terminator. This is a standard part of SQL grammar. Insignificant whitespace is generally ignored in SQL statements and queries and can be used to make such statements and queries more readable.

We'll now look at some SQL statements that correspond to SAP HANA modeling constructs that you're already familiar with.

**Creating Tables**

The short version of the SQL syntax to a create a table is as follows:

```
CREATE [<table_type>] TABLE <table_name>;
<table_type> ::= COLUMN | ROW | HISTORY COLUMN | GLOBAL TEMPORARY |
GLOBAL TEMPORARY COLUMN | LOCAL TEMPORARY | LOCAL TEMPORARY COLUMN |
VIRTUAL
```

This means that you have to type "CREATE TABLE BOOKS;" to create an empty table called BOOKS. In this example, <tablename> is BOOKS. You can choose what to type in place of the <tablename> placeholder.

Anything in square brackets, like [<table_type>], is optional. If you want to type something there, choose from the following list. If you want your table to be a column table, type "CREATE COLUMN TABLE BOOKS;", for example. If you do not specify the type of table, the system will create a row table, because that's what ANSI SQL expects. The following are important table types to keep in mind:

▶ **HISTORY COLUMN**
The HISTORY COLUMN table is a special SAP HANA table that stores historical database states. You can execute special SELECT statements with a "time-travel clause" on these types of tables to restore to a certain point in time. We can therefore read a table as it was at any point in time. This can be useful for tables that refer to financial transactions and can completely change the way that systems perform period closings.

▶ **GLOBAL TEMPORARY** and **GLOBAL TEMPORARY COLUMN**
These are temporary tables that are persisted in the database, even between sessions. Any user with the right privileges can read the table definition (metadata). The data in the GLOBAL TEMPORARY table can only be inserted and read by the owner of the table. When the session ends, the table is truncated (emptied).

▶ **LOCAL TEMPORARY** and **LOCAL TEMPORARY COLUMN**
These are temporary tables that are only available for the current session. No other user can read the table definition (metadata) or the data in this table. The data in the local temporary table can only be inserted and read by the owner of the table. When the session ends, the table is dropped (deleted).

### Reading Data

The query—the most common operation in SQL—uses the `SELECT` statement—for example:

```
SELECT [TOP <unsigned_integer>] [ ALL | DISTINCT ]
<select_list> <from_clause> [(<subquery>)] [<where_clause>]
[<group_by_clause>] [<having_clause>] [<order_by_clause>]
[<limit_clause>] [<for_update_clause>] [<time_travel_clause>];
```

One of the shortest statements that can be used to read data from table `BOOKS` is `SELECT * FROM BOOKS;`. This returns all the fields and data from table `BOOKS`, in effect putting the entire table in the result set. However, we recommend never using `SELECT *` especially not with column tables. Because SAP HANA uses primarily column tables, this type of `SELECT` statement should be avoided.

A better way is to specify the `<select_list>`—for example, `SELECT author, title, price FROM BOOKS;`. In this case, you only read the author, title, and price columns for all the books.

Note the `[<time_travel_clause>]` for use with `HISTORY COLUMN` tables.

### Filtering Data

In SAP HANA, we sometimes use a filter, by using the `WHERE` clause as part of a `SELECT` statement—for example:

```
SELECT author, title, price FROM BOOKS WHERE title LIKE '%HANA%';
```

### Creating Projections

Inside a projection node in SAP HANA views, you can rename fields. This is easily achieved via the `AS` keyword in SQL—for example:

```
SELECT author, title AS bookname, price FROM BOOKS;
```

The `title` field is now renamed to `bookname` in the result set.

### Creating Calculated Columns

Creating calculated columns looks almost the same as renaming fields, but there is an added formula, as shown:

```
SELECT author, title, price * discount AS discount_price FROM BOOKS;
```

In this case, we added a new calculated column called `discount_price`.

## Created Nested Reads and Aggregates

In SAP HANA views, we often have many layers; in SQL, we use nested `SELECT` statements. These nested queries are also known as *subqueries*. An example would be as follows:

```
SELECT author, title, price FROM BOOKS
WHERE price > (SELECT AVG(price) FROM BOOKS);
```

The `SELECT AVG(price) FROM BOOKS` statement returns the average price of all the books in table `BOOKS`. This helps return the books that are more expensive than the average price.

You can create aggregates, like with an aggregation node in a calculation view, using standard aggregation functions in SQL. We discussed aggregation in Chapter 4.

## Creating Joins

SAP HANA views normally have many joins. Here is an example of how to create an inner join between two tables:

```
SELECT BOOKS.author, BOOKS.title, BOOKS.price,
BOOK_SALES.total_sold FROM BOOKS
INNER JOIN BOOK_SALES
ON BOOKS.book_number = BOOK_SALES.booknumber;
```

The field on which both tables are joined is the `book_number` field.

## Creating Unions

Union nodes in calculation views can be performed by using the `UNION` operator—for example:

```
SELECT author, title, price FROM BOOKS
UNION
SELECT author, title, price FROM BOOKS_OUT_OF_PRINT;
```

You can also use the `UNION ALL` operator instead of `UNION`. The `UNION` operator returns only distinct values, whereas `UNION ALL` will return all records, including duplicate records.

### Conditional Statements

You can use the `if()` function in an expression in which you create a calculated column in SAP HANA. You can also handle if-then logic in SQL via the `CASE` statement—for example:

```
SELECT author, title, price,
CASE WHEN title LIKE '%HANA'%' then 'Yes' ELSE 'No' END
AS interested_in_book FROM BOOKS
```

Here, we have added a calculated column called `interested_in_book` to our query. If the book's title contains the word *HANA*, we indicate that we are interested in it.

## SQLScript

SQLScript exposes many of the memory features of SAP HANA to SQL developers. Column tables, parameterized information views, delta buffers, working with multiple result sets in parallel, built-in currency conversions at the database level, fuzzy text searching, spatial data types, and predictive analysis libraries makes SAP HANA unique. The only way to make this functionality available via SQL queries, even from other applications, is to provide it via SQL extensions.

We've come across many of these features in earlier chapters. In the next chapter (Chapter 9), we will look in more detail at the fuzzy text search, spatial functions, and predictive libraries in SAP HANA. We also will learn more about the Application Function Library (AFL) that include predictive and business functions that can be used with SQLScript.

In Chapter 4, we saw the spatial join type, used between a `ST_POINT` data type (like a location) and an `ST_POLYGON` (like a suburb). The spatial functions can be called from SQLScript to access and manipulate spatial data.

SAP HANA also has to cater for SAP-specific requirements—for example, limiting data to a specific "client" (e.g., 100) in the SAP business systems. In SAP HANA, you can use a `SESSION_CONTEXT(CLIENT)` function in the `WHERE` clause of a query to limit data in a session to a specific client.

In this section, we will look at the various features of SQLScript.

> **Note**
>
> In traditional client-server approaches, business logic is executed in the application server. With SAP HANA, much of this logic and the executions are pushed down into the SAP HANA database. This approach is different than the standard SQL way of working. SQLScript caters for these requirements.

**Separate Statements**

One of the unique approaches of SQLScript is the use of variables to break a large, complex SQL statement into smaller, simpler statements. This makes the code much easier to understand and it also helps with SAP HANA's performance, because many of these smaller statements can be run in parallel.

Let's look at an example:

```
books_per_publisher = SELECT publisher, COUNT (*) AS
num_books FROM BOOKS GROUP BY publisher;

publisher_with_most_books = SELECT * FROM
:books_per_publisher WHERE num_books >=
(SELECT MAX (num_books) FROM :books_per_publisher);
```

We would normally write this as a single SQL statement using a temporary table, or by repeating a subquery multiple times. In our example, we've broken this into two smaller SQL statements by using table variables.

The first statement calculates the number of books each publisher has and stores the entire result set into the table variable called `books_per_publisher`. This variable containing the entire result set is used twice in the second statement.

> **Tip**
>
> Notice that the table variable is prepended in SQLScript with a colon (:) to indicate that this is used as an input variable. All output variables use only the name, and all input variables have a colon prepended.

The second statement uses `:books_per_publisher` as input and uses a nested `SELECT` statement.

The SQLScript compiler and optimizer will determine how to best execute these statements, whether by using a common subquery expression with database hints or by combining them into a single complex query. The code becomes easier to write and understand and is more maintainable.

By breaking the SQL statement into smaller statements, we also mirror the way in which we have learned to build graphical information views in SAP HANA. Look at the calculation view in Figure 8.1; if you had to write all of this in SQL, it would be quite difficult to create optimal code.

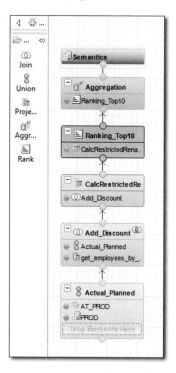

**Figure 8.1**  SAP HANA Calculation View in Layers

Just like we start building graphical information views from the bottom up, we do the same with our SQLScript code. We will not write all the SQLScript code here, but just some pseudocode to illustrate the point. We start with a union node in Figure 8.1:

```
union_output = SELECT * FROM AT_PROD UNION SELECT * FROM PROD;
```

The next node is a join node. It uses the output from the union node as the source for one side of the join:

```
join_output = SELECT * FROM :union_output
INNER JOIN SELECT * FROM get_employees_by_name_filter('Jones');
```

Each time, the output from the lower node becomes the input for the next higher node. As you can see, this is easy to write in SQLScript!

**Imperative Logic**

Most of the SQL and SQLScript we have worked with to this point has used *declarative logic*. In other words, we have used the set-oriented paradigm that contributes to SQL's performance. We have asked the database to hand us back all of the results immediately when the query has completed. Occasionally, you might prefer to receive the answers to a query one record at a time. This is most often the case when running SQL queries from application servers. In these cases, you will use *imperative logic*, meaning you'll "loop" through the results one at a time. You can also use conditionals, such as in if-then logic.

Imperative logic is (mostly) not available in ANSI SQL, and therefore SAP HANA provides it as part of SQLScript.

 **Hint**

Remember that imperative logic does not perform as well as declarative logic. If you require the best performance, try to avoid imperative logic.

There are different ways to implement imperative logic in SQLScript:

- WHILE loop
  The WHILE loop will execute some SQLScript statements as long as the condition of the loop evaluates to TRUE:

  ```
  WHILE <condition> DO
  … some SQLScript statements…
  END WHILE
  ```

- FOR loop
  The FOR loop will iterate a number of times, beginning with a loop counter starting value and incrementing the counter by one each time, until the counter is greater than the end value:

  ```
  FOR <loop-var> IN [REVERSE] <start_value> .. <end_value> DO
  … some SQLScript statements…
  END FOR
  ```

## Dynamic SQL and Security

Another powerful feature in SQLScript is the ability to create and execute dynamic SQL. Let's illustrate this via an example. Figure 8.2 shows a web form asking for the user's mobile telephone number at the top of the figure. We insert this mobile number into a partially prepared SQL statement, and then execute this SQL statement using the EXEC statement.

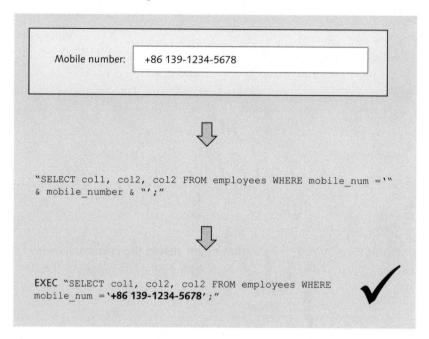

**Figure 8.2**   Dynamic SQL with Values from Web Form

Each user gets a unique SQL statement created especially for him or her. The performance is not as good as static SQL statements, but this is more powerful and flexible.

There is one problem: If you're not careful, hackers can use this setup to break into your system, which has been one of the top security vulnerabilities in web applications for many years now.

Let's look at the web form again. This time, in Figure 8.3, hackers enter more information than just the mobile telephone number. They add a closing quote and a semicolon. When this is inserted into our prepared SQL statement, it closes the current statement. (Remember that SQL statements are terminated by a semicolon.)

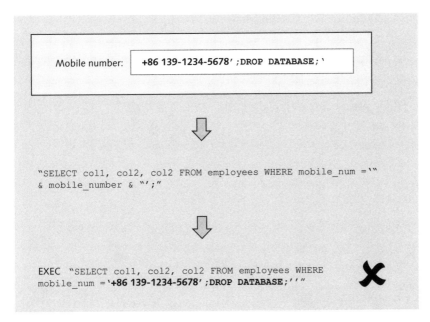

**Figure 8.3**  Dynamic SQL with SQL Injection from Web Form

Anything after this is executed as another SQL statement—so the hackers can enter something like DROP DATABASE that might delete the entire database. Or they can try various SQL statements to read or modify data values in the database.

SAP HANA SPS 11 includes some new features related to this problem, such as the new IS_SQL_INJECTION_SAFE function, which helps prevent such attacks.

If you remember to prevent security vulnerabilities like SQL injection, dynamic SQL can enable you to write some powerful applications. You can change data sources at any time, create new tables in real time and link them to applications, and build adaptive user interfaces.

### User-Defined (Table and Scalar) Functions

*User-defined functions* (UDFs) are custom read-only functions in SAP HANA. You write your own functions that can be called in a similar fashion as SQL functions.

There are two types of UDFs: *scalar functions* and *table functions*. The main difference is whether you want a function to return values as simple data types (like an integer) or in complete "table-like" result sets. A scalar function can return one or more values, but these values have to be single data types. A table function returns a set of data.

Both types of UDFs are read-only. You may not execute any DDL or DML statements inside these functions.

We create functions as shown in Listing 8.1.

```
CREATE FUNCTION <func_name> [(<parameter_clause>)]
   RETURNS <return_type>
   [LANGUAGE SQLSCRIPT]
   [SQL SECURITY <DEFINER | INVOKER>]
   [DEFAULT SCHEMA <default_schema_name>] AS
{ BEGIN
      <function_body>
 END }
```

**Listing 8.1**   Creating User-Defined Function

Here are a few important points to note with regards to UDFs:

▶ **RETURNS**
Depending on the type of data we return, RETURNS will be a scalar or a table function.

▶ **LANGUAGE**
We can only write UDFs in SQLScript.

▶ **SQL SECURITY**
Indicates against which user's security privileges this function will be executed:

  ▶ If we choose the DEFINER option, this function will be executed by the _ SYS_REPO system user.

  ▶ If we choose the INVOKER option, this function will be executed by the end user calling the function and all security privileges will be limited to that user's assigned authorizations.

  ▶ The default for scalar functions is INVOKER, and the default for table functions is DEFINER.

▶ **DEFAULT SCHEMA**
When we specify the default schema for this function, we do not have to prepend the schema name before every table name used. We can just write SELECT FROM table instead of SELECT from schema.table.

In the SAP HANA system, you can create UDFs as discussed in Chapter 5 (see also Figure 5.14).

We create .hdbscalarfunction objects for scalar functions, and ,hdbtable-function objects for table functions. Figure 8.4 shows a newly created table function in SAP HANA studio.

```
Table Function
   1  FUNCTION "SYSTEM"."sap.hana.democontent.epm.functions::demo_table_function" ( )
   2      RETURNS return_table_type
   3      LANGUAGE SQLSCRIPT
   4      SQL SECURITY INVOKER AS
   5  BEGIN
   6  /*****************************
   7      Write your function logic
   8  *****************************/
   9  END;
```

**Figure 8.4**  Newly Created (Blank) Table Function in SAP HANA Studio

The following two subsections look at examples of both scalar functions and table functions.

### Scalar Functions

Scalar UDF supports primitive SQL types as an input. Let's walk through an example to better understand their usage:

Start by creating a scalar function as in Listing 8.2 that takes the price of a book and a discount percentage as the two inputs and creates two output values. The first output value is the price of the book after the discount is applied, and the second is the discount amount.

```
FUNCTION apply_discount (book_price decimal(15,2),
book_discount decimal(15,2))
   RETURNS discounted_price decimal(15,2)
   LANGUAGE SQLSCRIPT
   SQL SECURITY INVOKER AS
BEGIN
   discounted_price := :book_price - ( :book_price * :book_discount);
   discount = :book_price * :book_discount;
END;
```

**Listing 8.2**  Scalar Function that Returns Two Values

You can call the scalar function with the following code:

```
SELECT apply_discount (59.50, 0.1). discounted_price as
your_book_price, apply_discount (59.50, 0.1).
discount as discount_amount from DUMMY;
```

In this case, you get two values back: 53.55 and 5.95.

Figure 8.5 shows a similar example of a scalar function from the SHINE demo content, as shown in SAP HANA studio.

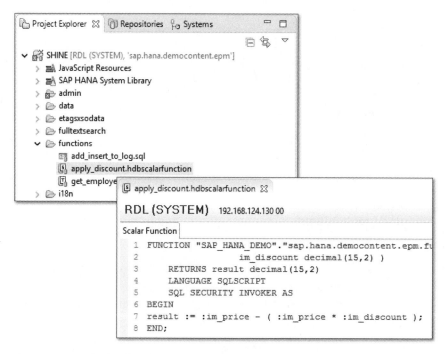

**Figure 8.5**   Example of Scalar Function Found in SHINE Content

### *Table Functions*

Table UDF supports table types as an input. Let's walk through an example to better under their usage:

Listing 8.3 shows a modified version of a table function found in the SHINE content. This code performs an inner join between an employee table and an address table to find the employee's email address. The neat trick here is in the WHERE clause: SAP HANA performs a fuzzy text search on the employee's last name. You will still get an email address, even if you mistyped the person's last name.

```
FUNCTION get_employees_by_name_filter" (lastNameFilter NVARCHAR(40))
   RETURNS table (EMPLOYEEID NVARCHAR(10),
                  "NAME.FIRST" NVARCHAR(40),
                  "NAME.LAST" NVARCHAR(40),
                  EMAILADDR NVARCHAR(255))
   LANGUAGE SQLSCRIPT
   SQL SECURITY INVOKER AS
BEGIN
RETURN
   SELECT a.EMPLOYEEID, a."NAME.FIRST", a."NAME.LAST", b.EMAILADDR,
   FROM Employees AS a INNER JOIN Addresses AS b
   ON a.EMPLOYEEID = b. EMPLOYEEID
   WHERE contains("NAME.LAST", :lastNameFilter, FUZZY(0.9));
END;
```

**Listing 8.3**  Table Function that Performs Fuzzy Text Search on Last Name
to Find Email Addresses

Figure 8.6 shows the table function from the SHINE demo content in SAP HANA
studio.

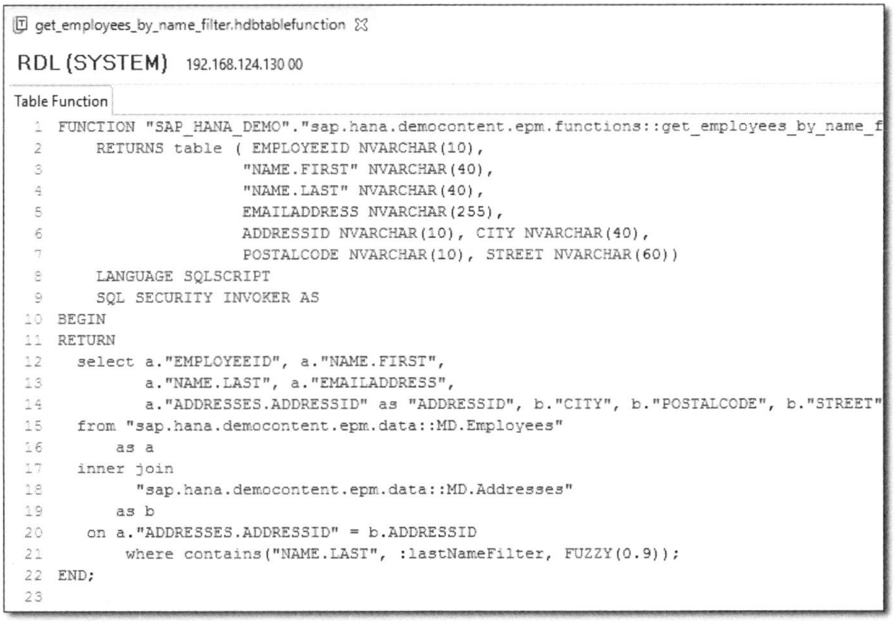

**Figure 8.6**  Example of Table Function Found in SHINE Content

We can use the table function from Figure 8.6 in a graphical calculation view. An example is shown in Figure 8.7, in which this table function is used in a join with the result set from a union node. (This is not really a good example—we should really join on the key field—but is used here purely to illustrate the point.)

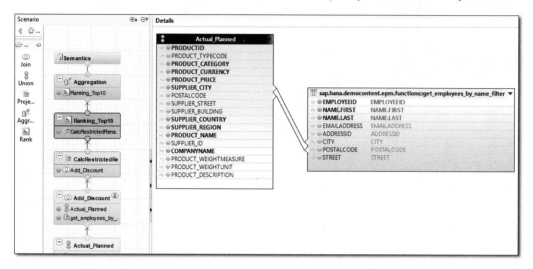

**Figure 8.7**   Using Table Function in Graphical Calculation View

**Procedures**

A *procedure* is a subroutine consisting of SQL statements. Procedures can be called or invoked by applications that access the database. Procedures are sometimes also known as *stored procedures*.

Procedures are more powerful than UDFs. Whereas UDFs are read-only and cannot change any data in the system, procedures can insert, change, and delete data. You can execute any DDL or DML statements inside a procedure. Whereas a table function can only return one result set, procedures can return many result sets.

Listing 8.4 illustrates how to create procedures.

```
CREATE PROCEDURE <proc_name> [(<parameter_clause>)]
   [LANGUAGE <SQLSCRIPT | R>]
   [SQL SECURITY <DEFINER | INVOKER>]
   [DEFAULT SCHEMA <default_schema_name>]
   [READS SQL DATA [WITH RESULTS VIEW <view_name>]] AS
```

```
{ BEGIN [SEQUENTIAL EXECUTION]
    <procedure_body>
  END }
```

**Listing 8.4** Creating Procedures

The following syntax are used in Listing 8.4:

▶ **LANGUAGE**

We can write procedures in SQLScript or in R. R is a popular open-source programming language and data analysis software environment for statistical computing.

▶ **SQL SECURITY**

Indicates against which user's security privileges this function will be executed:

  ▶ If we choose the DEFINER option, this function will be executed by the _ SYS_REPO system user.

  ▶ If we choose the INVOKER option, this function will be executed by the end user calling the function, and all security privileges will be limited to that user's assigned authorizations.

  ▶ The default for procedures is DEFINER (i.e., the _SYS_REPO user).

▶ **DEFAULT SCHEMA**

When we specify the default schema for this function, we do not have to prepend the schema name before every table name you use.

▶ **READS SQL DATA**

Marks the procedure as being read-only. The procedure then cannot change data or database object, and cannot contain DDL or DML statements. If we try to activate a read-only procedure that contains DDL or DML statements, we will get activation errors.

▶ **WITH RESULTS VIEW**

Specifies that a view (that we have to supply) can be used as the output of a read-only procedure. When a result view is defined for a procedure, it can be called by an SQL statement in the same way as a table or view!

▶ **SEQUENTIAL EXECUTION**

Forces sequential execution of the procedure logic; no parallelism is allowed.

Some important points to note with regards to these procedures:

▸ A procedure does not require any input and output parameters. Input and output parameters must be explicitly typed. The input and output parameters of a procedure can have any of the primitive SQL types or a table type. (Table types will be discussed in the next section.)

▸ If we require table outputs from a procedure, we have to use table types.

▸ Any read-only procedure may only call other read-only procedures. The advantage of using a read-only procedure is that certain optimizations are available for read-only procedures, such as not having to check for database locks; this is one of the performance enhancements in SAP HANA.

▸ Note that `WITH RESULTS VIEW` is a sub-clause of the `READS` SQL clause, so the same restrictions apply to it as those for read-only procedures.

We mentioned that if we require table outputs from a procedure, we have to use table types. In SQLScript, we can also define table types. Table types are similar to database tables, but do not have an instance. They are like a template for future use. They are used to define parameters for a procedure that needs to use tabular results.

Table types are created with the `CREATE TYPE` statement. The statement used to be `CREATE TABLE TYPE`, but this syntax has been deprecated. The definition is as follows:

```
CREATE TYPE <type_name> AS TABLE (<column_list_definition>)
```

The SQL syntax for defining table types is the same as that for defining new tables.

Let's switch gears. Similar to UDFs, we can create procedures as discussed in Chapter 5, illustrated by Figure 5.14. In this case, we create a `.hdbprocedure` object.

Figure 8.8 shows a newly created table function in SAP HANA studio.

Procedures are called with the `CALL` statement. You can call the procedure shown in Figure 8.8 with the following statement:

```
CALL "get_product_sales_price" ('HT-1000', ?);
```

The results of this call statement, as executed in the SQL Console in SAP HANA studio, are shown in Figure 8.9.

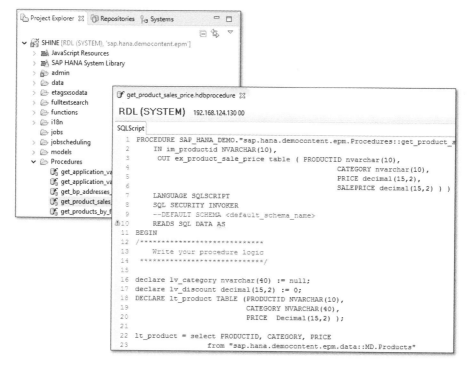

**Figure 8.8**  Example Procedure Found in SHINE Content

```
SQL   Result
    call "SAP_HANA_DEMO"."sap.hana.democontent.epm.Procedures::get_product_sales_price" ('HT-1000',?)

        PRODUCTID   CATEGORY   PRICE   SALEPRICE
1       HT-1000     Notebooks  956     764.8




Statement 'call "SAP_HANA_DEMO"."sap.hana.democontent.epm.Procedures::get_product_sales_price" ('HT-1000',?)'
successfully prepared


Statement 'call "SAP_HANA_DEMO"."sap.hana.democontent.epm.Procedures::get_product_sales_price" ('HT-1000',?)'
successfully executed in 12.519 seconds  (server processing time: 12.519 seconds)
Fetched 1 row(s) in 0 ms 15 µs (server processing time: 0 ms 0 µs)
```

**Figure 8.9**  Results of Calling a Procedure Directly from SQL Console

You can call procedure with multiple result sets, which reads and writes transactional data from an SAP HANA XS application using server-side JavaScript. The REST-style web services created will use HTTP GET for reading data and HTTP PUT for writing data.

You will notice that how we use procedures is quite different from how we use UDFs. We can use procedures in a similar way as functions if we specify the read-only and result view clauses.

In Listing 8.5, we create a procedure that uses a precreated result view called View4BookProc, and a table type called BOOKS_TABLE_TYPE.

```
CREATE PROCEDURE ProcWithResultView(IN book_num VARCHAR(13),
  OUT output1 BOOKS_TABLE_TYPE)
    LANGUAGE SQLSCRIPT
    READS SQL DATA WITH RESULT VIEW View4BookProc AS
BEGIN
    output1 = SELECT author, title, price FROM BOOKS WHERE
      isbn_num = :book_num;
END;
```

**Listing 8.5**   Read-Only Procedure Using Result View

We can now call this procedure from a SQL statement, just like a table function:

```
SELECT * FROM View4BookProc (PLACEHOLDER."$$book_num$$"=>'978-1-4932-
1230-9');
```

## Multilevel Aggregation

Sometimes, you may need to return multiple result sets with a single SQL statement. In normal SQL, this might not always be possible—but we can use multilevel aggregation with grouping sets to achieve this in SQLScript.

Let's start by looking at an example (Listing 8.6) in SQLScript of how we would create two result sets.

```
-- Create result set 1
books_pub_title_year = SELECT publisher, name, year, SUM(price)
FROM BOOKS WHERE publisher = pubisher_id
GROUP BY publisher, name, year;
-- Create result set 2
books_year = SELECT year, SUM(price) FROM BOOKS
GROUP BY year;
```

**Listing 8.6**   Creating Two Result Sets in SQLScript

You can create both of these result sets from a single SQL statement using GROUP-ING SETS, as shown in Listing 8.7.

```
SELECT publisher, name, year, SUM(price)
FROM BOOKS WHERE publisher = pubisher_id
GROUP BY GROUPING SETS ((publisher, name, year), (year))
```

**Listing 8.7**  Creating Multiple Result Sets from Single SQL Statement with Grouping Sets

You now have a good understanding of SQLScript and the powerful capabilities it brings to your modeling toolbox. Let's now look at when you should use this functionality and how to ensure that you use the latest variations of these features.

## Views, Functions, and Procedures

Taking a step back, let's look at how to best address our modeling requirements. In SAP HANA SPS 11 and later we have three main approaches: views, UDFs, and procedures.

Let's first discuss each of these options, and then we'll discuss when you should use each one.

### Information Views

We have discussed SAP HANA information views in detail in preceding chapters. You have built these views using the graphical environment, and you have now also learned how to also create these view using SQLScript.

Some of the characteristics of views include the following:

▶ Views are treated like tables. You can use SELECT, WHERE, GROUP BY, and ORDER BY statements on views.

▶ Views are static. They always return the same columns, and you look at a sets of data in the same way.

▶ They always return one result set.

▶ Views are mostly used for reading data.

**User-Defined Functions**

After learning about UDFs, you should be familiar with their characteristics, such as the following:

▶ Functions always return results. A table function returns a set, and a scalar function returns one or more values.

▶ Functions require input parameters.

▶ The code in UDFs is read-only. Functions cannot change, update, or delete data or database objects. You cannot insert data with functions, so you cannot use transactions or COMMIT and ROLLBACK in functions.

▶ Functions cannot call EXEC statements; otherwise, you could build a dynamic statement to change data and execute it.

▶ You can call the results of functions in SELECT statements and in WHERE and HAVING clauses.

▶ Functions can be used in a join.

▶ Table functions cannot call procedures, because procedures can change data. You have to hold to the read-only paradigm of functions.

▶ Functions use SQLScript code. This can include imperative logic in which you loop through results or apply an if-then logic flow to the results.

**Procedures**

Procedures are the most powerful of the three approaches. Some of the characteristics of procedures include the following:

▶ Procedures can use transactions, with COMMIT and ROLLBACK. They can modify tables and data, unless they are marked as read-only. Read-only procedures may only call other read-only procedures.

▶ Procedures can call UDFs, but UDFs cannot call procedures.

▶ Procedures do not have to return any values but may return multiple result sets. Procedures also do not need to specify any input parameters.

▶ Procedures provide full control, because all code functionality is allowed in procedures.

- Procedures can use `try-catch` blocks for errors.

- Procedures can also use dynamic SQL—but be aware of security vulnerabilities such as SQL injection when using dynamic SQL.

**When to Use What Approach**

After all that detail, the recommendation of when to use each of the three approaches is quite easy to make.

In order of functionality, we have views, then UDFs, and then procedures; that is, procedures have the most functionality.

In order of performance, we have the reverse. Views give the best performance, then UDFs (because they are permanently read-only), and then procedures.

Use the minimal approach to get the results you require.

If you can do it with views, then use views. If you cannot do it with views, then try using user-defined functions. If that still does not meet the requirements, create a procedure.

## Catching Up with SAP HANA SPS 11

Figure 8.7 illustrated how to use a table function in a graphical calculation view. This options changes how we approach modeling in SAP HANA projects. The emphasis has moved completely to the graphical modeling environment.

We can work graphically with our SAP HANA views, create UDFs or procedures for the occasional constraint, and bring these back into the graphical SAP HANA modeling environment. We can then continue building the remainder of our SAP HANA information models using the graphical information views.

Many of the SAP HANA modeling constructs and objects in SQLScript have changed to accommodate this shift in emphasis to the graphical environment. In the last few years, almost everything has changed!

Table 8.2 contrasts the old with the new.

| Action | The Old Method | The New Method |
|---|---|---|
| Create procedures | Create run-time objects<br>▸ Example:<br>  CREATE PROCEDURE | Create design-time objects<br>▸ Example:<br>  Create .hdbprocedure |
| Write SQLScript code | Use SQLScript "CE_" functions<br>▸ Example:<br>  CE_UNION_ALL(:A, :B) | Use SQL syntax<br>▸ Example:<br>  A UNION ALL B |
| Use SQLScript | SQLScript (scripted) calculation views | Table functions (.hdbtablefunction) |
| Create procedures | Create a procedure in the CONTENT area<br>or<br>Create a .procedure file | Create a .hdbprocedure file |
| Create table types | CREATE TABLE TYPE | CREATE TYPE |

**Table 8.2**  Changes in SQL and SQLScript

### Using the Latest Modeling Practices

To move from the old SQL and SQLScript modeling approaches to the newer techniques, use the following guidelines:

▸ Many modelers and developers used the SQL Console to create procedures. This created runtime objects, which cannot be transported to the production system. The recommended way is to create design-time objects—for example, .hdbprocedure objects—instead of using the CREATE PROCEDURE statement.

▸ In the early days of SAP HANA, there was a huge emphasis on using certain calculation engine functions (called CE-functions). The performance of these CE-functions was much better (back then) than using standard SQL syntax; you would use CE_UNION_ALL(:A, :B) instead of A UNION ALL B to improve performance. This has now changed, and the new recommendation is to forget about CE-functions and use the SQL syntax.

▸ There were two different ways to create procedures before—namely, in the context menu of a package (where we also create graphical views) and by using a .procedure file. Both of these methods are deprecated. You should now use a .hdbprocedure file to create procedures in SAP HANA.

▶ The old CREATE TABLE TYPE syntax to create a table type is now deprecated and replaced by the new CREATE TYPE syntax.

▶ When creating calculation views, there is still a dropdown option to create SQLScript calculation views. These are also known as scripted calculation views or script-based calculation views. We recommend not using this type of calculation view; instead, use table functions. In fact, as of SAP HANA SPS 11, the migration tool now migrates script-based calculation views to table functions for you.

We will now see how to use the migration tool to convert script-based calculation views to table functions.

### Migrating Scripted Calculation Views

Start the migration tool from the QUICK VIEW tab in the Modeler perspective. On the next screen (Figure 8.10), you'll see the migration tool dialog.

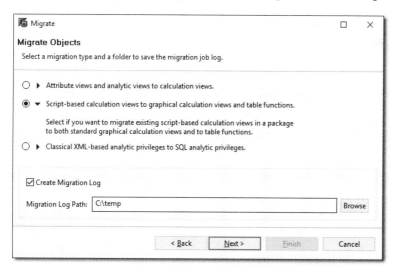

**Figure 8.10** Migration Tool

Here, we chose the option to migrate script-based calculation views to table functions. Figure 8.11 shows the next step, in which you select all the calculation views you want to migrate.

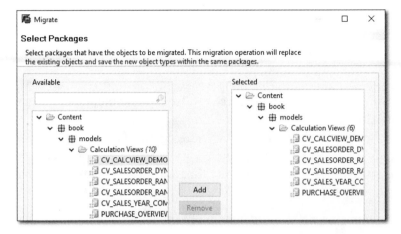

**Figure 8.11**   Selecting Scripted Calculation Views to Convert to Table Functions

Figure 8.12 shows a script-based calculation view before migration.

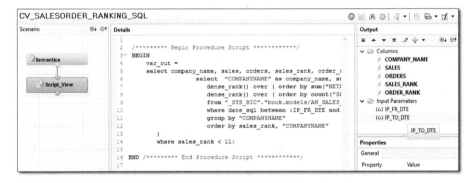

**Figure 8.12**   Script-Based Calculation View before Migration

The same script-based calculation view was converted to a table function. In Figure 8.13, you can see that both a table function (top part of the figure) and a graphical calculation view that uses this table function (bottom part of the figure) were created.

In this case, we did not have to create the table function manually; the migration tool created it for us.

**Figure 8.13**  Scripted Calculation View Migrated to Table Function and Graphical Calculation View

## Important Terminology

The following important terminology was used in this chapter:

▶ **SQL**
Structured Query Language (SQL) is a database programming language used to enhance your modeling process when you have requirements graphical views cannot fulfill.

▶ **SQLScript**
SQLScript exposes many of the memory features of SAP HANA to SQL developers. This includes working with column tables, parameterized information views, delta buffers, working with multiple result sets in parallel, built-in currency conversions at the database level, fuzzy text searching, spatial data

types, and predictive analysis libraries. The only way to make this functionality available via SQL queries, even from other applications, is to provide it via SQL extensions.

▶ **User-defined functions (UDF)**
UDFs are custom read-only functions in SAP HANA.

▶ **Procedures (stored procedures)**
A *procedure* is a subroutine consisting of SQL statements. Procedures can be called or invoked by applications that access the database.

▶ **Imperative logic**
Occasionally, you might prefer to receive the answers to a query one record at a time. This is most often the case when running SQL queries from application servers. In these cases, you will use *imperative logic*, meaning you'll "loop" through the results one at a time

▶ **Dynamic SQL**
Dynamic SQL is when you build up SQL strings on the fly using code, and then execute them.

## Practice Questions

These practice questions will help you evaluate your understanding of the topics covered in this chapter. The questions shown are similar in nature to those found on the certification examination. Although none of these questions will be found on the exam itself, they will allow you to review your knowledge of the subject. Select the correct answers and then check the completeness of your answers in the Practice Question Answers and Explanations section. Remember that on the exam you must select all correct answers and only correct answers to receive credit for the question.

1.   What paradigm describes the SQL language?

☐   **A.** Set-oriented

☐   **B.** Object-oriented

☐   **C.** Procedural

☐   **D.** Application-focused

2.   To what subset of SQL does the SELECT statement belong?

☐   **A.** DML

☐   **B.** DDL

☐   **C.** DCL

☐   **D.** DQL

3.   True or False: Delimited identifiers are treated as case-sensitive.

☐   **A.** True

☐   **B.** False

4.   What is used in SQL to indicate that there is no value?

☐   **A.** Zero

☐   **B.** Empty quotes

☐   **C.** NULL

☐   **D.** Spaces

5.   You want to use a table to store results for each session but do not want to recreate the table for every session. What type of table should you create?

☐   **A.** History column table

☐   **B.** Global temporary table

☐   **C.** Local temporary table

☐   **D.** Virtual table

6.   What character is used to terminate SQL statements?

☐   **A.** ? (question mark)

☐   **B.** : (colon)

☐   **C.** ; (semicolon)

☐   **D.** . (period)

7.   What SELECT statement is not recommended for use with column tables?

☐   **A.** SELECT *

☐   **B.** SELECT with a time-travel clause

☐   **C.** SELECT ALL

☐   **D.** SELECT in a subquery

8.  True or False: A union returns all values in a result set, even duplicate records.

☐   **A.** True

☐   **B.** False

9.  What character is prepended to a SQLScript variable when it is used as an input variable?

☐   **A.** ! (exclamation mark)

☐   **B.** : (colon)

☐   **C.** _ (underscore)

☐   **D.** & (ampersand)

10. What should you keep in mind when using imperative logic in SQLScript?

☐   **A.** It delivers the best possible performance.

☐   **B.** You can only use if-then logic.

☐   **C.** You can loop through records.

☐   **D.** It matches SQL's set-oriented paradigm.

11. What should you keep in mind when using dynamic SQL? (There are 2 correct answers.)

☐   **A.** It is always bad for security.

☐   **B.** It could be used for SQL injection.

☐   **C.** You can dynamically change your data sources.

☐   **D.** It delivers the best possible performance.

12. You created a user-defined function with a return type of BIGINT. What type of function have you created?

☐   **A.** SQL function

☐   **B.** Scalar function

☐ **C.** Table function

☐ **D.** Window function

13. In which programming languages can you create procedures in SAP HANA? (There are 2 correct answers.)

☐ **A.** SQLScript

☐ **B.** L

☐ **C.** JavaScript

☐ **D.** R

14. You created a user-defined function with the INVOKER security option. Which user's authorizations are checked when the function is executed?

☐ **A.** The owner of the function

☐ **B.** The _SYS_REPO user

☐ **C.** The SYSTEM user

☐ **D.** The user calling the function

15. You created a procedure without defining the security option. Which user's authorizations are checked when the procedure is executed in production?

☐ **A.** The user calling the function

☐ **B.** The system administrator that transported the procedure

☐ **C.** The _SYS_REPO user

☐ **D.** The developer that created the procedure

16. What is the preferred way to create a procedure?

☐ **A.** Use the CREATE PROCEDURE statement in the SQL Console.

☐ **B.** Create a .procedure file.

☐ **C.** Create a .hdbprocedure file.

☐ **D.** Use the context menu of a package.

17. With which statement can you call a table function? (There are 2 correct answers.)

☐  **A.** CALL

☐  **B.** INSERT INTO

☐  **C.** SELECT

☐  **D.** EXEC

18. What statement is allowed in a user-defined function?

☐  **A.** COMMIT

☐  **B.** EXEC

☐  **C.** INSERT

☐  **D.** JOIN

19. You want to call a procedure in a SELECT statement (like a table function). Which clauses do you have to specify? (There are 2 correct answers.)

☐  **A.** LANGUAGE SQLSCRIPT

☐  **B.** WITH RESULTS VIEW

☐  **C.** SEQUENTIAL EXECUTION

☐  **D.** READS SQL DATA

20. What statement do you have to run before you can return table results from a procedure?

☐  **A.** CREATE TABLE TYPE

☐  **B.** CREATE TYPE

☐  **C.** CREATE TABLE

☐  **D.** CREATE VIEW

21. What SQL construct do you use to return multiple result sets from a single SQL statement?

☐  **A.** GROUPING SETS

☐  **B.** SELECT subquery

☐  **C.** JOIN

☐  **D.** UNION

22. What can be used to return multiple result sets?

- ☐ **A.** Scalar function
- ☐ **B.** Table function
- ☐ **C.** Procedure
- ☐ **D.** View

23. What should you keep in mind about user-defined functions?

- ☐ **A.** They can use imperative logic.
- ☐ **B.** They can commit transactions.
- ☐ **C.** They can use dynamic SQL.
- ☐ **D.** They can call procedures.

24. What should you keep in mind about procedures? (There are 3 correct answers.)

- ☐ **A.** They can call views.
- ☐ **B.** They are NOT open to SQL injection.
- ☐ **C.** They must return values.
- ☐ **D.** They may have input parameters.
- ☐ **E.** They can call table functions.

25. What is a new and recommended way to work with SQL and SQLScript?

- ☐ **A.** Use CE-functions rather than SQL syntax.
- ☐ **B.** Use .procedure files rather than creating SQL and SQLScript via the package context menu.
- ☐ **C.** Use table functions rather than scripted calculation views.
- ☐ **D.** Create runtime objects rather than design-time objects.

26. Which tasks are part of the migration tool workflow? (There are 2 correct answers.)

- ☐ **A.** The tool requires a graphical calculation view as input.
- ☐ **B.** The tool requires a script-based calculation view as input.
- ☐ **C.** The tool produces only a table function.
- ☐ **D.** The tool produces a table function linked to a graphical calculation view.

## Practice Question Answers and Explanations

1. Correct answer: **A**

   SQL language uses a set-oriented paradigm. Object-oriented and procedural paradigms are used for application-level programming languages. SQL is database-focused rather than application-focused. (Imperative logic is more application-focused.)

2. Correct answer: **D**

   The SELECT statement belongs to the Data Query Language (DQL) subset of SQL. Data Manipulation Language (DML) refers to SQL statements like INSERT and UPDATE. Data Definition Language (DDL) refers to creating tables and so on. Data Control Language (DCL) refers to security.

3. Correct answer: **A**

   True. Yes, delimited identifiers are treated as case-sensitive. Undelimited (without quotes) identifiers are treated as if they were written in uppercase.

4. Correct answer: **C**

   NULL is used in SQL to indicate that there is no value.

5. Correct answer: **B**

   A GLOBAL TEMPORARY table stores results for each session, but you do not have to recreate the table for every session. It is persisted. History column and virtual tables are not related to sessions. A local temporary table deletes the table after each session.

6. Correct answer: **C**

   A semicolon (;) is used to terminate SQL statements.

7. Correct answer: **A**

   A SELECT * statement is not recommended for use with column tables. Column tables are stored per column, and SELECT * forces the database to read every column. It becomes much faster when it can ignore entire columns.

8. Correct answer: **B**

   False. A UNION ALL statement returns all values in a result set, even duplicate records. UNION only returns the unique records.

9. Correct answer: **B**

   A colon (:) is prepended to a SQLScript variable when it is used as an input variable.

10. Correct answer: **C**

    You can loop through records using imperative logic in SQLScript. It does NOT deliver the best possible performance. Declarative logic (the set-oriented paradigm) is much faster. The word *only* makes this statement "You can *only* use if-then logic" false, because we can also use loop logic with imperative logic.

11. Correct answers: **B, C**

    Dynamic SQL can be used for SQL injection, and you can dynamically change your data sources. The word *always* makes the "It is *always* bad for security" statement false. Dynamic SQL does NOT deliver the best possible performance.

12. Correct answer: **B**

    You create a scalar function when it has a return type of BIGINT. This returns a single value, and not a table-like result set. SQL functions and window functions are not user-defined functions.

13. Correct answers: **A, D**

    You can create procedures in SQLScript and R in SAP HANA.

14. Correct answer: **D**

    A user-defined function with the INVOKER security option checks the authorizations of the user calling the function when this function is executed. The _SYS_REPO user is used if the DEFINER security option is used. The owner of the function is no longer applicable once the function has been transported to the production system. The SYSTEM user is never used in this context.

15. Correct answer: **C**

    You first have to know that the default security option for a procedure is the DEFINER security option.

    The _SYS_REPO user is used if the DEFINER security option is used. The user calling the function is used for the INVOKER security option. The developer of the procedure is no longer applicable once the function has been transported to the production system.

16. Correct answer: **C**

    The preferred way to create a procedure is to create a .hdbprocedure file. All the other methods are deprecated! (This shows how much things have changed over the last few years.)

17. Correct answers: **C, D**

    You can call a table function with `SELECT` and `EXEC` statements. `EXEC` can be used to build a dynamic SQL statement that contains a `SELECT` statement, for example. You CANNOT use a function to `INSERT INTO`, because it's read-only. `CALL` is how procedures are called.

18. Correct answers: **C, D**

    `JOIN` is allowed in a user-defined function. `COMMIT`, `EXEC`, and `INSERT` are not read-only statements. A UDF will not even activate when you have these in the function.

19. Correct answers: **B, D**

    You need the `WITH RESULTS VIEW` and `READS SQL DATA` clauses to call a procedure in a `SELECT` statement.

20. Correct answer: **B**

    You have to run a `CREATE TYPE` statement before you can return table results from a procedure.

    `CREATE TABLE TYPE` is deprecated.

21. Correct answers: **C, D**

    `GROUPING SETS` can return multiple result sets from a single SQL statement. All the other statements use multiple sources, but return a single result set.

22. Correct answers: **C, D**

    Procedures can return multiple result sets. Table functions and views can only return single result sets. Scalar functions return (multiple) single values, not sets.

23. Correct answer: **A**

    UDFs can use imperative logic. They cannot commit transactions or use dynamic SQL (because they are read-only), and they cannot call procedures. (However, procedures can call UDFs.)

24. Correct answers: **A, D, E**

    Procedures can call views and table functions, and they may have input parameters. They may, but not *must*, return values. Because they can use dynamic SQL, they are open to SQL injection.

25. Correct answer: **C**

    We recommend using table functions rather than scripted calculation views.

26. Correct answers: **B, D**

The migration tool workflow requires a script-based calculation view as input, and it produces a table function linked to a graphical calculation view. Graphical calculation views do not need to be migrated. It produces not *only* a table function, but also a graphical calculation view.

## Takeaway

You have new tools and approaches in your modeling toolbox! We started by providing a basic understanding of SQL and how to use it with your SAP HANA information models. You learned about SQLScript in SAP HANA and discovered how it extends and complements SQL, especially by creating and using UDFs and procedures with your graphical SAP HANA information views.

We also discussed how the SAP HANA modeling environment with SQL and SQLScript has changed over the last few years and how to work with the new and recommended approaches.

## Summary

There is now less focus on SQL and SQLScript in our modeling workflow than in the past. We have new tools and approaches to accommodate the changes that have happened in SAP HANA over the last few years as it has matured. You should now be up-to-date with the SQL and SQLScript working environments and know how to use them in your SAP HANA information modeling.

In the next chapter, we will start using exciting features in SAP HANA for searching and analyzing text, utilizing spatial features, and leveraging predictive library functions.

# Text, Spatial, and Predictive Modeling

## Techniques You'll Master

- ▶ Know how to create a text search index
- ▶ Discover fuzzy text search, text analysis, and text mining
- ▶ Understand the key components of spatial processing
- ▶ Get to know the types of prediction algorithms
- ▶ Learn how to create a predictive analysis model

Now that you understand the basics of SAP HANA information modeling, it's time to take your knowledge to the next level. In this chapter, we will cover three different topics: text, spatial, and predictive modeling. These three topics are independent from each other but can be combined in projects; for an example, see the Real-World Scenario box.

We'll begin our discussion with text modeling—specifically, how to search and find text even if the user misspells it, how to analyze text to find sentiment, and how to mine text in documents. Next, we'll discuss spatial processing and how to combine business data with maps. Finally, we'll look at how to build a predictive analysis model for business users.

### Real-World Scenario

You are working on an SAP HANA project at a pharmaceutical company. The company has created a mobile web application with SAP HANA for its sales representatives. However, users are struggling to find products on their mobile phones, because the keyboard is small and the names of the pharmaceutical products are quite difficult to type correctly. Therefore, you implement a fuzzy text search, via which users type roughly what they want, and the SAP HANA system finds the correct products. The company later tells you that this also helped users avoid adding duplicate entries into the system.

You improve this mobile application by suggesting products to the sales reps. You create a predictive analysis model in SAP HANA to help with their sales forecasting by looking at the seasonal patterns to determine when people use certain products more—for example, in the winter.

You also notice that there were many comments about the company's products on Facebook and Twitter. You process these comments in SAP HANA and can quickly tell the marketing department which products people are talking about—and alert the company if people are making negative comments about any product. You provide special alerts to the sales reps to inform the customers about these products.

You finally add some what-if map-based analytics to the mobile app so that sales reps can change the areas where they are working and see the impact on their projected sales figures.

And of course, you win the "Best Employee" award for the year!

## Objectives of This Portion of the Test

The purpose of this portion of the SAP HANA certification exam is to test your knowledge of the SAP HANA modeling tools.

The certification exam expects you to have a good understanding of the following topics:

► How to create a text search index

► Fuzzy text search, text analysis, and text mining

► The key components of spatial processing

► The types of prediction algorithms

► How to create a predictive analysis model

 **Note**

This portion contributes up to 10% of the total certification exam score.

## Key Concepts Refresher

We've all heard of the website Google: You type in a few words, and the Google search engine returns a list of web pages that best meet your search query, ranked to your preferences. It is also used to indicate when you type a word incorrectly and suggests another spelling, with the question, DID YOU MEAN…? Now, however, the Google search engine has become so confident that it no longer suggests the correction with a qualifying question, but instead says SHOWING RESULTS FOR…. If you're convinced you're original entry is correct, it will allow you to SEARCH INSTEAD FOR [whatever you entered]. Even more revolutionary is the search engine's ability to predict what you want as you type.

Google search is a good example of what we can do with SAP HANA in information models: We can perform fuzzy text searches, like the "Did you mean" example; we can perform text mining to find the best document out of a large collection for a user; and we can perform predictive analysis.

In this chapter, we will also look at text and sentiment analysis and spatial and geo-spatial processing.

## Text

First, let's look at working with the text features in SAP HANA—namely, *fault-tolerant text searches*, *text analysis*, and *text mining*. However, before we can discuss each of these topics in more detail, you first need to create a full-text index.

### Text Index

To enable the text features in SAP HANA, you need a *full-text index*. Depending on what you specify when you create the full-text index, it gives access to one or more text features. The full-text index will use additional memory to provide the requested text features.

Listing 9.1 provides an example of a SQL statement to create a full-text index. In this case, we create a full-text index with the name DEMO_TEXT_INDEX on a column called SOME_TEXT in a column table.

```
CREATE FULLTEXT INDEX DEMO_TEXT_INDEX ON
    "TEXT_INDEX"."DEMO_TEXT" ("SOME_TEXT")
    LANGUAGE DETECTION ('EN')
    SEARCH ONLY ON
    FUZZY SEARCH INDEX ON
    TEXT ANALYSIS ON
        CONFIGURATION 'EXTRACTION_CORE_VOICEOFCUSTOMER'
    TEXT MINING OFF;
```

**Listing 9.1**  SQL Statement to Create a Full-Text Index

Let's examine the different text elements of the SQL statement in Listing 9.1:

▶ **CREATE FULLTEXT INDEX**
The first line creates a full-text index from the SOME_TEXT column in the DEMO_TEXT table.

▶ **LANGUAGE DETECTION**
SAP HANA will attempt to detect the language of your text. You can specify on what languages it should focus with this clause. In this case, we indicated that our text is all in English.

▶ **SEARCH ONLY ON**
This clause saves some memory by not copying the source text into the full-text index.

▶ **FUZZY SEARCH INDEX ON**
Enables or disables the fault-tolerant search feature. This feature is also called *fuzzy text search*.

▶ **TEXT ANALYSIS ON**
Enables or disables the text analysis feature.

▶ **CONFIGURATION**
Name of the configuration. The text analysis feature needs a configuration file. Some standard configurations ship with SAP HANA, and you can also create your own.

▶ **TEXT MINING OFF**
Enables or disables the text-mining feature.

 **Note**

You normally put the SQL statement in Listing 9.1 in a procedure (using a .hdb-procedure file). This way, you can deploy it later on the production system. The recommended way to create full-text indexes going forward is using Core Data Services (CDS). You can find the CDS syntax in the SAP HANA Search Developer Guide at *http://help.sap.com/hana_options_adp*.

You now can open the definition of the column table by double-clicking the table's name in the CATALOG area. In the INDEXES tab, you'll see the full-text index named DEMO_TEXT_INDEX that you just created. When you select this index, you'll see the details of the full-text index as shown in Figure 9.1.

You can see from the checkboxes that we enabled FUZZY SEARCH and TEXT ANALYSIS and disabled TEXT MINING in this index.

When fuzzy search is enabled for text-type columns, the full-text index increases the memory size of the columns by approximately an additional 10 percent. When text analysis is enabled, the increase in the memory size due to the full-text index depends on many factors, but it can be as large as that of the column itself.

SAP HANA will automatically create full-text indexes for columns with data types TEXT, BINTEXT, and SHORTTEXT.

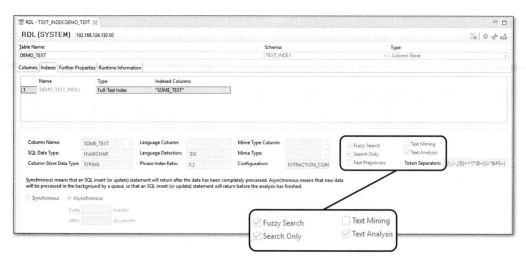

**Figure 9.1**  Full-Text Index Details

For other column types, you must manually create the full-text index. You can only manually create a full-text index for columns with the VARCHAR, NVARCHAR, ALPHANUM, CLOB, NCLOB, and BLOB data types.

When you manually create an index, SAP HANA attaches a hidden column to the column you indexed. This hidden column contains extracted textual data from the source column; the original source column remains unchanged. Search queries are performed on the hidden column, but the data returned is from the source column.

 **Tip**

> Remember that a full-text index is created for a specific column, not for the entire table. You will have to create a full-text index for every column that you wish to search or analyze.

**Text Search**

When you've created a full-text index with the FUZZY SEARCH option enabled, you can do fault-tolerant searches on your text data. (These are also called *fuzzy searches*.) This means we can misspell words, and SAP HANA will still find the text for us. The real-world scenario at the beginning of the chapter illustrates this point in a somewhat exaggerated manner.

SAP HANA will find alternative (US and UK) spellings for words like *color/colour*, *artifact/artefact*, *utilize/utilise*, and *check/cheque*. Incorrectly entered words such as typing *coat*, will still return the correct word, which was probably *cost*.

In Chapter 8, we discussed the LIKE operator in SQL. You can search for a random pharmaceutical product name (like Guaiphenesin) via the following SQL statement:

```
SELECT productname, price from Products where productname LIKE
'%UAIPH%';
```

This will find the name if you type the first few characters correctly. If you search for "%AUIPH%" instead, you won't find anything.


### CONTAINS Predicate

In SAP HANA, you can use the CONTAINS predicate to use the fuzzy text search feature. In this case, you use the following SQL statement:

```
SELECT SCORE(), productname, price from Products where
CONTAINS(productname, 'AUIPH', FUZZY(0.8)) ORDER BY SCORE() DESC;
```

 **Tip**

Remember that your users will not type SQL statements; you'll create these statements in a user-defined function (UDF) or a procedure and call them from your graphical calculation view or your SAP HANA XS application.

The CONTAINS predicate uses the column name you want to search on, the search string itself (even if misspelled), and how "fuzzy" you want the search to be. The fuzziness factor can range from zero (everything matches) to one (requires an exact match).

The SCORE() function helps sort the results from the most relevant to the least relevant.

If you want to search on all columns with a full-text search index, you can specify the CONTAINS predicate as follows:

```
CONTAINS (*,'AUIPH', FUZZY(0.8))
```

When you search on multiple columns at once, it's called a *freestyle search*. In this case, the asterisk (*) includes all columns. However, you also can specify which columns you want to include or exclude in the list.

There are some special characters you can use in the search string:

▶ **Double quotes (")**
Everything between the double quotes is searched for exactly as it appears.

▶ **Asterisk (\*)**
Replaces zero or more characters in the search string; for example, *cat\**
matches *cats*, *catalogues*, and so on.

▶ **Question mark (?)**
Replaces a single character in the search string; for example, *cat?* matches *cats*,
but not *catalogue*.

### SAP HANA Simple Info Access API

The *SAP HANA simple info access* (SINA) API is a client-side JavaScript API for
developing your own web-based search interfaces. Figure 9.2 shows a demo text
search application created with the SINA toolkit.

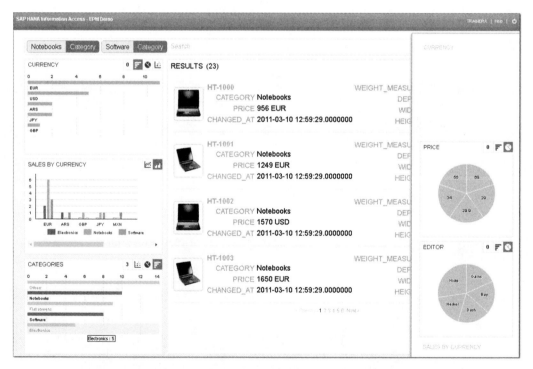

**Figure 9.2**   SAP HANA Simple Info Access Demo Search Application

> **Note**
>
> SAP HANA now includes an embedded search via the built-in `sys.esh_`
> `search()`procedure. With this procedure, you can use an existing ABAP SQL
> connection instead of an XS OData service for fuzzy text searches in SAP HANA
> from SAP business applications.
>
> For more information on this new API, see the SAP HANA Search Developer
> Guide at *http://help.sap.com/hana_options_adp*.

### *Fuzzy Text Search in Attribute Views*

To date, you can only use fuzzy text searches directly in attribute views; this is
one of the few reasons that SAP HANA SPS 11 still uses attributes.

Figure 9.3 shows the Search Properties tab in which you can see an output column's properties. Here, you can enable fuzzy text search for a column and with
a particular Fuzziness Threshold.

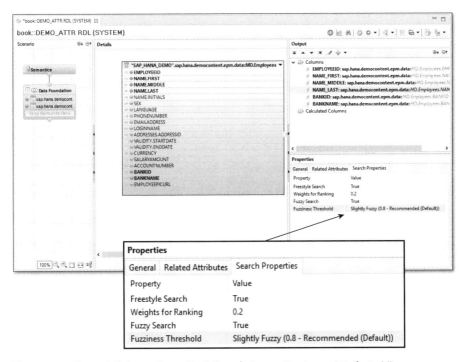

**Figure 9.3**   Output Column Fuzzy Text Search Properties in an Attribute View

### Text Analysis

Once you've created a full-text index with the TEXT ANALYSIS option enabled, you can analyze text with the SAP HANA text analysis feature, both via entity analysis and sentiment analysis.

#### *Working with Text Analysis*

You create text analysis via the full-text index. The abbreviated statement is as follows:

```
CREATE FULLTEXT INDEX INDEX_NAME ON TABLE_NAME ("COLUMN_NAME")
    TEXT ANALYSIS ON
        CONFIGURATION 'CONFIG_NAME';
```

You need the TEXT ANALYSIS ON clause and a CONFIGURATION NAME; there are a few built-in configurations, but you can also create your own industry-specific configuration files.

In the earlier example shown in Figure 9.1, we created the full-text index (called DEMO_TEXT_INDEX) on the DEMO_TEXT table. When you look at the table in the CATALOG area, you'll notice that SAP HANA has created an additional table: $TA_DEMO_TEXT_INDEX (see Figure 9.4). This is the name of the full-text index we created, prepended with $TA_.

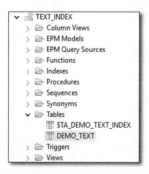

**Figure 9.4**  Source Table (DEMO_TEXT) and $TA_ Text Analysis Results Table

You'd expect $TA_ to denote *text analysis*—and that's exactly right. You get the text analysis request results back in table $TA.

 **Hint**

Table $TA is not the full-text index; it contains the results of the text analysis.

The original table included the following values in the `SOME_TEXT` column:

▶ `Laura likes apples. Laura dislikes chocolate.`

▶ `Colin loves running.`

▶ `Danie works for SAP.`

Figure 9.5 shows the text analysis request results.

| | ID | TA_RULE | TA_COUNTER | TA_TOKEN | TA_LANGUAGE | TA_TYPE | TA_NORMALIZED | TA_STEM | TA_PARAGRAPH | TA_SENTENCE |
|---|---|---|---|---|---|---|---|---|---|---|
| 1 | 1 | Entity Extraction | 1 | Laura | en | PERSON | ? | ? | 1 | 1 |
| 2 | 1 | Entity Extraction | 2 | Laura likes apples | en | Sentiment | ? | ? | 1 | 1 |
| 3 | 1 | Entity Extraction | 3 | Laura | en | Topic | ? | ? | 1 | 1 |
| 4 | 1 | Entity Extraction | 4 | likes | en | WeakPositiveSentiment | ? | ? | 1 | 1 |
| 5 | 1 | Entity Extraction | 5 | apples | en | Topic | ? | ? | 1 | 1 |
| 6 | 1 | Entity Extraction | 6 | Laura | en | PERSON | ? | ? | 2 | 2 |
| 7 | 1 | Entity Extraction | 7 | Laura dislikes chocolate | en | Sentiment | ? | ? | 2 | 2 |
| 8 | 1 | Entity Extraction | 8 | Laura | en | Topic | ? | ? | 2 | 2 |
| 9 | 1 | Entity Extraction | 9 | dislikes | en | WeakNegativeSentiment | ? | ? | 2 | 2 |
| 10 | 1 | Entity Extraction | 10 | chocolate | en | Topic | ? | ? | 2 | 2 |
| 11 | 2 | Entity Extraction | 1 | Colin | en | PERSON | ? | ? | 1 | 1 |
| 12 | 2 | Entity Extraction | 2 | Colin loves running | en | Sentiment | ? | ? | 1 | 1 |
| 13 | 2 | Entity Extraction | 3 | Colin | en | Topic | ? | ? | 1 | 1 |
| 14 | 2 | Entity Extraction | 4 | loves | en | StrongPositiveSentiment | ? | ? | 1 | 1 |
| 15 | 2 | Entity Extraction | 5 | running | en | Topic | ? | ? | 1 | 1 |
| 16 | 3 | Entity Extraction | 1 | Danie | en | PERSON | ? | ? | 1 | 1 |
| 17 | 3 | Entity Extraction | 2 | SAP | en | ORGANIZATION/COMMERCIAL | ? | ? | 1 | 1 |

**Figure 9.5**   $TA_ Text Analysis Results Table Content

The text analysis determined the following points:

▶ It identified Laura, Colin, and Danie as people.

▶ It classified SAP as an organization.

▶ It identified apples, chocolate, and running as topics.

▶ It rated Laura liking apples as a weak positive sentiment.

▶ It rated Laura disliking chocolate as a weak negative sentiment.

▶ It determined that Colin loving running is a strong positive sentiment.

With a different text analysis configuration file, we would have received different results.

Using the standard configuration files, you will be able to identify many of the attributes (master data) in your text data. Identifying measures is not always that easy, however.

### SAP HANA Text Analysis XS JavaScript API

From SAP HANA SPS 10 on, the SAP HANA Text Analysis XS JavaScript API is available. With this API, you can call text analysis without creating a full-text index or reading the results in the $TA table.

### Grammatical Role Analysis

SAP HANA SPS 11 makes the optional Grammatical Role Analysis (GRA) analyzer for English available. It identifies groups of three in the form of subject–verb–object expressions.

For an example, let's look at a well-known phrase:

```
The [SUBJECT]quick brown fox[/SUBJECT] [VERB]jumps[/VERB]
over the [DIRECTOBJECT]lazy dog[/DIRECTOBJECT]
```

### Text Mining

Fuzzy searches and text analysis work with a word, sentence, or paragraph—but with text mining, you can work with entire documents. These documents can be web pages, Microsoft Word documents, or PDF files that are loaded into SAP HANA.

*Text mining* uses the full-text indexing and text analysis processes. When using text mining in SAP HANA, you can perform the following tasks:

▶ Categorize documents

▶ Find top-ranked terms related to a particular term

▶ Analyze a document to find key phrases that describe the document

▶ See a list of documents related to the one you ask about

▶ Access documents that best match your search terms

You can call the text mining features from SQL functions or from web applications that can use the SAP HANA Text Mining XS JavaScript API.

 **Tip**

Remember that users will not work at the lower level that we have described in this chapter: They will want to use text features from a browser-based application interface. This is why SAP has focused on supplying various SAP HANA XS JavaScript APIs for SAP HANA modelers and developers.

Now that you know how to work with text data in SAP HANA and can use fault-tolerant text searches, text analysis, and text mining in SAP HANA modeling work, let's move on to spatial processing.

## Spatial

The next topic we'll discuss is understanding spatial processing in SAP HANA.

 **Tip**

*Geospatial processing* is a subset of spatial processing related to geography. *Spatial processing* can include CAD models or even the human body and uses a three-dimensional coordinate system that differs from the geospatial coordinates of longitude, latitude, and height above sea level.

We first mentioned spatial processing in Chapter 4 when we discussed spatial joins. Now, let's take a closer look at spatial joins in an SAP HANA system.

### Spatial Data Types and Joins

Figure 9.6 shows two tables that contain spatial data. One table contains shop locations, and the other table contains city suburb shapes.

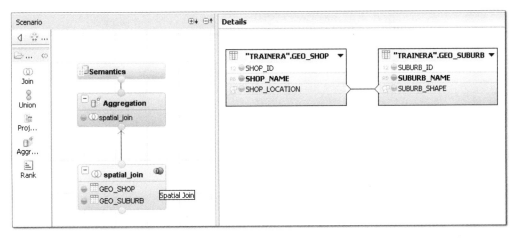

**Figure 9.6**  Two Tables Containing Spatial Data, with a Spatial Join

Here, we stored the shop locations in table GEO_SHOP, using the ST_POINT data type.

The following spatial data types are available:

▶ `ST_Geometry`
  This the supertype for all the other spatial data types; you can store objects like linestrings, polygons, and circles in this data type. Then you can use the `TREAT` expression to specify which data type you want to work with. For example, `TREAT( geometry1 AS ST_Polygon ).ST_Area()` will take a geometry, treat it like a polygon, and ask the size of the polygon's area.

▶ `ST_Point`
  A *point* is a single location in space with X and Y coordinates at a minimum. It can also have a Z coordinate for three-dimensional spatial data. Points are often used to represent addresses, as in the shop example in Figure 9.6.

▶ `ST_MultiPoint`
  A *multipoint* is a collection of points. For example, it could represent all the different locations (addresses) where a company has shops.

▶ `ST_LineString`
  A *linestring* is a line, which can be used to represent rivers, railroads, and roads. In the shop example, it could represent a delivery route.

▶ `ST_MultiLineString`
  A *multilinestring* is a collection of linestrings. In the shop example, this collection could include all the deliveries that a shop has to make on a certain day for which the driver goes to different customers or suppliers.

▶ `ST_Polygon`
  A *polygon* defines an area. In the shop example, this is used to represent the suburbs in the second table (Figure 9.6; most suburbs do not have regular square shapes).

▶ `ST_MultiPolygon`
  A *multipolygon* is a collection of polygons; for example, the suburbs could be combined to indicate the area of the city or town.

▶ `ST_CircularString`
  A *circularstring* is a connected sequence of circular arc segments, much like a linestring with circular arcs between points.

You can join different data spatial types together in a spatial join. Figure 9.7 shows the details of a spatial join. Notice that the Spatial Properties tab is available for this join type. The PREDICATE dropdown list in this tab allows you to specify how to join the fields.

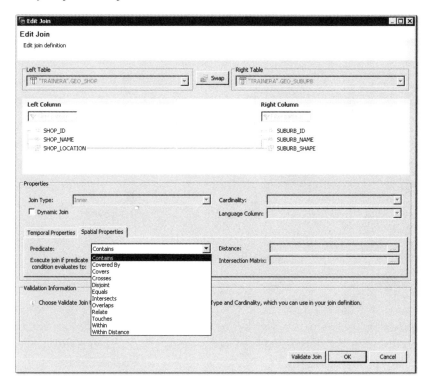

**Figure 9.7**   Spatial Join Details

In the shop example, we will use the CONTAINS option, because we want to see which suburb contains which shop addresses (locations).

> **Tip**
>
> Please don't confuse the CONTAINS option in the spatial joins with the CONTAINS predicate we used when executing a fuzzy text search.

### Importing and Exporting Spatial Data

In SAP HANA, you can import and export spatial data in the Well-Known Text (WKT) and the Well-Known Binary (WKB) formats. These formats are part of the Open Geospatial Consortium (OGC) standards. You can also import and export the extended versions of these formats, which are used by PostGIS.

In addition, SAP HANA can import ESRI shapefiles and export spatial data in the GeoJSON and Scalable Vector Graphic (SVG) file formats. The SVG file format is maintained by World Wide Web Consortium (W3C) and supported by all modern browsers.

### Spatial Functions

You saw an example of a spatial function earlier when we asked for the area of a polygon to be calculated—for example, `geometry1.ST_Area()`.

Referring back to Figure 9.7, you can ask if a shop's location is in a suburb as follows:

```
SUBURB_SHAPE.ST_CONTAINS(SHOP_LOCATION1)
```

You can also see how far two shops are from each other as follows:

```
SHOP_LOCATION1. ST_WITHINDISTANCE(SHOP_LOCATION2)
```

### Additional Resources

To learn more about spatial processing in SAP HANA, look at the examples in the SHINE demo content. Here, you can find examples like the one in Figure 9.8, in which you can work with shops on a map on the left of the screen and see their details in the area on the right.

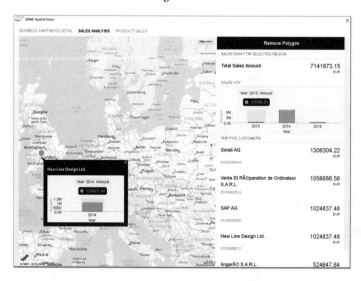

**Figure 9.8**  Spatial Data Used in a Business Application (SHINE Demo Content)

You can find more information about spatial data in the SAP HANA Spatial Reference Guide at *http://help.sap.com/hana_options_spatial*.

## Predictive

Now, let's discuss predictive analysis. We'll look at the SAP HANA predictive analysis libraries and how to use them to create a predictive analysis model.

In this section, we'll look at predicting future probabilities and trends and how you can use this functionality in business. In the real-world scenario at the beginning of the chapter, we described a use case in which you might create a predictive model in SAP HANA to help sales reps with their sales forecasting by looking at seasonal patterns; for example, people use more pharmaceuticals for allergies in the spring.

There are many use cases for the predictive analysis libraries built into SAP HANA: For financial institutions such as banks, you can detect fraud by looking at abnormal transactions. For fleet management and car rental companies, you can predict which parts will break soon in a vehicle and replace them before they actually break.

### Predictive Analysis Library

In SAP HANA, the predictive analysis functions are grouped together in the *Predictive Analysis Library* (PAL). PAL defines functions that you can call from SQLScript and use to perform various predictive analysis algorithms. The algorithms were chosen by looking at what SAP HANA applications need, what people commonly use, and what the market requests.

In PAL, predictive analysis algorithms are grouped in nine categories; we'll take a quick look at the nine categories and discuss a few popular algorithms in some of these categories. Figure 9.9 provides an overview. The categories are as follows:

▸ **Clustering**
  With clustering, you divide data into groups (clusters) of items that have similar properties. For example, you can group servers with similar usage characteristics, like email servers that all have a lot of network traffic on port 25 during the day. You might use the popular *K-means* algorithm for this purpose. Another example is computer vision, in which you cluster pictures of

human faces using the *affinity propagation* algorithm. Clustering is sometimes also called *segmentation*. The focus of clustering is the algorithm figuring out by itself what is the best way to group existing data together.

▶ **Classification**
The process of classification takes historical data and trains predictive models—using, for example, *decision trees*. You can then send new data to the predictive model you've trained, and the model will attempt to predict which class the new data belongs to. This process is often referred to as *supervised learning*. The focus here is on getting accurate predictions for unknown data.

▶ **Regression**
Regression plots the best possible line or curve through the historical data. You can then use that line or curve to predict future values. This could be used by the previously mentioned car rental company. The company has had 5,000 of these vehicles before, and so it has good information available to predict when certain parts in a similar vehicle will break.

▶ **Association**
For an example of an association, think of Amazon's suggestions: PEOPLE WHO BOUGHT THIS ITEM ALSO BOUGHT THE FOLLOWING ITEMS. The *apriori algorithm* can be used to analyze shopping baskets. It can identify products that are commonly purchased together and group them together in the shop—for example, flashlights and batteries. You could even offer a discount on the flashlights because you know that people will need to buy batteries for them, and you can make enough profit on the batteries. (Notice however that the inverse is not necessarily true; a discount on the batteries will not encourage people to buy flashlights.)

▶ **Time series**
For an example of a time series, think of the real-life scenario at the beginning of the chapter, in which we built a predictive model to forecast sales by looking at seasonal patterns. You might also see, for example, a monthly pattern in shops of higher sales after paydays.

▶ **Preprocessing**
This category of algorithms is used to prepare data before further processing. These algorithms may improve the accuracy of the predictive models by reducing the noise. You can also identify outliers, or invalid and missing values.

▶ **Statistics**

This category includes some statistical algorithms to find out how closely variables are related to—or independent they are from—each other. One example is the *Grubbs' test* algorithm, which is used to detect outliers. This could be used in the fraud detection use case we mentioned earlier, in which certain transactions are different from the others. (Often, we first use a clustering algorithm to group transactions together, and then detect outliers for each group/cluster after.)

▶ **Social network analysis**

Currently, the only algorithm in this category is the *link prediction* algorithm, used to predict the likelihood of a future association between two people who have no association yet. This is used by companies like Facebook and LinkedIn.

▶ **Miscellaneous**

Two algorithms fall under this category: The *ABC analysis* algorithm can be used to identify which 20 percent of our customers account for 80 percent of the revenue, and *weighted score tables* can be used to help you decide what to buy when some criteria are more important than others—for example, if you want to buy an SAP HANA server. The speed of the memory weighs more heavily in that decision than disk speeds.

Figure 9.9 shows the PAL algorithms, per category, that are available in SAP HANA SPS 11.

You can find information about each of the PAL predictive functions in the SAP HANA Predictive Analysis Library (PAL) Reference Guide at *http://help.sap.com/hana_platform/*.

### Installing PAL

PAL is part of the Application Function Library (AFL) that ships with all SAP HANA systems. AFL is an optional component; if you want to use the predictive analysis algorithms in PAL, you have to install AFL via SAP HANA Application Lifecycle Management. AFL also includes a Business Function Library (BFL).

After the installation, you have to ensure that the script server is started and make sure you have the `AFL_SYS_AFL_AFLPAL_EXECUTE` role assigned to your SAP HANA user. (Roles, and how to assign them, are discussed in Chapter 13.)

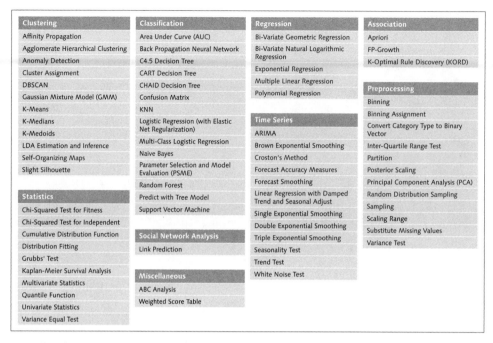

| Clustering | Classification | Regression | Association |
|---|---|---|---|
| Affinity Propagation | Area Under Curve (AUC) | Bi-Variate Geometric Regression | Apriori |
| Agglomerate Hierarchical Clustering | Back Propagation Neural Network | Bi-Variate Natural Logarithmic Regression | FP-Growth |
| Anomaly Detection | C4.5 Decision Tree | Exponential Regression | K-Optimal Rule Discovery (KORD) |
| Cluster Assignment | CART Decision Tree | Multiple Linear Regression | |
| DBSCAN | CHAID Decision Tree | Polynomial Regression | **Preprocessing** |
| Gaussian Mixture Model (GMM) | Confusion Matrix | | Binning |
| K-Means | KNN | | Binning Assignment |
| K-Medians | Logistic Regression (with Elastic Net Regularization) | **Time Series** | Convert Category Type to Binary Vector |
| K-Medoids | | ARIMA | |
| LDA Estimation and Inference | Multi-Class Logistic Regression | Brown Exponential Smoothing | Inter-Quartile Range Test |
| Self-Organizing Maps | Naive Bayes | Croston's Method | Partition |
| Slight Silhouette | Parameter Selection and Model Evaluation (PSME) | Forecast Accuracy Measures | Posterior Scaling |
| | Random Forest | Forecast Smoothing | Principal Component Analysis (PCA) |
| **Statistics** | Predict with Tree Model | Linear Regression with Damped Trend and Seasonal Adjust | Random Distribution Sampling |
| Chi-Squared Test for Fitness | Support Vector Machine | Single Exponential Smoothing | Sampling |
| Chi-Squared Test for Independent | | Double Exponential Smoothing | Scaling Range |
| Cumulative Distribution Function | **Social Network Analysis** | Triple Exponential Smoothing | Substitute Missing Values |
| Distribution Fitting | Link Prediction | Seasonality Test | Variance Test |
| Grubbs' Test | | Trend Test | |
| Kaplan-Meier Survival Analysis | **Miscellaneous** | White Noise Test | |
| Multivariate Statistics | ABC Analysis | | |
| Quantile Function | Weighted Score Table | | |
| Univariate Statistics | | | |
| Variance Equal Test | | | |

**Figure 9.9**   Predictive Functions Available in SAP HANA SPS 11, Grouped by Category

You can check if AFL is installed on a system by opening the `AFL_FUNCTIONS` view in the `SYS` schema. If you see lots of entries in this view, then AFL has been installed on that system.

### Creating a Predictive Model

Once PAL is installed, you can create predictive models graphically via the application function modeler (AFM). In Chapter 5, we discussed the steps to create a flowgraph model:

1. Create a .hdbflowgraph file in your project in the developer perspective.

2. Give your predictive model a name, and choose FLOWGRAPH FOR ACTIVATION AS STORED PROCEDURE.

> **Note**
>
> You can also create a predictive model using SQLScript, which is the traditional way to build such models. Building the models graphically using the AFM only became available in the last few releases of SAP HANA.

If you find .aflpmml files, which are AFL models, you will have to convert these to AFM flowgraphs. SAP HANA SPS 11 can still run these files, but you cannot edit them in the AFM.

In the AFM, build a flowgraph model. Start on the left side and work towards the right side, as shown in Figure 9.10. First, drag a table with data into the left side of the work area. Next, select a PAL function from the palette on the right and drag it to the work area. Then, connect the table to the PAL function; the PAL functions are grouped into the categories that we discussed earlier.

In Figure 9.10, we started building the end-to-end scenario to predict segmentation of new customers for a supermarket, as described in the PAL reference guide. The guide describes how to do this by using SQLScript, but it's a good exercise to try to do it via a graphical flowgraph model.

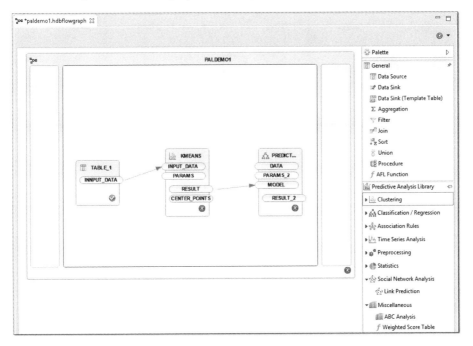

**Figure 9.10**   Creating a Flowgraph Model in the AFM Tool

Sometimes, you might want to train your model, and then use it later to make predictions. Figure 9.11 shows such a model: It starts with some training data that you feed into a *C4.5 decision tree*. The data is used to train the classification model. You then feed the trained classification model into a prediction function and also give the prediction function some new data. The prediction function applies the trained model to the new data and provides the predicted results in an output table.

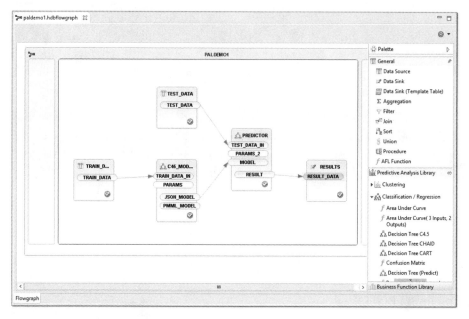

**Figure 9.11**   Predictive Model Created in AFM

SAP HANA automatically converts the graphical flowgraph model into a SQL-Script procedure, and you can then call this procedure when you want to use the predictive model as part of your other SAP HANA information models.

## Important Terminology

In this chapter, we looked at the following important terms:

▸ **Full-text index**
Depending on what you specify when you create the full-text index, it gives access to one or more text features. The full-text index will use additional memory to provide the requested text features.

▸ **Fuzzy text search**
Enables or disables the fault-tolerant search feature.

- **SAP HANA simple info access (SINA)**
  The SINA API is a client-side JavaScript API for developing your own web-based search interfaces.

- **Text analysis**
  Text analysis provides a vast number of possible entity types and analysis rules for many industries in many languages.

- **SAP HANA Text Analysis XS JavaScript**
  With this API, you can call text analysis without creating a full-text index or reading the results in the $TA table.

- **Text mining**
  When using text mining in SAP HANA, you can perform the following tasks:

  - Categorize documents

  - Find top-ranked terms related to a particular term

  - Analyze a document to find key phrases that describe the document

  - See a list of documents related to the one you ask about

  - Access documents that best match your search terms

- **Spatial processing**
  Simply put, spatial processing uses data to describe, manipulate, and calculate the position, shape, and orientation of objects in a defined space.

- **Predictive Analysis Library (PAL)**
  Defines functions that you can use to perform various predictive analysis algorithms.

# Practice Questions

These practice questions will help you evaluate your understanding of the topics covered in this chapter. The questions shown are similar in nature to those found on the certification examination. Although none of these questions will be found on the exam itself, they will allow you to review your knowledge of the subject. Select the correct answers, and then check the completeness of your answers in the Practice Question Answers and Explanations section. Remember that on the exam you must select all correct answers and only correct answers to receive credit for the question.

1. Which text feature do you use to find sentiment in textual data?

   ☐ **A.** Full-text index

   ☐ **B.** Fuzzy text search

   ☐ **C.** Text analysis

   ☐ **D.** Text mining

2. You create a full-text index. For what text feature clause do you need to specify a configuration?

   ☐ **A.** SEARCH ONLY

   ☐ **B.** FUZZY SEARCH INDEX

   ☐ **C.** TEXT MINING

   ☐ **D.** TEXT ANALYSIS

3. What is the recommended way to create full-text indexes going forward?

   ☐ **A.** User-defined functions

   ☐ **B.** Procedures

   ☐ **C.** Core Data Services

   ☐ **D.** SQL statements in the SQL Console

4. For which data types does SAP HANA automatically create full-text indexes? (There are 3 correct answers.)

   ☐ **A.** NVARCHAR

   ☐ **B.** SHORTTEXT

   ☐ **C.** BINTEXT

   ☐ **D.** CLOB

   ☐ **E.** TEXT

5. What predicate do you use for fuzzy text search in the WHERE clause of a SQL statement?

   ☐ **A.** LIKE

   ☐ **B.** ANY

☐   **C.** IN

☐   **D.** CONTAINS

6.  What do you use in a SQL query to sort fuzzy text search results by relevance?

☐   **A.** RANK()

☐   **B.** SCORE()

☐   **C.** SORT BY

☐   **D.** TOP

7.  What API would you use in SAP HANA SPS 11 to display search results in an ABAP system?

☐   **A.** The esh_search procedure

☐   **B.** SAP HANA Simple Info Access API (SINA)

☐   **C.** SAP HANA Text Mining XS JavaScript API

☐   **D.** SAP HANA Text Analysis XS JavaScript API

8.  In what type of view can you use fuzzy text search directly?

☐   **A.** Analytic views

☐   **B.** Calculation views of type dimension

☐   **C.** Calculation views of type cube

☐   **D.** Attribute views

9.  True or False: The full-text index is stored in table $TA.

☐   **A.** True

☐   **B.** False

10. What spatial data type would you use to store multiple shop locations?

☐   **A.** ST_Point

☐   **B.** ST_MultiPoint

☐   **C.** ST_Polygon

☐   **D.** ST_MultiLineString

11. Which spatial data formats can you import into SAP HANA? (There are 2 correct answers.)

☐  **A.** Scalable Vector Graphic (SVG)

☐  **B.** Well Known Text (WKT)

☐  **C.** ESRI shapefiles

☐  **D.** GeoJSON

12. What PAL algorithm category can you use for supervised learning?

☐  **A.** Classification

☐  **B.** Clustering

☐  **C.** Association

☐  **D.** Social network analysis

13. What PAL algorithm would you use to analyze shopping baskets?

☐  **A.** K-means

☐  **B.** Decision tree

☐  **C.** Apriori

☐  **D.** Link prediction

14. What must be installed for PAL to work?

☐  **A.** SAP HANA BFL

☐  **B.** SAP HANA AFL

☐  **C.** SAP HANA AFM

☐  **D.** SAP HANA SINA

15. What SAP HANA information object does AFM create?

☐  **A.** Attribute view

☐  **B.** Calculation view

☐  **C.** Table function

☐  **D.** Procedure

## Practice Question Answers and Explanations

1. Correct answer: **C**

   You use to text analysis (also called *sentiment analysis*) to find sentiment in textual data.

2. Correct answer: **D**

   You need to specify a configuration with the TEXT ANALYSIS clause when you create a full-text index.

3. Correct answer: **C**

   The recommended way going forward to create full-text indexes is using CDS. We never recommend using SQL statements in the SQL Console, because you will have to retype everything again in the production system. Procedures are acceptable and usable, but CDS is the recommended way going forward.

4. Correct answers: **B, C, E**

   SAP HANA automatically creates full-text indexes for TEXT, BINTEXT, and SHORTTEXT. For NVARCHAR and CLOB, you have to create full-text indexes manually.

5. Correct answer: **D**

   You use the CONTAINS predicate for fuzzy text search in the WHERE clause of a SQL statement. The LIKE predicate only uses exact matching, not fuzzy text search.

6. Correct answer: **B**

   You use the SCORE() function in a SQL query to sort fuzzy text search results by relevance. RANK, SORT BY, and TOP cannot be used to sort SAP HANA fuzzy text search results.

7. Correct answer: **A**

   You use the sys.esh_search procedure in SAP HANA SPS 11 to display search results in an ABAP system. You can use the current ABAP SQL connection rather than having to use XS JavaScript. SAP HANA SINA is the older SAP HANA XS-based API.

8. Correct answer: **D**

   You use fuzzy text search directly in attribute views; this is currently the only way to use it. This is one of the few reasons to still use attribute views in SAP HANA SPS 11.

9.  Correct answer: **B**

    False. The full-text index is NOT stored in the `$TA` table.

10. Correct answer: **B**

    Use a `ST_MultiPoint` data type to store multiple shop locations. `ST_Point` can only store a single shop location, and `ST_Polygon` and `ST_Multi-LineString` cannot be used for shop locations.

11. Correct answers: **B, C**

    You can import Well Known Text (WKT) and ESRI shapefiles into SAP HANA. You can only export Scalable Vector Graphic (SVG) and GeoJSON file formats.

12. Correct answer: **A**

    You can use the algorithms in the PAL classification category for supervised learning. Clustering is sometimes also called *unsupervised learning*.

13. Correct answer: **C**

    Use the apriori PAL algorithm to analyze shopping baskets.

14. Correct answer: **B**

    You must install AFL for PAL to work. BFL is part of AFL, but completely separate from PAL. AFM is the modeling tool used for graphically designing predictive models, and SAP HANA SINA is the API used for text search.

15. Correct answer: **D**

    AFM creates a procedure.

## Takeaway

You now know how to create a text search index for use with the fuzzy text search, text analysis, and text mining features in SAP HANA. You can use these features to provide fault-tolerant searches, sentiment analysis, and document references for the users of your information models.

You should now also understand the key components of spatial processing, which spatial data types are available, and how to perform spatial joins in SAP HANA information views.

Finally, we also discussed the categories and some of the algorithms in PAL and learned how to create a predictive analysis model.

## Summary

We discussed a few aspects of text analysis: how to search and find text even if the user misspells it, how to analyze text to find sentiment, and how to mine text in documents. We explained how to use spatial processing and how to combine business data with maps, and you learned how to build a predictive analysis model for business users.

In the next chapter, we'll look at how to improve SAP HANA information models to achieve optimal performance.

# Optimization of Information Models

## Techniques You'll Master

- ▶ Understand the performance enhancements in SAP HANA
- ▶ Get to know techniques for optimizing performance
- ▶ Learn how to use the SAP HANA optimization tools
- ▶ Implement good modeling practices for optimal performance
- ▶ Create optimal SQL and SQLScript

During our exploration of SAP HANA, we've frequently come across the topic of performance. SAP HANA is well-known for the improvements it brings to business process runtimes and its real-time computing abilities.

In this chapter, we'll discuss some of these performance enhancements built into SAP HANA and review the techniques you've learned previously. We'll then look into new ways of pinpointing performance issues and discuss how to use the optimization tools built into SAP HANA.

Finally, we'll examine some guidelines and best practices when modeling and writing SQL and SQLScript code.

### Real-World Scenario

The CEO of your company reads a 2009 study by Akamai that says that 40 percent of online shoppers will abandon a website that takes longer than three seconds to load.

Therefore, you are tasked to help achieve a response time of less than three seconds for most reports and analytics that sales representatives use. Many such users work on tablets, especially when they are visiting customers. You decide to use a mobile-first approach, creating interactive analytics and reports to reduce network requirements.

Some of the reports currently take more than two minutes to run on SAP HANA. Using your knowledge of optimization, you manage to bring these times down to just a few seconds.

## Objectives of This Portion of the Test

The purpose of this portion of the SAP HANA certification exam is to test your knowledge of the SAP HANA modeling tools.

The certification exam expects you to have a good understanding of the following topics:

▸ Performance enhancements in SAP HANA

▸ Techniques for optimizing performance

- ▶ Using the Explain Plan tool, the Visualize Plan tool, the Administration Console, and the Performance Analysis Mode

- ▶ Good modeling practices for optimal performance

- ▶ Creating optimal SQL and SQLScript

**Note**

This portion contributes up to 10% of the total certification exam score.

# Key Concepts Refresher

In the preceding chapters, we've discussed many performance enhancements that are built into the design of SAP HANA; in this chapter, we'll walk through various optimization topics in SAP HANA.

## Architecture and Performance

The largest and most fundamental change that comes with SAP HANA technology is the move from *disks* to *memory*. The in-memory technology that SAP HANA is built on has been one of the biggest contributors of performance improvements. The decision to break with the legacy of disk-based systems and use in-memory systems as the central focus point (and everything that comes with this) has led to significant changes in performance.

The next step was to combine *memory* and *multicore CPUs*. If we store everything in memory and have plenty of processing power, we do not have to store calculated results. We just recalculate them when we need them—which opens the door to *real-time computing*. Real-time computing requires that results be recalculated each time they're needed, because the data might have changed since the last query.

This combination of memory and CPU processing power led to new innovations. Now, you can combine OLTP and OLAP together in the same system: The OLAP components don't need the storage of precalculated cubes and can be recalculated without impacting the performance of the OLTP system.

Another innovations prompted by combining memory and CPU is *data compression*. This both reduces memory requirements and helps to better utilize CPUs by loading more data in the level 1 CPU cache. Loading more data into CPUs once again improved performance.

To improve compression, SAP HANA prefers *columnar storage*. Along with many advantages, columnar storage also has a few disadvantages: Inserting new records and updating existing records are not handled as efficiently in column tables as in row tables. To solve this, SAP HANA implemented the *insert-only principle* with *delta buffers*. We use row storage for delta buffers to improve insert speeds and then use *delta merges* to bring the data back to columnar storage, which leads to better read performance.

> **Tip**
>
> The performance improvements in SAP HANA do not mean that we can be negligent in modeling. For example, you should not use SELECT * statements or choose any unnecessary fields in queries, because doing so decreases the efficiency of the column storage.

Using multicore processors, everything in SAP HANA was designed from the ground up to run in parallel. Even a single aggregation value is calculated using parallelism. This led to SAP HANA growing from a single hardware appliance to a distributed scale-out system that can work across multiple server nodes and finally to multitenant database containers. Tables can now also be partitioned across multiple servers. With more servers, the scale and performance of SAP HANA systems has vastly advanced.

## Redesigned and Optimized Applications

While combining memory and processors, we also saw that moving data from memory to application servers is not the optimal way to work with an in-memory database. It makes more sense to push down some of the application logic to the SAP HANA system for fast access to the data in memory and plenty of computing resources for calculations.

SAP started by making SAP HANA available as an accelerator and sidecar solution to improve issues with long-running processes in current systems. Over time, SAP business applications were migrated to SAP HANA and re-engineered to make use of the advantages it offers.

With SAP S/4HANA, we now have a system that uses views instead of material-ized aggregates in lookup tables, significantly reducing the size of the system, simplifying the code, and enriching the user experience.

## Information Modeling Techniques

In previous chapters, we discussed some techniques that can help optimize infor-mation models, such as the following:

▸ Limit data as quickly as possible. Do this by defining filters on the source data, applying variables in your SAP HANA views, and selecting only the fields that you require in your query results. Also, let SAP HANA perform the calcula-tions and send only the results to a business application, instead of sending lots of data to the application and performing the calculations there.

▸ Perform calculations as late as possible. For example, perform aggregation before calculation in analytic views.

▸ Use referential joins when your data has referential integrity. When working with referential integrity, you do not have to evaluate the join for all queries.

▸ Similarly, use dynamic joins to optimize the join performance for certain que-ries.

▸ Join tables on key fields.

▸ Use a union instead of a join for combining large sets of data; make unions even more efficient by using union pruning.

▸ Only use a single fact table in a data foundation of a star join view.

▸ Build up your information views in layers.

If you use these techniques, you will avoid many optimization hazards. These techniques should be part of your everyday workflow.

 **Tip**

The best optimization is no optimization. If you avoid the pitfalls in this chapter, you will not need to optimize later.

In spite of your best efforts, sometimes you need to optimize an information model.

## Optimization Tools

When optimizing an SAP HANA information model, a number of tools are at your disposal. You need to know when to pick which optimization tool and how to use it.

### SAP HANA Engines

SAP HANA has several internal components called *engines*. Each of these engines is optimized to provide specific functionality for the processing of SAP HANA information models:

▸ **Row engine**
The row engine is used for processing data from row tables and certain features that are traditionally expected from relational databases.

▸ **Column engine**
This engine processes data from the column table and associated features.

▸ **Join engine**
Dimension views almost exclusively use joins between tables and therefore send most of their processing to the join engine.

▸ **OLAP engine**
Star join views are OLAP "cubes." The OLAP engine specializes in handling cube-type processes and is traditionally associated with analytic views.

▸ **Calculation engine**
Calculation views and calculated columns use the calculation engine. The spatial engine is added functionality in the calculation engine that provides the spatial capabilities of SAP HANA.

▸ **SQL engine**
This engine is used for processing the SAP HANA Live models, which are mostly focused on relational processes.

These engines work together to process information models. However, transferring information from one engine to another can affect performance.

 **Tip**

Reduce the amount of data transferred between the engines.

A better idea of how this process between engine works can be seen when using a star join view with calculated columns. In this case, SAP HANA might use the OLAP engine for processing the star join view and the calculation engine for processing the calculated columns. If you plan to use a calculation view of type cube on top of the star join view later, it might make sense to move the calculated columns to the calculation view of type cube. This is in line with our general recommendation to calculate as late as possible.

**Note**

As SAP HANA improves and matures, there will be less emphasis on the engines and the transfer between engines. With SAP HANA now providing a migration tool to help move to calculation views, this implies less emphasis on knowing about and compensating for the transfer between engines.

Now that you have a better understanding of SAP HANA's engines, in the next section we'll begin discussing the tools available for optimizing performance.

### Explain Plan

One of the purposes of the *Explain Plan* tool is to show which engines are used when processing an information model and if there is a transfer between engines involved. It also shows what operators are processed—for example, a join, a column table, a column search, or a filter. This tool does not provide any information about the actual processing, such as how many records were processed or how long it took.

You can access the Explain Plan tool from the context menu of the SQL Console.

**Tip**

There is a quick way to reach any SAP HANA view from the SQL Console window: Right-click the name of the view in the CONTENT area and select the GENERATE SELECT SQL option from the context menu. This will open a SQL editor with an equivalent SQL query for the selected information view.

Figure 10.1 shows the Purchase Overview calculation view, opened from the SHINE content. From the context menu in the SQL Console, choose the EXPLAIN PLAN option to launch the tool for this SQL query.

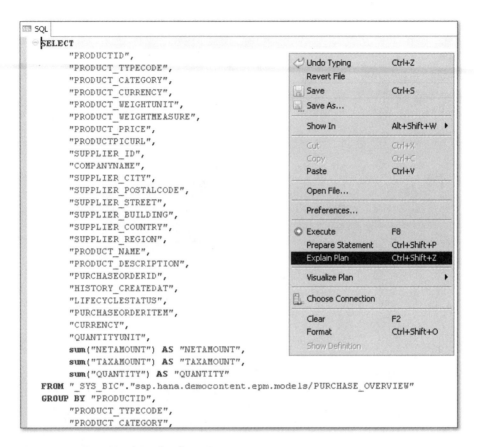

**Figure 10.1**   Open Explain Plan from Context Menu

Figure 10.2 shows the Explain Plan with the SQL query on the top and the execution engines and the names of the operators used when running the SQL query. In the OPERATOR DETAILS column, you can see which tables are used here.

**Visualize Plan**

From the same context menu in the SQL Console, you can also launch the *Visualize Plan* tool. The Visualize Plan tool has two options, as shown in Figure 10.3: PREPARE and EXECUTE.

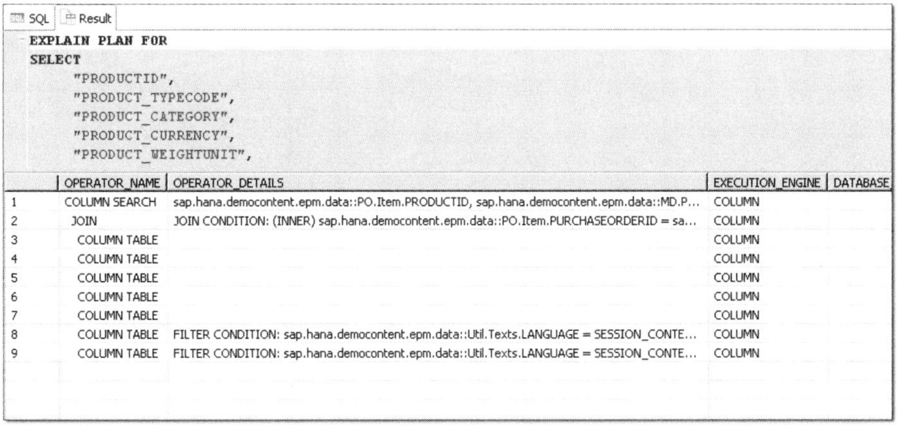

**Figure 10.2** Explain Plan

**Figure 10.3** Visualize Plan Context Menu Options in SQL Console

The Visualize Plan tool visually shows how the SQL query will be prepared and executed. Figure 10.4 illustrates the prepared execution plan. The bottom row shows the various column tables that will be read, and the lines going to the next block up (a join node) show how many records will be read from each table. The join node output again shows the number of rows.

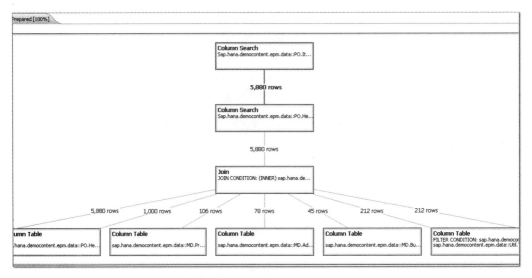

**Figure 10.4**   Prepared Execution Plan Visualized

This information is helpful when you want to reduce the data transferred between layers as quickly as possible or filter as early as possible, as recommended. You can view the prepared plan and find out how many records will be generated in the result set. Then, you can apply a filter, for example, and rerun the prepared plan to see the difference.

Once you've viewed the prepared execution plan, you can execute the SAP HANA information model and call the Visualize Plan tool for the executed plan. You will see the OVERVIEW tab (Figure 10.5).

From the OVERVIEW tab, you can see how long the query took, how much memory it used, the number of tables that were used, and how many records were returned in the result set.

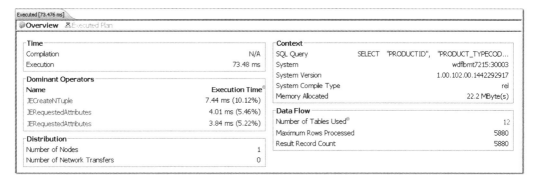

**Figure 10.5**  Executed Plan Overview Tab

Next to the OVERVIEW tab is the EXECUTED PLAN tab, which shows the executed plan visually, with the execution times for each operator block. You can expand an operator block by clicking on the small triangle at the top-right of the block (see Figure 10.6). Here, you can see the execution time for every block and how many records are passed between the operations.

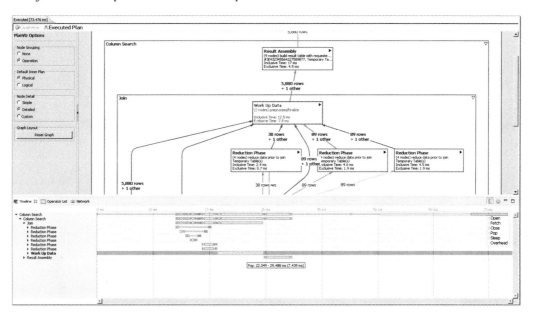

**Figure 10.6**  Executed Plan Visualization and Timeline View

Figure 10.6 also shows the *timeline view*, which presents timelines for various operations. The top and bottom portions of the screen are linked, so if you select a line on the timeline view, the corresponding operations block in the top graph is selected as well.

Next to the TIMELINE tab, you'll see the OPERATOR LIST tab (Figure 10.7), which provides more detail on every operator used when executing the query.

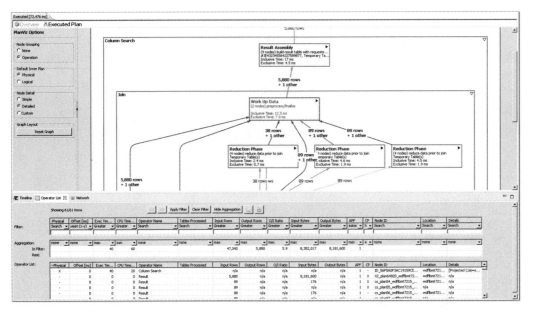

**Figure 10.7**   Executed Plan Visualization and Operator List

As you can see, the Visualize Plan is a powerful tool that can help you optimize SAP HANA information models.

### Administration Console

We briefly mentioned the Administration Console in Chapter 5. There are three tabs that are especially relevant to optimization:

▶ PERFORMANCE
The PERFORMANCE tab has several subtabs. The SQL PLAN CACHE subtab (shown in Figure 10.8) contains a list of all the SQL statements executed in the SAP HANA system. You can sort this list according to certain criteria, such as the amount of memory used, the number of rows returned, and execution time. That way, you can find the 10 statements that took the most memory

quickly and discover where the memory in your SAP HANA system disappeared to.

You can open any of the SQL statements in the Visualize Plan or in the SQL Console, where you can test variations and measure the impact of your changes.

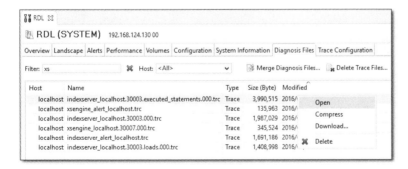

**Figure 10.8**    SQL Plan Cache Subtab in Administrator Console

▶ DIAGNOSIS FILES
  Next is the DIAGNOSIS FILES tab. Figure 10.9 shows a list of trace and log files. We filtered this list to the "xs" search string, meaning that it only shows files that have "xs" in the file name. You can read these files in SAP HANA studio, or if they're too large, you can download them. You can download them as-is or compressed in a ZIP file.

**Figure 10.9**    Filtered List of Trace and Log Files in Diagnosis Files Tab

These trace and log files can provide detailed process information, and SAP HANA can trace very specific events; for example, you can limit a trace file to a specific user or application.

▶ TRACE CONFIGURATION
To set up specific traces, use the TRACE CONFIGURATION tab, shown in Figure 10.10. This tab allows you to set up various trace configurations. We won't go into any detail about available trace configurations here; this information is discussed in SAP HANA technical training, because these traces are normally executed by SAP HANA database or system administrators. You'll need to work with your SAP HANA administrator if you want to run any traces.

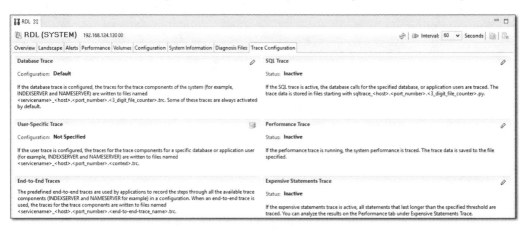

**Figure 10.10**   The Trace Configuration tab of the Administration Console.

## Performance Analysis Mode

The last tool that we will look at in this chapter is *Performance Analysis Mode*, available from the top-right toolbar when you build SAP HANA information views.

You can switch this mode on or off when designing information views. The tool will analyze your view and suggest possible improvements.

Figure 10.11 shows the dropdown menu for Performance Analysis Mode. The first menu option allows you to switch this mode on or off.

**Figure 10.11**   Performance Analysis Mode Menu

Before we discuss the main features of Performance Analysis Mode, let's briefly detour to look at the last option on the menu shown in Figure 10.11. The VISU-ALIZE VIEW IN PLANVIZ EDITOR option opens a simplified graphical flow of the information view (Figure 10.12).

When you select a node, you can see the attributes and measures on the left of the graphical flow and the input and output fields on the right.

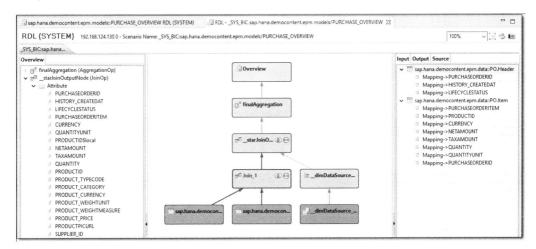

**Figure 10.12**   Visualize View Called from Performance Analysis Mode Menu

Go back to the Performance Analysis Mode and you will notice that a new tab, PERFORMANCE ANALYSIS, has been added to the VIEW EDITOR in which you design the information view. When you select a node—for example, the join node—in your view, and then then open the PERFORMANCE ANALYSIS tab (top middle), you will now see improvement recommendations from the SAP HANA system.

Figure 10.13 returns to the Purchase Overview calculation view from the SHINE content.

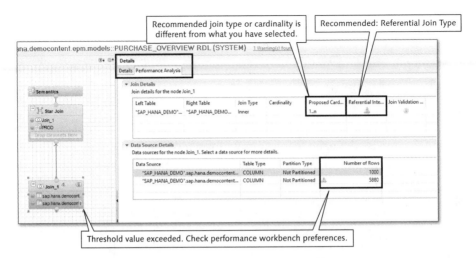

**Figure 10.13**  Performance Analysis Mode Optimization Suggestions

As shown in Figure 10.13, we've highlighted three possible improvement suggestions:

► **Recommended join type or cardinality is different from what you have selected.**
In this case, we did not specify any cardinality on the join. SAP HANA analyzed the data and view and suggested that a 1..n cardinality should be set. Setting the cardinality will allow SAP HANA to execute the view faster, because it won't have to calculate what the cardinality is first.

► **Recommended: Referential join type.**
SAP HANA looked at the data to see if referential integrity was ensured. Because there is referential integrity in this case, SAP HANA suggested that a referential join would be better in the join node of this view.

► **Threshold value exceeded. Check performance workbench preferences.**
Here, SAP HANA looked at how many records will be returned by the join. If the number of records exceeds a threshold, SAP HANA suggests that partitioning the table could speed up the join. The system shows us information about the number of rows and the partitions.

Figure 10.14 shows additional information for when you're joining tables from remote sources using SAP HANA smart data access (SDA). (We will discuss SDA in Chapter 14.)

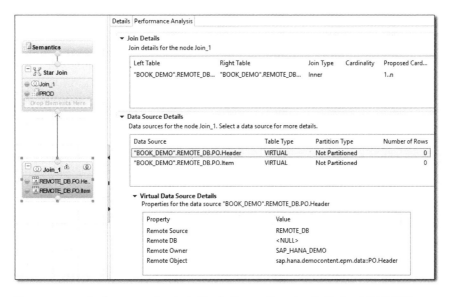

**Figure 10.14**   Performance Analysis Mode Suggestions to Optimize SAP HANA Information View Built on Virtual Tables

You can set validation rules related to performance in the SAP HANA studio preferences. From the WINDOW menu, select PREFERENCES • SAP HANA • MODELER • VALIDATION RULES. Figure 10.15 shows validation rules related to performance.

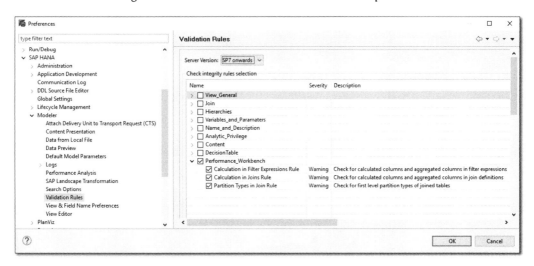

**Figure 10.15**   Validation Rules Related to Performance in SAP HANA Studio

## Best Practices for Optimization

Performance Analysis Mode suggested some improvements we could make to our information view with regards to specifying the cardinality, using a referential join, and potentially partitioning our tables. In this last section, we will discuss some additional best practices for modeling in SAP HANA. Remember that we mentioned a few earlier in the chapter when we summarized concepts you've learned previously in the book.

We can divide these best practices into two areas—namely, those related to the graphical view design and those related to SQL and SQLScript.

### Graphic Information Modeling Best Practices

The following are some additional best practices to optimize graphical information models:

▸ Minimize data transfer between SAP HANA execution engines.

▸ Reduce data transfer between information views.

▸ Implement filters at a table level.

▸ Don't send all information to the analytics and reporting tools; instead, make your reports more interactive and make multiple smaller requests from SAP HANA. The SAP HANA system will use less memory, be more efficient, and respond faster. With less data moving across the network, the user experience improves. In addition, by sending less information to the analytics and reporting tools, you make these tools more mobile-friendly.

▸ Select only the fields you require; columnar databases don't like working with all the columns.

▸ Specify the cardinality in a join.

▸ Use left outer rather than right outer joins.

▸ Investigate whether partitioning your tables is a valid option.

▸ Let SAP HANA do hard work like aggregations and calculations.

**Tip**

Remember that SAP HANA uses authorizations as a filter. If a user is only allowed to see one cost center, then SAP HANA will use that as a filter to speed up the query. In this case, security is not an overhead as in many other systems but an optimization technique.

### SQL and SQLScript Guidelines

We mentioned several best practices for optimizing SQL and SQLScript in Chapter 8, including the following:

▶ Do not use SELECT * statements.

▶ Try to avoid imperative logic with a loop or branch logic. SQL uses a set-oriented approach for best performance.

▶ Break large, complex SQL statements into smaller independent steps using SQLScript variables. This can improve the parallelization of the execution of the query.

▶ Use procedures or GROUPING SETS to return multiple results sets.

 **Tip**

For more optimization and performance tips, watch Werner Steyn's excellent one-hour session, named DMM208, from SAP TechEd 2015 at *http://events.sap.com/teched/en/session/26543*.

You can also attend the HA215 training course. You can find more information about this course at *https://training.sap.com/shop/course/ha215-sap-hana-monitoring-and-performance-tuning-classroom-010-g-en/*.

## Important Terminology

In this chapter, we covered the following important topics:

▶ **Architecture and performance**
We started this chapter by reviewing the architecture design principles of SAP HANA and how everything contributes to optimal system performance. We

also summarized some of the best practices you've already learned in your information modeling journey.

▸ **Explain Plan**
The Explain Plan tool shows the different engines used by SAP HANA to execute a query, along with a list of operators.

▸ **Visualize Plan**
The Visualize Plan tool shows graphical flows for both the prepared and the executed plans. We can see the number of records returned per operator in the prepared plan and the number of records along with the time each step of the query took in the executed plan. We can also combine the graphical flow with a timeline and an operator list.

▸ **Administration Console**
The Administration Console provides access to the SQL cache of all SQL statements previously run in the SAP HANA system. We can also create and read trace files for identifying exactly what happens in the SAP HANA system when a query is executed.

▸ **Performance Analysis Mode**
The Performance Analysis Mode provides suggestions while we are designing a view to potentially improve performance. This tool looks, for example, at join types, referential integrity, cardinality, and partitioning.

▸ **Best practices**
Finally, we looked at some best practices for ensuring that SAP HANA information models perform optimally.

## 🐾 Practice Questions

These practice questions will help you evaluate your understanding of the topics covered in this chapter. The questions shown are similar in nature to those found on the certification examination. Although none of these questions will be found on the exam itself, they will allow you to review your knowledge of the subject. Select the correct answers and then check the completeness of your answers in the Practice Question Answers and Explanations section. Remember that on the exam you must select all correct answers and only correct answers to receive credit for the question.

1. What combination enabled real-time computing?

   ☐ **A.** In-memory technology with solid-state disks

   ☐ **B.** In-memory technology and multicore CPUs

   ☐ **C.** Multicore CPUs and solid-state disks

   ☐ **D.** Multicore CPUs with large level 1 caches

2. What are the advantages of columnar storage? (There are 2 correct answers.)

   ☐ **A.** Improved compression

   ☐ **B.** Improved data reading performance

   ☐ **C.** Improved data writing performance

   ☐ **D.** Improved performance when all fields are selected

> **Tip**
>
> The following five items list almost exactly the same question, but the answers are different each time.

3. What performance technique should you implement to improve join performance?

   ☐ **A.** Use joins instead of unions for combining large data sets.

   ☐ **B.** Join on key fields between tables in a dimension view.

   ☐ **C.** Do NOT use dynamic joins if you require optimal performance.

   ☐ **D.** Always use referential joins in star join views.

4. What performance techniques should you implement to improve join performance? (There are 3 correct answers.)

   ☐ **A.** Use unions instead of joins for combining large data sets.

   ☐ **B.** Always specify the cardinality of a join.

   ☐ **C.** Join as many tables as possible in an analytic view's data foundation.

   ☐ **D.** Use left outer joins instead of right outer joins.

   ☐ **E.** Always mark joins as dynamic to improve performance.

5.  What performance technique should you implement to improve the performance of SAP HANA information views?

☐   **A.** Build single large views.

☐   **B.** Implement union pruning conditions.

☐   **C.** Output as many fields as possible.

☐   **D.** Supply reporting tools with all the data in one transfer.

6.  What performance technique should you implement to improve the performance of SAP HANA information views that include SQLScript?

☐   **A.** Use imperative logic.

☐   **B.** Use SELECT *.

☐   **C.** Break large statements into smaller steps.

☐   **D.** Use dynamic SQL.

7.  What performance techniques should you implement to improve the performance of SAP HANA information views? (There are 3 correct answers.)

☐   **A.** Perform calculation before aggregation in your analytic views.

☐   **B.** Minimize the transfer of data between the execution engines.

☐   **C.** Investigate partitioning of large tables.

☐   **D.** Apply filters as late as possible.

☐   **E.** Push down aggregations to SAP HANA.

8.  What engine executes the spatial queries?

☐   **A.** Calculation

☐   **B.** OLAP

☐   **C.** Join

☐   **D.** SQL

9.  What information can you find in the Explain Plan tool? (There are 2 correct answers.)

☐   **A.** The execution engines used

☐   **B.** The number of records returned in each step

☐   **C.** The time taken for each step

☐   **D.** The list of operators

10.  What information can you find in the Visualize Plan tool? (There are 2 correct answers.)

☐   **A.** The execution engines used

☐   **B.** The number of records returned in each step

☐   **C.** The time taken for each step

☐   **D.** The SQL Plan Cache

11.  What information can you find in the Administration Console? (There are 2 correct answers.)

☐   **A.** The execution engines used

☐   **B.** The trace and log files

☐   **C.** The list of operators

☐   **D.** The SQL Plan Cache

12.  What information can you find in Performance Analysis Mode when you view the analysis for a join node? (There are 2 correct answers.)

☐   **A.** The suggested filter for the tables in the join node

☐   **B.** The total number of records returned by the node

☐   **C.** The time taken by the join

☐   **D.** The tables used by the join in the node

## Practice Question Answers and Explanations

1.  Correct answer: **B**

The combination of in-memory technology and multicore CPUs enabled real-time computing. Solid-state disks are still disks and relatively slow compared to memory. Multicore CPUs with large level 1 caches help, but also need in-memory technology.

2. Correct answers: **A, B**

The advantages of columnar storage include improved compression and data-reading performance. (Because data is compressed, you can read more data at the same IO speed.) Improved data-writing performance is for row storage. Neither column nor row has improved performance when all fields are selected via SELECT *.

3. Correct answer: **B**

Joining on key fields between tables in a dimension view will improve join performance. The answer "Use joins instead of unions for combining large data sets" has joins and unions swapped around: You should use unions rather than joins. Dynamic joins are created to improve performance. The word *always* makes the "Always use referential joins" answer wrong.

4. Correct answers: **A, B, D**

The following are the correct performance techniques to improve join performance:

▸ Use unions instead of joins for combining large data sets.

▸ Always specify the cardinality of a join.

▸ Use left outer joins instead of right outer joins.

You should try to use only one table in an analytic view's data foundation. The word *always* makes the "Always mark joins as dynamic" answer wrong.

5. Correct answer: **B**

Implementing union pruning conditions will improve the performance of SAP HANA information views. You should not build a single large view; instead, build views up in layers. Use SAP HANA Live as an example. "Output as many fields as possible" is another way of saying "Use SELECT *"; don't do it. Instead, supply reporting tools with only the data they need right now, make them interactive, and use multiple small requests.

6. Correct answer: **C**

Breaking large statements into smaller steps will improve the performance of SAP HANA information views that include SQLScript. Do NOT use imperative logic, SELECT *, or dynamic SQL if you need optimal performance.

7. Correct answers: **B, C, E**

The following are the performance techniques you can implement to improve the performance of SAP HANA information views:

► Minimize the transfer of data between execution engines.

► Investigate partitioning of large tables.

► Push down aggregations to SAP HANA.

"Calculation before aggregation" is reversed; to be correct, it should say "aggregation before calculation." Filters should be applied as early as possible.

8. Correct answer: **A**

   The calculation engine executes the spatial queries.

9. Correct answers: **A, D**

   The Explain Plan tool shows the execution engines used and the list of operators.

10. Correct answers: **B, C**

    The Visualize Plan tool shows the number of records returned and the time taken in each step.

    The Explain Plan tool shows the execution engines used, and the Administration Console shows the SQL Plan Cache.

11. Correct answers: **B, D**

    The Administration Console shows the SQL Plan Cache and the trace and log files. The Explain Plan tool shows the execution engines used. The Explain Plan and Visualize Plan tools show the operators used.

12. Correct answers: **B, D**

    Performance Analysis Mode shows the total number of records returned and the tables used.

## Takeaway

You now have a checklist of modeling practices to ensure optimal performance for SAP HANA information models, including guidelines for creating optimal SQL and SQLScript.

You have learned how to use the Explain Plan tool to identify the execution engines used and the Visualize Plan tool to find the time taken and number of records returned for every step in a query.

You can use the Administration Console to identify long-running and expensive statements and to perform traces of specific queries and user activities. Performance Analysis Mode helps improve your SAP HANA information models by providing optimization suggestions.

## Summary

You've seen that SAP HANA has been built from the ground up with many performance enhancements to enable high-performing processes. However, you still have to do your part if you expect the best results.

You've now created SAP HANA information models with graphical views and with SQL and SQLScript. You've also learned how to optimize your information models.

In the next chapter, we'll look at how to deploy your finished SAP HANA information models to a production environment.

# Administration of Information Models

**11**

## Techniques You'll Master

▶ Learn how to validate information models

▶ Understand the activation process

▶ Explain the difference between design-time and runtime objects

▶ Learn the transport process for importing and exporting objects

▶ Understand schema mapping

▶ Describe delivery units

▶ Perform refactoring techniques on information models

▶ Document modeling work

▶ Translate information models into other languages

Up to this point, we provided overviews of and instructions for creating information models. In this chapter, we'll look at the steps you need to take to ensure your models are valid. In addition, we'll walk through how to bring these models into a production environment so end users can utilize them. You'll learn how to validate, activate, transport, refactor, document, and translate your information models.

> ### Real-World Scenario
>
> You have created new information models for your project. All the modeling work was performed in your development system. You feel confident about the work you have delivered, so now it's time to take it to the production system. You need to transport your information models through the SAP HANA landscape. Before end users can use your information models in the production system, your models need to be activated in the production system.
>
> As the project progresses, new customer requirements arise. Your information models need to adapt to changing business conditions. You ensure they do so by using the refactoring tools built into the SAP HANA modeling tools. Also, because your end users are scattered across the globe, you have to translate your information models into various languages.
>
> As your project approaches the final go-live date, you must ensure that your information models are properly documented.

## Objectives of This Portion of the Test

The objective of this portion of the SAP HANA certification is to test your understanding of how to administrate the information models you have built.

The certification exam expects SAP HANA data modelers to have a good understanding of the following topics:

- Validating and activating models
- The difference between design-time and runtime objects
- The transport process, exporting and importing information objects, delivery units, and schema mapping

▶ Refactoring information models

▶ Documenting and translating information models

 **Note**

This portion contributes up to 10% of the total certification exam score.

## Key Concepts Refresher

Many of the concepts in this chapter will help you deploy the solutions you build into a live environment for end users. As such, you will start working more closely with an SAP HANA system administrator at this point. Typically, export and import duties are performed mostly by the system administrator.

Some other concepts, like refactoring, are used in larger projects to ensure your modeling work stays fresh and useful. The idea is similar to gardening: You need to mow the lawn, pull weeds, and prune the roses to maintain a beautiful garden. This idea of upkeep can be applied to the administration of your data models.

### Validating and Activating Information Models

Before end users can use your information models, you need to ensure that they are both valid and available to the users. In SAP HANA, *validation rules* are used to check for possible errors that may affect the usability of your models. Once you've worked out all the kinks, you'll need to activate the models to make them available.

#### Validation Rules

SAP HANA has built-in validation rules for the different types of information models and modeling objects. These validation rules check for possible syntax errors and missing properties. When you request a validation run, SAP HANA applies the relevant validation rules to your information model.

Here are some example validation checks:

▶ That a language column is specified when you use a text join (without a specified language column, the text join will not have a 1:1 cardinality)

▶  That a dimension view has at least one attribute specified as the key attribute

▶  If filter values are valid

▶  That a calculation view does not have any floating (orphan) nodes

▶  That there there are no unjoined (orphan) tables in a view

▶  If attributes or measures are defined for large object data types (e.g., `BLOB` or `CLOB`)

You can access the validation rules (see Figure 11.1) in SAP HANA studio by selecting PREFERENCES from the WINDOW menu. Drill down the tree to SAP HANA • MODELER • VALIDATION RULES.

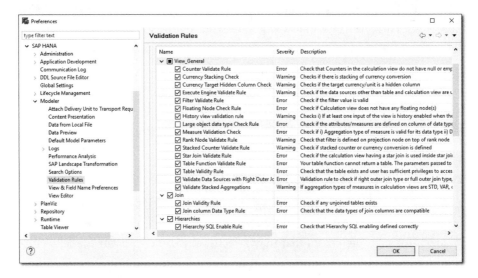

**Figure 11.1**    Validation Rules in SAP HANA Studio

When your information model is ready, you can validate it by clicking the SAVE AND VALIDATE button on the toolbar, as shown in Figure 11.2. You can also SAVE the model and then use the model's context menu to VALIDATE it.

If the system finds an error during validation, you will see a message in the JOB LOG tab in SAP HANA studio (Figure 11.3). Double-click the error message to open the dialog box shown in Figure 11.4. Read the message carefully to understand why SAP HANA does not accept the model as valid. (In this case, you did not specify one of the attributes as a key attribute. To fix this, you will specify one of your attributes as a key attribute in the semantic layer.)

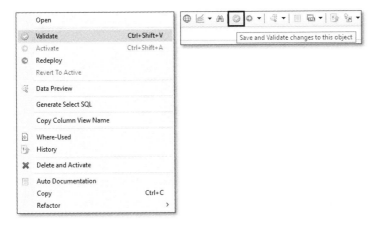

**Figure 11.2**  Validating an Information Model

**Figure 11.3**  Error Found When Validating an Information Model

**Figure 11.4**  Validation Error Dialog Box

**Tip**

With complex data models, the problem often lies in the way you created the joins, so recheck your joins. Often, the easiest way to fix a problem with joins is to delete and recreate the joins.

**Activation**

The next step to get your information models ready for use is to *activate* them. When you click the Save and Activate button on the toolbar (Figure 11.5), SAP HANA creates an "active" copy of the information model. This active copy is then used by end users.

**Figure 11.5**    Activating an Information Model

**Tip**

We recommend that you get into the habit of using the Save and Activate button. It saves the information model, checks it against the relevant validation rules, and creates an active version. You do not need to perform a Save and Validate action first.

We have seen modelers become confused when using the Activate menu option alone. They try to activate their model and get errors. After solving the errors, they try to activate again, but keep getting the same errors. This is because they forget to click the Save button before activating the model again. Therefore, SAP HANA activated the last saved copy on the server, which still has the same error. Only when they save their changes to the server will SAP HANA activate the latest version that includes the corrections.

By using the Save and Activate button as we recommend, you can avoid this kind of situation.

Let's dive a little deeper into this activation process.

When you create and validate an information model, it is saved in the Content area of the Systems view. The objects stored here are called *repository objects* or *design-time objects*. These objects are merely definitions (metadata) for what SAP

HANA should create when running the information models. They are seen as the "inactive" versions, and end users cannot run them.

When you activate an information model, SAP HANA first checks the model against the validation rules. It then creates an "active copy" of the model in the _SYS_BIC schema. When you activate the calculation view CV_CALCVIEW_DEMO, you will find the "active copy" of that model in the COLUMN VIEWS folder of the _SYS_BIC schema, as shown in Figure 11.6.

This "active copy" is referred to as the *runtime version* of the object. End users can only run the active versions of objects. All runtime versions are stored in the CATALOG area of the SYSTEMS view.

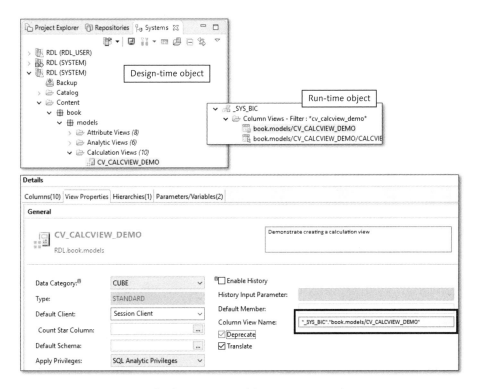

**Figure 11.6**  Active Copy of Information Models in _SYS_BIC Schema

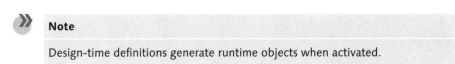

**Note**

Design-time definitions generate runtime objects when activated.

If you edit and save (without activating) this information model, you will have two copies of the object on the server: An active runtime version, which users can still use, and a new inactive *design-time version* that you are busy modifying.

You can switch between the active and the inactive versions in the SAP HANA modeling tools via the dropdown menu (see Figure 11.7). If your new model won't activate or contains any sort of similar error, you can compare the two versions to see what was changed and adjust accordingly.

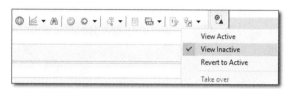

**Figure 11.7**  Switching between Active and Inactive Information Model Versions

If you do not want to keep changes to the information model, choose the REVERT TO ACTIVE option (see Figure 11.7). SAP HANA then discards your changes and resets the design-time version back to the runtime version. You can only revert to a changed version you saved, but have not yet activated. Once you've activated the new version, you cannot revert to a previous version any longer.

If you are happy with your changes, you can activate the new version with the changes made. The existing runtime version is replaced by the newer version of the information model, provided your model passes the validation rules.

SAP HANA uses the _SYS_REPO user to execute activated models. To do this, the _SYS_REPO user must be able to read the tables in your schema. Otherwise, your information views cannot be activated. We discuss how to do this in Chapter 13.

## Transporting Information Models

When working with SAP systems, you will have to deal with *transports*. SAP systems are used by many of the largest corporations in the world and for mission-critical systems. These corporations expect the SAP production (live) systems to be exceptionally stable and robust. If someone frequently makes changes directly to a running production system, the chance of making a mistake becomes quite large. For this reason, SAP established a standard way to deploy SAP systems and update them to increase stability.

In a standard SAP environment, you will find three systems instead of just a single production system, as shown in Figure 11.8:

▶ **Development system**
This is where all of your modeling and development work is done. Once the development work is finished, it is copied ("transported") to the quality assurance system.

▶ **Quality assurance system**
This is where all testing is done before moving to the production system. The quality assurance system is normally a recent copy of the production system. Any errors created in this system would also create errors in the production system. By catching them here, we can ensure an error-free production environment. When all errors have been fixed, the error-free development and modeling work is finally transported to the production system. This setup is important for ensuring stable business systems.

▶ **Production system**
This is the area where companies' business activities occur and where end users perform functions for their daily work.

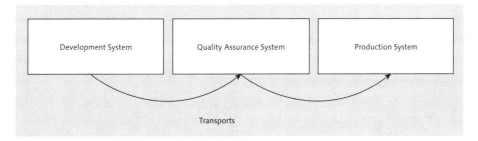

**Figure 11.8**  Standard SAP System Landscape

You can copy all your SAP HANA packages, information models, and objects to quality assurance and production systems using transports. You can also use transports to update the sandbox ("playpen") and training systems.

In SAP HANA, you can combine several packages with all their modeling objects into a single artifact called a *delivery unit*. A delivery unit therefore consists of one or more packages. Each package in a delivery unit can contain many information models.

> **Note**
>
> You can only transport design-time objects with delivery units (i.e., those con-
> tained in the REPOSITORY or CONTENT areas). You cannot transport runtime objects
> (e.g., tables with their content).

In the following subsections, we will discuss the different methods for importing and exporting information models in SAP HANA. We'll begin with a general
discussion on importing and exporting content, before diving into special topics
including using the SAP HANA Application Lifecycle Manager, exporting extra
data, importing objects via scheme mapping and mass copy, and comparing
native vs. imported objects.

### Importing and Exporting from the Development System to the Quality Assurance and Production Systems

The first method that you can use to transport your SAP HANA modeling work
is to export it from the development system and then import it into the quality
assurance and production systems.

You can access the IMPORT and EXPORT options from either the QUICK VIEW menu
in the Modeling perspective or from the FILE • EXPORT and FILE • IMPORT menu
options.

Figure 11.9 shows the EXPORT dialog screen.

Here, we opened the SAP HANA CONTENT folder in the dialog box to export SAP
HANA content. The following options are found in this folder:

▶ CHANGE AND TRANSPORT SYSTEM (CTS)
  This option is used by SAP HANA system administrators in cases in which a
  company has many other SAP business systems. They will use the Change and
  Transport System (CTS) of SAP Solution Manager to manage all of the company's SAP transports. This provides control over large volumes of transports
  from all SAP development systems to their respective production systems.

▶ DELIVERY UNIT
  You can use this option to export and import delivery units.

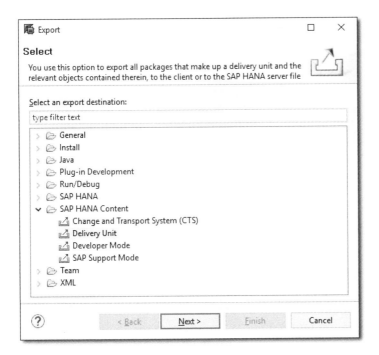

**Figure 11.9**   Importing and Exporting Content from SAP HANA

▶ DEVELOPER MODE
You can manually transport a few selected or individual information models from one system to another by exporting them and importing them into the quality assurance or production system. You can also use this to mode make backups of your own information models.

▶ SAP SUPPORT MODE
When you encounter problems with your SAP HANA system, you can log an SAP message with SAP Support. Sometimes, SAP Support will ask you to send some of your information models so that it can replicate the problem on its own servers. SAP Support will not use your system to try and solve the problem. You can export the relevant information models to SAP Support via this mode.

Figure 11.10 shows the options for exporting a delivery unit. Select the name of the delivery unit you want to export. You can also choose the time period of the latest changes to objects in the delivery unit. Optionally, you can choose whether the delivery unit should be exported to the server or to your client machine (e.g., your laptop).

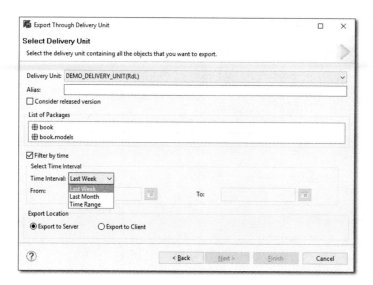

**Figure 11.10**    Exporting a Delivery Unit

    **Tip**

You cannot export and import a package alone. You can transport packages contained in a delivery unit, or you can transport the objects contained inside a package using the developer mode. If you want to transport a single package, the easiest way is to create a new delivery unit containing just that one package.

### Using the SAP HANA Application Lifecycle Manager

Another method you can use to transport your SAP HANA modeling work is to use the SAP HANA Application Lifecycle Manager, shown in Figure 11.11.

You can access this built-in transport tool from the context menu of your SAP HANA system. This is especially useful for companies that do not have other SAP systems or SAP Solution Manager to manage their transports. This web-based interface also works well on larger mobile phones and tablets.

### Exporting Data (Extra)

There is a special method to export and import tables with their data between systems. This method is not automated like transports, but it can still be quite useful—for example, to build a training system.

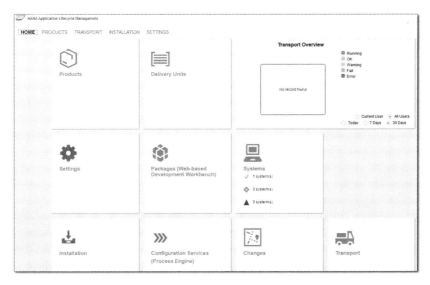

**Figure 11.11**  Transporting SAP HANA Objects Using the SAP HANA Application Lifecycle Manager

Access the same IMPORT and EXPORT menu options as for the transports, but in this case open the SAP HANA folder in the dialog box and select CATALOG OBJECTS (see Figure 11.12) to export SAP HANA data tables.

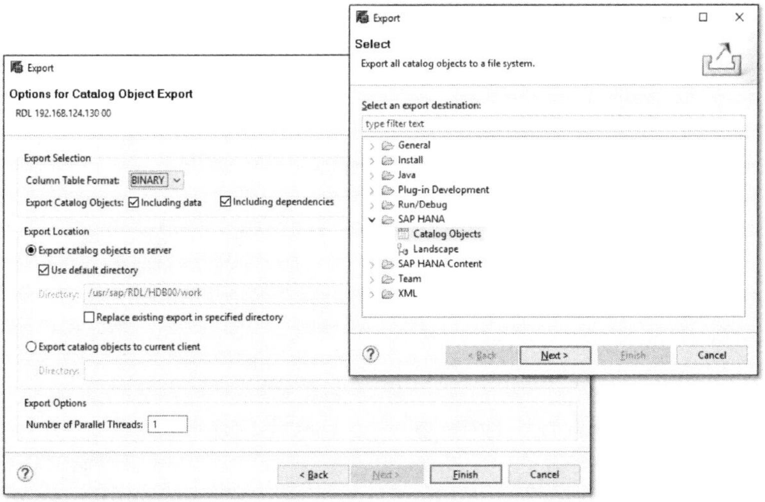

**Figure 11.12**  Exporting Data Tables

You can export the tables in either CSV or binary format.

### Importing Objects with Schema Mapping

Sometimes, you may find that a schema in a development system is named differently than a similar schema in the production system. If someone named the original schema SALES_DEV in a development system, such a name makes no sense in the production system. Therefore, it's renamed to SALES in the production system. When you create information models in the development system using the PRODUCTS tables from the SALES_DEV schema, SAP HANA uses the naming convention <schema name>.<table name> (e.g., SALES_DEV.PRODUCTS) for tables used in the models. If you now transport these information models to the production system, the models expect the PRODUCTS table in the SALES_DEV schema. The table has to exist already in this exact location. If the schema or table is not found, you will receive an activation error. In this example, the schema is now simply called SALES, so you will receive an error when transporting the models.

You can work around this problem by using *schema mapping*. You can create such a schema mapping in the production system, as shown in Figure 11.13. You can find the SCHEMA MAPPING functionality in the QUICK VIEW menu (see Figure 11.13).

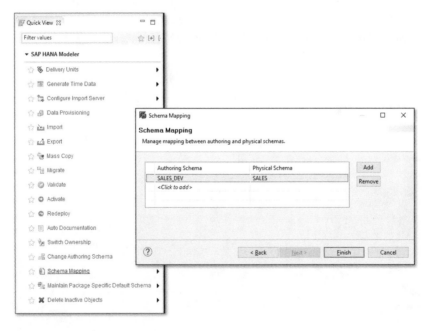

**Figure 11.13**   Schema Mapping

The original schema name in the development system is called the AUTHORING SCHEMA. The target schema in the production system is called the PHYSICAL SCHEMA.

After you set up the schema mapping and import the data models, all references to the SALES_DEV.PRODUCTS table are automatically changed to refer to the SALES.PRODUCTS table. In this case, you do not receive activation errors because the PRODUCTS table already exists in the SALES schema in your production system.

**Hint**

Schema mapping is applied on information models as part of the import process.

### Maintaining a Default Schema for a Package

We can use schema mapping to map multiple authoring schemas to a single target schema. For example, the BOOK_DEMO and SAP_HANA_DEMO authoring schemas might both map to the physical BOOKS schema in the production schema. If you do this, SAP HANA studio might not be able to determine which authoring schema an information model must reference when doing schema mapping.

You can therefore specify the default schema for models in a package. When you import information models contained in such a package into the target schema, SAP HANA studio knows what the authoring schema is, and can perform the mapping to the physical target schema. This is a new feature in SAP HANA SPS 11.

Figure 11.14 shows that the BOOK package is mapped to the BOOK_DEMO schema as its default schema, and the SAP.HANA.DEMOCONTENT package is mapped to the SAP_HANA_DEMO schema as its default schema.

You can leave the PACKAGE NAME field open. In Figure 11.14, we have a blank PACKAGE NAME field, and a DEFAULT SCHEMA named DEFAULT_SCHEMA_FOR_OTHER_PACKAGES. In this case, all other packages in the system that do not have a default schema specified will use this DEFAULT_SCHEMA_FOR_OTHER_PACKAGES schema for their default schema.

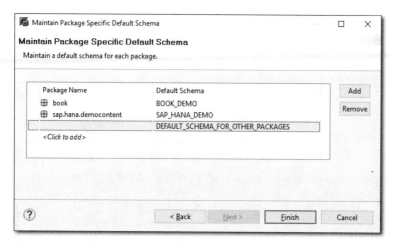

**Figure 11.14**   Maintain Default Schemas for Packages

### Importing Objects with Mass Copy

In the QUICK VIEW menu (see Figure 11.13), you can find the MASS COPY option. Mass copy allows you to copy many information models at the same time and keep the references between the copied models consistent. All references are updated automatically. For example, you could create a limited SAP HANA sandbox (playpen) environment to quickly test some modeling and reporting functionality.

You could also think of this as a "Mass Import" option. The MASS COPY option can be used to import SAP HANA application content created by SAP or SAP partners into your SAP HANA landscape. This application content can consist of many SAP HANA information models and objects.

### Native vs. Imported Objects

To further ensure the stability of production systems, SAP HANA marks all transported objects as *imported objects* in the production system. In the development system, where they were created, they are marked as *native objects*. SAP-created objects will be marked as imported objects in all your systems—even in your development system—because you did not create them.

**Hint**

Imported objects should not be edited. If you want to make changes, you can make a copy of the relevant objects and modify the copy. This ensures that you do not lose all your changes when SAP updates SAP-provided content. When the new version of the SAP content is imported, it will overwrite all the current objects. All your changes would be lost if you modified the imported objects directly.

## Core Data Services

SAP takes the concept of design-time versus runtime objects to the next level with *Core Data Services* (CDS) in SAP HANA (CDS was discussed in Chapter 4). You can think of CDS as a more intelligent activation process that combines with transports to allow activation in other SAP HANA systems as well.

CDS data sources are fully transportable. Previously, you had to ensure that all tables required by your information models were available in the target system before you could import your models, but with CDS data sources, you can now import and activate the data sources together with your information models.

The SHINE demo package is a good example of CDS data sources in action. You do not have to create a schema, tables, or import data into these tables. When SHINE is imported into your SAP HANA system, it automatically creates all that content for you using CDS statements. This means there is no need to do schema mapping in your target system.

## Refactoring Information Models

*Refactoring* is the process of restructuring your information models without changing their external behavior (i.e., their result sets). You do this to improve, simplify, and clarify the design of your models—for example, when you move information models inside the system from one package to another, or when you rename an information model.

You can access the REFACTOR option from the context menu of an information model, as shown in Figure 11.15.

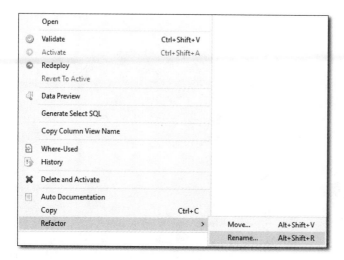

**Figure 11.15**   Refactoring Information Models

Renaming or moving an information model is not always a trivial task. If the information model is used in many other models, you will have to update those models as well. You can easily find yourself having to update hundreds of information models when simply trying to rename a single dimension view.

The REFACTOR option in SAP HANA takes care of this process for you. The only case in which you will still have to manually help with the refactoring process is when the information model is also used in some SQL or SQLScript code, and with updating the security authorization when you move the models to another package.

### Refactoring and Restructuring Nodes in a Graphical Calculation View

Figure 11.16 shows the context menu of a node in a graphical calculation view. From this menu, you can rename the node.

In this case, you can also go further and replace the data sources used in the node, or even replace or delete the entire node. However, such actions are not normally part of refactoring because the result set of the information model will change.

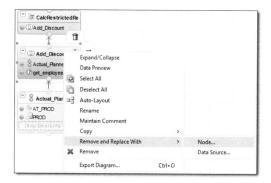

**Figure 11.16** Restructuring and Refactoring Nodes in Graphical Calculation View

 **Tip**

Replacing the data source in a node is useful when you have to create different information models that are based on similar data tables. You can make a copy of an existing view, and then change the data source to a similar table. SAP HANA will ask you to verify the mapping of the old data source to the new data source. It will then keep as much of the current information intact as possible. This can save you many hours of building similar information models.

**Where-Used**

In the refactoring process, you may have to figure out where a specific information model is used. Figure 11.17 shows the context menu of an information model. By selecting the WHERE-USED menu option, SAP HANA finds all the places where that information is used.

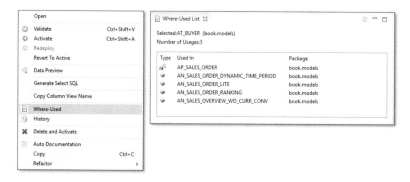

**Figure 11.17** Where-Used List

The WHERE-USED functionality was used in older versions of SAP HANA to find out where to rename an information model. This feature shows you a list of models that use your information model. These models will be affected when you rename the information model, and will therefore also need updating. The new REFACTOR • RENAME feature makes this task much easier. It renames the information model and updates all the models where it is used to ensure everything still works post-renaming. This feature became available as of SAP HANA SPS 10.

### History

Just below the WHERE-USED menu option in the context menu of an information model (Figure 11.17), you will see the HISTORY menu option. The HISTORY feature shows which users updated and activated the current and previous versions of an information model.

### Deprecate

Sometimes, you create a new variation of an information model that is better than the older version. However, you cannot simply get rid of the older version; it might be used in many other information models, and you do not have time to make the necessary changes in all those models. In this case, you can go to the properties of your information model and mark the information model as *deprecated* by selecting the DEPRECATE checkbox, as shown in Figure 11.18.

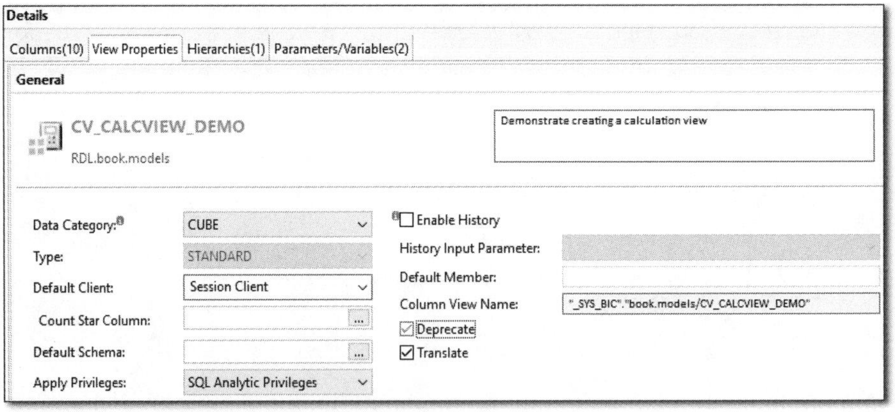

**Figure 11.18**  Deprecating an Information Model

This does not stop the old version of the information model from working. However, it will produce a warning if you or any of your colleagues try to use the old version when creating new models. The MODEL IS DEPRECATED message indicates that everyone should use the newer variation of the information model.

## Documenting Information Models

As you near the end of a modeling project, documentation becomes important. You need to hand your modeling work over to someone else. There are always good reasons for the many decisions you make, such as why the various nodes of a calculation view are in a specific order. Documentation tools and features in SAP HANA allow you to communicate that information to anyone who may work on your project in the future.

### Comments

In SAP HANA, you can document various aspects of information models using comments. Figure 11.19 shows what the comments look like.

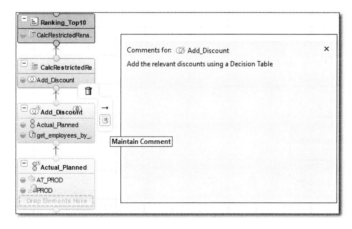

**Figure 11.19**   Documenting a Join Node of a Graphical Calculation View

A yellow comments popup will open when you click on the STICKY NOTE icon.

### Auto Documentation

In the context menu of an information model (see Figure 11.20), you'll find another useful documentation feature: AUTO DOCUMENTATION.

**Figure 11.20**    Auto Documentation Option in an Information Model's Context Menu

The AUTO DOCUMENTATION feature documents graphical information models in SAP HANA. Figure 11.21 shows an example of the output generated.

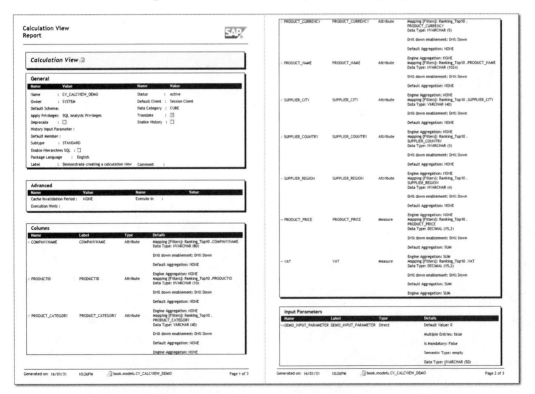

**Figure 11.21**    Example Documentation Generated by Auto Documentation

## Translating Information Models

SAP HANA also provides functionality to help you prepare your information models for consumption by end users who communicate in other languages. In this section, we will focus on the translation of labels and how to use the Repository Translation Tool (RTT).

### Translating Labels

You can open the MULTI-LANGUAGE SUPPORT dialog box (see Figure 11.22) by clicking on the WORLD icon (leftmost icon resembling a globe) on the information model toolbar (refer back to Figure 11.5).

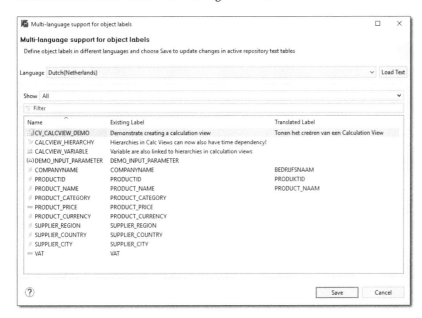

**Figure 11.22**  Translating Information Model Labels

Select the language that you require from the LANGUAGE dropdown menu, and click the LOAD TEXT button. You can then translate all the labels in your information model.

### Repository Translation Tool

SAP HANA also provides a command-line tool known as the *Repository Translation Tool* for exporting, uploading, downloading, and importing language files.

These language files contain all the text of repository objects and are in a standard format for customer or partner usage. Because RTT is a command-line tool, you will need to ask your SAP HANA system administrator for access to it.

## Important Terminology

In this chapter, we covered the following important terminology:

▶ **Validation rules**
SAP HANA has built-in validation rules for the different types of information models and modeling objects. Validation rules check for possible syntax errors and missing properties. When you request a validation run, SAP HANA applies the relevant validation rules to your information model.

▶ **Repository objects (design-time objects)**
These objects are definitions (metadata) for what SAP HANA should create when running information models and are saved in the CONTENT area of the SYSTEMS view. They are seen as the "inactive" versions, and end users cannot run them.

▶ **Runtime version**
When you activate an information model, SAP HANA checks the model against the validation rules, then creates an "active copy" of the information model in the _SYS_BIC schema. This active copy is called a runtime version.

▶ **Development system**
This is where all of your modeling and development work is done.

▶ **Quality assurance system**
This is where all testing is done before moving to the production system. The quality assurance system is normally a recent copy of the production system. Any errors created in this system would also create errors in the production system. By catching them here, you can ensure an error-free production environment.

▶ **Production system**
This is the area where companies' business activities occur and where end users perform functions for their daily work.

▶ **Delivery unit**

A single artifact made up of combined packages that contain all modeling objects. A delivery unit therefore consists of one or more packages. Each package in a delivery unit can contain multiple information models.

▶ **Change and Transport System (CTS)**

Used by SAP HANA system administrators to manage the company's SAP transports.

▶ **Developer Mode (importing and exporting)**

Used to manually transport a few selected or individual information models from one system to another by exporting them and importing them into the quality assurance or production system. You can also use this to mode make backups of your own information models.

▶ **SAP Support Mode (importing and exporting)**

When you encounter problems with your SAP HANA system, you can log an SAP message with SAP Support. You can export the relevant information models to SAP Support via this mode.

▶ **SAP HANA Application Lifecycle Manager**

Built-in transport tool that supports all phases of application lifecycle. This is especially useful for companies that do not have other SAP systems or SAP Solution Manager to manage their transports. This web-based interface also works well on larger mobile phones and tablets.

▶ **Schema mapping**

Used to transport SAP HANA objects from one system to another when physical schema in the target system does not match the authoring scheme in the source system.

▶ **Authoring schema**

Schema used in the development system when building information models.

▶ **Mass copy**

Mass copy allows you to duplicate an information model and where all references from the other models are updated automatically.

▶ **Imported objects**

Objects that originated from another system. These are normally transported objects in the production system. SAP-created objects will be marked as imported objects in all your systems—even in your development system—because you did not create them.

▶ **Native objects**
Original objects in the development system.

▶ **Refactoring**
The process of restructuring your information models without changing their external behavior to improve, simplify, and clarify the design of your models.

▶ **Auto Documentation**
Feature that documents graphical information models in SAP HANA.

## Practice Questions

These practice questions will help you evaluate your understanding of the topics covered in this chapter. The questions shown are similar in nature to those found on the certification examination. Although none of these questions will be found on the exam itself, they will allow you to review your knowledge of the subject. Select the correct answers and then check the completeness of your answers in the Practice Question Answers and Explanations section. Remember that on the exam you must select all correct answers and only correct answers to receive a point for the question.

1.   For which of the following tasks can you use Auto Documentation?

☐   **A.** Documenting all transported information models

☐   **B.** Documenting all graphical information models

☐   **C.** Documenting all activated information models

☐   **D.** Documenting all created information models

2.   Which are valid descriptions of delivery units? (There are 2 correct answers.)

☐   **A.** Always consist of one package

☐   **B.** Are used to transport runtime objects

☐   **C.** Can be exported

☐   **D.** Can be imported

3. Which of the following describe design-time objects? (There are 3 correct answers.)

☐ **A.** Repository objects

☐ **B.** Native objects

☐ **C.** Catalog objects

☐ **D.** Inactive

☐ **E.** Active

4. Which of the following are examples for validation rules? (There are 2 correct answers.)

☐ **A.** Check that tables contain data

☐ **B.** Check formulas in calculated columns

☐ **C.** Check that attribute views have a key attribute specified

☐ **D.** Check that graphical calculation views have no orphan nodes

5. Schema mapping is used during which process?

☐ **A.** Importing

☐ **B.** Activation

☐ **C.** Exporting

☐ **D.** Validation

6. True or False: CDS can improve security in a production environment.

☐ **A.** True

☐ **B.** False

7. Which of the following statements describe a standard SAP system landscape used for transports?

☐ **A.** It consists of only a quality assurance and a production system.

☐ **B.** The quality assurance system is normally a recent copy of the production system.

☐ **C.** Transports go from production to quality assurance.

☐ **D.** You perform development in the quality assurance system.

8.  True or False: CDS only works with runtime objects.

☐  **A.** True

☐  **B.** False

9.  Which statements describe the mass copy feature in SAP HANA? (There are 2 correct answers.)

☐  **A.** It can be used to create a sandbox (playpen) environment.

☐  **B.** It is used to import an application from an SAP partner.

☐  **C.** It is used to transport data tables.

☐  **D.** It can be used to fix models when schemas have different names.

10. In which schema does SAP HANA store an activated graphical calculation view?

☐  **A.** SYSTEM

☐  **B.** SYS

☐  **C.** _SYS_BI

☐  **D.** _SYS_BIC

11. Which tab in SAP HANA studio shows validation check errors?

☐  **A.** PROBLEMS

☐  **B.** PROPERTIES

☐  **C.** HISTORY

☐  **D.** JOB LOG

12. What happens when you activate an information model? ? (There are 2 correct answers.)

☐  **A.** It generates a runtime object.

☐  **B.** It reverts to the active version.

☐  **C.** It checks the validation rules.

☐  **D.** It exports an active version.

13. You want to use a web-based transport system on your Apple iPad. What tool do you use?

□   **A.** SAP Solution Manager

□   **B.** SAP HANA Application Lifecycle Manager

□   **C.** Developer mode

□   **D.** CTS

14. True or False: When you mark an information model as deprecated, it no longer works.

□   **A.** True

□   **B.** False

15. Refactoring is used with which of the following actions?

□   **A.** Improving your modeling design

□   **B.** Translating

□   **C.** Transporting

□   **D.** Documenting

16. Which export option can you use to make backups of your own information models?

□   **A.** CTS

□   **B.** Delivery units

□   **C.** Developer mode

□   **D.** SAP Support mode

17. For what tasks would you use the Where-Used feature in SAP HANA?

□   **A.** To find all places a transport is imported

□   **B.** To find all places where translations exist

□   **C.** To find all places a user updated information models

□   **D.** To find all places an information model is used

18. When do you always have both an active and an inactive version of an information model available in the SAP HANA development system?

☐ **A.** When you edit an existing model

☐ **B.** When you create a new model

☐ **C.** When validation of a model fails

☐ **D.** When you selected REVERT TO ACTIVE on an inactive version

19. Your schemas in development and production have different names. What do you use to ensure you do not receive activation errors when importing information models into production?

☐ **A.** Mass copy

☐ **B.** Schema mapping

☐ **C.** Refactoring

☐ **D.** CDS

20. In which subfolder of the _SYS_BIC schema do you find activated information models?

☐ **A.** COLUMN VIEWS

☐ **B.** PROCEDURES

☐ **C.** VIEWS

☐ **D.** FUNCTIONS

21. Which actions does refactoring typically use? (There are 2 correct answers.)

☐ **A.** Transporting

☐ **B.** Deleting

☐ **C.** Moving

☐ **D.** Renaming

## Practice Question Answers and Explanations

1. Correct answer: **B**

   Auto Documentation is for documenting graphical views (see Figure 11.18). It does not document scripted calculation views. All the other options could contain scripted views. Watch out for the word *all* in the answers.

2. Correct answers: **C, D**

   See Figure 11.9. Delivery units can contain more than one package. Watch out for the word *always* in the answers. Delivery units transport design-time objects, not runtime objects. Once the design-time objects are imported into the SAP HANA system, activation is used to create the corresponding runtime objects.

3. Correct answers: **A, B, D**

   Design-time objects are inactive repository objects, stored in the CONTENT area, and need to be activated. During activation, runtime objects are created in the CATALOG area.

4. Correct answers: **C, D**

   "Check that attribute views have a key attribute specified" is a valid rule (see Figure 11.4 as an example).

   "Check that graphical calculation views have no orphan nodes" is mentioned in the list of examples described just before Figure 11.1. There is no validation rule to check that tables contain data. Checking formulas in calculated columns is done in the Expression Editor.

5. Correct answer: **A**

   Schema mapping is used during the importing process. During the export, you don't know what schemas are available in the target system. Activation and validation are running in the same system and are unrelated to schema mapping. See just below Figure 11.12.

6. Correct answer: **A**

   Core Data Services (CDS) can improve security because you do not need to give someone authorization to create tables and schemas in a production system. If no one has those authorizations, then you have improved the security. See the Core Data Services section for more information.

**Tip**

Remember that simple true or false questions do not occur in the certification exam. The other questions with at least four answers are more representative of the questions you will find in the certification exam.

7.  Correct answer: **B**

    The quality assurance system is normally a recent copy of the production system is one of the aspects of a standard SAP system landscape used for transports.

    Watch out for the word *only* in the first answer, which makes it a wrong answer. It consists NOT only of a quality assurance and a production system, but also a development system. See Figure 11.8 for a correct illustration. Transports go from quality assurance to production, not the other way around. You do NOT development in the quality assurance system, but in the development system.

8.  Correct answer: **B**

    CDS objects are design-time objects. They create runtime objects when they are activated. The word *only* makes this statement false. See the Core Data Services section.

9.  Correct answers: **A, B**

    The mass copy feature in SAP HANA can be used to create a sandbox (playpen) environment, and is used to import an application from an SAP partner. Mass copy does not transport data tables. You need to perform an export and import to transport data tables, because they are runtime objects. CDS addresses this problem by making them design-time objects. Schema mapping is used to fix models when schemas have different names, not mass copy. See the Importing Objects with Mass Copy section.

10. Correct answer: **D**

    SAP HANA store activated graphical calculation views in the _SYS_BIC schema (see Figure 11.6).

11. Correct answer: **D**

    SAP HANA studio shows validation check errors in the JOB LOG tab (see Figure 11.3).

12. Correct answers: **A, C**

    When you activate an information model it checks the validation rules and generates a run-time object. Remember that activation also triggers a validation, hence answer C is also correct. See the Activation section.

    Reverting to the active version is not done at activation, but *before* activating a newer version, to go back to older active version. Active (run-time) versions are not exported. Design-time versions are exported. Remember, activation also triggers a validation.

13. Correct answer: **B**

    SAP HANA Application Lifecycle Manager is a web-based transport system that you can use on your Apple iPad (see Figure 11.11). SAP Solution Manager and Change and Transport System (CTS) are the traditional SAP transport tools. Developer Mode is the mode to export, for example, single SAP HANA views. This is normally run from SAP HANA studio, which does not run on your Apple iPad.

14. Correct answer: **B**

    When you mark an information model as deprecated, it *does* still work. It merely warns developers or modelers who want to use it that there is an updated version available.

15. Correct answer: **A**

    Refactoring is used to improve your modeling design. You can use it, for example, to rename SAP HANA models. Translating is used to translate your models to other languages (e.g., Chinese). Transporting is taking your modeling work from the development system to the production system. Documenting is writing documents and explaining your modeling work.

16. Correct answer: **C**

    The Developer Mode allows you use to make backups of your own information models (see the description of Figure 11.9). The Change and Transport System (CTS) and delivery units are used to transport your information models to the production system. SAP Support Mode is used to send your information models to SAP if you have a problem with your SAP HANA models.

17. Correct answer: **D**

    You use the Where-Used feature in SAP HANA to find all the places an information model is used (see Figure 11.17). You would use the Change and Transport System (CTS) to find all places a transport is imported. You could use the semantic node in an SAP HANA view to find all places where translations exist for specified fields. You use HISTORY to find which information models a user updated.

18. Correct answer: **A**

    You only have both an active and an inactive version of an information model available in the SAP HANA development system when you edit an existing model. With a new model, there is no active version yet. When validation fails, both versions could (perhaps) exist, but this not guaranteed; for example, when validating a new model there is not yet an active version. Watch out for partially true answers. The word *always* in the question makes this answer wrong! If you have already clicked the REVERT TO ACTIVE button, then the inactive version is gone. At that point, you only have the active version.

19. Correct answer: **B**

    "Your schemas in development and production have different names." This sentence immediately indicated that we are asking about schema mapping (see Figure 11.13).

    With mass copy, you normally do not have the development schema or system, as these belong to either SAP or a third-party developer/partner. Refactoring is used for renaming and moving SAP HANA information models inside the same system, not between systems as the question indicates. CDS does not fix different schema names.

20. Correct answer: **A**

    You find activated information models in the COLUMN VIEWS subfolder of the _SYS_BIC schema (see Figure 11.6).

21. Correct answers: **C, D**

    Refactoring typically uses moving and renaming (see Figure 11.15).

## Takeaway

You should now know how to validate and activate information models and understand what happens behind the scenes when you activate a model. The concept of transporting design-time objects is important when preparing a project for the go-live date. You might have to implement techniques such as schema mapping to ensure a smooth transport process for your information models.

Like gardening to maintain an attractive lawn, you might also need to refactor your modeling work to keep it up-to-date. You've also learned how to document and translate your information models to make them useful for as many people as possible.

## Summary

In previous chapters, we focused on how to create information models. In this chapter, we discussed how to validate, activate, transport, refactor, document, and translate your information models.

By now, you should have a good idea of how to set up an SAP HANA production environment for end users who will use your information models in their every-day business.

With this we have completed the modeling topics inside SAP HANA as a plat-form. The next chapter concentrates on how SAP is using calculations views with business transactional systems like SAP ERP, using SAP HANA as the database.

# SAP HANA Live

## Techniques You'll Master

- Understand the concepts behind SAP HANA Live

- Get to know the two architecture options for SAP HANA Live

- Learn about SAP HANA Live's virtual data model and understand what you are allowed to use and modify within it

- Choose the correct SAP HANA Live views for your reports

- Know how to use the SAP HANA Live Browser tool

- Know how to use the SAP HANA Live Extension Assistant

- Design your own SAP HANA Live views

- Extend and adapt standard SAP HANA Live views for your reporting requirements

Thus far, we have primarily discussed using SAP HANA as a modeling and development platform (see the sections on the sidecar and platform architecture deployment scenarios in Chapter 3). In this chapter, we'll turn our attention to the architecture deployment scenario, in which SAP HANA—via SAP HANA Live—is used as the database for SAP business systems such as SAP Enterprise Resource Planning (ERP), SAP Customer Relationship Management (CRM), and SAP Supply Chain Management (SCM).

### Real-World Scenario

Imagine that you are asked to help design and develop some new reports for a company—but these are not the usual management reports. The company wants to streamline its product deliveries.

The company has been struggling to continuously plan the shipping of its products during the day. The company receives a shipping schedule from the data warehouse system every morning, but traffic jams and new customer orders quickly render this planned schedule useless. This causes backlogs at the loading zones and costs the company more in shipping because it can't combine various customer orders in a single shipment.

Someone has tried using a Microsoft Excel spreadsheet, but the data is not kept up-to-date, and it cannot consolidate the data from all the data sources. After hearing about SAP HANA's ability to analyze data in real time, the company asks you to create some real-time delivery planning reports.

You know that there are prebuilt SAP HANA Live information models available for the SAP ERP system, and you can use a few of these SAP HANA Live information models to meet this business need quickly.

## Objectives of This Portion of the Test

The objective of this portion of the SAP HANA certification is to test your knowledge of SAP HANA Live concepts. The certification exam expects you to have a good understanding of the following topics:

- SAP HANA Live concepts and architecture
- A high-level overview of SAP HANA Live implementation

- ▶ The architecture of SAP HANA Live with the virtual data model (VDM)

- ▶ How to find and consume the right SAP HANA Live information models using the SAP HANA Live Browser

- ▶ How to extend and modify the available SAP HANA Live models to address business requirements

> **Note**
>
> This portion contributes up to 10% of the total certification exam score.

## Key Concepts Refresher

Simply put, SAP HANA Live uses predelivered content in the form of calculation views for real-time operational reporting. In this chapter, we'll look first at the real-world scenario again. Then we'll walk through the history of business information systems to understand the problem posed in this scenario better and determine how using SAP HANA Live addresses this problem. Then, we'll look at what necessitated SAP HANA Live, similar to Chapter 3, in which we discussed the impact SAP HANA's fast memory had on systems that traditionally used slower disk memory.

From there, we'll dive into the architecture of SAP HANA Live, its VDM, its many views, and steps for installation and administration. After we've covered these foundational topics, we'll shift our attention to the primary tools used within SAP HANA Live: SAP HANA Live Browser and SAP HANA Live Extension Assistant. Finally, we'll discuss the steps for modifying SAP HANA Live information models.

### Background Information

Many years ago, SAP only had a single product, called *SAP R/3*. This offering blossomed into the SAP ERP system that we still use today. SAP ERP did everything for companies, from finances to manufacturing, procurement and sales to delivery, and payroll to stores management. The SAP ERP system was a transactional system, what we now call an *online transactional processing* (OLTP) system (also called an *operational system*). All reports were run from within this system, although they tended to be simple "listing" reports.

Over time, the need arose for more complex reports. In response, more advanced analytics and dashboard tools were provided. Through these tools, people learned how to use *cubes* to analyze data. When developers tried to build these new analytics into the transactional system, they discovered that these new reporting features had a huge impact on the performance of the SAP ERP system. A single reporting user running a large cube could consume more data from the database than hundreds of transactional users. It was unacceptable that a single user could slow the entire system down.

To address performance issues, all reporting data from the transactional system was copied to a newly invented *reporting system*. The era of data warehouses had arrived. All reporting data is updated from the transactional system to the data warehouse during the night. This way, the performance of the transactional system remained acceptable during the workday. The new data warehouses were called *online analytical processing* (OLAP) systems, and OLTP and OLAP went their separate ways (see Figure 12.1).

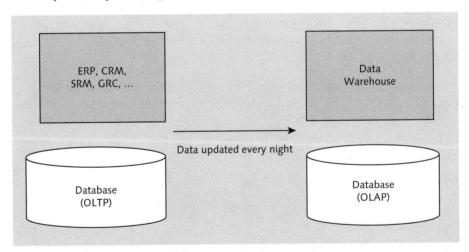

**Figure 12.1**  Separate OLTP and OLAP Systems

This departure helped the performance of both systems but eventually led to countless other headaches. Reports were always outdated now because yesterday's data was used for the reports. We could not see what was happening in the OLTP system in real time. People then started using Microsoft Excel spreadsheets to address some of the issues, which in turn led to more problems and risks (e.g., reports that didn't agree, wrong formulas, and an inability to consolidate information).

> **Note**
>
> Our real-world scenario at the start of the chapter provides a good example in which yesterday's data cannot address today's traffic jams.

How did SAP address these new issues with SAP HANA? By introducing SAP HANA Live, which moves the operational reporting functionality from the data warehouse back into the operational system.

A question quite often arises: "Can SAP HANA just replace an entire data warehouse like SAP Business Warehouse (BW)?"

The short answer is: "No, SAP HANA cannot fully replace SAP BW." Data warehouses are multipurpose. In the real-world scenario we used for this chapter, we only looked at the operational reporting aspects of data warehouses, which are not particularly strong points for such systems. If you had a single operational system with a single warehouse for reporting, you could do everything with SAP HANA—but reality tends to be more complex.

Most companies use their data warehouses to consolidate data from many systems, as shown in Figure 12.2. They use data warehouse features such as the following:

▸ Data governance

▸ Preconfigured content in the form of cube definitions and reports

▸ Data lifecycle management, including data aging and a complete history of business transactions

▸ Cross-system consistency and integration

▸ Planning, consolidation, and consumption

> **Tip**
>
> It makes no sense to try to get rid of data warehouses completely due to operational reporting issues. A better solution is to focus on addressing the few problematic areas in which data warehouses are not optimal.

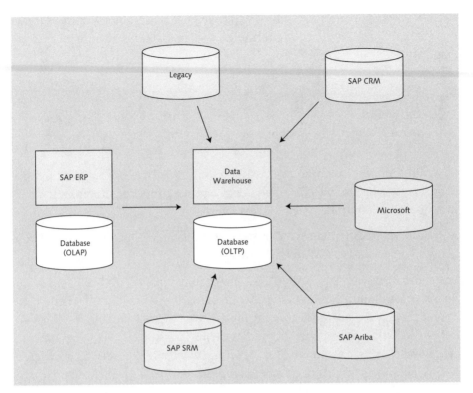

**Figure 12.2**  Data from Multiple Business Systems Consolidated into Data Warehouse for Reporting, Transactional History, and Aging

Because SAP BW is now primarily used for data warehousing, operational reporting needed to be shifted back to SAP ERP. To enable this functionality, SAP ERP uses SAP HANA as a database. This allows companies to run their operational reports, even with complex analytics, on real-time SAP ERP data directly from the underlying SAP HANA database via information models.

SAP HANA Live is the tool used to install, select, maintain, and modify these information models. SAP HANA Live is not only limited to SAP ERP, but also is available for many other SAP business systems, such as SAP CRM, SAP SCM, SAP Governance, Risk, and Compliance (GRC), and SAP Product Lifecycle Management (PLM).

Some of the benefits of SAP HANA Live include the following:

▶ Real-time reporting and analytics on up-to-date information.

▶ SAP HANA does not need to store precalculated aggregates in cubes.

- OLTP and OLAP run in the same system, which can help reduce the total cost of ownership (TCO).

- Open for access by any reporting tool or application.

- Customers and partners can extend it to suit their needs.

Now that you have a better understanding of how SAP HANA Live came to be, the following subsections will dive further into SAP HANA Live's architecture, virtual data model (VDM), views, installation and administration procedures, and modifications.

## Architecture

SAP HANA Live needs an SAP HANA database. Connecting to an SAP HANA database can be achieved in two ways (in this case, we just concentrate on the SAP ERP system, but this also applies to all the other SAP business systems like SAP CRM, SAP SCM, SAP GRC, and SAP PLM; see Figure 12.3):

- **SAP HANA as a database**
  The first option is to migrate an SAP ERP system's database to SAP HANA. No additional systems are required. This is also known as the integrated scenario.

- **SAP HANA as a sidecar**
  The second option is to keep the SAP ERP database and install an SAP HANA system as a sidecar (as discussed in Chapter 3). Then, replicate the required database tables to the SAP HANA system using SAP LT Replication Server (SLT). You can find more information about SLT in Chapter 14. SLT enables real-time replication so that SAP HANA always has the latest data available. For this scenario, you need to install the SLT and SAP HANA systems as well. This is also known as the side-by-side scenario.

After you've connected to an SAP HANA database, you can build reports, analytics, and dashboards directly on the SAP HANA Live content. Other applications can also call this content directly.

 **Note**

In both architectural scenarios, SAP HANA Live is installed in the SAP HANA database.

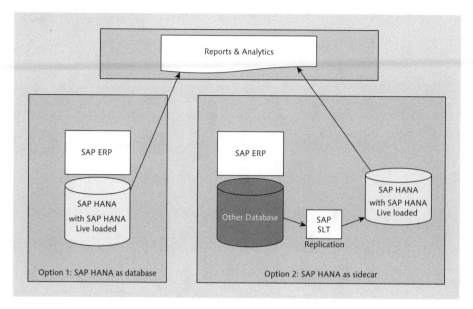

**Figure 12.3**    Architecture Options for SAP HANA Live

## Virtual Data Model

SAP HANA Live content consists primarily of calculation views that are designed, created, and delivered by SAP. These calculation views are built for operational reporting instead of analytical reporting purposes, and therefore use mostly join nodes. The information models are relational rather than dimensional (cube-like), and therefore use the SQL engine rather than the calculation engine. A system administrator loads the SAP HANA Live content into the SAP HANA database. These calculation views are layered in a structure called the SAP HANA Live *virtual data model* (VDM). SAP HANA Live is structured internally as shown in Figure 12.4.

The VDM consists of the following types of views:

▶ **Private views**
These are built directly on the database tables and on other private views. These denormalize the database source data for use in the reuse views.

▶ **Reuse views**
These structure the data in a way that business processes can use. These views can be reused by other views.

► **Query views**

These can be consumed directly by analytical tools and applications. They are not reused by other views. These views are used when designing reports.

► **Customer query views**

These are created either by copying SAP-provided query views or by creating your own query views. You can add your own filters, variables, or input parameters to these views. You can also expose additional data fields or hide fields that are not required.

► **Value help views**

These are used as lookups (i.e., dropdown lists or filter lists) for selection lists in analytical tools and business applications. They make it easier for users to filter data by providing a list of possible values to choose from. Value help views are not used in other VDM views; they are consumed directly by analytical tools and business applications.

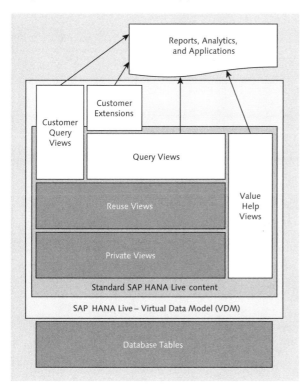

**Figure 12.4**   SAP HANA Live Virtual Data Model

> **Tip**
>
> You should never call private and reuse views directly.

You can build your reports, analytics, or business applications directly on query views. These can be either SAP-provided query views or custom query views. When you run your report, these query views are called. They in turn call the relevant reuse views, which call the relevant private views, which in turn read the relevant database tables. The value help views are called whenever drop-down lists are used to display possible values that a user can choose from.

> **Note**
>
> It is not recommended to modify any SAP-provided VDM views because all SAP-provided VDM views are overwritten when a newer version of the SAP HANA Live content is installed. There is no mechanism like the one in ABAP, in which the system asks if you want to keep any customer changes.
>
> Therefore, you should always make a copy of a VDM query view to modify, rather than modifying the original.

## SAP HANA Live Views

Most of the SAP-provided SAP HANA Live views are calculation views. All the SAP HANA modeling techniques that you've learned are relevant to these views. Figure 12.5 shows an example of such a calculation view.

You will notice several characteristics of these calculations views in Figure 12.5:

▶ They contain several layers (nodes). This is to denormalize the source data. Normalizing data is normal in an OLTP system to improve performance but is not required for analytics.

▶ There are many joins. These are used to combine reuse views to create the VDM query view.

▶ The views might have variables, input parameters, and calculated attributes. The use of input parameters has been limited due to the fact that some reporting tools have difficulty using them. Default values are always supplied for the input parameters.

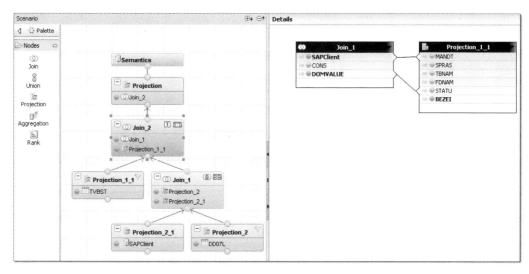

**Figure 12.5**   SAP-Provided Calculation View (OverallBillingBlockStatus) in SAP HANA
Live for SAP ERP

▶ Calculation views use the SQL engine instead of the OLAP engine. We discussed these engines in Chapter 10. There are several reasons for using the
SQL engine instead of the OLAP engine. The main reason is that we are working with data from an OLTP system, which consists of line-level transactions
rather than aggregates, so we do not require the features of the OLAP engine.
Another good reason is for performance; for example, we do not want to pass
data between execution engines.

### Installation and Administration

SAP HANA Live is installed in the SAP HANA database. A system administrator
will normally install the SAP HANA Live content package.

All SAP HANA Live information can be found at *http://help.sap.com/hba*.

You will need to define a schema mapping (see Chapter 11) before importing the
SAP HANA Live content package. The schema name that SAP used to develop the
SAP HANA Live information models will not be the same as the schema name of
your source system.

Once you've installed SAP HANA Live on an SAP HANA system, you will see the
content in the CONTENT folder, under SAP • HBA, as shown in Figure 12.6. You can

explore the calculation views in SAP HANA studio or the SAP HANA web-based development workbench. We do not recommend that you change the views here. All the SAP-provided VDM views are overwritten when a newer version of the SAP HANA Live content is installed. There is no mechanism in place within SAP HANA Live to ask if you want to keep any customer changes, so you could lose all your hard work during an SAP HANA Live update.

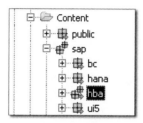

**Figure 12.6**   SAP HANA Live Content Package in SAP HANA Studio

> **Note**
>
> SAP HANA Live has its own release cycles and timelines. SAP HANA Live content updates do not have to correspond to the SAP HANA system update cycles and timelines.

In the SAP • HBA package, you will also find various web-based tools for working with SAP HANA Live content:

▸ **SAP HANA Live Browser**
This tool is used to find the right query views for your reporting needs.

▸ **SAP HANA Live Extension Assistant**
This tool helps you copy and modify views based on your business requirements.

If you have set up the SAP HANA database in a sidecar configuration, you also need to do the following:

▸ Install SLT.

▸ Replicate the relevant tables from the source database to the SAP HANA database. The SAP HANA Live Browser tool will help you select the correct tables for the views you require (see the SAP HANA Live Browser section for more information).

In the SAP documentation, you will also find references to a *rapid deployment solution* (RDS) for SAP HANA Live. This is an optional consulting service that SAP offers (for a fee) to help you install SAP HANA Live on your SAP systems.

In the next section, we'll look at the full breadth of SAP HANA Live Brower's functionality.

## SAP HANA Live Browser—Browse and Use Views

The SAP HANA Live Browser tool is a web-based (HTML5) application that enables you to find the correct views for your reporting or analytics requirements. Sometimes, you might need to ask an SAP functional person that knows the source system well to help you find the required views. Fox example, to find sales information in an SAP ERP system, you might need the advice of an SAP Sales and Distribution (SD) consultant.

You can find the SAP HANA Live Browser tool (Figure 12.7) by accessing *http://<SAP HANA server hostname>:8000/sap/hana/hba/explorer*. (This assumes that the instance number is 00.)

In this section, we will walk through the different areas found in SAP HANA Live, the ALL VIEWS  toolbar, and the SAP HANA Live version for business users.

### Areas

We start by looking at the ALL VIEWS section of the tool (see Figure 12.7).

Here you can search for views by typing a part of the name of the view in the FILTER field. For each view, you can see the following information:

► View name

► Description of the view

► View category (private, reuse, or query view)

► View type (mostly calculation views)

► To which area of the application the view is applicable

► In which SAP HANA package the view is located

Figure 12.8 shows a partial list of views that we can use for procurement reports.

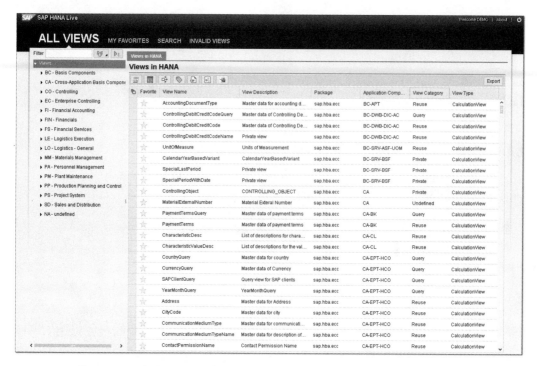

**Figure 12.7**   SAP HANA Live Browser

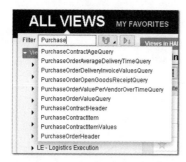

**Figure 12.8**   Filter String Entry to Find Views

You can easily mark an SAP HANA Live view as a favorite by clicking on the empty star to the left of the view name (Figure 12.9). From the MY FAVORITES tab in the SAP HANA Live Browser, you can see a list of all your favorite views.

You also can see a list of invalid views (Figure 12.10). Views can appear on this list if they are missing underlying tables or dependent views. Such views will not activate, either.

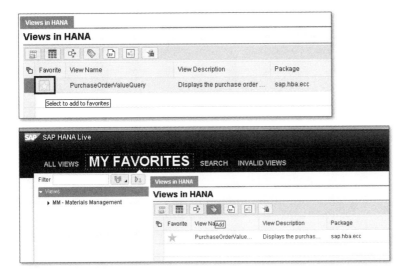

**Figure 12.9**  Mark SAP HANA Live Views as Favorites

**Figure 12.10**  List of Invalid SAP HANA Live Views

### All Views Toolbar

You can access many features in SAP HANA Live Browser from a provided toolbar (see Figure 12.11).

**Figure 12.11**  SAP HANA Live Browser Toolbar

The following functions are available from the toolbar:

▶ OPEN DEFINITION ▦

The OPEN DEFINITION tab (Figure 12.12) shows the metadata of the SAP HANA Live view. These fields are available for your reports and analytics. If you need other fields, you will have to use the SAP HANA Live Extension Assistant.

| Views in HANA | sap.hba.ecc:PurchaseOrderValueQuery × | | | | | | | | |
|---|---|---|---|---|---|---|---|---|---|

| Name | | | Package | | | | Type | | |
|---|---|---|---|---|---|---|---|---|---|
| PurchaseOrderValueQuery | | | sap.hba.ecc | | | | CalculationView | | |

**Columns**

| Column Na... | Position | SQL Data T... | Length | Column Sto... | Is Nullable | Default Value | Compressi... | Index Type | Comments |
|---|---|---|---|---|---|---|---|---|---|
| SAPClient | 1 | NVARCHAR | 3 | STRING | TRUE | | DEFAULT | FULL | |
| Vendor | 2 | NVARCHAR | 10 | STRING | TRUE | | DEFAULT | FULL | |
| VendorName | 3 | NVARCHAR | 35 | STRING | TRUE | | DEFAULT | FULL | |
| Plant | 4 | NVARCHAR | 4 | STRING | TRUE | | DEFAULT | FULL | |
| PlantName | 5 | NVARCHAR | 30 | STRING | TRUE Click to Select TRUE | | DEFAULT | FULL | |
| Material | 6 | NVARCHAR | 18 | STRING | TRUE | | DEFAULT | FULL | |
| MaterialName | 7 | NVARCHAR | 40 | STRING | TRUE | | DEFAULT | FULL | |
| YearMonth | 8 | VARCHAR | 6 | STRING | TRUE | | DEFAULT | FULL | |
| YearWeek | 9 | VARCHAR | 6 | STRING | TRUE | | DEFAULT | FULL | |
| CompanyC... | 10 | NVARCHAR | 5 | STRING | TRUE | | DEFAULT | FULL | |
| EffectivePur... | 11 | NVARCHAR | 5 | STRING | TRUE | | DEFAULT | FULL | |
| EffectivePur... | 12 | DECIMAL | 26 | FIXED | TRUE | | DEFAULT | FULL | |

**Figure 12.12**  Open Definition Tab Showing SAP HANA Live View Metadata

▶ OPEN CONTENT ▦

The OPEN CONTENT tab (Figure 12.13) shows a preview of the data an SAP HANA Live view will produce.

▶ OPEN CROSS REFERENCE ⇨

The OPEN CROSS REFERENCE tab (Figure 12.14) shows an interactive and graphical depiction of all the related tables and views used by this specific SAP HANA Live view. You can also see an outline version instead of the graphical version.

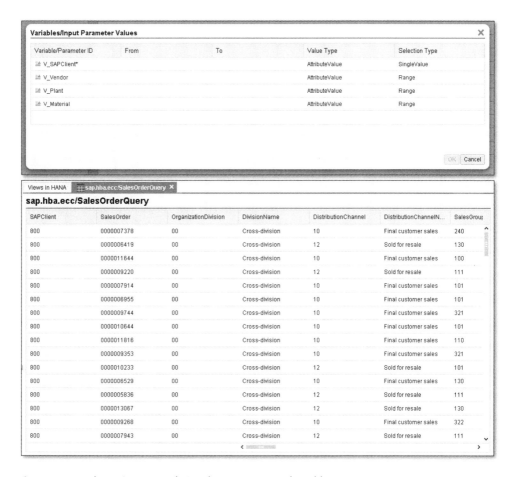

**Figure 12.13**  Show Content Tab Displaying Data Produced by an SAP HANA Live View

▶ TAG 🏷️
   The TAG tab (Figure 12.15) allows you to add your own keywords (tags) to describe SAP HANA Live views. You can use these tags to group some SAP HANA Live views that you would like to use in your reporting, analytics, or dashboards.

▶ GENERATE SLT FILE 📄
   The GENERATE SLT FILE icon allows you to generate configurations for SLT in order to replicate only the tables that you require for your reporting or analytics. This function is only required if you are using SAP HANA Live in a sidecar configuration. You will not replicate the entire source system to the SAP HANA database, but only the tables used by the business end users.

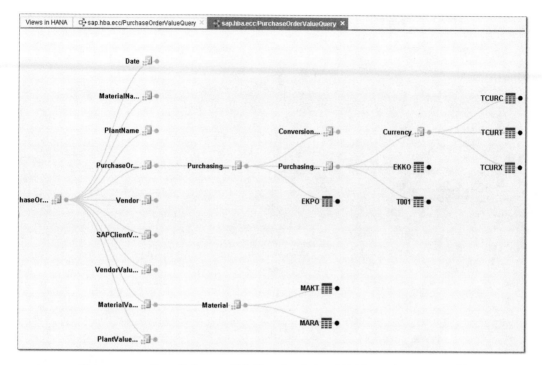

**Figure 12.14**    Cross Reference Tab Showing Related Tables and Views Used by This SAP HANA Live View (Graphical Version)

**Figure 12.15**    Adding Tags to an SAP HANA Live View

▶   OPEN VIEW IN SAP LUMIRA 🔲 and OPEN VIEW IN ANALYSIS OFFICE 🔲
The last two tabs on the SAP HANA Live Browser toolbar allow you to open the specified SAP HANA Live view in either SAP Lumira (Figure 12.16) or the SAP Analysis for Office reporting tools. This allows you to create reports easily and quickly.

The SAP HANA Live Browser does not show you the actual models or where they are used in your reports. Use SAP HANA studio or the SAP HANA web-based development workbench to view SAP HANA Live models.

**Figure 12.16**   Output of an SAP HANA Live View for Sales in SAP Lumira

## SAP HANA Live Browser for Business Users

Up until now, we have discussed the developer edition of the SAP HANA Live Browser. There is also a business user version of SAP HANA Live Browser available at *http://<SAP HANA server host>:8000/sap/hana/hba/explorer/buser.html*.

This version only allows you to find a model, preview the content, and open the view in SAP Lumira or SAP BusinessObjects Analysis, edition for Microsoft Office. It is meant for nontechnical users, such as functional consultants or specialists.

Advanced features like generating SLT files, viewing broken models, tagging a model, or opening graphical cross references are not available in the business user edition of the SAP HANA Live Browser.

## SAP HANA Live Extension Assistant—Modify Views

Figure 12.5 showed an example of an SAP HANA Live view, which is similar to any other view in SAP HANA. There are two ways to modify SAP HANA Live views.

We can use SAP HANA studio and the SAP HANA web-based development workbench to modify, preview, test, debug, and trace SAP HANA Live information models, similar to all the other SAP HANA views we created in previous chapters.

 **Tip**

Here are some guidelines for creating your own SAP HANA Live views:

▶ Try to use graphical calculation views of type cube, with an aggregation node as the top node.

▶ Set the calculation view to execute using the SQL engine.

▶ Do not use attribute or analytic views.

▶ You can combine standard SAP HANA Live views with your own custom views.

Another tool that can be used to modify SAP HANA Live views is the *SAP HANA Live Extension Assistant*.

Figure 12.17 shows the SAP HANA Live Extension Assistant tool.

SAP HANA Live views do not expose all their attributes and measures; SAP has carefully chosen a subset of these elements for the most common business processes. However, there are many hidden fields. You can use the SAP HANA Live Extension Assistant to change which fields are hidden or shown in a particular view.

 **Tip**

Don't delete the fields you're not using; just mark them as hidden. SAP HANA's optimization is very good, and hiding a field does not increase the run time of queries.

You can extend reuse and query views, and you can extend a particular view multiple times.

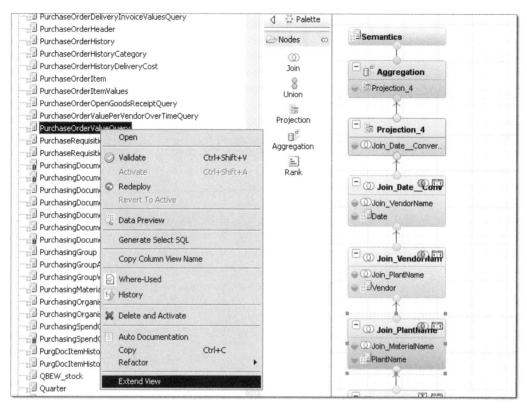

**Figure 12.17**   SAP HANA Live Extension Assistant in SAP HANA Studio

The SAP HANA Live Extension Assistant has a few restrictions that you need to be aware of:

▶ It cannot extend a query view that contains a union node.

▶ It cannot extend a query view that contains an aggregation node as one of the middle nodes. An aggregation node as the top node is normal and allowed.

▶ It cannot extend your own custom views. It only recognizes SAP-delivered views.

 **Tip**

You should not extend SAP-delivered views. Make a copy, and extend that instead.

## Important Terminology

In this chapter, we covered the following important terminology:

▶ **Operational reporting**
Operational reporting is reporting that is done on transactional data (e.g, sales and deliveries) to enable people to do their work today (e.g., like delivering a sold item). SAP BW reports are normally the next day only, and do not help with, for example, today's deliveries. SAP HANA Live is meant only for operational reporting requirements in SAP operational systems like SAP ERP.

▶ **SAP HANA Live**
SAP HANA Live consists of SAP-created calculation views (for the most part) and several tools for working with these SAP HANA views.

▶ **SAP HANA Live views**
The SAP HANA Live views are organized in an architectural structure called the *virtual data model (VDM)*. The different SAP HANA Live views are:

  ▶ *Private views*: These are built directly on the database tables and on other private views. These denormalize the database source data for use in the reuse views.

  ▶ *Reuse views*: These structure the data in a way that business processes can use. These views can be reused by other views.

  ▶ *Query views*: These can be consumed directly by analytical tools and applications. They are not reused by other views. These views are used when designing reports.

  ▶ *Customer query views*: These are created either by copying SAP-provided query views or by creating your own query views. You can add your own filters, variables, or input parameters to these views. You can also expose additional data fields or hide fields that are not required.

  ▶ *Value help views*: These are used as lookups (i.e., dropdown lists or filter lists) for selection lists in analytical tools and business applications. They make it easier for users to filter data by providing a list of possible values to choose from. Value help views are not used in other VDM views; they are consumed directly by analytical tools and business applications.

▸ **SAP HANA Live Browser**
The SAP HANA Live Browser tool is a web-based (HTML5) application that enables you to find the correct views for your reporting or analytics requirements.

▸ **SAP HANA Live Extension Assistant**
The SAP HANA Live Extension Assistant tool is used to modify SAP HANA Live views.

# Practice Questions

These practice questions will help you evaluate your understanding of the topics covered in this chapter. The questions shown are similar in nature to those found on the certification examination. Although none of these questions will be found on the exam itself, they will allow you to review your knowledge of the subject. Select the correct answers and then check the completeness of your answers in the Practice Question Answers and Explanations section. Remember that on the exam you must select all correct answers and only correct answers to receive credit for the question.

1.  Where is SAP HANA Live installed?

☐   **A.** On SLT

☐   **B.** On the SAP ERP application server

☐   **C.** In the reporting tool

☐   **D.** In the SAP HANA database

2.  Which engine do most SAP HANA Live views use?

☐   **A.** SQL engine

☐   **B.** OLAP engine

☐   **C.** Join engine

☐   **D.** Calculation engine

3. Which of the following views can you extend with the SAP HANA Live Extension Assistant?

☐ **A.** Query views with a union

☐ **B.** Reuse views

☐ **C.** All SAP-delivered views

☐ **D.** Your own custom views

4. Which sentence best describes SAP HANA Live?

☐ **A.** Operational reporting moving back to the OLTP system

☐ **B.** Analytical reporting moving back to the OLAP system

☐ **C.** Operational reporting moving back to the OLAP system

☐ **D.** Analytical reporting moving back to the OLTP system

5. Which of the following are features of a data warehouse? (There are 3 correct answers.)

☐ **A.** Consolidation

☐ **B.** Data governance

☐ **C.** Both OLTP and OLAP in one system

☐ **D.** Real-time reporting

☐ **E.** A full transactional history

6. What tool generates files to help configure SLT table replication?

☐ **A.** SAP HANA Live Extension Assistant

☐ **B.** Authorization Assistant

☐ **C.** SAP HANA studio

☐ **D.** SAP HANA Live Browser

7. True or False: You can create custom query views by directly modifying SAP-delivered query views.

☐ **A.** True

☐ **B.** False

8. True or False: When you upgrade SAP HANA Live content, you can choose to keep your modifications.

☐ **A.** True

☐ **B.** False

9. Which of following are features associated with SAP HANA Live? (There are 2 correct answers.)

☐ **A.** A new data warehouse

☐ **B.** Hundreds of predeveloped views

☐ **C.** Web-based tools

☐ **D.** Precalculated aggregates stored in cubes

10. Which of the following terms are associated with an operational system? (There are 2 correct answers.)

☐ **A.** OLTP

☐ **B.** OLAP

☐ **C.** Transactional

☐ **D.** Data warehouse

11. True or False: SAP HANA Live replaces SAP BW.

☐ **A.** True

☐ **B.** False

12. True or False: You can view metadata of SAP HANA Live views with the business user version of the SAP HANA Live Browser.

☐ **A.** True

☐ **B.** False

13. In which package in SAP HANA will you find the SAP HANA Live views?

☐ **A.** */sap/hana/democontent*

☐ **B.** */public*

☐ **C.** */sap/hba*

☐ **D.** */sap/bc*

14. As what are most of the views in SAP HANA Live created?

☐  **A.** Table functions

☐  **B.** Calculation views

☐  **C.** CDS data sources

☐  **D.** Cubes

15. Which of the following VDM views can be called by applications and reports? (There are 2 correct answers.)

☐  **A.** Reuse views

☐  **B.** Value help views

☐  **C.** Private views

☐  **D.** Query views

## Practice Question Answers and Explanations

1. Correct answer: **D**

   In the SAP HANA database (see Figure 12.3). The SAP LT Replication Server (SLT) is only used for the sidecar scenario. You still need to install SAP HANA Live, even if we do not have a sidecar scenario, so this is obviously wrong. We have ABAP code in the SAP ERP application server, not SAP HANA calculation views. Reporting tools have nothing to do with SAP HANA. They can use SAP HANA views, but they cannot be run in the reporting layer.

2. Correct answer: **A**

   Most SAP HANA Live views use the SQL engine. See the last bullet point after Figure 12.5.

3. Correct answer: **B**

   You can extend reuse and query views with the SAP HANA Live Extension Assistant. You cannot extend query views with a union node or your own custom views.

4. Correct answer: **A**

   Operational reporting moving back to the OLTP (operational) system. See the Background Information section.

5. Correct answers: **A, B, E**

   Data warehouse features include consolidation, data governance, and a full transactional history. Please note that the question did not specify that this is an SAP BW on SAP HANA system. It asked about a generic data warehouse. Having both OLTP and OLAP in one system is only available for SAP HANA real-time reporting. For a full list of data warehouse features, refer to Figure 12.2.

6. Correct answer: **D**

   The SAP HANA Live Browser can help generate files for SLT replication. SAP HANA Live Extension Assistant is used for modifying SAP HANA Live views. The Authorization Assistant helps with creating users and roles for SAP HANA Live. The SAP HANA studio does not have this functionality See the SAP HANA Live Browser section for more information.

7. Correct answer: **A**

   This is actually a "bad" question. It is clear from this chapter that you *should not* create custom query views by directly modifying SAP-delivered query views. However, the question asked if you *can* do it. Technically, it's possible—but you will lose all your hard work during the next update of the SAP HANA Live content.

8. Correct answer: **B**

   When you upgrade the SAP HANA Live content, there is no option for you to keep your modifications. All changes to SAP-delivered content will be lost. This is different than the process in ABAP systems, which do ask if you want to save your modifications.

   This question was very similar to the previous question. In the certification exam you will not find one question providing the answer to another. The SAP team ensures that this does not happen.

9. Correct answers: **B, C**

   SAP HANA Live consists of hundreds of predeveloped views, as well as some web-based tools. SAP HANA Live is not a new data warehouse, as we clearly specified that it will not replace SAP BW. With SAP HANA we do not store pre-calculated aggregates in cubes. This is only done in old non-SAP HANA data warehouses. See the Architecture section.

10. Correct answers: **A, C**

An operational system is the transactional (OLTP) system. See the Background Information section.

11. Correct answer: **B**

SAP HANA Live does *not* replace SAP BW. Only the operational reporting portion moves back from the data warehouse to the transactional system.

12. Correct answer: **B**

You cannot view the metadata of SAP HANA Live views within the business user version of the SAP HANA Live Browser. This version is meant for non-technical users. See the SAP HANA Live Browser for Business Users section.

13. Correct answer: **C**

The SAP HANA Live views are in the */sap/hba* subpackage. Figure 12.6 shows the SAP HANA Live content in SAP HANA studio.

14. Correct answer: **B**

Most of the views in SAP HANA Live are calculation views. See Figure 12.5 in the SAP HANA Live Views section.

15. Correct answers: **B, D**

Query views and value help views can be called by applications and reports (see Figure 12.4). Reuse views and private views may not be called directly.

## Takeaway

You should now know what SAP HANA Live is, the concepts behind it, and the architecture options. You will also have an idea of what is involved with the installation.

You can use your understanding of the VDM to choose which views can be used, modified, or extended, and you can use the SAP HANA Live Browser tool to help design your reports.

## Summary

In this chapter, you used your knowledge of SAP HANA modeling in a scenario in which SAP HANA is used as a database for SAP business systems like SAP ERP.

The difference here is that SAP has developed hundreds of SAP HANA views already, and you can tap into this vast resource to build powerful analytical reports quickly.

We have now covered the pure modeling topics. The next chapters will focus on complementary actions and requirements—for example, security, how to load data into SAP HANA, and which reporting tools to use with SAP HANA.

# Security

13

## Techniques You'll Master

- Know when to use SAP HANA security
- Understand how users, roles, and privileges work together
- Know how to create new users and roles
- Learn the various types of privileges
- Explain analytic privileges

In this chapter, we'll discuss how to implement security on the information models you've built. Security is frequently a specialist area, with people dedicated to looking after system security and user administration.

We will not go into all the details of SAP HANA security in this chapter, but we'll give you a good overview to help you with most of the scenarios you will encounter in your day-to-day information modeling work and those that are covered on the exam.

### Real-World Scenario

You get an error message in SAP HANA indicating that you do not have sufficient privileges to do a certain task. In cases like these, you will need to know how to resolve this kind of error message. For this situation, the answer is simply granting a right to a special user. In some cases, you may need to build special roles and privileges.

In other cases, you may be asked by the project manager to assist with setting up the security on the information models. Because you built these information models in SAP HANA, you will have a good idea of which users should have certain privileges.

## Objectives of This Portion of the Test

The purpose of this portion of the SAP HANA certification exam is to test your knowledge of SAP HANA security.

The certification exam expects you to have a good understanding of the following topics:

▶ When to use SAP HANA security, and when to use application security

▶ How users, roles, and privileges work together

▶ Understanding system users and how to create new users

▶ Building a new role

▶ Assigning the various types of privileges to a role

▶ Working with analytic privileges

▶ Migrating old analytic privileges in SAP HANA SPS 11

**Note**

This portion contributes up to 5% of the total certification exam score.

# Key Concepts Refresher

Security determines what people are allowed to do and see in business applications. Although we want to stop any unauthorized people from getting access to company information, we also want to allow business users to do their work without hindrance. There are various ways to achieve this balance in SAP HANA.

In this section, we will discuss the basic use cases for security in SAP HANA and important security concepts. We will then look at how to create users, how these users can access the system, and what roles and privileges these users should get to achieve their goals.

## Usage and Concepts

Let's begin by looking at when to use security measures in SAP HANA before tackling important concepts.

### Use Cases

The use cases for implementing security in SAP HANA depend on the deployment scenario. Let's look at the different deployment scenarios and their security management:

▶ **SAP HANA as a database**
In a deployment scenario in which SAP HANA is used as the *database* for business applications like SAP ERP, SAP CRM, and SAP BW, you do not need to create SAP HANA users and roles for the business users. These users log into the various SAP systems via the SAP NetWeaver application servers and all end user security is managed by these applications. This is shown on the left side of Figure 13.1. You will still need to create a few SAP HANA users and roles for the system administrator users, but you do not need to create anything for the business users.

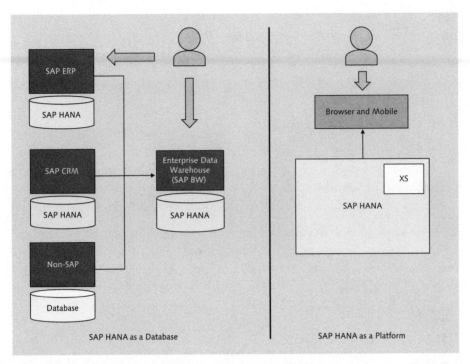

**Figure 13.1**   Security for SAP HANA as Database vs. Platform

▶ **SAP HANA as a sidecar or platform**
In deployment scenarios in which SAP HANA is used as a *sidecar* or a *platform*, end users need to log in and work directly in the SAP HANA system. In such cases, you definitely need to create users and assign roles for these users. In this chapter, we will focus primarily on these scenarios.

▶ **SAP HANA Live**
For SAP HANA Live, you also need end users to log in and work in the SAP HANA system. However, sometimes they also work in SAP HANA Live models via SAP applications. In this case, you need to manage the users in the SAP applications and use the *Authorization Assistant* tool to automatically create the correct SAP HANA Live users and roles inside the SAP HANA system. This chapter will not focus on this use case.

We've mentioned users and their roles in this section. In the next section, we'll look at how these concepts work together in SAP HANA.

**Security Concepts**

Figure 13.2 illustrates how privileges, roles, and users fit together in SAP HANA:

▸ **Privileges**
*Privileges* are the individual rights you can grant to a role or a user.

▸ **Roles**
A *role* in SAP HANA is a collection of granted privileges. You can combine several roles into another role, which is called a *composite role*.

▸ **Users**
*Users* are identities in the SAP HANA system that you assign to business people using your system. You do not assign privileges directly to users, even though it is possible to do so in SAP HANA. The best practice is to assign privileges to a role and then assign that role to users.

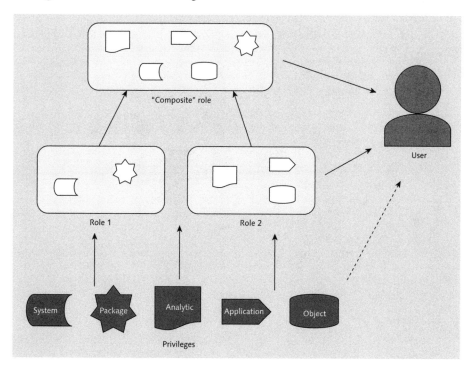

**Figure 13.2**   Assign Privileges to Roles and Roles to Users

We start the security process shown in Figure 13.2 with privileges; assign certain privileges to a role, and then assign that role to the users.

> **Note**
>
> In SAP HANA, the default behavior is to deny access. You cannot do anything in the system until you have been granted a privilege.

These privileges and roles all add up to give a complete portfolio of what users are allowed to do. If something is not specified in a granted role or privilege, SAP HANA denies access to that action.

### Using Security in SAP HANA

To begin using security in SAP HANA, go to the SECURITY area of the SYSTEMS tab in SAP HANA studio, or open the SAP HANA web-based development workbench and select the SECURITY block, as shown in Figure 13.3. You can also go to this area directly in your browser via *http://<servername>:8000/sap/hana/ide/security/*, where "8000" is the port number (if your SAP HANA system is installed as instance 00).

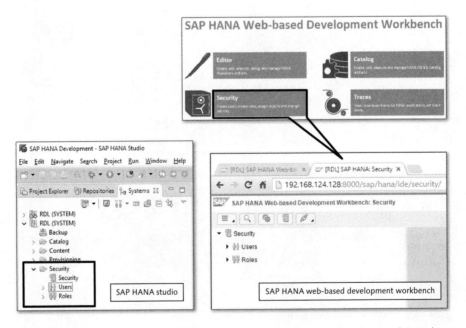

**Figure 13.3**  Security Areas in SAP HANA Studio and SAP HANA Web-Based Development Workbench

In this area, you can begin creating users and roles, which we'll discuss next.

## Users

In this section, we'll look at the two important system users in SAP HANA and the steps for creating users.

### System Users

Figure 13.4 shows a list of all the users in the USERS area of SAP HANA studio. The system users are SYS, SYSTEM, and a few _SYS_ users.

```
v  📂 Security
      🗎 Security
   v  👥 Users
         👤 DEMO_USER
         👤 RDL_USER
         👤 SYS
         👤 SYSTEM
         👤 XSSQLCC_AUTO_USER_3094F258A8978F
         👤 XSSQLCC_AUTO_USER_D5D3B0C4F06A7
         👤 _SYS_AFL
         👤 _SYS_EPM
         👤 _SYS_REPO
         👤 _SYS_STATISTICS
         👤 _SYS_TASK
         👤 _SYS_XB
   >  👥 Roles
```

**Figure 13.4**   Users in SAP HANA System

There are two important system users in SAP HANA:

- SYSTEM

  The SYSTEM user is the main SAP HANA user. When the system is installed, this user can do everything. However, do not be surprised when you later get authorization messages saying that the SYSTEM user does not have privileges to perform certain tasks. Remember that SAP HANA by default denies access to everything. Any models that you have created since the system installation are new objects. You have to explicitly grant access to these new models to the SYSTEM user before it is allowed to use them.

**Note**

Auditors normally require that the SYSTEM user is locked and disabled in an SAP HANA system to improve security.

▶ _SYS_REPO

The _SYS_REPO user is the owner of all the activated objects in the SAP HANA system. We discussed activation in Chapter 11, and showed that an activated copy of an object is created in the _SYS_BIC schema (see Figure 11.6). SAP HANA uses the _SYS_REPO user to execute activated models.

To be able to do this, the _SYS_REPO user must be able to read the tables in your schema. If not, your information views cannot be activated. One of the most common questions on SAP HANA forums is from people asking why they cannot activate newly created information views when they are the owners of the views.

**Tip**

You must grant SELECT rights for your schema to the _SYS_REPO user via the GRANT SELECT ON SCHEMA "SCHEMA_NAME" TO _SYS_REPO WITH GRANT OPTION; statement.

### Creating Users

You can create your own users from the context menu in the USERS area. Right-click and select the NEW USER option, as shown in Figure 13.5.

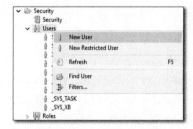

**Figure 13.5**  Creating New User via the Context Menu

On the next screen, as shown in Figure 13.6, you can enter the details for the new user. You can choose a name for the user, a validity period, and the default session client. This is the fifth time we've set the default session client when working with SAP business applications. The other four were as follows:

▶ Setting the preferences in SAP HANA studio (Chapter 5)

▶ Setting the default client in the semantics node of any information view (Chapter 6)

▶ Creating a filter by using the `$$client$$` variable (Chapter 7)

▶ Using the `SESSION_CONTEXT(CLIENT)` statement (Chapter 8)

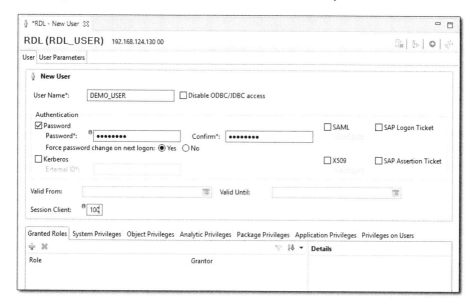

**Figure 13.6**   Screen for Creating a New User

Except for these standalone fields, the screen is divided into two main areas. The area near the top is for authentication, and the bottom area is for authorization:

▶ **Authentication**
*Authentication* answers the question, "Who are you?" It is concerned with identifying users when they log in and making sure they really are who they claim to be.

▶ **Authorization**
*Authorization* answers the question, "What are you allowed to do?" This identifies which tasks a user can perform in the system.

In the AUTHENTICATION area, you can specify if you can log in using a username and password, or whether you should use one of the many *single sign-on* options available in SAP HANA. The most popular single sign-on option is Kerberos, which most companies use together with their Microsoft Active Directory services. When a user logs into the company's network infrastructure, the Kerberos server issues a security certificate. When that user gets to the SAP HANA system and the Kerberos option is enabled for that SAP HANA user, the system will automatically ask for and validate this certificate and will then allow the user access to the SAP HANA system. With single sign-on, users do not have to enter a username and password each time they use the SAP HANA system.

In the AUTHORIZATIONS area at the bottom of Figure 13.6, you can assign roles (or privileges) to the new user. Click the plus sign ✚ in the GRANTED ROLES tab for a list of available roles in the SAP HANA system, as shown in Figure 13.7. You can select one or more roles from the list (press ⌨Ctrl⌨ to select multiple roles).

You can save your changes by pressing ⌨Ctrl⌨+⌨S⌨ or by clicking the DEPLOY button on the top-right of the screen.

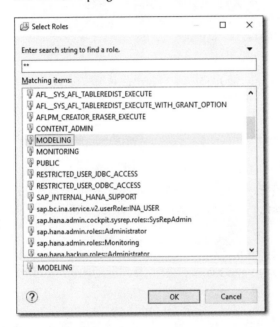

**Figure 13.7**   Choosing Roles

Once you have selected a role for the new user, it is shown in the AUTHORIZATIONS area. In this example, we chose the CONTENT_ADMIN role for the user (Figure 13.8). The blank PUBLIC role is automatically added for all users in the SAP HANA system.

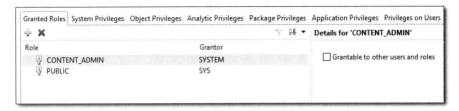

**Figure 13.8**   Roles Assigned to User

**Tip**

Users in an SAP HANA system are not transportable. You cannot create users in a development system and transport them to the production system with all their roles and privileges.

## Roles

In the previous section, we looked at creating users and assigning them roles. In this section, we will take a deeper dive into SAP HANA's roles and discuss the various template roles available and the steps for creating a role in the system.

### Template Roles

You can see all the roles in SAP HANA in the ROLES area of the SYSTEMS tab of SAP HANA studio (see Figure 13.9).

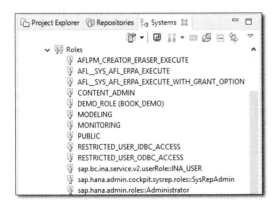

**Figure 13.9**   Some SAP HANA Template Roles

SAP provides a few *template roles* that you can use as examples for building your own, or you can use them as a starting point and extend them. We do not recommend modifying any of the template roles directly; instead, copy them and modify the copy.

The following two template roles are important:

▸ **MONITORING**
This is a role that provides read-only access to the SAP HANA system. You provide this, for example, to a system administrator or monitoring tool that needs to check your system. Users that have this role assigned cannot modify anything in the system.

▸ **MODELING**
This role is given to modelers so they can create information models in the SAP HANA system. We do not recommend giving this role to any user in the production system. Users with this role assigned can create and modify objects in the system and can read all data, even sensitive or confidential data.

**Creating Roles**

You can create custom roles from the context menu in the ROLES area. Select the NEW ROLE option from the context menu. In the next screen, as shown in Figure 13.10, enter the details for your new role.

**Figure 13.10**   Creating New Role

Once you have provided the ROLE NAME and details, you can save and deploy your role by clicking on the DEPLOY button in the top-right corner of the screen.

You can also take another role and extend it. You can, for example, have a custom role built for your team members. You can then create a new custom role for the project manager by taking the team member role and extending it with a few more privileges. In Figure 13.10, we selected the CONTENT_ADMIN role by clicking on the plus sign  in the GRANTED ROLES tab. We can now extend this role by adding more privileges to our new role.

 **Tip**

There is no concept in SAP HANA of taking away privileges, because the default behavior is to deny access.

### Runtime vs. Design-Time Roles

If you use SAP HANA studio to create roles, they are created as *runtime objects* and cannot be transported to the production system. (For more details about the difference between design-time and runtime objects, see Chapter 12.)

However, you can create the roles as design-time files in the SAP HANA web-based development workbench. By using the EDITOR area rather than the SECURITY area shown in Figure 13.3, you can create roles as repository objects.

In Figure 13.11, we create a new ROLE from the context menu in our package. This creates an .hbdrole file in the repository. In the SAP HANA web-based development workbench, we can then edit this role exactly like any other role, as shown in the middle of Figure 13.11. If we try to edit this .hbdrole file in SAP HANA studio, however, we can use only a text editor instead of the usual graphical editor.

 **Tip**

When creating roles, we recommend that you create them as .hbdrole files in the SAP HANA web-based development workbench. These roles are the design-time objects and can be transported to the production system. This improves security, because you need someone with rights to create roles in the production system.

Creating a new .hdb role file in the web-based editor

Adding privileges to the design-time role

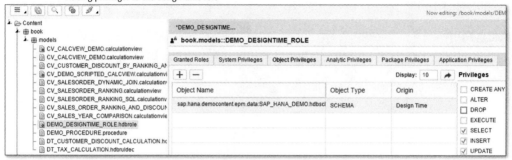

The SAP HANA studio cannot edit the .hdb role file graphically

**Figure 13.11**   Creating Design-Time Roles in SAP HANA Web-Based Development Workbench

## Privileges

In SAP HANA, there are five types of privileges:

▶ System

▶ Object

▶ Analytic

▶ Package

▶ Application

When you build or extend a role, you can assign a type of privilege. Each of these privileges has its own tab in the role editing screen. You can add new privileges in each tab by clicking on the plus sign button.

A dialog box will present a list of relevant privileges to choose from. All of these dialog boxes have a text field in which you can type some search text. The list of available privileges will be limited according to the search text you type.

You can select multiple privileges from the list by clicking on the first privilege and then holding the `Ctrl` key while selecting the other privileges.

In this section, we will discuss the different types of privileges available in SAP HANA.

### System Privileges

*System privileges* can be associated with the phrase "system administration." These privileges grant users the rights to work with the SAP HANA system. Most of the system privileges are applicable to database and system administrators. Figure 13.12 shows some examples of system privileges.

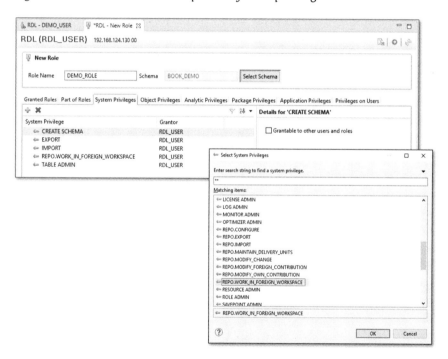

**Figure 13.12**   Assigning System Privileges to Roles

There are a few system privileges shown that are relevant to information modelers:

▸ `REPO.EXPORT` and `REPO.IMPORT`
These are required to export and import delivery units. You need these if you want to transport modeling work to the production system.

▸ `REPO.MAINTAIN_DELIVERY_UNITS`
This allows you to create and edit delivery units.

▸ `REPO.WORK_IN_FOREIGN_WORKSPACE`
This system privilege is useful if a team member is away on summer vacation and you need to activate some of his or her information models.

## Object Privileges

*Object privileges* are used to assign rights for users to data source objects, including schemas, tables, virtual tables, procedures, and table functions.

Granting object privileges requires very basic knowledge of SQL syntax. This makes sense, because you're working with data sources. You will have to know basic `SELECT`, `INSERT`, `UPDATE`, and other SQL statements. The right side of Figure 13.13 shows the options for assigning object privileges.

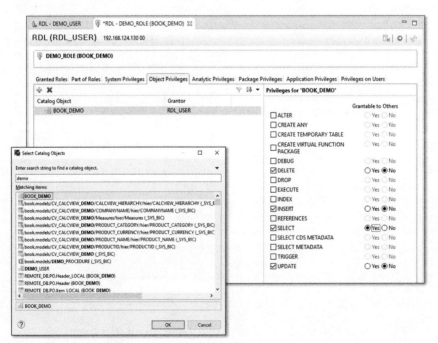

**Figure 13.13**   Assigning Object Privileges to Roles

**Analytic Privileges**

With object privileges, you can grant rights for someone to read all the data from a data source—but how do you limit access to sensitive and confidential data, or limit access to the data that people can see or modify to certain areas only? For example, you may need to ensure that managers can only edit data of employees reporting directly to them, that someone responsible for only one cost center accesses only the correct information, or that only board members can see financial results before they are announced.

*Analytic privileges* can be used to limit data at the row level. This means that you can limit data—for example, to show only rows that contain data for 2016, or your employees, or your cost center.

 **Tip**

> We are sometimes asked how to limit data at the column level. For example, a company wants to allow employees to see all their colleagues' details, except their salaries. How do we hide the Salaries column?
>
> This is not possible with analytic privileges, but it is with *views*. Simply create a view on the employees table and make sure the Salaries column is not part of the output field list, and then grant everyone access to the view.

Figure 13.14 shows how to assign analytic privileges to a role. The figure shows only a small portion of the work involved. Here, we assign the precreated analytic privileges to a role. We will look at how to create these analytic privileges later in this section.

 **Tip**

> In Figure 13.14, we assigned an analytic privilege called _SYS_BI_CP_ALL to a role. Be careful when assigning this analytic privilege; it grants access to the entire dataset of the information views involved. This analytic privilege should not be granted to end users in a production system.
>
> Also note that this privilege is part of the MODELING role. Once again, the MODELING role should not be granted to any end users in a production system.

Think about how analytic privileges behave when they are used with *layered information views*. Assume you need access to information about your cost center. Let's view this from the reporting side. You run a report that is calls view A.

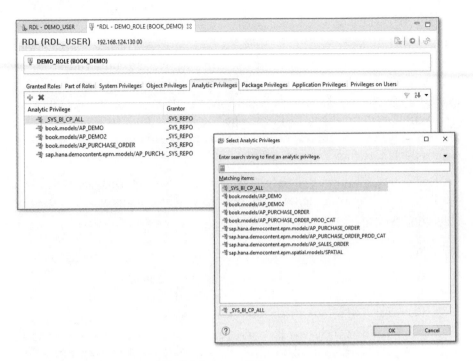

**Figure 13.14**   Assigning Analytic Privileges to Roles

View A then calls another view, called B. (View A is built on top of view B.) You can only see your cost center information if you have an analytic privilege that allows you to see the information being assigned to both views. If you have the analytic privilege assigned to only one of the two views, you will not be able to see your cost center information.

Now that you have a basic understanding of analytic privileges, in the next two subsections we will discuss how to create and maintain them.

### Creating Analytic Privileges

You can create analytic privileges in the same context menu where you created all your SAP HANA information views. In the context menu, select New • Analytic Privilege…, as shown in Figure 13.15.

In the dialog box (Figure 13.16), enter the name of the new analytic privilege. The default choice for Type is SQL Analytic Privilege.

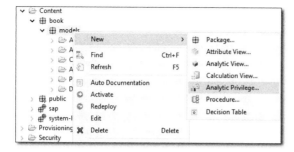

**Figure 13.15**   Context Menu for Creating New Analytic Privilege

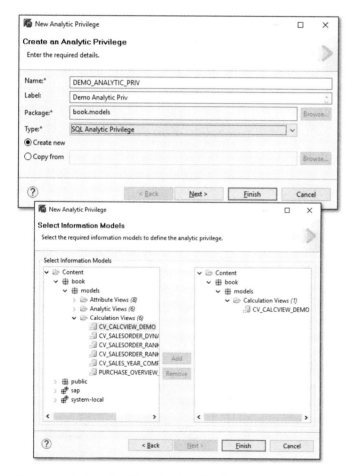

**Figure 13.16**   Creating New Analytic Privilege

**SQL-Based Analytic Privileges**

In SAP HANA SPS 10, the new SQL-based analytic privileges became the default choice. In SAP HANA SPS 11, we now have a migration tool to convert the old XML-based analytic privileges to the new SQL-based analytic privileges. (The old XML-based analytic privileges are also called *classical analytic privileges*.)

The new SQL-based analytic privileges are more powerful, allowing you, for example, to use hierarchies in your analytic privileges. This is useful when working with many company structures, like an HR structure or a financial cost center hierarchy.

In the next step, choose the information views that you want to restrict access to.

Once you have selected the information views, you can create the row-level access restrictions. On the left side of the screen in Figure 13.17, you can add more information views. On the right side of the screen, create your restrictions.

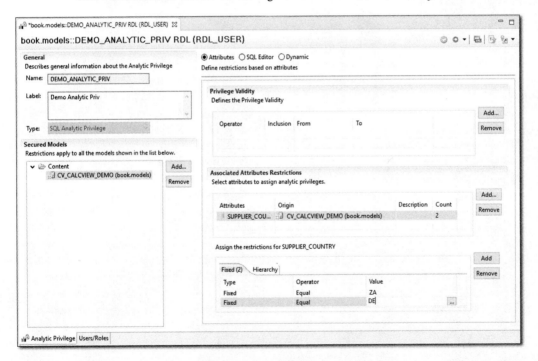

**Figure 13.17**  Assigning Analytic Privilege Restrictions

There are three ways to specify the restrictions:

▶ ATTRIBUTES

With this option, you first select the attributes that you want to create the restrictions on. In this example, we chose the SUPPLIER_COUNTRY field. You then have to specify the restrictions. In this example, we restrict the suppliers to be from ZA (South Africa) or DE (Germany) only. You can see this more clearly in Figure 13.18

Restrictions based on attributes

Restrictions based on a SQL expression

```
1   ((("SUPPLIER_COUNTRY" = 'ZA') OR ("SUPPLIER_COUNTRY" = 'DE')))
```

Restrictions based on a procedure

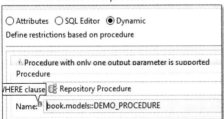

**Figure 13.18** Three Ways to Assign Analytic Privilege Restrictions

▶ SQL Editor

If you used the running example with the Attributes option and then changed the selection to SQL Editor, SAP HANA studio automatically converts this to a SQL WHERE clause—in this example:

```
((SUPPLIER_COUNTRY = 'ZA') OR (SUPPLIER_COUNTRY = 'DE'))
```

▶ Dynamic

The last option is the most powerful. You can base your restrictions on the result set from a procedure. The procedure must be a read-only procedure that only has one output parameter. You must also ensure that the _SYS_REPO user can execute the procedure.

Finally, you have to ensure that the relevant information views can use the new SQL analytic privileges, which you can do in the semantics node of the information view by setting the Apply Privileges field to SQL Analytic Privileges. (See Figure 13.19.)

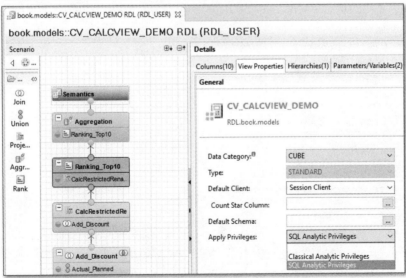

**Figure 13.19**  Ensuring Information Views Can Use SQL-Based Analytic Privileges

If you do not set this option correctly, you will receive warnings that the SQL analytic privileges will have no effect on the information view. The SQL analytic privileges will also send warnings that you cannot use hierarchies in the information view.

With the focus now firmly on the new SQL analytic privileges, let's see how we can migrate our old analytic privileges to the new SQL analytic privileges.

### Migrating Analytic Privileges

A new feature in SAP HANA SPS 11 is the ability to migrate older modeling content to the newer formats. Instead of having to recreate your information views, scripted calculation views, and analytic privileges in the newer formats, SAP has provided a migration wizard to assist you.

Start the migration process by going to the QUICK VIEW tab in the Modeler perspective in SAP HANA studio. SAP HANA SPS 11 includes a number of new options in the QUICK VIEW tab. Select the MIGRATE option to start the process, as shown in Figure 13.20.

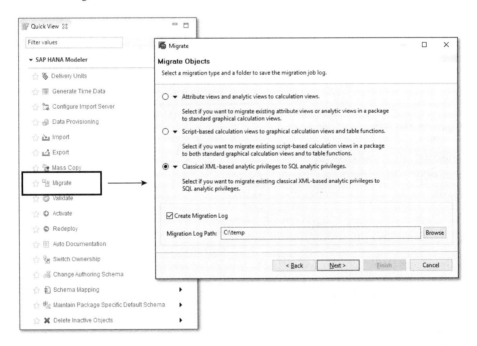

**Figure 13.20**  Starting Migration: Classical XML-Based Analytic Privileges to SQL Analytic Privileges

In the next dialog box, select the CLASSICAL XML-BASED ANALYTIC PRIVILEGES TO SQL ANALYTIC PRIVILEGES option (Figure 13.20).

You can then select all the analytic privileges you need to migrate. Finally, the migration wizard shows you a summary screen before processing the analytic privileges (see Figure 13.21).

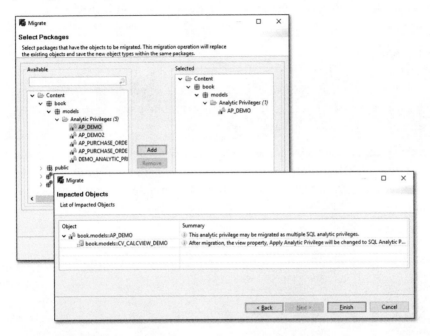

**Figure 13.21**  Migration Summary

The migration process will even update the affected information views by automatically setting the APPLY PRIVILEGES option TO SQL ANALYTIC PRIVILEGES. (See Figure 13.19 for an example of this setting.)

## Package Privileges

*Package privileges* are granted rights to work in packages in the CONTENT area of the SYSTEMS tab in SAP HANA studio. Packages contain all the information views and modeling objects.

*Packages* are normally in a tree structure, with packages, subpackages, and sub-sub-packages. When you are granted access to a higher-level package via a package privilege, you automatically also get access to all the subpackages underneath it. For example, if you have access to the BOOK package as shown in Figure 13.22, you also have access to the BOOK.MODELS subpackage.

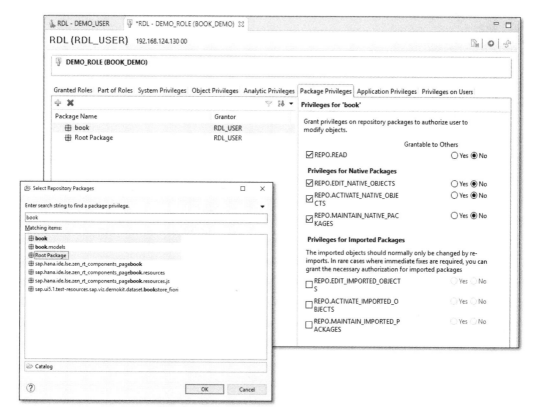

**Figure 13.22**  Assigning Package Privileges to Roles

There also is a special ROOT PACKAGE privilege that grants access to all packages in the SAP HANA system, even packages that will be created at a later date.

The right side of Figure 13.22 shows you how to grant privileges to repository (design-time) packages. For SAP HANA Live, you will need the top REPO.READ or read privilege, as well as PRIVILEGES FOR NATIVE PACKAGES.

### Application Privileges

*Application privileges* are used to grant rights to SAP HANA XS applications. These application privileges are created by the developers of these web applications. In this step, you merely assign these privileges to a role.

In Figure 13.23, we assign the SAP.HANA.DEMOCONTENT.EPM::ADMIN application privilege to the role. This specific privilege allows a user to administrate the SHINE demo application.

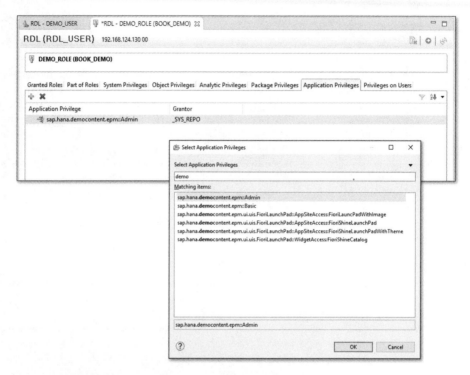

**Figure 13.23**   Assigning Application Privileges to Roles

We have now assigned the various types of privileges to a role. Once you are satisfied with the role, you can assign it to users.

## Testing Security

Often, when you are building a role and assigning privileges, you need to test whether the role is working correctly. You can do this easily in SAP HANA studio by connecting to the same SAP HANA system with two different users.

In Figure 13.24, we connected to the RDL system with both the SYSTEM user and RDL_USER. When we look in the CONTENT areas of both, they look similar—but in the RDL_USER user area everything we run is checked against the authorizations of the RDL_USER user, whereas everything in the SYSTEM user area is checked against the authorizations of the SYSTEM user.

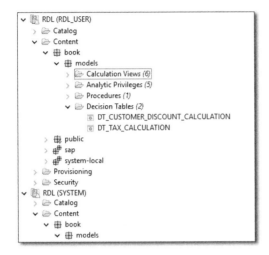

**Figure 13.24**  Testing User Authorizations in SAP HANA Studio

This makes it easy to check one user area while fixing any mistakes in the other user area.

## Important Terminology

In this chapter, we covered the following terminology:

▶ **Users**
Identities in the SAP HANA system that you assign to business people using your system. The best practice is to assign privileges to a role and then assign that role to users. The following are two important system users:

  ▶ SYSTEM: The main SAP HANA user. When the system is installed, this user can do everything.

  ▶ _SYS_REPO: The owner of all the activated objects in the SAP HANA system. SAP HANA uses the _SYS_REPO user to execute activated models.

▶ **Roles**
A *role* in SAP HANA is a collection of granted privileges. You can combine several roles into another role, which can be called a *composite role*.

▶ **Template roles**
Templates that you can use to build your own roles. The following two template roles are important:

  ▶ MONITORING: Provides read-only access to the SAP HANA system. Users that have this role assigned cannot modify anything in the system.

  ▶ MODELING: Given to modelers so they can create information models in the SAP HANA system. Users with this role assigned can create and modify objects in the system and can read all data, even sensitive or confidential data.

▶ **Authentication**
Identifies users when they log in and ensures they are who they claim to be.

▶ **Authorization**
Identifies which tasks a user can perform in the system.

▶ **Privileges**
The individual rights you can grant to a role or a user. In SAP HANA, there are five types of privileges:

  ▶ *System privileges*: These privileges grant users the rights to work with the SAP HANA system. Most of the system privileges are applicable to database and system administrators.

  ▶ *Object privileges*: These privileges are used to assign rights for users to data source objects, including schemas, tables, virtual tables, procedures, and table functions. Requires very basic knowledge of SQL syntax.

  ▶ *Analytic privileges*: These privileges control access to SAP HANA data models. There are two types of analytic privileges: classic XML-based analytic privileges and the new SQL-based analytic privileges that came with SAP HANA SPS 10. In SAP HANA SPS 11, there is a migration tool to convert the old XML-based analytic privileges to the new SQL-based analytic privileges.

  ▶ *Package privileges*: These privileges grant rights to work in packages. Packages contain all the information views and modeling objects.

  ▶ *Application privileges*: These privileges are used to grant rights to SAP HANA XS applications.

▶ **Restrictions in analytic privileges**
You can implement row-level access restrictions using analytic privileges.

# 🧩 Practice Questions

These practice questions will help you evaluate your understanding of the topic. The questions shown are similar in nature to those found on the certification examination. Although none of these questions will be found on the exam itself, they will allow you to review your knowledge of the subject. Select the correct answers and then check the completeness of your answers in the Practice Question Answers and Explanation section. Remember that on the exam you must select all correct answers and only correct answers to receive credit for the question.

1. Which are the recommended assignments in SAP HANA? (There are 2 correct answers.)

   ☐ **A.** Privileges to users

   ☐ **B.** Roles to users

   ☐ **C.** Roles to roles

   ☐ **D.** Roles to privileges

2. In which SAP HANA deployment scenarios will end users be created as users in the SAP HANA system? (There are 2 correct answers.)

   ☐ **A.** SAP BW powered by SAP HANA

   ☐ **B.** SAP S/4HANA

   ☐ **C.** SAP HANA as a platform

   ☐ **D.** SAP HANA Live

3. True or False: The default behavior of SAP HANA is to allow access.

   ☐ **A.** True

   ☐ **B.** False

4. Your newly created information view does NOT want to activate. For which system user must you grant read access to your schema?

   ☐ **A.** _SYS_REPO

   ☐ **B.** SYSTEM

   ☐ **C.** SYS

   ☐ **D.** _SYS_TASK

5.  What do you have to assign to users to allow single sign-on?

☐   **A.** SQL analytic privileges

☐   **B.** Kerberos authentication

☐   **C.** TRUST ADMIN system privilege

☐   **D.** Application privileges

6.  Where do you graphically create a design-time role in SAP HANA?

☐   **A.** In the SECURITY area of the SAP HANA web-based development work-bench

☐   **B.** In the ROLES area under SECURITY in SAP HANA studio

☐   **C.** In the REPOSITORY area in the development perspective in SAP HANA studio

☐   **D.** In the EDITOR area of the SAP HANA web-based development workbench

7.  What system privilege do you need to create a delivery unit?

☐   **A.** REPO.EXPORT

☐   **B.** REPO.IMPORT

☐   **C.** REPO.MAINTAIN_DELIVERY_UNITS

☐   **D.** REPO.WORK_IN_FOREIGN_WORKSPACE

8.  True or False: Object privileges on a table with SELECT rights will allow you to access to all the data.

☐   **A.** True

☐   **B.** False

9.  What can you use to limit users to see only 2016 data? (There are 2 correct answers.)

☐   **A.** An object privilege

☐   **B.** A SQL analytic privilege

☐   **C.** A view with a filter

☐   **D.** A view with a restricted column

10. You have two calculation views for viewing manufactured products. The WORLD calculation view shows worldwide information. The INDIA calculation view is built on top of the WORLD calculation view and shows information for Indian products. What privilege must you assign to see your department's specific data in a report built on the INDIA calculation view?

    ☐ **A.** An analytic privilege on the WORLD calculation view
    ☐ **B.** An analytic privilege on the INDIA calculation view
    ☐ **C.** An analytic privilege on the both calculation views
    ☐ **D.** An object privilege on the WORLD calculation view

11. True or False: You can limit access to a subpackage if you have given access to the higher level package.

    ☐ **A.** True
    ☐ **B.** False

12. You have created a SQL analytic privilege on an information view. Where do you tell the view to enable SQL analytic privileges?

    ☐ **A.** In the semantic node of the information model
    ☐ **B.** In the restrictions settings of the SQL analytic privilege
    ☐ **C.** In the SAP HANA studio preferences
    ☐ **D.** In the migration tool

13. What does the migration tool allow you to migrate?

    ☐ **A.** XML analytic privileges to table functions
    ☐ **B.** XML analytic privileges to SQL analytic privileges
    ☐ **C.** SQL analytic privileges to XML analytic privileges
    ☐ **D.** Object privileges to SQL analytic privileges

## Practice Question Answers and Explanations

1. Correct answers: **B, C**

   We can assign roles to other roles and roles to users in SAP HANA. We can assign privileges to users, but this is not recommended. We cannot assign roles to privileges. We can only assign privileges to roles.

2. Correct answers: **C, D**

   End users are created as users in the SAP HANA system in the SAP HANA as a platform deployment scenario. With SAP HANA Live, users are created in the SAP application server, and they are automatically created by the Authorization Assistant in SAP HANA. With SAP BW on SAP HANA and SAP S/4HANA, users are created in the SAP application servers, not in SAP HANA.

3. Correct answer: **B**

   False. The default behavior of SAP HANA is to deny access. Please note that True or False questions are included to help your understanding, but the actual certification exam does not have such questions.

4. Correct answer: **A**

   You must grant read access to your schema for the _SYS_REPO user if your newly created information view does NOT want to activate.

5. Correct answer: **B**

   You have to assign Kerberos authentication to users to allow single sign-on

6. Correct answer: **D**

   You can graphically create a design-time role in the EDITOR area of the SAP HANA web-based development workbench. In the SECURITY area of the workbench, you can create only runtime roles. In the ROLES area under SECURITY in SAP HANA studio, you can create only runtime roles. In the REPOSITORY area in the development perspective in SAP HANA studio, you can only create a design-time role as a text file, not graphically.

7. Correct answer: **C**

   The REPO.MAINTAIN_DELIVERY_UNITS system privilege allows you to create a delivery unit. REPO.EXPORT and REPO.IMPORT are used for transporting, not for creating delivery units. REPO.WORK_IN_FOREIGN_WORKSPACE allows you to activate colleagues' information views and is not related to delivery units.

8. Correct answer: **A**

   True. Yes, an object privilege on a table with SELECT rights will allow you to access all the data.

9. Correct answers: **B, C**

   You can use a view with a filter or a SQL analytic privilege to limit users to see only 2016 data. A view with a restricted column will show all the data in all the fields, except in the restricted column.

10. Correct answer: **C**

    An analytic privilege on both calculation views.

11. Correct answer: **B**

    False. You cannot limit access to a subpackage if you have given access to the higher-level package.

12. Correct answer: **A**

    You tell the view to enable SQL analytic privileges in the semantic node of the information model.

13. Correct answer: **B**

    The migration tool migrates XML analytic privileges to SQL analytic privileges.

## Takeaway

You should now have a good overview of security in SAP HANA, especially as it relates to information modeling. You should understand when to use SAP HANA security and how users, roles, and privileges work together.

You know how to create new users and roles and how to assign the various types of privileges, and you can explain analytic privileges, how to create them, and how to migrate them to the newer SQL-based analytic privileges.

In your journey, you also learned best practices and picked up practical tips to work with in your SAP HANA projects.

## Summary

We started by looking at when to use SAP HANA security and when to use an application's security. We then went into the details of creating users and roles and assigning privileges. Along the way, we went into more details on analytic privileges, which these are particularly applicable to our modeling knowledge.

In the next chapter, we will explain how to get data from various outside sources into SAP HANA for use with your information models.

# Data Provisioning

14

## Techniques You'll Master

- ▶ Learn what data provisioning is
- ▶ Understand the basic data provisioning concepts
- ▶ Get to know the various SAP data provisioning tools available for SAP HANA
- ▶ Know when to use the different SAP data provisioning tools in the context of SAP HANA
- ▶ Identify the benefits of each data provisioning method
- ▶ Gain a working knowledge of some features in a few of the SAP provisioning tools

In this chapter, we will cover how to provide data to SAP HANA information models and the basic principles and tools used for data provisioning in SAP HANA. For our information models to work properly, we need to ensure that we get the right data into SAP HANA at the right time.

There are people who specialize in each of the data provisioning tools discussed, and there are special training courses for every one of these tools. Our aim, therefore, is not to dive deep into detail about the various concepts and tools, but to give you a high-level working knowledge of what each tool does, to understand the concepts involved when provisioning data into SAP HANA, to enable you to have a meaningful conversation on the topic, and to help you when choosing the right tool for your business requirements.

### Real-World Scenario

You start a new project that involves SAP HANA, and you are asked to provide data for the SAP HANA system.

You start by asking important questions about the expected data provisioning: Where is the data stored currently? Is the data clean? Will the data be updated in the source systems, or is this a once-off data provisioning process? Does the business need the data in real time, or is a delay of some hours acceptable? Does the data need to be stored in the SAP HANA system? Does the business already have a data provisioning tool that you can re-use? Will the data provisioning process be limited to SAP HANA only?

After evaluating all these factors, you recommend the right data provisioning tool to the business, one that is applicable to its budget, circumstances, and requirements.

## Objectives of This Portion of the Test

The objective of this portion of the SAP HANA certification is to test your high-level understanding of the various SAP data provisioning tools available for getting data into an SAP HANA system.

The certification exam expects you to have a good understanding of the following topics:

- General data provisioning concepts

- Different SAP data provisioning tools

- Similarities and differences between the various provisioning tools

- When to use a particular SAP provisioning tool

- High-level understanding of features of some of the SAP data provisioning tools

> **Note**
>
> This portion contributes up to 5% of the total certification exam score.

## Key Concepts Refresher

In Chapter 4, we started by looking at the basic information modeling concepts. Figure 4.11 presented an overview diagram of the different types of information models in SAP HANA and how they all work together to help solve business requirements. This overview diagram is shown again in Figure 14.1. This diagram can be considered a summary of the entire book!

So far, we have focused our attention on the bottom half of the diagram: on information modeling inside SAP HANA. In this chapter, our attention shifts to the upper left corner of the diagram. You need to know how to supply your SAP HANA information models with the data they require.

SAP HANA does not really differentiate whether the data comes from SAP or from non-SAP source systems. Data is data, regardless of where it comes from. Combined with the fact that SAP HANA is a full platform—and not just a dumb database—this makes it an excellent choice for all companies. SAP HANA is meant not only for traditional SAP customers but also for a wide range of other companies, from small startups to large corporations. In fact, SAP now actively supports thousands of startups, helping them use SAP HANA to deliver innovative solutions that are "nontraditional" in the SAP sense.

In this chapter, we will look at the various data provisioning concepts and tools.

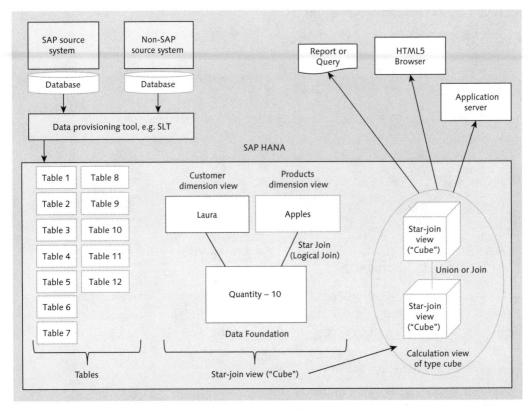

**Figure 14.1**  Overview Diagram and Where Data Provisioning Fits

## Concepts

*Data provisioning* is used to get data from a source system and provide that data to a target system. In our case, we get this data from various source systems, whether they're SAP or non-SAP systems, and our target is always the SAP HANA system.

We are not too concerned in this chapter about the different types of data—whether financial transactional data, spatial data, real-time sensor data, social media data, or aggregated information. We will focus instead on the process of providing the data to SAP HANA.

Data provisioning goes beyond merely loading data into the target system. With SAP HANA and some of its new approaches to information modeling, we also have more options available to us when working with data from other systems. We do not always have to store the data we use in SAP HANA as with traditional data loading. We now also have the ability to consume and analyze data once, never to be looked at again.

### Extract, Transform, and Load

Extract, Transform, and Load (ETL) is viewed by many people as the traditional process of retrieving data from a source system and loading it into a target system. Figure 14.2 illustrates the traditional ETL process of data provisioning.

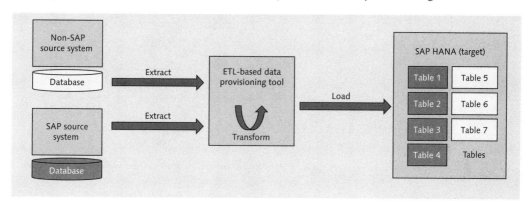

**Figure 14.2**   Extract, Transform, and Load Process

The ETL process consists of the following phases:

▸ **Extraction**
During this phase, data is read from a source system. Traditional ETL tools can read many data sources, and most can also read data from SAP source systems.

▸ **Transform**
During this phase, the data is transformed. Normally this means cleaning the data, but it can refer to any data manipulation. It can combine fields to calculate something (e.g., sales tax, or filter data, or limit the data to the year 2016). You set up transformation rules and data flows in the ETL tool.

▸ **Load**
In the final phase, the data is written into the target system.

The ETL process is normally a batch process. Due to the time required for the complex transformations that are sometimes necessary, tools do not deliver the data in real time.

With SAP HANA, the process sometimes changes from ETL to *ELT*. This is because SAP HANA has some data provisioning components built in, as shown in Figure 14.3. In this case, we *extract* the data, *load* it into SAP HANA, and only then *transform* the data

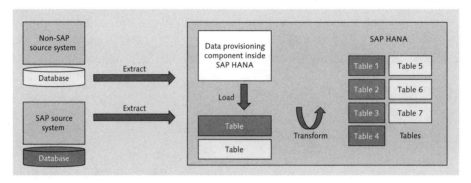

**Figure 14.3**   Extract, Load, and Transform Process

### Initial Load and Delta Loads

It is important to understand that loading data into a target system happens in two distinct phases, as illustrated in Figure 14.4.

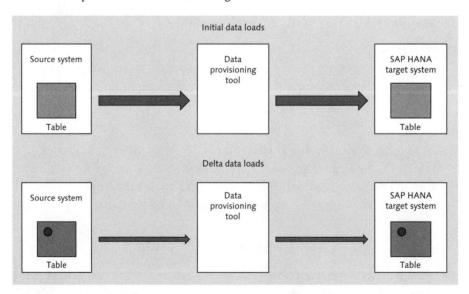

**Figure 14.4**   Initial Load of Tables and Subsequent Delta Updates

We always start by making a full copy of the data that we need from the source system. If we require an entire table, we make a copy of the table in the target system. This is called the *initial load* of the data. We can limit the initial load with a filter (e.g., to load only the latest 2016 data).

Sometimes this step is enough and we do not need to do anything more. If we set up a training or a testing system, we do not need the latest data in these systems.

Many times, however, we need to ensure that our copy of the data in the target system stays up-to-date. Business carries on, and items are bought and sold. Each new transaction can change the data in the source system. We need a mechanism to update the data in the target system. We could just delete the data in the target system and perform the initial load again. For small sets of data, this approach can work, but it quickly becomes inefficient and wasteful for large datasets.

A more efficient method is to look at the data that has changed and apply the data changes to our copy of the data in the target system. These data changes are referred to as the *delta*, and applying these changes to the target system is called a *delta load*. The various data provisioning tools can differ substantially in the way they implement the delta load mechanism.

**Replication**

Replication emphasizes a different aspect of the data loading process.

ETL focuses on ensuring that the data is clean and in the correct format in the target system. Replication does less of that, but gets the data into the target system as quickly as possible. As such, the replication process appears quite simple, as shown in Figure 14.5.

The extraction process of ETL tools can be demanding on a source system. Because they have the potential to dramatically slow down the source system due to the large volumes of data read operations, the extraction processes are often only run after hours.

*Replication* tools aim to get the data into the target system as fast as possible. This implies that data must be read from the source system at all times of the day and with minimal impact to the performance of the source system. The exact manner in which different replication tools achieve this can range from using database triggers to reading database log files.

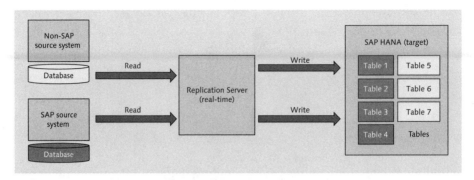

**Figure 14.5**   Replication of Tables

With SAP HANA as the target system, we achieve real-time replication speeds. (We've worked on projects where the average time between when a record is updated in the source system to when the record is updated in SAP HANA was only about 50 milliseconds!)

 **Tip**

> We often use real-time replication with SAP HANA to leverage the speed of SAP HANA for our data analysis.

### SAP Extractors

Normally, we think of data provisioning as reading the data from a single table in the source system and then writing the same data to a similar table in the target system. However, it is possible to perform this process differently, such as reading the data from a group of tables and delivering all this data as a single integrated data unit to the target system. This is the idea behind SAP *extractors*.

The standard approach for taking data from an SAP business system to an SAP BW system (Figure 14.6) uses extractors. There are thousands of extractors predelivered by SAP for SAP business systems. Extractors are only found in SAP systems.

In the scenario shown in Figure 14.6, the extractor gathers data from multiple tables in the SAP source system. It neatly packages this data for consumption by the SAP BW system in a flat data structure (datasource). Extractors provide both initial load and delta load functionality. All this happens in the SAP source system.

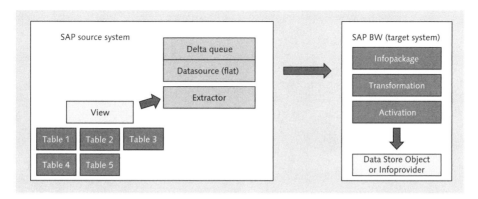

**Figure 14.6** Extractors in SAP Business Systems Loading Data into SAP BW

In the SAP BW target system, you create an *InfoPackage* to help schedule delta loads. SAP BW receives the data from the remote data source and applies the transformation and activation processes to the data before storing it in SAP BW. The data can be stored in a *DataStore Object* (DSO) or *InfoProvider*. A report can read the data from the SAP BW InfoProvider.

SAP BW rose in popularity with many companies due to the large number of extractors that SAP provides with it. These extractors are well-documented and make it easy to find the data you are looking for.

For example, say you want to create a report using procurement data. You find the extractors that contain the data you need and select the best one for your needs. You activate this extractor: It then automatically creates the correct data structures for you in the SAP BW system and populates them with the data you asked for. You then build your report on these data structures. Even if the provided data structures are not 100% what you were looking for, it is easier to modify something that is 95% complete than to create it all from scratch.

### Database Connections

SAP HANA provides drivers known as SAP HANA clients that allow you to connect to other types of databases. Let's look at some of the common database connectivity terminology you might encounter:

▶ **Open Database Connectivity (ODBC)**
ODBC acts as a translation layer between an application and a database via an ODBC driver. You write your database queries using a standard application

programming interface (API) for accessing database information. The ODBC driver translates these queries to database-specific queries, making your database queries database and operating system independent. By changing the ODBC driver to that of another database and changing your connection information, your application will work with another database.

▶ **Java Database Connectivity (JDBC)**
JDBC is similar to ODBC but specifically aimed at the Java programming language.

▶ **Object Linking and Embedding, Database for Online Analytical Processing (ODBO)**
ODBO provides an API for exchanging metadata and data between an application and an OLAP server (like a data warehouse using cubes). You can use ODBO to connect Microsoft Excel to SAP HANA.

▶ **Multidimensional expressions (MDX)**
MDX is a query language for OLAP databases, similar to how SQL is a query language for relational (OLTP) databases. The MDX standard was adopted by a wide range of OLAP vendors, including SAP.

▶ **Business Intelligence Consumer Services (BICS)**
BICS is an SAP-proprietary database connection. It is a direct client connection that performs better and faster than MDX or SQL. Hierarchies are supported, negating the need for MDX in SAP environments. Because this is an SAP-only connection type, you can only use it between two SAP systems—for example, from an SAP reporting tool to SAP BW.

The fastest way to connect to a database is via dedicated database libraries. ODBC and JDBC insert another layer in the middle that can impact your database query performance. Many times, however, convenience is more important than speed.

## SAP Data Services

*SAP Data Services* is a powerful ETL tool. It can read most known data sources, transform and clean data, and load data into target systems. It has been available for many years, and was previously called SAP BusinessObjects Data Services.

SAP Data Services runs on its own server, as shown in Figure 14.7, and requires a database to store job definitions and metadata. In many cases, this database is Microsoft SQL Server, but could be an SAP HANA database as well.

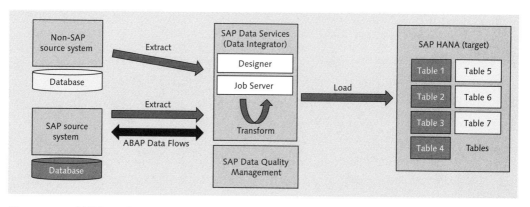

**Figure 14.7**   SAP Data Services

In this section, we'll look at using SAP Data Services for extracting data, transforming and cleansing data, and finally round-out our discussion by looking at its primary benefits.

### Extracting Data

The extraction capabilities of SAP Data Services are well-known in the industry. It can read many data sources—even obscure ones, like old COBOL copybooks. However, SAP Data Services can also read all the latest social media feeds available on the Internet, and it can communicate with most databases and large business applications.

SAP Data Services can get data from SAP business systems in various ways. We can use it to directly read a system's databases. We could also use some of the built-in extractors we discussed in the SAP Extractors section. However, it cannot use all the SAP extractors. For example, if you need extractors that require activation afterwards, then the SAP Direct Extractor Connection (DXC) discussed in the SAP Direct Extractor Connection section could be a better tool to use. If, on the other hand, you are already extensively using SAP Data Services in your company, and you do not require all the extractors, SAP Data Services is a better choice.

Another way SAP Data Services can get data from SAP business systems is by using an ABAP data flow. *ABAP* is the programming language that SAP uses to write the SAP Business Suite systems. SAP Data Services can write some ABAP code that you can load into the SAP source system. This code becomes part of an

ABAP data flow and is a faster and more reliable way to extract the data from an SAP source system.

### Transforming and Cleaning Data

There is no better SAP tool than SAP Data Services for providing complex transformations. SAP Data Services is actually several products combined. When people refer to SAP Data Services, they normally refer to the data provisioning product called *Data Integrator*. Another product called *SAP Data Quality Management* is also combined under the SAP Data Services product name.

All SAP Data Services products ensure that you have clean and reliable information to work with. You may have heard the old saying, "garbage in, garbage out." If you have rubbish data going into your reporting system, you get rubbish data in your reports. SAP HANA's great performance does not make this go away. It just changes that old saying to, "garbage in, garbage out *fast!*"

### Benefits of SAP Data Services

Use SAP Data Services for data provisioning when:

▶ A strong ETL tool is required because no other tool can read certain data sources (e.g., legacy systems)

▶ Transformation of data is required—for example, when data is not clean

▶ Real-time data provisioning is not a business requirement

▶ A customer already has an instance of SAP Data Services running and requires you to use the current infrastructure and skills available

## SAP LT Replication Server

*SAP LT Replication Server* (SLT) is a data provisioning tool that uses replication to load data into SAP HANA. Remember that the focus of a replication server is to load data into the target system as fast as possible.

SLT started as a tool that SAP developed and used internally to help companies migrating data between SAP systems—for example, when companies wanted to consolidate systems after a merger or acquisition. SLT is written in ABAP and runs on the SAP NetWeaver platform, just like SAP ERP and other SAP business systems. SLT was successfully used for years for data migrations, but became more popular and well-known with the arrival of SAP HANA.

> **Tip**
>
> SLT is one of the most popular SAP data provisioning tools for SAP HANA. This is due to its real-time replication capabilities, and the fact that it understands SAP source systems well due to it running on the SAP NetWeaver platform.

SLT works with both SAP and non-SAP source systems. It uses the same database libraries as the SAP Business Suite and therefore supports all the same databases as the SAP business systems, including SAP HANA, SAP ASE, SAP MaxDB, Microsoft SQL Server, IBM DB/2, Oracle, and Informix. We recommend that SLT be installed on its own server, as shown in Figure 14.8, even though you can install it inside an SAP NetWeaver–based source system.

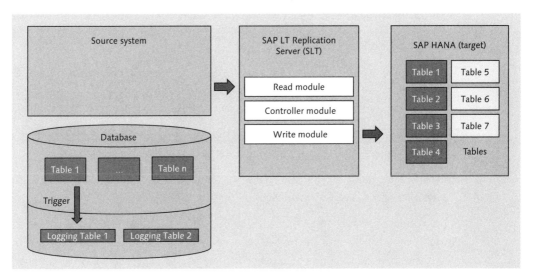

**Figure 14.8** SLT Replication Server

### Trigger-Based Replication

The method that SLT uses for real-time replication is trigger based. A *trigger* is a feature that all databases have, whereby they can trigger an action when data changes in a table. For example, if data is updated or deleted or new data is inserted in a specific table, you can set up a database trigger to also write these changes to a special replication log table. SLT replication is also known as *trigger-based replication*. The impact of the SLT replication on the source systems is minimal because database triggers are quite efficient.

SLT performs the initial load of the database tables without the use of triggers. The delta load mechanism is trigger based. SLT creates triggers in the source systems on the tables it replicates. Any changes made to the source tables after the initial load are collected in logging tables in a separate database schema. SLT then quickly applies all these changes to the SAP HANA target tables and empties the logging tables in the source system. The logging tables are therefore normally kept very small.

Some database administrators do not like triggers on their critical legacy production systems. In such cases, you should consider using SAP Replication Server, which has even less of an impact on source systems than SLT.

**SLT Replication Process**

SLT consists of a few modules: The *read module* reads the delta data from the logging tables in the source system, the *controller module* controls the replication, and the *write module* loads the data into the SAP HANA target system.

The write module uses a database connection to the target SAP HANA system, as shown in Figure 14.9. SLT can also load data into other target databases.

All the SLT modules are written in ABAP. The controller and write modules are always run within the SLT system.

If the source system is an SAP system, which also uses ABAP code, then the read module is run from within the SAP source system. ABAP modules in different systems communicate with each other using a *remote function call* (RFC) connection.

If the source system is not an SAP system, then the read module ABAP code cannot run in the source system. In this case, the read module is run in the SLT system, and a database connection is used to read the delta data from the logging tables in the source system's database.

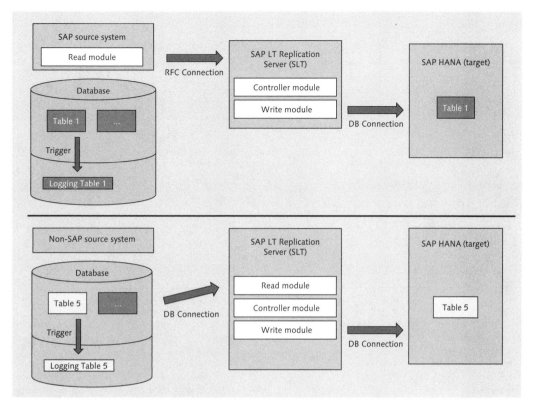

**Figure 14.9**   SLT Replication Process for SAP and non-SAP Source Systems

### Other SLT Replication Features

You can perform filtering and simple transformations as you load the data into SAP HANA by calling ABAP code inside SLT. Because SLT uses ABAP code, you can create more complex transformations, but this would interfere with the real-time advantages of SLT. If you require complex transformations or data cleaning, consider using SAP Data Services.

Because SLT can read data from older SAP systems, it can also read non-Unicode data from these systems. SLT converts this data to Unicode while it is replicated to SAP HANA. This is required, because SAP HANA uses Unicode.

### Creating and Managing an SLT Replication Configuration

Figure 14.10 shows the last summary step for creating an SLT replication configuration. You can see that the source system is an SAP system because we specified an RFC connection.

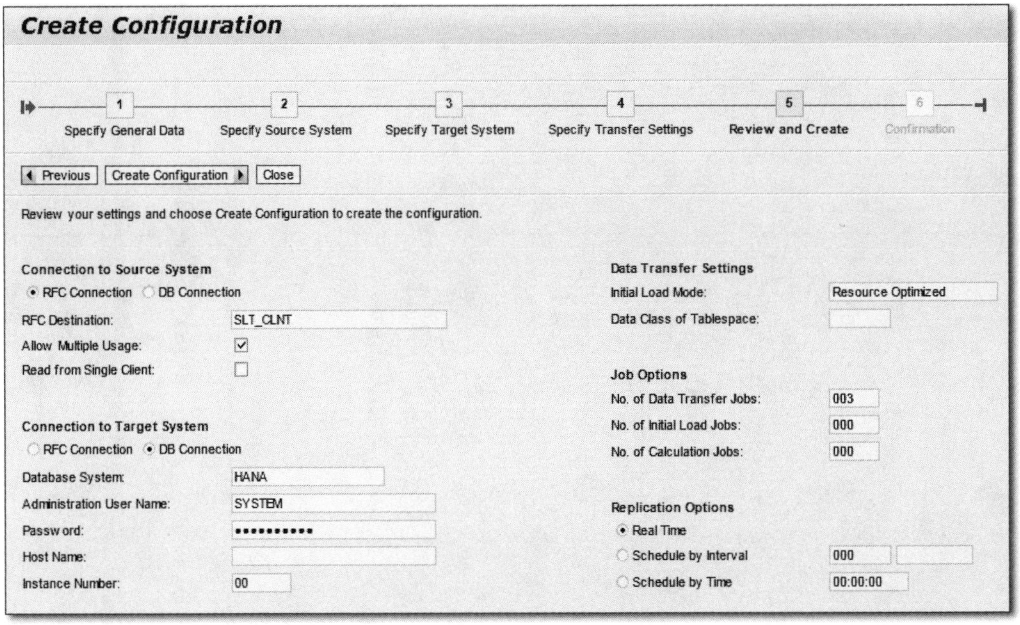

**Create Configuration**

| 1 | 2 | 3 | 4 | 5 | 6 |
|---|---|---|---|---|---|
| Specify General Data | Specify Source System | Specify Target System | Specify Transfer Settings | Review and Create | Confirmation |

◀ Previous | Create Configuration ▶ | Close

Review your settings and choose Create Configuration to create the configuration.

**Connection to Source System**
● RFC Connection   ○ DB Connection
RFC Destination:            SLT_CLNT
Allow Multiple Usage:       ☑
Read from Single Client:    ☐

**Connection to Target System**
○ RFC Connection   ● DB Connection
Database System:            HANA
Administration User Name:   SYSTEM
Password:                   ●●●●●●●●●●
Host Name:
Instance Number:            00

**Data Transfer Settings**
Initial Load Mode:          Resource Optimized
Data Class of Tablespace:

**Job Options**
No. of Data Transfer Jobs:  003
No. of Initial Load Jobs:   000
No. of Calculation Jobs:    000

**Replication Options**
● Real Time
○ Schedule by Interval      000
○ Schedule by Time          00:00:00

**Figure 14.10**   Setting Up SLT Replication Configuration

Within the SLT replication server, we can also monitor, manage, and troubleshoot the replication.

### Monitoring SLT from SAP HANA Studio

You can also monitor and control the replication from SAP HANA studio. From the QUICK VIEW menu in the Modeler perspective, select the DATA PROVISIONING option. Figure 14.11 shows the resulting SLT data provisioning screen.

You can choose which tables you want replicated to the SAP HANA target system with the LOAD and REPLICATE buttons on the right. The LOAD button will perform only an initial load of the selected tables, whereas the REPLICATE button will perform an initial and a continuous delta load of the selected tables.

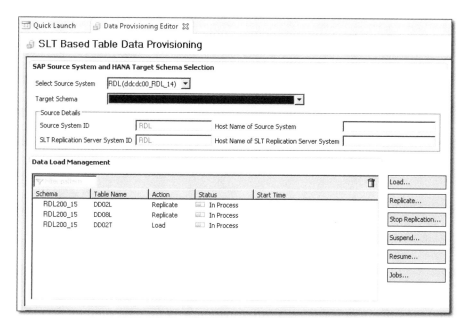

**Figure 14.11**   Controlling SLT Replication from SAP HANA Studio

To speed up the selection of tables from the source system, SLT always replicates
tables DD02L, DD08L, and DD02T. These tables contain the list of tables available in
the source system. Having the full list of available tables in SAP HANA speeds up
the table selection for the data provisioning administrator.

Once the replication is running, you can SUSPEND and RESUME the replication
with the appropriate buttons. You can use these options to pause the SLT replication when needed, such as when you need to perform maintenance on any of
the replication servers.

If you no longer wish to replicate the tables, you can permanently stop the replication by using the STOP REPLICATION button.

**Benefits of SLT**

Use SLT for your data provisioning needs when:

▶ Replication of data is preferred to transformation

▶ There is a business requirement or preference to get the data into SAP HANA
in real time

▶ The use of triggers is acceptable

▶ Replication of data from older SAP systems is required

### SAP Replication Server

*SAP Replication Server* (SRS), previously called Sybase Replication Server, also uses replication to load data into SAP HANA. The focus of a replication server is to load the data into the target system as fast as possible, with minimal impact on the source system.

#### Log-Based Replication

SRS differs from SLT in that it uses the database log files for real-time replication, as shown in Figure 14.12. Its delta load mechanism is log-based. As data changes in tables, all databases write these changes into a database log file. SRS reads these database log files to enable table replication. SRS replication is also known as *log-based replication*. This log file replication mechanism has even less of an impact on the source system than SLT.

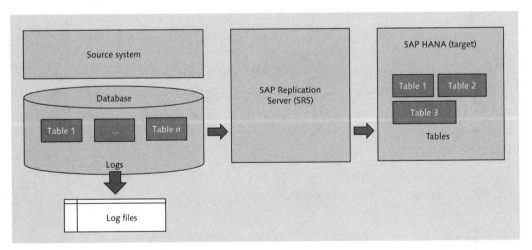

**Figure 14.12**  SAP Replication Server

SRS works with both SAP and non-SAP source systems and supports many databases.

Replication servers do not focus on the filtering or transformation of data before loading the data into SAP HANA.

The database log files contain all the changes in a database. SAP Replication Server can use this information to replicate entire databases. For example, SAP ASE databases use SRS to replicate the database log files for disaster recovery purposes.

SLT became more popular with increased use of SAP HANA systems because SLT understands SAP systems.

**Benefits of SAP Replication Server**

Consider using SRS for your data provisioning needs when:

▶ Replication of data is preferred to transformation

▶ There is a business requirement or preference to get the data into SAP HANA in real-time

▶ The use of triggers is not acceptable

▶ No pool or cluster tables need to be replicated

▶ The business requires minimal impact on the source system

▶ Database replication is needed for disaster recovery purposes

## SAP Direct Extractor Connection

The purpose of *SAP Direct Extractor Connection* (DXC) is to use extractors from SAP systems to load data into SAP HANA. When the extractors require activation, SAP Data Services might not be able to use these complex extractors. A good business case for DXC is to use it to load some financial data from an SAP Business Suite system into SAP HANA with minimal modeling effort.

 **Tip**

DXC only works with SAP source systems, because only SAP systems use extractors.

You can replicate the multiple financial tables from the SAP source system using SLT, but you will end up with many tables inside SAP HANA, as shown in the top process diagram in Figure 14.13. You will then have to create a complex data model to join all the tables and manipulate the data in SAP HANA.

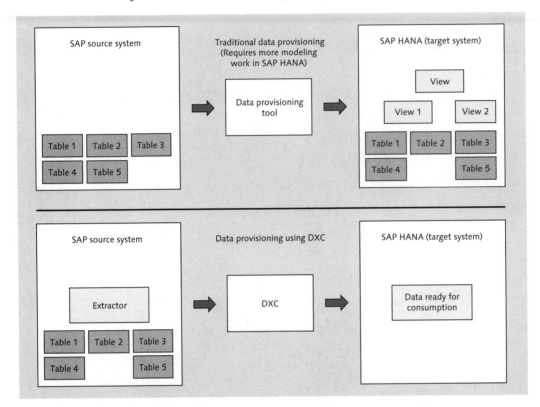

**Figure 14.13** Replication vs. Extractors for Data Provisioning

By using the extractors via DXC, financial data is delivered to you in SAP HANA in a nicely packaged way that is immediately usable, and you don't have to create a complex data model in SAP HANA (see the bottom process diagram in Figure 14.13). The disadvantage of this option is that these extractors are not available in real time. If you require real-time replication, then SLT or SRS is a better option.

As we discussed in the SAP Extractors section, SAP extractors were created to easily load data from SAP business systems into SAP BW. Even though SAP Data Services can use some of the extractors, only an SAP BW system can use all of the available extractors.

There may be times when you want to use SAP extractors to load data into SAP HANA, but without your data making a pit stop at SAP BW before moving into SAP HANA, which wastes both time and disk space. DXC provides an alternative option.

The only system that really can read all the available extractors is an SAP BW system. Instead of installing yet another SAP BW system for providing data to SAP HANA, we use the embedded SAP BW in the SAP source system. SAP business systems are all built on the SAP NetWeaver platform, and SAP BW is part of the SAP NetWeaver platform. Therefore, all ABAP-based SAP NetWeaver systems have an SAP BW system embedded. Normally, this embedded SAP BW system is not activated; it just lies dormant.

Figure 14.6 illustrated how extractors normally work with SAP BW; compare that to Figure 14.14. Normally, the SAP BW system is external to the SAP source system, but in this case, we activate the embedded SAP BW system inside the SAP source system.

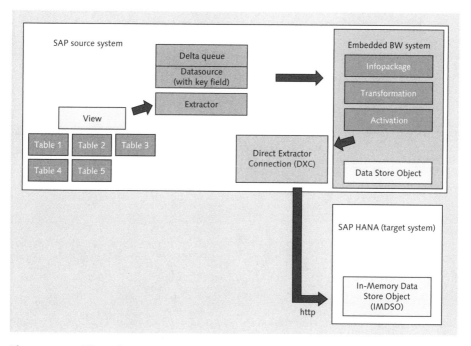

**Figure 14.14**   Direct Extractor Connection

The process flow is almost exactly the same. You have an SAP extractor, it puts the data in the data source and populates the delta queue, the InfoPackage schedules the loading of the delta data into the SAP BW system, and we transform and activate the data.

There are a few notable exceptions, however:

▸  The data source in this case requires a key field.

▸  DXC is also installed in the SAP system. The SAP BW system thinks it is writing the data into a DSO, but DXC instead intercepts the data writing process and sends it to SAP HANA via an HTTP connection.

▸  Inside SAP HANA, DXC writes the data into an *In-Memory DataStore Object* (IMDSO)—the SAP HANA memory-optimized version of an SAP BW DSO.

Consider using DXC for your data provisioning needs when:

▸  All the source systems are SAP systems.

▸  The business wants to use SAP extractors to minimize the modeling effort in SAP HANA.

▸  Real-time data provisioning is not a business requirement.


## SAP HANA Smart Data Access

*SAP HANA smart data access* (SDA) provides SAP HANA with direct access to data in a remote database. In this case, we do not store the data in the SAP HANA database; we can access it at any time. We merely consume the remote data when required.


### Virtual Tables

SDA allows you to create *virtual tables*, empty tables that point to tables or views inside another database somewhere (see Figure 14.15). Some databases have a similar feature called *proxy tables*, also sometimes called *data federation*.

SDA has various database *adapters* it uses to connect these virtual tables to a large number of databases. These adapters include the following:

▸  SAP HANA, SAP ASE, SAP IQ, and SAP MaxDB

▸  Hadoop (Hive), Spark, and SAP HANA Vora

- IBM DB2 and IBM Netezza

- Microsoft SQL Server

- Oracle

- Teradata

SDA can also use an ODBC framework to connect to other databases via ODBC connectivity.

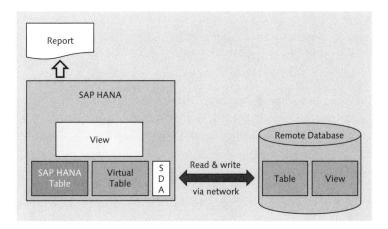

**Figure 14.15**   SDA and Virtual Tables

When you ask for data from a virtual table, SAP HANA connects to the remote database across the network, logs in, and requests the relevant data from the remote table or view. You can combine the data from the remote database table with data stored in SAP HANA. You can use a virtual table in SAP HANA information models, just like native SAP HANA tables. SDA will automatically convert the data types from those used in the remote database to SAP HANA data types.

**SDA Virtual Tables vs. SAP HANA Native Tables**

You cannot expect the same performance from SDA virtual tables as from SAP HANA native tables. SAP HANA tables are loaded in the memory of SAP HANA. The data from the virtual table is fetched from a relatively slow disk-based database across the network.

Keep in mind that SDA reads data from remote tables directly, as it is stored. It cannot do any data cleansing as it reads data from remote tables. SAP HANA also does not have any scheduling tool, so SDA cannot be used for ETL processes or replication. It just reads the data from the remote tables as the need arises; for example, a reporting query requires data to be stored in a remote table.

SAP HANA provides optimizations for SDA virtual tables:

▶ SAP HANA caches data that it reads from remote databases. If the data is found in the cache, the data is read from the cache and no request is sent to the remote database.

▶ SAP HANA can use *join relocation*. If you join two virtual tables from different remote databases, it can copy the smaller remote table to a temporary table in the remote system with the larger table. It then requests the second remote system to join the larger table to the temporary table.

▶ SAP HANA can push down queries to remote databases if it will execute faster in the remote database, rather than copy lots of data via the network. For example, a remote database can calculate an aggregate faster on half a million records than it will take to the copy these records across the network for SAP HANA to aggregate.

▶ SAP HANA also has optimization features for aggregating data. It uses functional compensation to compensate for certain (missing) features in other databases.

### Implementing SDA

It's easy to create and use virtual tables with SDA. Once the relevant database adapter is set up, you can create a new virtual table, as shown in Figure 14.16.

In the SYSTEMS tab, open the PROVISIONING folder. From the context menu, select NEW REMOTE SOURCE. On the right side of the screen, you can see the settings for connecting to the remote database. In this case, it shows a remote SAP HANA system.

Once the remote source is created, you can drill down in the REMOTE SOURCES folder to find the remote table you want to use.

From the context menu of the remote table, select ADD AS VIRTUAL TABLE, provide a name for your virtual table, select a schema in your local SAP HANA system, and click on CREATE (see Figure 14.17). You can find the newly created virtual table in your local SAP HANA schema.

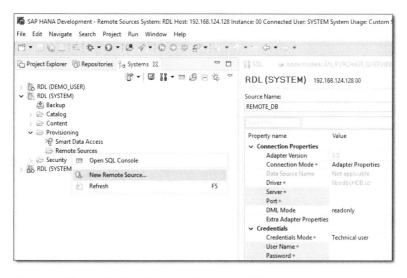

**Figure 14.16**   Create New Remote Source for SDA

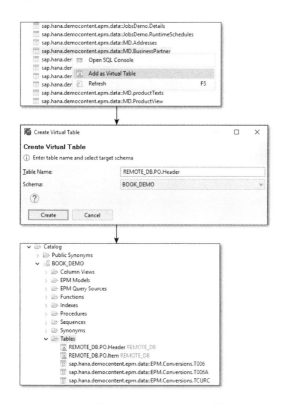

**Figure 14.17**   Adding a New Virtual Table in SAP HANA

You can use your newly created virtual tables in SAP HANA information models (Figure 14.18), just like you would do normally with SAP HANA in-memory tables.

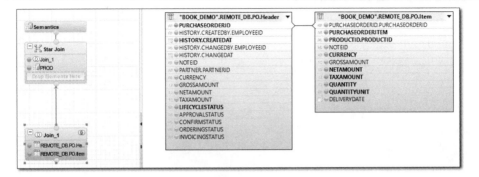

**Figure 14.18**   Using Virtual Tables in SAP HANA Modeling

All features of SAP HANA information models are available. Figure 14.19 shows what the PERFORMANCE ANALYSIS information looks like for an SAP HANA calculation view using two virtual tables.

**Figure 14.19**   Performance Analysis Mode for Calulation View with Virtual Tables

### Big Data Use Case

We often hear about people wanting to put all their data into a single physical data warehouse to analyze it there. Some variations are called *data lakes*. This scenario is referred to as *big data* (see Figure 14.20, left).

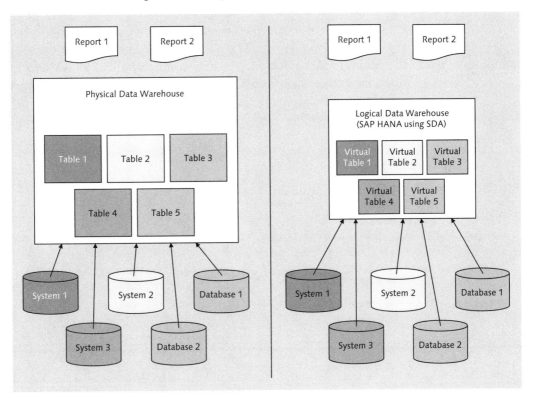

**Figure 14.20**  Logical Data Warehouse Use Case for SDA

There are a few problems with the physical data warehouse approach:

▶ You have to duplicate all your data, so your data is double the size, and you now need more storage. You essentially have doubled your cost and effort.

▶ You have to copy all of that data via the network, which slows your network.

▶ The data in the new data warehouse is never up-to-date, and as such, the data is never consistent.

▶ The single data warehouse system itself cannot handle all the different types of data requirements, such as unstructured data, graph engine data, key–value pairs, spatial data, huge varieties of data, and so on.

These are some of the issues we deal with in the physical data warehouse scenario, and with such issues, it might be better to consider a *logical data warehouse*. You keep the data in your source systems, don't duplicate it via the network, and don't store copies of it. This is where SDA fits in. You create virtual tables for the various data sources. All the data is stored inside SAP HANA and behaves just as in a single data warehouse. You get the data from the various source databases only when required, and can then access those bits of specific data, combine them with other data, and report on it (see Figure 14.20, right).

**Data Archiving Use Case**

SDA can help implement data archiving of SAP HANA data, as shown in Figure 14.21.

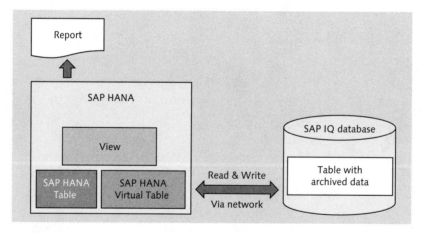

**Figure 14.21**   Data Archiving Use Case for SDA

Let's think about a retail company. Retail companies have millions of transactional records in their databases. For example, they have a few reports that analyze and compare this year's Mother's Day sales to last year's Mother's Day sales. Most of their reports, however, only use the last six weeks of data, analyzing and comparing items such as this month's payday sales to last month's sales.

The retail company does not want to load all its retail data into SAP HANA. Why would you load rarely used data into expensive memory? Using SDA, a company can write the rarely used data—anything older than six weeks—into an *SAP IQ* database (a columnar disk-based database) for archiving. This is called *warm data*. The data in SAP HANA is called *hot data*.

The company can now create a simple view that combines the warm archived data in SAP IQ with the hot data in SAP HANA.

For all reports on newer (hot) data only, the SAP HANA system still delivers typical fast reporting times. If you request a report that uses older (warm) data, the report will be somewhat slower because it will combine data from SAP HANA and SAP IQ. However, this slower response is acceptable because these types of reports are not run very often, and the cost savings justify the slower responses.

 **Tip**

Although the virtual table technology for SDA seems quite simple, the implemented use cases can have a huge impact.

**Benefits of SDA**

Consider using SDA for your data provisioning needs when

- You do not need to store all the data inside SAP HANA

- You use a logical data warehouse or are presented with a big data scenario

- You need integration with Hadoop

- You use a smaller SAP HANA system

- Real-time data provisioning is not a business requirement

- SAP HANA performance is not required

- You have no need to transform or clean data

## SAP HANA Enterprise Information Management

*SAP HANA smart data integration* (SDI) and *SAP HANA smart data quality* (SDQ) together are referred to as *SAP HANA Enterprise Information Management* (EIM). Both are optional SAP HANA components that you can purchase.

As shown in Figure 14.22, SDI and SDQ can work similarly to ELT (refer back to Figure 14.3).

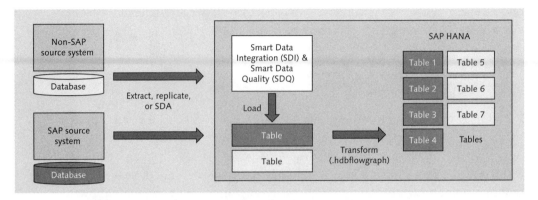

**Figure 14.22**   Smart Data Integration and Smart Data Quality Modules in SAP HANA

Using various adapters, including SDA adapters, we can replicate or consume data into SAP HANA. Then, using SDQ capabilities, we can transform and clean that data.

### SAP HANA Smart Data Integration

SDI can use various adapters to replicate, load, or consume data into SAP HANA.

Via SDA adapters, SDI can consume data from a large list of databases using virtual tables. SDI has some real-time adapters, for example, reading the database log files of source systems like Oracle, Microsoft SQL Server, and IBM DB2 databases. These same adapters can be used to read data from SAP systems like SAP ERP. SDI also has a real-time adapter for Twitter, as well as batch adapters for reading web services via OData and for reading data from Hadoop Hive.

The difference between the log-based adapters for SDI and SRS is that SDI is limited to SAP HANA as your target system for your data provisioning, whereas a standalone SRS system can have many target systems.

### SAP HANA Smart Data Quality

SDQ has similar advantages as SAP Data Services for data cleaning and transformation, and you would choose it for the same reasons. It also provides complex transformations of your data. The data flows in SDQ use the hdbflowgraph features inside SAP HANA and therefore also use AFM. (We used this tool for predictive models in Chapter 9.) These data flows work differently than in SAP Data

Services. You will therefore not be able to simply copy and paste your SAP Data Services data flows into SDQ.

SDQ is limited to SAP HANA as your target system for your data provisioning, whereas a standalone SAP Data Services system can have many target systems.

### Benefits of SAP HANA Enterprise Management

Consider using SAP HANA EIM (SDI and SDQ) for your data provisioning needs when:

▶ An ELT tool is required

▶ Transformation of the data is required, such as when the data is not clean

▶ Real-time data provisioning might be a business requirement

▶ Replication of data is required, with later transformation of the data

▶ The only data provision target is SAP HANA

## SAP HANA Smart Data Streaming

*SAP HANA smart data streaming* (SDS) provides SAP HANA with the ability to observe, process, and analyze fast-moving data. This was previously a standalone product called Sybase Event Stream Processing (ESP). It is now part of SAP HANA and extends the capabilities of the SAP HANA platform with the addition of real-time event stream processing.

Just like SDI and SDQ, SDS is an optional SAP HANA component that you can purchase.

### Data Streaming

Let's look at an example of why you might use data stream processing.

Say that you want to monitor some manufacturing equipment. Sensor data tells you the equipment temperature, but that data alone is not very interesting. If the equipment temperature is 90°C and the pressure is high, that might be normal. However, if the temperature is 180°C when the pressure is high, that could indicate a dangerous situation in which equipment could be blown apart, causing accidents and manufacturing losses. You want to receive an alert before a situation becomes critical and to analyze the temperature and pressure trends over time and the relationship between these factors.

The temperature data is not important, and you do not want to store this data. The data, once exposed and processed, is no longer useful. You just want to find the trend, see the relationships between the data, and react when certain conditions are met within a certain time period.

Data streaming and the processing of such information is different than a single event, like a database trigger. Figure 14.23 illustrates the data streaming process.

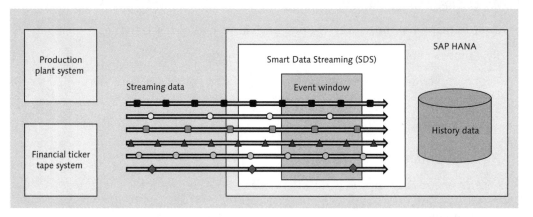

**Figure 14.23**   Smart Data Streaming

Another example to illustrate the use of SDS is in stock trade. You can have many streams of financial data coming in at very high speeds. How do you react to these continual data streams in a short span of time? What do you react to? A single stock going down may not be a problem, but if many stock prices start going down quickly within a certain time window—say, five minutes—that could indicate a stock market crash. The single price values are of little importance. The important information is found in combining many trends and finding the trend in a certain time window.

The *Internet of Things* (IoT) is not in the future: It's already here. Millions of devices are now connected and delivering information. We even have lightbulbs with built-in Wi-Fi that can be controlled from an app on your smartphone. How do you take advantage of all the data that's available? How do you collect it and analyze it?

With SDS, you can not only analyze data streams but also store this data and perform deeper, wider analytics of it at a later stage. In this way, SDS and SAP HANA complement each other.

### Computation Continuous Language

With SDS, you can define continuous queries on streaming data and specify how the system must react to these events (see Figure 14.24).

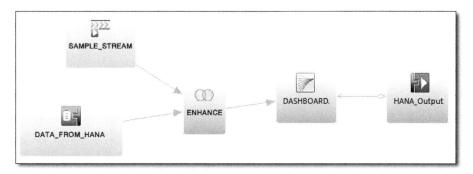

**Figure 14.24**   Example CCL Flow in Visual Editor for Smart Data Streaming

You can define streaming *projects*, which define input streams, continuous queries, and outputs. These projects are defined in the stream processing language called *Computation Continuous Language* (CCL). A streaming plug-in for SAP HANA studio provides both a CCL editor and a visual editor, along with testing tools. SDS uses AFM.

### Benefits of SDS

Consider using SDS for your data provisioning needs when:

▶ You need to analyze real-time streaming data for events in a certain time window and react to the same

▶ Fast-moving data is observed, processed, and analyzed, but not stored

▶ Data is processed as-is: There is no data cleaning, but you have to find a signal in spite of the noisy data

## Flat Files or Microsoft Excel Datasheets

*Flat files* (also called *CSV files*) or *Microsoft Excel datasheets* are the simplest way to provision data to SAP HANA. Especially in proof-of-concept (POC) or sandbox testing projects, you can waste time connecting SAP HANA to the various source systems. You do not need the latest data; you just want to find out if an idea you have for information modeling will work.

As such, it makes sense to ask the business to provide you with the data in flat files, and then you can load the data into SAP HANA for the POC or sandbox development (see Figure 14.25).

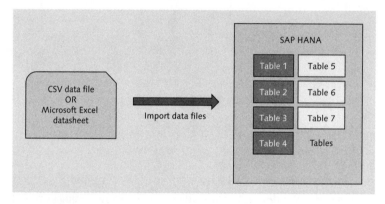

**Figure 14.25**   Loading Data into SAP HANA from Text Files or Microsoft Excel Datasheets

Just watch out for security concerns. Many companies have a rule that data at rest (i.e., on disk) should be encrypted. In this case, security policies will prevent you from using this method.

Loading data files into SAP HANA is simple and quick. From the IMPORT menu, select DATA FROM LOCAL FILE (Figure 14.26). On the following screen, specify the file and where you want to import it to in SAP HANA.

If you are importing multiple files to the same database table—for example, 2014, 2015, and 2016 data files—you will be asked to map the data fields. The import process only allows a simple 1:1 mapping, as shown in Figure 14.27. This mapping is used if some of the fields in the data files are in a different order than the previously imported data files.

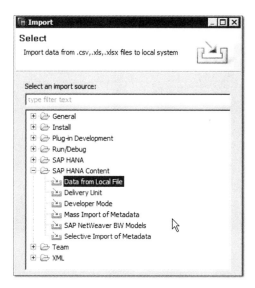

**Figure 14.26**   Importing Data from a File Stored on Your Personal Computer

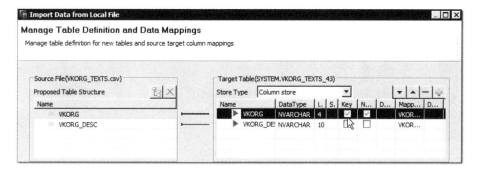

**Figure 14.27**   Simple Mapping of Fields

Consider using data files for your data provisioning needs when:

▸ You only need to load the data once

▸ There is no connection available to the source systems

▸ You need simple and quick loading of data

▸ Data security is not a concern

### Web Services (OData and REST)

We won't discuss web services in detail in this text, but of course you can consume data from a source system that provides it via web services. You can consume these web services using the SAP HANA XS development environment inside SAP HANA.

The SAP HANA XS engine can consume OData and REST web services, as shown in Figure 14.28. The data is normally transferred in JavaScript Object Notation (JSON) format rather than XML format.

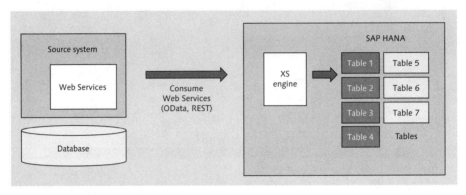

**Figure 14.28**   Data Provisioning via Web Services

Consider using web services for your data provisioning needs when the source systems only expose their data as *web services*. This is typical of *web and cloud applications*.

## Important Terminology

In this chapter, we cover the following important terms:

▶ **Data provisioning**
Get data from a source system and provide that data to a target system.

▶ **Extract, Transform, and Load (ETL)**
The ETL process consists of the following phases:

  ▶ *Extraction*: Data is read from a source system. Traditional ETL tools can read many data sources, and most can also read data from SAP source systems.

▶ *Transform*: Data is transformed. Normally this means cleaning the data, but it can refer to any data manipulation.

▶ *Load*: Data is written into the target system.

▶ **Initial load**
The process of making a full copy of data from the source system. If we require an entire table, we make a copy of the table in the target system.

▶ **Delta load**
Look at the data that has changed and apply the data changes to the copy of the data in the target system. These data changes are referred to as the *delta*, and applying these changes to the target system is called a *delta load*.

▶ **SAP extractors**
Reads data from a group of tables, and delivers the data as a single integrated data unit to the target system.

▶ **Open Database Connectivity (ODBC)**
ODBC acts as a translation layer between an application and a database via an ODBC driver. Database queries are written using a standard API for accessing database information. The ODBC driver translates these queries to database-specific queries, making your database queries database and operating system independent. By changing the ODBC driver to that of another database and changing your connection information, your application will work with another database.

▶ **Java Database Connectivity (JDBC)**
JDBC is similar to ODBC but specifically aimed at the Java programming language.

▶ **Object Linking and Embedding, Database for Online Analytical Processing (ODBO)**
ODBO provides an API for exchanging metadata and data between an application and an OLAP server (like a data warehouse using cubes). You can use this to connect Microsoft Excel to SAP HANA.

▶ **Multidimensional Expressions (MDX)**
MDX is a query language for OLAP databases, similar to how SQL is a query language for relational (OLTP) databases. The MDX standard was adopted by a wide range of OLAP vendors, including SAP.

▶ **Business Intelligence Consumer Services (BICS)**

BICS is an SAP-proprietary database connection. It is a direct client connection that performs better and faster than MDX or SQL. Hierarchies are supported, negating the need for MDX in SAP environments. Because this is an SAP-only connection type, you can only use it between two SAP systems—for example, from an SAP reporting tool to SAP BW.

▶ **SAP Data Services**

Solution used to integrate, improve the quality of, profile, process, and deliver data.

▶ **SAP LT Replication Server (SLT)**

Uses replication to load data into SAP HANA. Remember that the focus of a replication server is to load data into the target system as fast as possible.

▶ **SAP Replication Server (SRS)**

Uses replication to load data into SAP HANA. SRS differs from SLT in that it uses the database log files for real-time replication. SRS reads these database log files to enable table replication. SRS replication is also known as *log-based replication*.

▶ **SAP Direct Extractor Connection (DXC)**

Uses extractors from SAP systems to load data into SAP HANA using the embedded SAP BW system in SAP NetWeaver Systems.

▶ **SAP HANA smart data access (SDA)**

Provides SAP HANA with direct access to data in a remote database.

▶ **SAP HANA smart data integration (SDI)**

Uses various adapters to replicate, load, or consume data into SAP HANA.

▶ **SAP HANA smart data quality (SDQ)**

Used to cleanse and enrich data persisted in the SAP HANA database.

▶ **SAP HANA smart data streaming (SDS)**

Allows you to observe, process, and analyze fast-moving data. You can create continuous projects in CCL to model streaming information. You can then issue continuous queries to analyze the data.

## 🔧 Practice Questions

These practice questions will help you evaluate your understanding of the topic. The questions shown are similar in nature to those found on the certification examination. Although none of these questions will be found on the exam itself, they will allow you to review your knowledge of the subject. Select the correct answers and then check the completeness of your answers in the Practice Question Answers and Explanations section. Remember that on the exam you must select all correct answers and only correct answers to receive credit for the question.

1. Which of the following SAP data provisioning tools can provide real-time data provisioning? (There are 3 correct answers.)

   ☐ **A.** SDI
   ☐ **B.** SAP Data Services
   ☐ **C.** SRS
   ☐ **D.** DXC
   ☐ **E.** SLT

2. What is the correct sequence for loading data with SAP Data Services?

   ☐ **A.** Extract • Load • Transform
   ☐ **B.** Load • Transform • Extract
   ☐ **C.** Load • Extract • Transform
   ☐ **D.** Extract • Transform • Load

3. You are loading data into SAP HANA using DXC. Which of the following are executed in the embedded SAP BW system? (There are 3 correct answers.)

   ☐ **A.** InfoPackage
   ☐ **B.** Transformation
   ☐ **C.** Extractor
   ☐ **D.** Activation
   ☐ **E.** IMDSO

4.  Which of the following database terms are used when providing OLAP data with hierarchies? (There are 3 correct answers.)

☐  **A.** ODBC

☐  **B.** ODBO

☐  **C.** BICS

☐  **D.** JDBC

☐  **E.** MDX

5.  Which of the following data provisioning tools can provide a delta load of a table from the source system?

☐  **A.** SDS

☐  **B.** SDA

☐  **C.** DXC

☐  **D.** Flat files

6.  Which of the following data operations can you perform with SDA? (There are 3 correct answers.)

☐  **A.** Data federation

☐  **B.** Logical data warehouse

☐  **C.** Physical data warehouse

☐  **D.** Big data

☐  **E.** Real-time replication

7.  You get the following requirements from a customer: They have a lot of purchasing data in their SAP system which they wish to analyze in SAP HANA. They want to have reports every morning showing the total expenditure per department. Their SAP BW developers have not yet had any SAP HANA training. Which data provisioning tool would you recommend?

☐  **A.** SLT

☐  **B.** SDA

☐  **C.** EIM

☐  **D.** DXC

8. You want to pause the SLT replication in SAP HANA studio. What do you select to achieve this?

☐ **A.** Quick View • Data Provisioning • Stop

☐ **B.** Quick View • Import • Selected Import of Metadata

☐ **C.** Quick View • Data Provisioning • Suspend

☐ **D.** Quick View • Configure Import Server

9. Which programming language do you use for streaming projects?

☐ **A.** CCL

☐ **B.** JavaScript

☐ **C.** SQL

☐ **D.** SQLScript

10. You want to retrieve data from a web application. Which of the following could you use? (There are 3 correct answers.)

☐ **A.** JSON

☐ **B.** REST

☐ **C.** JDBC

☐ **D.** BICS

☐ **E.** OData

11. True or False: SAP Data Services can read all the SAP extractors.

☐ **A.** True

☐ **B.** False

12. Why would you recommend SAP Replication Server?

☐ **A.** If the data contains some rubbish information in several places.

☐ **B.** If database administrators do not want triggers in their database.

☐ **C.** If the data is financial ticker tape data.

☐ **D.** If the source data is in a virtual table.

13. Which data provisioning tools can use SAP HANA adapters? (There are 2 correct answers.)

☐  **A.** SDA

☐  **B.** SDS

☐  **C.** SDI

☐  **D.** SRS

14. Which of the following data provisioning tools can you use to read data directly from Twitter? (There are 3 correct answers.)

☐  **A.** SRS

☐  **B.** SAP HANA XS engine

☐  **C.** SAP Data Services

☐  **D.** SDI

☐  **E.** SDA

## Practice Question Answers and Explanations

1. Correct answers: **A, C, E**

   SDI, SRS, and SLT. Also see Table 14.1 for a quick reference.

2. Correct answer: **D**

   EXTRACT • TRANSFORM • LOAD. SAP Data Services is an ETL tool.

3. Correct answers: **A, B, D**

   InfoPackage for scheduling the data provisioning, transformation, and activation. The in-memory DSO is in SAP HANA. The extractor is in the SAP source system (see Figure 14.15).

4. Correct answers: **B, C, E**

   ODBO (used with Microsoft Excel), BICS (used between SAP systems only), and MDX (query language for OLAP, like SQL is a query language for relational databases). See the Database Connections section.

5. Correct answer: **C**

   DXC provides delta loads. SDS performs neither initial nor delta loads. SDA and flat files could only perform an initial load.

6. Correct answers: **A, B, D**

   Data federation, logical data warehouse, and big data. SDA is not used to load data for a physical data warehouse because there is no delta load mechanism. SDA cannot perform real-time replication because there is no delta load mechanism.

7. Correct answer: **D**

   DXC. The data is in an SAP system. "Their SAP BW developers" implies that they know SAP BW well. They want to do minimal modeling in SAP HANA because they do not know it very well yet. A report with total expenditure per department is a simple aggregation report in SAP HANA, provided all the data is in a single unit—which DXC provides.

8. Correct answer: **A**

   QUICK VIEW • DATA PROVISIONING. STOP will permanently stop the replication. The other two answers are not valid. Note that the two invalid answers do exist in the system. In the SAP HANA certification exams, all answer options have to exist in the system.

9. Correct answer: **A**

   CCL. See the Computation Continuous Language section.

10. Correct answers: **A, B, E**

    JSON, REST, and OData are all associated with web services (see the Web Services (OData and REST) section).

    Web applications (in the cloud or on the Internet) do not allow JDBC database connections.

    Web applications are not necessarily SAP systems that understand BICS. Again, a web application will not allow database connections via the Internet for security reasons.

11. Correct answer: **B**

    False. SAP Data Services cannot read all the SAP extractors (see Figure 14.7).

12. Correct answer: **B**

    Database administrators do not want triggers in their database. This means that you cannot use SLT, so SRS is an option. If the data contains some rubbish information, it will need cleaning, and you will want to use SAP Data Services or SDQ. Financial ticker tape data means that this is streaming data, so use SDS. If the data is a pool table, then you should use SLT (or possibly SAP Data Services; look back at one of the previous questions).

13. Correct answers: **A, C**

SDA and SDI use the SDA adapters. To use the built-in adapters, the data provisioning tools also have to be built in. SDS reads streaming data, but not by using the adapters. SRS reads database log files. Even though SDI can use log-based adapters, SRS does not use these because SRS is not built into SAP HANA.

14. Correct answers: **B, C, D**

Twitter does have web services. This is not specified in the book, so in the actual exam this option would not appear because it makes too many assumptions. For the purposes of this book, we assumed that everyone knows what Twitter is and that it has web services. SAP Data Services can read social media feeds. Refer to the Extracting Data section. SDI has a Twitter adapter. See the SAP HANA Smart Data Integration section.

## Takeaway

You should now have a high-level understanding of the various SAP data provisioning tools available for getting data into an SAP HANA system and what each one does.

When asked to recommend an SAP data provisioning tool during a project, you can use Table 14.1 as a quick reference.

| Business Requirement | Data Provisioning Tool |
|---|---|
| Real-time replication | SLT, SRS, or SDI |
| ETL, data cleaning | SAP Data Services or SDQ |
| Extractors | SAP Data Services or DXC |
| Streaming data | SAP ESP or SDS |
| Federation, big data | SDA |
| POC, dev, testing | Flat files or Microsoft Excel datasheets |

**Table 14.1**  Choosing a Data Provisioning Tool

# Summary

You've learned the various data provisioning concepts and looked at the different SAP data provisioning tools available in the context of SAP HANA. They all have their own strengths, and you now know when to use the various tools.

In this chapter, we looked at how to get data into SAP HANA. In the next chapter, we will do the opposite—that is, get data out of SAP HANA.

# Utilization of Information Models

## Techniques You'll Master

- Get insight into business intelligence concepts
- Understand the strategic direction of SAP business intelligence tools
- Differentiate between authors and consumers of business information
- Learn about the different SAP business intelligence tools
- Get to know the characteristics and high-level features of some business intelligence tools
- Identify when to use which SAP business intelligence tool
- Discover alternatives for providing information from SAP HANA to business users

This chapter is the last step to making your SAP HANA information models useful to people and businesses. In your work, you need to find ways to present the right information to the right people, at the right time, in the right way. You need to help end users with their responsibilities, analysts and decision makers to find new and innovative ways to grow their businesses into new areas, and executives to achieve their vision.

The focus of this chapter is business intelligence and how it relates to SAP HANA. Each of the SAP business intelligence tools have dedicated training courses, and there are specialists in each of the analytics topics. The objective of this chapter, and this particular portion of the exam, is therefore not to dive into all the deep details of the various tools. Rather, we aim to give you high-level working knowledge of what each tool does, present the concepts involved when consuming data from SAP HANA, and help you decide which tools are right for your particular business requirements.

### Real-World Scenario

You are working on an SAP HANA information modeling project and have created a few calculation views for a new business process.

In SAP HANA studio, you used the OPEN DATA PREVIEW feature to give managers an idea of what information they can expect from the calculation views. They like what they see, and want to deploy this solution to the users in the business. They ask you which business intelligence tool they should use.

You know that business needs are just as important as the technical capabilities of each tool and ask relevant questions in light of this fact. After evaluating business and technical requirements, you recommend the right business intelligence tool for the circumstances.

## Objectives of this Portion of the Test

The objective of this section of the SAP HANA certification is to test your high-level understanding of the various methods available to present information from an SAP HANA system to business users.

The certification exam expects you to have a good understanding of the following topics:

▶ General concepts of business intelligence for consumers of SAP HANA information models.

▶ List the connectivity methods for the business intelligence tools.

▶ Different SAP business intelligence tools.

▶ Characteristics and high-level features of the various business intelligence tools.

▶ When to use a particular SAP business intelligence tool with SAP HANA.

▶ Alternatives for providing information from SAP HANA to business users.

 **Note**

This portion contributes up to 5% of the total certification exam score.

## Key Concepts Refresher

In Chapter 14, we discussed how to provide data to SAP HANA systems. We started with the overview diagram shown in Figure 14.1, which we said could be viewed as a summary of the entire book.

We are now at the last step in the modeling process, in which you present your SAP HANA information models to the world!

 **Tip**

It will be useful to take another look at the Database Connections section in Chapter 14, which we will build on in this chapter.

Let's start by looking at *reporting* and the evolution of business intelligence.

### Business Intelligence Concepts

If you worked with data and modeling in the 1990s, you might have used something like Microsoft Visual Basic or Borland Delphi. Back then, you created reports for end users via reporting tool like Crystal Reports, which was one of the most-used reporting tools of the era. Another tool that financial people and engineers often used was Microsoft Excel. Both these tools surprisingly are still in use today and are discussed in this chapter.

*Reports* mostly consisted of thousands of lines of transactional line items, printed out on reams of papers. To make sense of all this data, you need to see the patterns or exceptions in all that text and form a mental picture. Over time, reporting tools improved and allowed you to embed simple graphs. You could develop more complex reports that resembled tax forms, with lots of blocks and lines. Instead of filling in these forms with a pen, they were populated from a database and then printed. (Workflows were still largely paper based.)

During those days, you needed programming skills to use reporting tools, as well as a working knowledge of databases. Reports were therefore developed by IT and were quite prescriptive. Developing these reports took time, and they could not be changed easily. Because running these reports was time-consuming, they were scheduled to be run and printed at night. Each morning, you would find your printed reports on your desk.

Business Objects acquired Crystal Reports from Seagate in 2003, and SAP acquired Business Objects in 2007. Today, we still have SAP Crystal Reports, albeit a largely improved version. However, this is no longer the only reporting tool available.

We have moved from simple reporting to the concept of business intelligence, which includes powerful analytics, data mining, and data science. "Reporting" as we once knew it is now merely a subsection of a much wider topic. We have moved from paper-based forms and workflows to web-based options and mobile consumption, and we now have the tools to enable it all.

In this chapter, we will only focus on the tools that are relevant for SAP HANA. Most of the tools are generic tools; that is, they are not specific to SAP HANA alone. Therein lies some of the complexity when choosing the right tool for the job!

*Business intelligence* can be described as taking raw (transactional) business data and transforming it into useful information for the purpose of business analysis. Building information models in SAP HANA can be seen as part of this process. We enable people to process large volumes of data to find new opportunities based on insights gained from our information models. Hopefully, this can provide businesses with a competitive market advantage and long-term sustainability.

Business intelligence can consist of the following:

▶ *Reporting* of historical and current information. We described reporting in the previous section. A *report* is a document that can contain information organized in a tabular or a graphical format.

▶ *Analytics*, through which we discover meaningful patterns in data and use visualization techniques to promote insight.

▶ *Complex event processing*, such as SAP HANA smart data streaming (SDS).

▶ *Predictive analytics*, through which we attempt to forecast what will happen.

▶ *Prescriptive analytics*, through which a business acts on predictive analytics— for example, by replacing a part in a machine before it breaks, because the predictive analytics indicate a high chance of the part breaking soon.

▶ *Text mining*, *data mining*, and *process mining*.

▶ *OLAP*—that is, SAP BW systems and data warehouses can be seen as a subsection of business intelligence.

### Convergence of SAP's Business Intelligence Tools

Over the years, SAP has collected and developed a large number of business intelligence tools. Some were added when SAP acquired Business Objects. Others were business intelligence tools developed for use with SAP Business Warehouse (BW). Others are new tools recently developed to make use of SAP HANA or to add new business intelligence features, such as visualization and predictive analysis.

The middle column of Table 15.1 shows a list of the available SAP business intelligence tools: There are 15 tools listed! SAP realized that this list is too long and decided to trim it to just five, which are shown in the right column. SAP calls this the *convergence* of its business intelligence tools.

**Convergence of SAP BI Tools**

| Office Integration | ▸ SAP BusinessObjects Analysis, edition for Microsoft Office (Analysis Office) ▸ Live Office ▸ EPM Add-In ▸ BEX Analyzer | ▸ SAP BusinessObjects Analysis, edition for Microsoft Office (Analysis Office) |
|---|---|---|
| Applications and Dashboards | ▸ SAP BusinessObjects Design Studio ▸ SAP BusinessObjects Dashboards ▸ SAP BusinessObjects Analysis, edition for online analytical processing (Analysis OLAP) ▸ BEX Web Application Designer | ▸ SAP BusinessObjects Design Studio |
| Data Discovery | ▸ SAP Lumira Desktop ▸ SAP Lumira Server ▸ Set Analysis ▸ SAP BusinessObjects Explorer | ▸ SAP Lumira |
| Reporting | ▸ SAP Crystal Reports ▸ SAP BusinessObjects Web Intelligence ▸ SAP BusinessObjects Desktop Intelligence | ▸ SAP Crystal Reports ▸ SAP BusinessObjects Web Intelligence |

**Table 15.1**   Convergence of SAP Business Intelligence Tools

SAP split the list of tools into four types, grouped by use cases rather than by features and functions. For each category (shown in the left column of Table 15.1), SAP selected only one or two business intelligence tools that will be actively developed and improved going forward. The tools not on this list will *converge* into the selected SAP business intelligence tool(s) for each category. These older tools will not stop working or disappear; they will still be maintained and supported, but they will not continue to be developed.

SAP also will not force people to migrate to the new, shorter list of tools. Because many of the tools have been in use for more than 20 years, it is not a simple matter to just "kill" the old products. Millions of reports are still running daily using these old tools. Such large-scale migrations are not feasible.

SAP recommends that all new projects should preferably use the list of SAP business intelligence tools in the right column. All the unique features might not yet be available in these five SAP BI tools, but they will be included over time.

The selected SAP business intelligence tools for each of the four content types are as follows:

▶ **Microsoft Office integration**
The SAP reporting tool going forward is SAP BusinessObjects Analysis, edition for Microsoft Office. This tool runs as a Microsoft Office plug-in.

▶ **Applications and dashboards**
SAP BusinessObjects Design Studio is a relatively young tool for creating dashboards and web applications.

▶ **Data discovery**
SAP Lumira is also a young tool, one that integrates very well with SAP HANA. It is strong with visualization and working with all different kinds of information. It is an easy tool to learn, so end users can quickly create impressive results.

▶ **Reporting**
The tools selected here are SAP BusinessObjects Web Intelligence and SAP Crystal Reports.

All five of the selected tools work well together, so you can publish results from one tool and consume it in another.

You should focus mainly on these five SAP business intelligence tools. SAP Business Explorer (BEx) tools are specifically for SAP BW and will not be discussed in this chapter.

**Creators and Consumers**

*Creators* use SAP's business intelligence tools to build models, reports, and analytics. *Consumers* use the same tools, but only to view the results. The dividing line is not always clear. It can be blurred with power users, who do a bit of both.

> **Tip**
>
> What is important here is that all of these people use the same business intelligence tools; they just use them in totally different ways. How each group uses these tools factors into deciding which tool to use.

**Professionally Authored and Self-Service**

Because people use these business intelligence tools differently, it is easy to see that some tools suit one group of people more, and other tools suit another group more.

Some SAP business intelligence tools suit an approach called *professionally authored*. These types of tools expect IT folks, creators, analysts, data scientists, and power users to be the creators and designers. Other tools suit a more relaxed approach. They make it easy for average end users, decision makers, and power users to find, discover, visualize, and consume information. This is the *self-service* approach.

> **Note**
>
> You can use the same tools with either approach. Some tools just seem to encourage a certain approach, as we will discuss when we look at individual tools.

There is also a group that lies in between these approaches. This group includes analysts who author business intelligence content for their own use or for use within their department or line of business (LOB).

These different groups are shown in Figure 15.1, which nearly summarizes the entire chapter. By looking at the usage patterns, the types of users, and the business intelligence tool categories, you can start to make a decision about which tool to use.

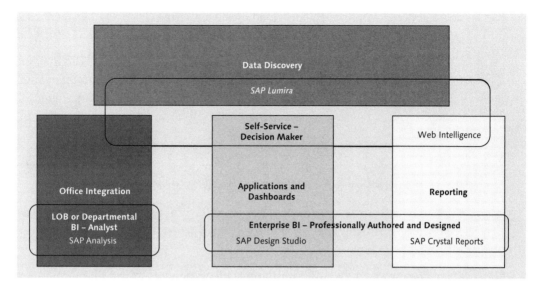

**Figure 15.1**   Four Types of SAP Business Intelligence Tools and Three Types of Users

## Trusted Data

The concept of *professionally authored* is associated with a concept called *trusted data*. SAP BusinessObjects Design Studio is an example of a trusted visualization and dashboard creation tool. With these types of tools, you are restricted to trusted data sources, such as universes, BEx queries, and SAP HANA views. These data sources are seen as "trusted" because they are managed and governed by IT. Although SAP BusinessObjects Design Studio leans towards creating professionally authored dashboards and applications, it is specifically focused to consume trusted data sources. It does not even allow you to connect to some types of data sources. SAP Lumira, on the other hand, allows you to be as open and free for your data discovery needs and allows you to connect it to a large variety of information sources.

## SAP Cloud for Analytics

In all areas of SAP, there is an emphasis on making sure products also work in the cloud. We have seen that even SAP HANA has cloud deployment (see the Cloud Deployments section in Chapter 3), and SAP business intelligence tools are no exception. SAP created a new cloud product offering called *SAP Cloud for Analytics*, which provides analytics functionality on SAP HANA Cloud Platform (HCP).

In this chapter, we will focus our attention on the on-premise SAP business intelligence tools. This does not mean that we will completely ignore the cloud; for example, you can publish directly from SAP Lumira, an on-premise SAP BI tool, to the cloud.

## Business Intelligence Tools for Microsoft Office Integration

Tools that integrate with parts of Microsoft Office fall within this section as they relate to SAP HANA. They mostly focus on Microsoft Excel but can also use Microsoft PowerPoint.

The convergence of the SAP's business intelligence tools means that we will not pay any attention in this chapter to Microsoft Live Office, the EPM Add-In, or the BEx Analyzer.

We'll look at two tools specifically: Microsoft Excel; and SAP BusinessObjects Analysis, edition for Microsoft Office (occasionally referred to as Analysis Office).

 **Note**

The official name is SAP BusinessObjects Analysis, edition for Microsoft Office. Analysis Office is not an official abbreviation, but we have seen it used in several publicly available SAP slide sets and published YouTube videos. You will also find it commonly used in online forms, such as those at SAP Community Network (SCN).

In the certification exam, the official name of an SAP product is always used. Sometimes, the exam will display the abbreviated name as well—for example, SAP HANA smart data access (SDA).

### Microsoft Excel

Let's start with Microsoft Excel, which is obviously not an SAP tool, but has probably been the most widely used and best-known business intelligence tool available for more than 30 years.

As much as financial and engineering departments love Microsoft Excel, many IT departments hate it. The difference lies in their approach to the same tool. People with a self-service approach love it, whereas people with a professionally authored approach hate it. IT does not control and manage it, so it is seen as "unprofessional."

### Fact Sheet

Figure 15.2 presents many useful facts about Microsoft Excel. We will use Microsoft Excel as an example to describe the layout of the fact sheet. We use this same layout to help you learn the features for each of the SAP business intelligence tools that we discuss in this chapter. The features presented in the fact sheets were selected to help you choose the correct tools when consuming your SAP HANA information models.

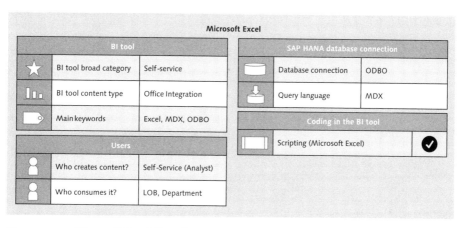

**Figure 15.2** Microsoft Excel Fact Sheet

Let's start at the top left of the fact sheet. Microsoft Excel is a self-service business intelligence tool and falls into the Office Integration category because it is actually a part of Microsoft Office. What do we learn from this?

▶ Because it is a self-service tool, this tells us that the users are self-service users or analysts, who consume it themselves or in their department. (Look again at Figure 15.1.)

▶ Because it falls into the Microsoft Office integration category, we know that the tool environment is Excel-based. Other business intelligence tools can, for example, be Eclipse-based or web-based. The end user also consumes the content created with this business intelligence tool in Microsoft Excel, either on their desktops or their tablets with the Microsoft Excel mobile app. Other end user consumption environments include dashboards, web applications, printed reports, web pages, or mobile apps.

Microsoft Excel uses the ODBO driver to connect to SAP HANA. It is the only business intelligence tool that uses this driver. The ODBO driver implies that it uses MDX, which means it can read cubes. This means that Microsoft Excel is able to consume SAP HANA analytic and calculation cube views. By knowing that ODBO uses MDX and that MDX reads cubes, you just have to remember that Microsoft Excel uses ODBO.

### *Using Microsoft Excel with SAP HANA*

Microsoft Excel is the ultimate self-service business intelligence tool. However, despite all its flexibility, it is also easy to use it "incorrectly." If you import 700,000 records into Microsoft Excel and then build a pivot table on that data, you are not using Excel in the best possible way. If you use it that way, you use Microsoft Excel as a database—and it is not meant to be a database. You are also straining the network while transferring that much data.

A better way to use Microsoft Excel is to connect it to SAP HANA, as shown in Figure 15.3. You can then build the pivot table directly on the SAP HANA view. In this case, SAP HANA performs all the calculations, and Microsoft Excel displays the results. The 700,000 records stay in SAP HANA, and the minimum amount of data is transferred via the network. SAP HANA usually also uses less memory and thus is faster.

The best way to test if you are using business intelligence tools correctly is to ask, will it work on a mobile device, like a tablet? If you load 700,000 records into Microsoft Excel, it will not work on your tablet. The tablet simply does not have enough memory, and your mobile data costs will be high. With the "correct" way, on the other hand, you could probably get this setup working on the mobile app version of Microsoft Excel if you had the correct driver installed.

An added benefit is that your reports and analytics become interactive; for example, drilldowns are easy to implement.

Connect to an SAP HANA system.

A pivot table with SAP HANA data.
All calculations are done by SAP HANA.

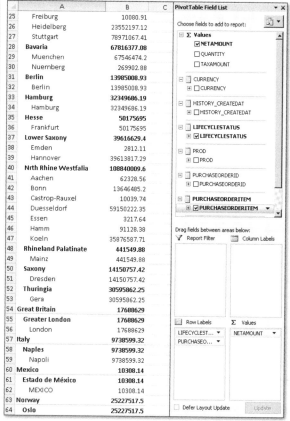

**Figure 15.3**   Use SAP HANA Information Models with Hierarchies in Pivot Table

## SAP BusinessObjects Analysis, Edition for Microsoft Office

SAP BusinessObjects Analysis, edition for Microsoft Office consists of plug-in tools for Microsoft Excel and Microsoft PowerPoint and therefore is a Microsoft Office integration type of business intelligence tool. The main user group for this is analysts, as the product name indicates.

Like Microsoft Excel, SAP BusinessObjects Analysis, edition for Microsoft Office is a self-service business intelligence tool. In this case, however, the focus is on working with trusted data (see Figure 15.4).

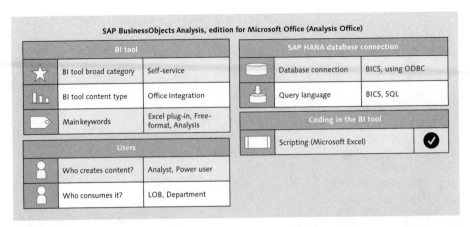

**Figure 15.4** SAP BusinessObjects Analysis, Edition for Microsoft Office Fact Sheet

Because SAP BusinessObjects Analysis, edition for Microsoft Office focuses on trusted OLAP data sources and is an SAP business intelligence tool, the preferred BICS connection is expected.

Figure 15.5 provides a snapshot of SAP BusinessObjects Analysis, edition for Microsoft Office.

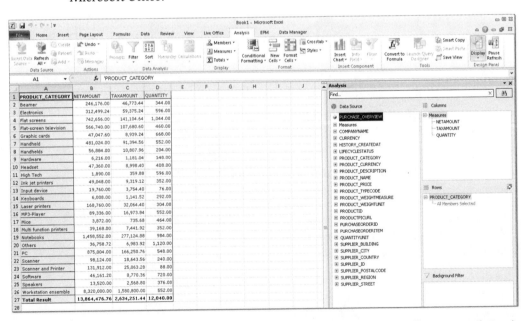

**Figure 15.5** SAP BusinessObjects Analysis, Edition for Microsoft Office Microsoft Excel Plug-In

On the top of the screen, notice that there is a new menu option and ribbon bar available inside Microsoft Excel after you've installed the plug-in. The ANALYSIS screen on the right looks very similar to the pivot table that Microsoft Excel users are accustomed to.

## Business Intelligence Tools for Applications and Dashboards

SAP business intelligence tools for applications and dashboards are used for tasks such as creating dashboards for executives and decision makers and web applications for end users. This category of tools focuses on professionally authored results for trusted data.

We will look at SAP BusinessObjects Design Studio in this section. The other SAP business intelligence tools in this category will converge to SAP BusinessObjects Design Studio, which is the main tool in the applications and dashboards category.

SAP BusinessObjects Design Studio is used to create dashboards, OLAP web applications, and guided analytics. It features native (direct) connections to SAP BW and SAP HANA.

SAP BusinessObjects Design Studio concentrates on trusted data, and therefore uses BICS connectivity. The SAP BusinessObjects fact sheet is shown in Figure 15.6.

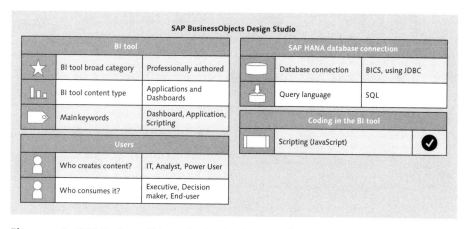

**Figure 15.6** SAP BusinessObjects Design Studio Fact Sheet

SAP BusinessObjects Design Studio was built with mobility in mind, so it features both Apple iPad support and an HTML5 user interface.

SAP BusinessObjects Design Studio falls into the professionally authored category, in which analytic content is centrally governed. It tends to be more of a developer's tool, so some knowledge of JavaScript is required to get the most out of it. In addition, it draws a strong distinction between creators and consumers. The creators are normally IT professionals, and the consumers are normally executives and decision makers. Remember that these lines between creators and consumers can blur; for example, a CIO is the executive in charge of IT.

SAP BusinessObjects Design Studio has an Eclipse-based what you see is what you get (WYSIWYG) design environment, as shown in Figure 15.7.

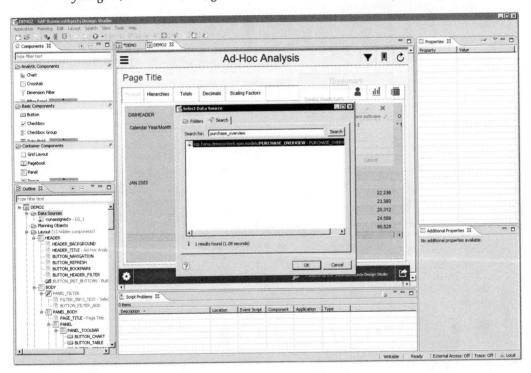

**Figure 15.7**   Designing a Dashboard in SAP BusinessObjects Design Studio

## Business Intelligence Tools for Data Discovery

SAP's business intelligence tools for data discovery focus on self-service and visualization. These tools are easy to learn and have a wide audience. They also connect to more data sources than other business intelligence tools that focus on trusted data only.

SAP's business intelligence tools in this category will converge to SAP Lumira. We will look at two SAP BI tools: SAP Lumira and SAP Predictive Analytics, which runs on SAP Lumira.

### SAP Lumira

SAP Lumira is a comparatively new tool for the self-service and visualization of analytics. It was designed with SAP HANA in mind, so it leverages SAP HANA features to deliver fast results.

SAP Lumira had separate desktop, server, and cloud versions, but these are now converging into a new version of SAP Lumira. The new SAP Lumira integrates with SAP Cloud for Analytics. It is also easy to consume SAP Lumira content on mobile devices via the SAP BusinessObjects BI Mobile app.

SAP Lumira is well suited for ad hoc types of analytics; you can view and visualize any type of data in the way you like with minimal effort. In contrast to SAP BusinessObjects Design Studio, it does not focus only on trusted data; SAP Lumira connects to all the SAP HANA information models, like dimension views and OLAP views (see Figure 15.8).

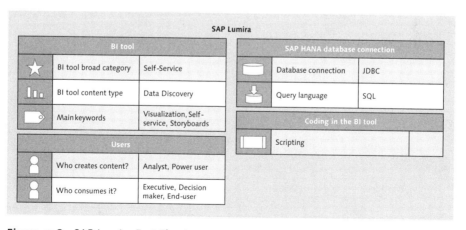

**Figure 15.8**   SAP Lumira Fact Sheet

Figure 15.9 shows the visualization options available in SAP Lumira. Here, you can see information from the SAP HANA Interactive Education (SHINE) procurement views displayed on a geo cloropleth map. On a *cloropleth* map, the countries that sold more products are a darker green color than the countries that sold less.

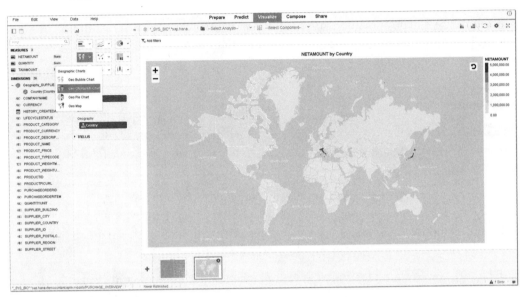

**Figure 15.9**   Data from SAP HANA Information Model on Geo Cloropleth Chart

You can combine multiple graphs (see Figure 15.10) or tables with information to create storyboards in SAP Lumira. You can then publish these storyboards to the web or to the cloud.

For more information on features such as infographics that are updated in real time and Smart Bus Cockpits, go to *http://help.sap.com/lumira*. You can download SAP Lumira at *http://www.saplumira.com*.

### SAP Predictive Analytics

SAP Predictive Analytics is based on SAP Lumira technology. It is a combination of SAP Lumira and two older products: SAP Predictive Analytics and SAP InfiniteInsight.

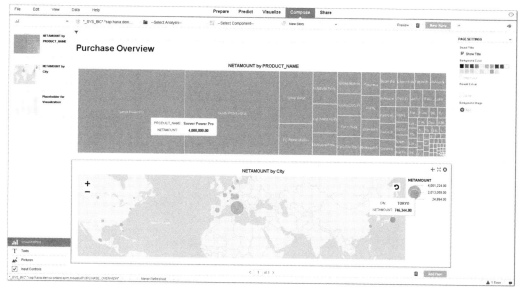

**Figure 15.10**   SAP Lumira Storyboard

SAP Predictive Analytics' features are similar to those of SAP Lumira. However, a large amount of extra functionality is available for this product, especially for data scientists, a very small group of people that will use this functionality. Self-service tools like SAP Lumira cater to about 97% of the business intelligence audience. Designers of tools that create professionally authored content are about 3% of the business intelligence audience. Data scientists are perhaps only 0.01% of the audience.

You can use SAP Predictive Analytics to build predictive models, which can use an automated predictive library. Data scientists can also use the advanced features of SAP Predictive Analytics to integrate their own R language code, for example.

An example of how to use predictive models is to analyze the "churn" of banking customers. By looking at all the customers' transactions and historical data, predictive models can be taught to identify when banking customers are likely to change to another bank. A personal banker can then get an alert to contact the customer and fix any issues before they leave the bank.

Executives and decision makers generally will not use predictive models, but they will be able to act on the results of these models.

## Business Intelligence Tools for Reporting

In this section, we will look at two SAP business intelligence tools in the reporting category: SAP BusinessObjects Web Intelligence and SAP Crystal Reports.

### SAP BusinessObjects Web Intelligence

SAP BusinessObjects Web Intelligence, popularly called Webi, is one of the most popular SAP business intelligence tools because it is easy to work with, yet powerful and fast enough to get the job done. You might hear SAP business intelligence people say, "When in doubt, use WebI." See Figure 15.11.

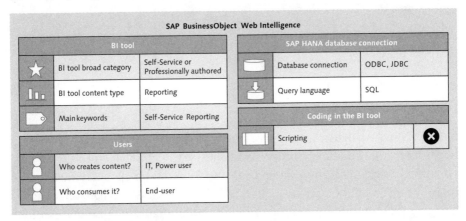

**Figure 15.11**   SAP BusinessObjects Web Intelligence Fact Sheet

SAP BusinessObjects Web Intelligence is useful for many users and can be used for both self-service purposes and professionally authored reports. It was one of the first self-service style business intelligence tools from SAP. Because self-service BI tools allow users to use most business intelligence information sources, SAP BusinessObjects Web Intelligence can use all the SAP HANA tables and views.

End users can consume SAP intelligence reports using the mobile app or via a browser.

### SAP Crystal Reports

We mentioned SAP Crystal Reports in the Business Intelligence Concepts section earlier in this chapter. In this section, we'll dive deeper into the product details. There are two versions of SAP Crystal Reports to note: SAP Crystal Reports for Enterprise and SAP Crystal Reports 2011/2013. In this section we will specifically look at SAP Crystal Reports for Enterprise.

SAP Crystal Reports for Enterprise is used to create reports, which often have the exact specifications and look of the existing paper forms. The term "pixel-perfect" describes this requirement. It focuses on professionally authored reports, which can be viewed on desktops, browsers, and offline. Figure 15.12 shows the fact sheet.

SAP Crystal Reports for Enterprise can use a wide variety of data sources, including SAP HANA tables and views.

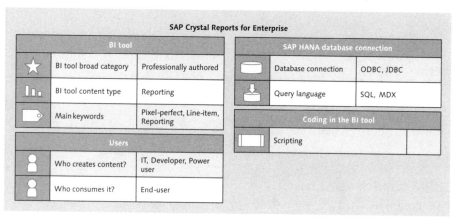

**Figure 15.12**  SAP Crystal Reports for Enterprise Fact Sheet

## Choosing the Right Business Intelligence Tool

You should now have a high-level understanding of the various SAP business intelligence tools available and what each one does. When asked to recommend an SAP business intelligence tool on a project, you can use Table 15.2 as a quick reference.

| Business Requirement | SAP Business Intelligence Tool |
| --- | --- |
| Microsoft Office integration | SAP BusinessObjects Analysis, edition for Microsoft Office |
| Dashboards | SAP BusinessObjects Design Studio |
| Web applications | SAP BusinessObjects Design Studio |
| Reporting | SAP BusinessObjects Web Intelligence or SAP Crystal Reports |
| Self-service | SAP Lumira or SAP BusinessObjects Web Intelligence |
| Professionally authored | SAP BusinessObjects Design Studio or SAP Crystal Reports |
| Only uses trusted data | SAP BusinessObjects Analysis or SAP BusinessObjects Design Studio |
| Can consume all data | SAP Lumira, SAP BusinessObjects Web Intelligence, or SAP Crystal Reports |
| Uses BICS connectivity | SAP BusinessObjects Analysis, edition for Microsoft Office and SAP BusinessObjects Design Studio |
| Uses MDX | Microsoft Excel and SAP Crystal Reports for Enterprise |

**Table 15.2**  SAP Business Intelligence Tool Options

See if you can expand this table. What SAP business intelligence tool would analysts use? Which would you recommend for trend analysis?

## Alternative Consumption Methods for SAP HANA

To this point, we have only discussed which business intelligence tools you can use to consume SAP HANA information models—but SAP HANA views can also be used in many other ways to show business information.

### SAP HANA Studio Preview

Another way that we can view information created by SAP HANA views is with the Data Preview feature in SAP HANA studio or the SAP HANA web-based development workbench. We discussed this feature in Chapter 5 in the Data Preview and Catalog Area sections (see Figure 5.5 and Figure 5.18).

In the Data Preview of SAP HANA studio, you can show raw data, apply filters to data, show distinct values, and analyze data. We hinted at this way of consuming SAP HANA information in the real-world scenario presented at the start of the chapter.

### Using SAP HANA Information Models in SAP HANA XS

In Chapter 3, in the SAP HANA as a Platform section, we discussed the SAP HANA Extended Application Services (XS) component that is built into SAP HANA. SAP HANA is more than just a database. Although the primary focus of both this book and the exam are modeling, there is also another capability that makes SAP HANA invaluable: developing custom web applications using information models, OData and REST services, and the SAPUI5 framework. This method of development is also known as Model-View-Controller (MVC).

The following looks at the three layers used in MVC:

▸ **Models**
The types of models are same SAP HANA information models that we have created in this book—for example, calculation views. You can also create the models in SQLScript.

▸ **Controllers**
Controllers are the "glue" holding models and views together. You can use OData or REST services with XSJS (XS JavaScript) to expose SAP HANA information models as web services. These web services consume the information in information models—provided of course that the end users have the necessary authorizations. The information gathered by the controllers is sent to the views using the normal HTTP protocol used by the web. The OData or REST web services are available to the web and can be used via RESTful HTTP commands such as GET, PUT, POST, and DELETE. The data is sent to the SAPUI5 views in either XML or JavaScript Object Notation (JSON) format. Controllers are written with server-side JavaScript.

▸ **SAPUI5 views**
These are not the same as calculation views in SAP HANA; they refer to the HTML5 screens displayed in the web browser. SAPUI5 uses client-side JavaScript.

Note the differences in where the JavaScript runs. For controllers, the Java-Script runs on the SAP HANA server. The views are displayed in the browser, so the JavaScript code runs inside the browser on the end user's device.

 **Further Information**

The SAP HA450 training course and the free openSAP training courses on SAP HANA development go into more details on this topic.

### Using SAP HANA Information Models in SAP BW

We discussed SAP BW running on SAP HANA in the SAP HANA as a Database section of Chapter 3 (see also Figure 3.11).

SAP BW has its own information modeling objects—for example, InfoCubes and Data Store Objects (DSOs). The objects in SAP BW are built in the application server layer. Even if SAP BW is powered by SAP HANA and these SAP BW objects are optimized for SAP HANA, they are still completely different from the normal SAP HANA information models, like calculation views.

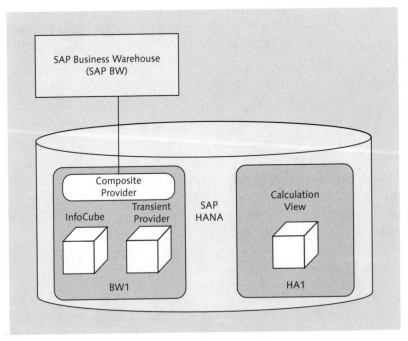

**Figure 15.13**   SAP BW Information Objects and SAP HANA Information Models Together

You can have a single SAP HANA system in which one portion is used as the SAP HANA database for an SAP BW system and another portion is used for SAP HANA as a platform. Let's call the SAP BW portion *BW1* and the SAP HANA platform portion *HA1*, as shown in Figure 15.13.

The BW1 portion will contain SAP BW modeling objects, and the HA1 portion will contain SAP HANA calculation views.

In a system like this, we can perform the following tasks:

▶ Enable the SAP BW system to consume the SAP HANA calculation views from the HA1 portion.

▶ Get the SAP BW system to generate normal SAP HANA views in HA1 to expose the SAP BW information for consumption by SAP HANA.

You can use the HA1 portion with all the standard SAP HANA modeling, data provisioning, and utilization techniques.

### SAP BW Consuming SAP HANA Information Models

Say that you have built a calculation view in the HA1 portion. You can use that calculation view in the BW1 portion and make it available for the SAP BW application server by creating a Transient Provider in SAP BW. You can combine this calculation view with another SAP BW cube by using a Composite Provider. In this way, you can combine historical data in the SAP BW system with operational data in the SAP HANA system.

### SAP BW Generating SAP HANA Views

SAP BW powered by SAP HANA is also able to automatically create a calculation view in the HA1 portion. This calculation view exposes the data in an SAP BW cube or DSO. You can then combine the SAP BW–created calculation view with other SAP HANA views, and can then consume SAP BW data inside SAP HANA.

When you change the structure of your SAP BW information objects, the SAP BW–created calculation view will be recreated automatically.

## Important Terminology

In this chapter, the following important terms were discussed:

▶ **Business intelligence**
Taking raw (transactional) business data and transforming it into useful information for the purpose of business analysis. Building information models in SAP HANA can be seen as part of this process. Business intelligence can contain the following:

  ▶ Reporting

  ▶ Analytics

  ▶ Complex event processing

  ▶ Predictive analytics

  ▶ Prescriptive analytics

  ▶ Text mining, data mining, and process mining

  ▶ OLAP

▶ **Report**
A document that can contain information organized in a tabular or a graphical format.

▶ **Professionally authored tools**
These types of tools expect IT folks, creators, analysts, data scientists, and power users to be the creators and designers.

▶ **Self-service tools**
These types of tools allow the average end users, decision makers, and power users to find, discover, visualize, and consume information.

## 🖱 Practice Questions

These practice questions will help you evaluate your understanding of the topics covered in this chapter. The questions shown are similar in nature to those found on the certification examination. Although none of these questions will be found on the exam itself, they will allow you to review your knowledge of the subject. Select the correct answers, and then check the completeness of your answers in the Practice Question Answers and Explanations section. Remember that on the exam you must select all correct answers and only correct answers to receive credit for the question.

1. You need a business intelligence tool that is Microsoft Excel-based and can use parent-child hierarchies. Which tool do you use?
   □ **A.** SAP Lumira
   □ **B.** SAP BusinessObjects Design Studio
   □ **C.** SAP BusinessObjects Web Intelligence
   □ **D.** SAP BusinessObjects Analysis, edition for OLAP

2. You are given an old government paper form with lines, blocks, and fields. You are asked to create a report that looks like this form. Which business intelligence tools do you use?
   □ **A.** SAP BusinessObjects Web Intelligence
   □ **B.** SAP Crystal Reports for Enterprise
   □ **C.** SAP BusinessObjects Design Studio
   □ **D.** SAP Lumira

3. You have a discussion with board members of a company. They want your recommendation on a business intelligence tool that they can use on their Apple iPad to display KPI dashboards. They also want a WYSIWYG design environment that allows scripting, should it be required. Which tool do you recommend?
   □ **A.** SAP BusinessObjects Design Studio
   □ **B.** SAP Lumira
   □ **C.** SAP Crystal Reports for Enterprise
   □ **D.** SAP BusinessObjects Web Intelligence

4. What do you use a Transient Provider for?
   □ **A.** To use an SAP HANA calculation view in Microsoft Excel
   □ **B.** To expose an SAP HANA calculation view as an OData web service
   □ **C.** To expose an SAP BW information object inside SAP HANA
   □ **D.** To use an SAP HANA calculation view in the SAP BW application

5.  You want to publish your business intelligence content directly to SAP Cloud for Analytics. Which tool do you use? (There are 2 correct answers.)

☐  **A.** SAP Predictive Analytics

☐  **B.** SAP Lumira

☐  **C.** SAP Crystal Reports for Enterprise

☐  **D.** SAP BusinessObjects Analysis, edition for Microsoft Office

6.  Which business intelligence tool queries SAP HANA using MDX?

☐  **A.** SAP BusinessObjects Analysis, edition for Microsoft Office

☐  **B.** SAP Lumira

☐  **C.** SAP BusinessObjects Web Intelligence

☐  **D.** Microsoft Excel

7.  Which business intelligence tools use BICS connectivity to SAP HANA? (There are 2 correct answers.)

☐  **A.** Microsoft Excel

☐  **B.** SAP BusinessObjects Analysis, edition for Microsoft Office

☐  **C.** SAP Lumira

☐  **D.** SAP BusinessObjects Design Studio

8.  Which business intelligence tool can publish storyboards?

☐  **A.** SAP BusinessObjects Analysis, edition for Microsoft Office

☐  **B.** SAP BusinessObjects Design Studio

☐  **C.** SAP BusinessObjects Web Intelligence

☐  **D.** SAP Predictive Analytics

9.  Which of the following ways of publishing SAP HANA information model content could require some JavaScript knowledge? (There are 2 correct answers.)

☐  **A.** Creating business intelligence content with SAP BusinessObjects Design Studio

☐  **B.** Creating a composite provider in SAP BW

☐   **C.** Creating a report in SAP Crystal Reports for Enterprise

☐   **D.** Creating a REST web service in the SAP HANA XS engine

## Practice Question Answers and Explanations

1. Correct answer: **C**

   SAP BusinessObjects Analysis, edition for Microsoft Office is Excel-based and can handle parent-child hierarchies.None of the other three business intelligence tools are Excel-based

2. Correct answer: **B**

   SAP Crystal Reports for Enterprise create pixel-perfect reports. SAP BusinessObjects Design Studio is not a reporting tool. SAP BusinessObjects Web Intelligence SAP Lumira are not used for creating pixel-perfect reports.

3. Correct answer: **A**

   SAP BusinessObjects Design Studio can display results on a mobile device, has a WYSIWYG design environment and scripting, and can be used to create dashboards. SAP Lumira and SAP BusinessObjects Web Intelligence are not dashboard-building tools.

4. Correct answer: **C**

   You use a Transient Provider to expose an SAP BW information object inside SAP HANA. See SAP BW Consuming SAP HANA Information Models.

5. Correct answers: **A, B**

   SAP Lumira can publish your business intelligence content directly to the SAP Cloud for Analytics. SAP Predictive Analytics is built on SAP Lumira. See the SAP Cloud for Analytics section.

6. Correct answer: **D**

   Microsoft Excel queries SAP HANA using MDX via the ODBO driver. See Figure 15.2. It is the only business intelligence tool in this chapter that uses the ODBO driver.

7. Correct answers: **B, D**

   SAP BusinessObjects Analysis and SAP BusinessObjects Design Studio use BICS.

8. Correct answer: **D**

   SAP Predictive Analytics is based on SAP Lumira, and SAP Lumira can publish storyboards.

9. Correct answers: **A, D**

   JavaScript knowledge may be required for SAP BusinessObjects Design Studio (see Figure 15.6) and when creating a REST web service (see Using SAP HANA Information Models in SAP HANA XS). You create a composite provider in SAP BW via the application server, and the process does not require coding. Creating a report in SAP Crystal Reports for Enterprise does not require JavaScript.

## Takeaway

You now should understand general concepts of business intelligence when using SAP HANA information models. You learned about the different SAP business intelligence tools, their characteristics and high-level features, and when to use a particular tool.

In addition, you learned about some of the alternatives for providing information from SAP HANA to business users—for example, using the SAP HANA XS engine or SAP BW.

## Summary

In this chapter, we looked at various business intelligence concepts—for example, differentiating between creators and consumers of business information. Once we had discussed the strategic direction of the different SAP business intelligence tools, we covered the tools in more detail and summarized their features in the fact sheets. We also discussed when to use which tool, and we presented alternative ways of utilizing SAP HANA information models.

This chapter completes your learning experience with SAP HANA modeling. We wish you the best of luck with your SAP HANA certification exam.

# The Author

**Rudi de Louw** is an SAP HANA architect for SAP in South Africa, as well as an international speaker and trainer, principal consultant, and mentor. He has been working with SAP HANA for more than 5 years, and is the SAP HANA and big data market unit champion. He helped to set up several SAP HANA certification exams and is also the content owner for the SAP HANA professional certification examination.

Rudi has provided software and technology solutions to businesses for more than 25 years, and has been with SAP since 1999. He has a passion for sharing knowledge, understanding new technologies, and finding innovative ways to leverage these to help people in their development.

# Index

## A

ABAP, 477
ABC analysis algorithm, 329
Accelerator deployment, 84
  profitability analysis, 84
ACID-compliant database, 75
Administration, 367, 368
Administration Console, 152, 163, 343, 352, 360, 365
  diagnosis files, 163
  performance, 163
Affinity propagation, 328
Aggregation node, 197, 213, 216, 219
  calculated columns, 226
  restricted columns, 232
Aggregations, 129, 136, 344
Algorithms, 327
Amazon Web Services (AWS), 47, 49, 88, 94
American National Standards Institute (ANSI), 271
Analytic privileges, 449, 460, 465
  assign to role, 450
  create, 450
  migration, 455, 463
Analytic views, 123, 136, 137, 144, 182, 208, 215
  calculate before aggregation, 229
  create, 186
  migration, 209
  temporal joins, 220
  vs. calculation views of type cube with star join, 208
Analytics, 159, 517, 538
API, 318, 333
  SAP HANA simple info access (SINA), 318
  SAP HANA Text Analysis XS JavaScript, 322
  SAP HANA Text Mining XS JavaScript, 322
Application Function Library (AFL), 278, 329
Application Function Modeler (AFM), 179, 330, 331, 332, 336
  editor, 168
  PAL, 168

Applications, 344
  development, 167
  privileges, 457
Apriori algorithm, 328
Architects, 25
Architecture, 69, 90, 343, 359
Association algorithms, 328
Asynchronous replication, 79
Attribute views, 123, 136, 144, 182, 205, 217
  create, 186
  derived, 207
  migration, 185, 209
  vs. calculation view of type dimension, 205
Attributes, 101, 120, 121, 135
  calculated columns, 228
  geographic, 254
  restricted columns, 232
  restrictions, 453
  vocabulary, 252
Authentications, 441
Authorization Assistant, 436
Authorizations, 359, 441, 442
Auto Documentation, 387, 392, 397
Automated predictive library, 531
Average, 129

## B

Backups, 76, 154
Best practices, 134
BEx Analyzer, 522
Big data, 493
  limitations, 493
BIGINT, 307
Bookmark questions, 59
Bottlenecks, 69
Branch logic, 359
Bring-your-own-license, 89
Business Explorer (BEx), 519
Business Function Library (BFL), 329
Business information, 513

Business intelligence, 513, 514
  *applications and dashboards*, 527
  *choosing the right tool*, 533
  *consuming information models*, 515
  *convergence of tools*, 517
  *data discovery*, 529
  *fact sheet*, 523
  *history*, 516
  *reporting*, 532
  *tools*, 519
Business Intelligence Consumer Services
  (BICS), 476, 504, 526, 540
Business rules, 250
BW362, 29, 38

# C

C_HANAIMP, 27
C_HANAIMP_11, 17, 24
  *scoring*, 33
C_HANATEC, 27, 29
C4.5 decision tree, 331
Caching, 127
Calculated columns, 102, 223, 225, 226, 258,
  260, 276, 278
  *analytic views*, 263
  *counters*, 230
  *create*, 226
  *input parameters*, 244
Calculation engine, 346, 365
Calculation view of type cube, 124, 136, 144,
  183, 214, 216
  *aggregation node*, 219
  *create*, 188
Calculation view of type cube with star join,
  123, 136, 144, 183, 208, 210, 214, 220
  *advantages*, 209
  *create*, 188
  *star join node*, 200, 219
  *vs. analytic views*, 208
Calculation view of type dimension, 123,
  136, 144, 183, 189, 205, 214, 217
  *create*, 187
  *migration*, 210
  *projection node*, 219

Calculation views, 126, 185, 263, 346, 536
  *adding data sources*, 192
  *adding nodes*, 191
  *create*, 186
  *creating joins*, 193
  *default nodes*, 190
  *output area*, 246
  *save and activate*, 196
  *selecting output fields*, 194
  *variables*, 241
Calculations, 134, 345
CALL statement, 290
Cardinality, 106, 193, 356, 358, 361
  *many-to-many*, 107
  *many-to-one*, 107
  *one-to-many*, 106
  *one-to-one*, 106
  *types*, 106
Catalog, 178
  *SAP HANA studio*, 155, 156, 176
  *SAP HANA web-based development
    workbench*, 171
  *table context menu*, 156
  *table preview*, 172
  *tables*, 156
CDS views, 117, 135, 139
  *ABAP*, 118
  *benefits*, 117
  *data sources*, 118
Certification
  *prefixes*, 26
  *track*, 23
Change and Transport System (CTS), 376
Characteristics, 120
Circularstring, 324
Classical analytic privileges, 204
Classification algorithms, 328
Classroom training, 36
Clients, 168
Client-side JavaScript, 86
Cloud, 170
  *deployments*, 87
Clustering algorithms, 327, 329
Cold data, 79
Column, 103
  *engine*, 346

Column (Cont.)
  *store*, 156
  *table*, 78, 157, 272
  *views*, 156
Column Views folder, 373
Columnar storage, 344, 361
Column-based
  *databases*, 73
  *input parameters*, 243, 259
  *storage*, 73
  *table*, 68, 156, 176
Column-oriented tables, 103
Comments, 387
Complex event processing, 517, 538
Composite Provider, 537
Compression, 62
Computation Continuous Language
  (CCL), 499
Conditional statements, 278
Consumers, 520
Consumption, 534
Contains predicate, 317
Content, 159
  *create modeling object*, 162
  *packages*, 159
  *SAP HANA studio*, 155, 159
  *SHINE package*, 161
  *subpackages*, 159
Context menu, 156
Controllers, 535
Convergence, 517
Core Data Services (CDS), 101, 117, 145,
  184, 213, 315, 383, 393
Count, 129
Counters, 230, 258
  *new*, 231
CPU
  *in parallel*, 71
  *speed*, 64
Create Fulltext Index, 314
Creators, 520
CSS, 86, 151
CSV files, 500
Cubes, 101, 119, 135, 137, 144
Currency, 246, 248
  *conversion*, 247, 248

Currency (Cont.)
  *conversion options*, 249
  *conversion schema*, 249
  *decimal shift*, 248
  *decimal shift back*, 249
  *source and target*, 247
Currency conversions, 102, 223, 259, 261,
  278, 299
Customer query views, 411, 424

# D

Dashboards, 534
Data
  *aging*, 72, 79
  *archiving*, 494
  *backups*, 76
  *category*, 187, 188
  *compression*, 343, 361
  *discovery*, 519, 529
  *federation*, 488
  *filter*, 276
  *foundation*, 122, 126, 135, 145, 251, 345
  *integration specialist*, 25
  *lakes*, 493
  *noise*, 328
  *persistence*, 77
  *provisioning specialist*, 25
  *read*, 276, 361
  *records*, 272
  *scientists*, 25
  *sources*, 184, 213
  *streaming*, 497
  *types*, 273
  *volume*, 76, 77, 78, 79, 99
Data Control Language (DCL), 273, 306
Data Definition Language (DDL), 273,
  284, 306
Data foundation node, 215
Data Manipulation Language (DML), 273,
  306
Data modeling
  *artifacts*, 127, 136
  *concepts*, 101
  *limit and filter*, 134
Data preview, 157
  *analysis*, 159

Data preview (Cont.)
  distinct values, 159
  sort current dataset, 158
  sort entire dataset, 158
  sorting and exporting, 158
Data provisioning, 467, 502
  concepts, 470
  replication vs extractors, 486
  tools, 469
Data Query Language (DQL), 273, 301, 306
Database
  administrators, 25
  column-oriented, 68
  connections, 475
  deployment, 82, 83
  development, 167
  migration, 82, 90
  to platform, 69
  views, 104
Datahub, 54
Datasets, 54
DataStore Object (DSO), 475
Decimal shift, 262
Decision
  tables, 102, 184, 213
  trees, 328
Decision tables, 223, 250, 261, 263
  create, 251
  nodes, 252
  output fields, 252
Declarative logic, 281
Dedicated hardware, 79
Default schema, 284, 289
Default view node, 190
Definer, 284
Delimited identifiers, 274, 306
Delivery units, 367, 375, 376, 391, 397, 462
Delta, 503
  buffer, 73, 74, 278, 299, 344
  load, 473, 484, 503
  merge, 73, 74, 344
  store, 74
Deployment, 61
  accelerator, 84
  cloud, 87
  database, 82, 83

Deployment (Cont.)
  development platform, 84, 85
  scenarios, 61, 79, 93
  sidecar solution, 80
  virtual machine, 87
Deprecate, 204, 216, 386
Derived attribute views, 207
Derived From Procedure/Scalar Function
  input parameter, 243, 259
Derived From Table input parameter,
  243, 259
Design-time
  definitions, 373
  objects, 368
  roles, 445
Design-time objects, 372, 390, 393
  CDS, 383, 398
  delivery units, 397
Developer Mode, 377, 391, 399
Developer perspective, 153, 164
  Repositories tab, 153
  Systems tab, 153
Developers, 25
Development
  object, 167
  system, 250, 375, 390
Development platform deployment, 84
  programming languages, 85
  SAP HANA XS, 85
Diagnosis Files tab, 163, 353
Dictionary compression, 68
Dimension tables, 119, 120, 125, 135
Dimension views, 123, 125, 136, 183, 185,
  200, 205, 217, 361
Direct input parameter, 243, 258
Disaster recovery, 79
Distinct values, 159
Distributed database, 75
Documentation, 387
Domain fix values, 238, 258, 260
Dynamic
  data tiering, 79
  join, 110, 116, 135, 194, 345
  restrictions, 454
  SQL, 282, 295

# E

E_HANAAW ABAP certification, 29
E_HANABW SAP BW on SAP HANA
  certification, 29
E_HANAINS installation certification, 29
Eclipse, 151, 153
Editor, 173
  *SAP HANA web-based development
    workbench*, 173
E-learning, 36
Elimination technique, 58
Engines, 346, 358, 362
Entity analysis, 320
Exam
  *objects*, 31
  *process*, 33
  *questions*, 56
  *structure*, 31
EXEC statement, 282
Execution plan, 350, 351
Explain Plan, 343, 347, 360, 362, 365
Export, 376, 379, 395
  *delivery units*, 368
  *information models*, 368
Expression Editor, 228
  *calculated columns*, 227
  *elements*, 228
  *functions area*, 228
  *operators area*, 228
  *restricted columns*, 233
Expressions, 223, 273
Extract, Transform, and Load (ETL), 471, 502
Extraction, 471

# F

Facets, 120
Fact tables, 101, 119, 121, 122, 126, 135
Fault-tolerant text search, 314, 316
Fields
  *hide*, 216
  *original*, 215
  *output*, 194
  *rename*, 215
Filters, 169, 236, 258, 345, 358, 462
  *expressions*, 223, 237, 263

Filters (Cont.)
  *operations*, 223
  *operators*, 236
  *variables*, 239
Flat files, 500
  *use cases*, 501
Flowgraph, 164, 167
For loop, 281
Free access, 46
Freestyle search, 317
Full outer join, 108, 110, 194
Full-text index, 314, 316, 320, 332, 334
  *columns*, 315
  *hidden column*, 316
Functions, 156, 274
Fuzzy text search, 207, 210, 278, 286, 299,
  311, 313, 315, 316, 319, 332, 335
  *alternative names*, 317

# G

Generate SLT File, 419
GeoJSON, 326
Geospatial processing, 323
Global Temporary, 275
Global Temporary Column, 275
Google, 313
Grammatical Role Analysis (GRA), 322
Granted Roles tab, 442, 445
Graphical calculation views, 173, 174, 186,
  385, 422
  *decision tables*, 250
  *refactoring and restructuring*, 384
Graphical data models, 70, 97
Graphical flowgraph model, 331
Graphical information models, 358
Group by, 197, 216
Grouping sets, 359
Grubbs' test algorithm, 329
Guidelines, 134

# H

HA100, 37
HA215, 38
HA300, 38
HA400, 38

HA450, 38, 536
Hardware, 51
Hierarchies, 101, 132, 133, 223, 253
  BICS, 254
  create, 254
  MDX, 254
  time-dependent, 207, 256
  value help, 257
High availability, 75
  shared disk storage, 75
History, 386
  column, 275
Hot data, 79, 495
HTML5, 85, 86, 151, 170
Hybrid cloud, 88, 91

# I

Identifiers, 273, 274
if(), 228, 278
Imperative logic, 281, 302, 359
Import, 376, 379
  delivery units, 368
  information models, 368
  objects, 382, 383, 391
Index server, 77
Indexes, 156
InfoCubes, 536
InfoPackage, 475, 508
InfoProvider, 475
Information modelers, 25
Information models, 536
  activate, 368, 369, 372, 394
  administration, 367, 368
  Auto Documentation, 387
  build, 125
  comments, 387
  deprecated, 386, 395
  documentation, 367, 369, 387
  labels, 389
  mass copy, 382
  refactoring, 367, 369, 383, 392
  SAP BW, 536
  SAP HANA XS, 535, 542
  schema mapping, 380
  techniques, 345
  translation, 367, 369, 389

Information models (Cont.)
  transport, 368, 374
  utilization, 126, 513
  validate, 21, 367, 368, 369
Information views, 122, 181
  characteristics, 293
  data sources, 184, 217
  parameterized, 272
  performance, 362
  use, 124
Infrastructure as a Service (IaaS), 87
Initial load, 473, 480, 503
In-memory, 67, 72
  data movement, 70
  technology, 61, 63, 89, 361
In-Memory DataStore Object (IMDSO), 488
Inner join, 108, 109, 111, 135, 137, 144, 194
Input parameters, 102, 223, 242, 258
  create, 243, 244
  date, 246
  expressions, 245
  types, 243, 258
Insert-only, 74
  principle, 344
International Organization for
  Standardization (ISO), 271
Internet of Things (IoT), 498
Interval, 239, 258
Invoker, 284
  security, 307

# J

Java, 151
Java Database Connectivity (JDBC), 476, 503
Java Virtual Machines, 151, 170
JavaScript, 85, 151
  server-side, 86
Join node, 253, 260
  calculated columns, 226
Joins, 102, 104, 107, 110, 135, 181, 193,
  294, 356
  basic, 108
  dynamic join, 116
  engine, 346
  node, 191, 200, 213
  performance, 361

Joins (Cont.)
   *referential join*, 111
   *relocation*, 490
   *self-joins*, 110
   *spatial join*, 115
   *star joins*, 122
   *temporal join*, 113
   *text join*, 112
   *types*, 108

# K

Kerberos, 462, 464
Key
   *field*, 104
   *figures*, 119
K-means, 327

# L

Language, 284, 289
   *detection*, 314
Layered information views, 449
Lazy load, 78, 99
Left outer join, 108, 109, 113, 135, 144, 194,
   220, 361
Level hierarchies, 132, 134, 254, 262
Line of business (LOB), 520
Linestring, 324
Link prediction algorithm, 329
Load, 471
Local Temporary, 275
Local Temporary Column, 275
Log
   *backups*, 77, 78
   *buffer*, 78
   *volume*, 77, 79, 99
Log-based replication, 484
Logical
   *data warehouse*, 494
   *joins*, 122
Loops, 302, 307, 359

# M

Main table, 107
Managed Cloud as a Service (MCaaS), 88

Many-to-many cardinality, 107
Many-to-one cardinality, 107
Mapping property, 194, 215, 219
Mass
   *copy*, 382, 394, 398
   *import*, 382
Master data, 122, 135, 145, 214
Materialized views, 105
Maximum, 129
Measures, 101, 119, 121, 135, 138, 145
   *calculate before aggregation*, 229
   *calculated columns*, 228
   *restricted columns*, 232
Memory
   *blocks*, 76
   *dump*, 78
Microsoft Azure Cloud, 47, 49
Microsoft Excel, 540
   *datasheets*, 500
   *on SAP HANA*, 524
Microsoft Live Office, 522
Microsoft Office integration, 519, 534
Microsoft PowerPoint, 522
Migration, 211
Miscellaneous algorithms, 329
Mobile, 170
Modeler perspective, 153, 176
Modeling role, 444, 449, 460
Models, 535
Model-View-Controller (MVC), 85, 535
Monitoring role, 444, 460
Moore's Law, 63
Multicore CPUs, 343, 361
Multidimensional expressions (MDX), 476,
   524
Multilevel aggregation, 292
Multilinestring, 324
Multiple choice questions, 56
Multiple response questions, 56
Multipoint, 324
Multipolygon, 324
Multitenancy, 86
Multitenant database container (MDC), 86,
   184, 213

# N

Native objects, 382, 392
Nodes, 181
NoSQL databases, 75
NULL, 274, 301, 306

# O

Object Linking and Embedding, Database
    (OLE DB), 503
Object Linking and Embedding, Database for
    Online Analytical Processing, 476
Object privileges, 448, 460
OData, 38, 85, 502, 509
    service, 319
ODBO driver, 524
OLAP, 92, 343, 517, 538
    engine, 346, 347, 413
    vs. OLTP, 67
OLTP, 92, 343
    vs. OLAP, 67
One-to-many cardinality, 106
One-to-one cardinality, 106
Online analytical processing, 406
Online transactional processing, 405
Open Content, 418
Open Cross Reference, 418
Open Database Connectivity (ODBC), 475,
    503
Open Definition, 418
Open Geospatial Consortium (OGC), 325
Open View in Analysis Office, 420
Open View in SAP Lumira, 420
openHPI, 44
openSAP, 44, 536
    certifications, 45
Operating system, 51
Operational reporting, 424, 426
Operators, 233, 273, 348, 352
Optimization, 341
    best practices, 358
    tools, 346
Oracle, 272
Outliers, 329
Output fields, 105, 194

# P

P_HANAIMP, 28
Package privileges, 456
Page manager, 76, 77, 99
Pages, 76
Parallelism, 71, 344
Parameters, 290
Parent-child hierarchies, 132, 134, 254, 256,
    260, 534
Partitioned tables, 75
Partitioning, 75
Performance, 343
    analysis, 492
    enhancements, 341
    tab, 163, 352
Performance Analysis Mode, 179, 343, 354,
    355, 360, 363, 365
Persistence layer, 61, 74, 75, 90
Perspectives, 152
    change, 153
    list, 153
    modeler vs. developer, 153
PHP, 151
PL/SQL, 272
Plan visualization, 153
Platform as a Service (PaaS), 87
Point, 324
Polygon, 324
PostGIS, 325
Predicates, 273, 325
Predictive, 327
    analytics, 517, 538
    modeling, 311, 327, 330
Predictive Analysis Library (PAL), 168, 327,
    331, 333, 336
    algorithms, 329
Preprocessing algorithms, 328
Prescriptive analytics, 517, 538
Primary storage, 76
Private cloud, 88, 91
Private views, 410, 424
Privileges, 437, 460
    analytic privileges, 449
    application privileges, 457
    object privileges, 448
    package privileges, 456

Privileges (Cont.)
  *system privileges*, 447
  *types*, 446
Procedures, 288, 293, 300, 303
  *characteristics*, 294
  *create*, 288
  *parameters*, 290
  *read-only*, 292
Production system, 250, 375, 390
Professionally authored, 520, 534
Project Explorer, 153, 166
Projection node, 198, 213, 260
  *calculated columns*, 226
  *filters*, 237
Projections, 127, 136, 276
Projects, 52, 53
Proof-of-concept (POC), 500
Provisioning, 155
Proxy tables, 488
Pruning configuration table, 201
Public cloud, 88, 91, 98

## Q

Quality assurance system, 250, 375, 390
Queries, 274
Query views, 411, 412, 424
Quick View tab, 152, 154, 455

## R

R language, 85, 307, 531
Range, 239, 258
Rank node, 198, 213, 216
  *columns*, 199
  *sorting*, 198
Ranking, 128, 136
Raw
  *data*, 157
  *tab*, 176
RDL_USER, 459
Reads SQL data, 289
Real-time
  *computing*, 343, 361
  *data*, 127
  *reporting*, 105
Recursive tables, 110

Refactoring, 367, 383, 384, 392, 395, 396
  *deprecate*, 386
  *history*, 386
  *nodes in a graphical calculation view*, 384
  *Where-Used*, 386
Referential integrity, 111, 144
Referential join, 110, 111, 112, 114, 135,
  137, 144, 194, 220, 345, 356
  *star joins*, 122
Regression algorithms, 328
Release notes, 39
Replication, 79, 82, 473
  *log-based*, 484
  *trigger-based*, 479
REPO.EXPORT, 448
REPO.IMPORT, 448
REPO.MAINTAIN_DELIVERY_
  UNITS, 448
REPO.WORK_IN_FOREIGN_
  WORKSPACE, 448
Report writers, 25
Reporting, 515, 517, 519, 538
  *system*, 406
Reports, 516
Repository
  *create*, 165
  *icon*, 165
  *objects*, 372, 390, 445
  *tab*, 165
  *workspace*, 165
Repository Translation Tool (RTT), 389
REST, 38, 85, 502
Restricted columns, 223, 231, 232, 258
  *create*, 233
  *operators*, 233
  *using calculated columns*, 235
Restrictions, 452, 453
Restructuring, 384
Returns, 284
Reuse views, 410, 412, 424
Right outer join, 108, 110, 138, 144, 194
Right-click menu, 156
Roles, 433, 437, 443, 459
  *choosing*, 442
  *composite role*, 437, 459
  *create*, 444
  *new*, 444

Roles (Cont.)
*template roles*, 443, 444
Root package privilege, 457
Row, 103
*engine*, 346
*storage*, 344
*store*, 156
Row-based
*databases*, 73
*storage*, 73
*tables*, 68, 156, 176
Row-oriented tables, 103
Ruby, 151
Runtime information, 157
Runtime objects, 368, 397
*CDS*, 383
Runtime roles, 445
Runtime version, 373, 390

# S

Sales forecasting, 327
Sandbox, 500
SAP Basis, 27
SAP Business Suite, 479
SAP Business Warehouse (BW), 82
SAP BusinessObjects Analysis, edition for
Microsoft Office, 519, 522, 525, 539, 541
*information*, 526
*plug-in*, 526
SAP BusinessObjects BI Mobile, 529
SAP BusinessObjects Design Studio, 519,
521, 527, 529, 539, 540
*dashboard*, 528
*information*, 527
SAP BusinessObjects Web Intelligence,
519, 532
*information*, 532
SAP BW, 121, 156, 435, 475, 486, 517, 536
*consume calculation views*, 537
*consume information models*, 537, 541
*generate SAP HANA views*, 537
SAP BW on SAP HANA, 38, 51, 82, 156, 464
SAP Cloud Appliance Library, 49, 50
SAP Cloud for Analytics, 522, 529, 540
SAP Community Network (SCN), 41
SAP CRM, 435

SAP Crystal Reports, 519, 532
SAP Crystal Reports 2011/2013, 533, 539
SAP Crystal Reports for Enterprise, 533,
539, 540
*information*, 533
SAP Data Quality Management, 478
SAP Data Services, 476, 505
*benefits*, 478
*extracting data*, 477
*transforming and cleaning data*, 478
SAP Direct Extractor Connection (DXC), 477,
485, 487
SAP Education, 35
SAP ERP, 408, 435
SAP ERP on SAP HANA, 156
SAP extractors, 474, 503
SAP Fiori, 86
SAP HANA
*as a database*, 82, 83
*as a development platform*, 84, 85
*as a sidecar solution*, 80, 81
*as a virtual machine*, 87
*as an accelerator*, 84
*clients*, 475
*in the cloud*, 87
*reference guides*, 40
*training courses*, 35, 37
SAP HANA Academy, 41
SAP HANA application function modeler
(AFM), 168
SAP HANA Application Lifecycle Manager,
329, 378, 391
SAP HANA as a database, 409
*security*, 435
SAP HANA as a platform, 90
*security*, 436, 461
SAP HANA as a sidecar, 409
*security*, 436
SAP HANA Business Function Library (BFL)
Reference, 41
SAP HANA certifications
*associate level*, 27
*professional level*, 28
*specialist level*, 28
SAP HANA Cloud Platform, 47, 48, 87,
89, 522
SAP HANA Developer Center, 46

SAP HANA Developer Guide, 41
SAP HANA Developer Quick Start Guide, 41
SAP HANA Enterprise Cloud (HEC), 88, 89,
    91, 94
    *private cloud*, 89
SAP HANA Enterprise Information
    Management, 495
SAP HANA Interactive Education (SHINE),
    39, 530
SAP HANA Live, 364, 403, 404, 461, 464
    *architecture*, 410
    *background information*, 405
    *definition*, 405
    *installation*, 413, 425
    *rapid deployment solution*, 415
    *security*, 436
    *SQL engine*, 346
    *tags*, 419
    *views*, 403, 412, 422, 424
SAP HANA Live Browser, 403, 414, 415, 425
    *all views*, 416
    *for business users*, 421, 430
    *invalid views*, 416
    *my favorites*, 416
    *toolbar*, 418
SAP HANA Live Extension Assistant, 403,
    414, 422, 425, 426
    *restrictions*, 423
SAP HANA Modeling Guide, 39
SAP HANA Predictive Analysis Library (PAL)
    Reference, 41
SAP HANA Security Guide, 40
SAP HANA simple info access (SINA) API,
    318, 333
SAP HANA smart data access (SDA), 79,
    356, 488
    *adapters*, 488
    *benefits*, 495
    *data archiving*, 494
    *implementation*, 490
    *virtual tables*, 488
SAP HANA smart data integration (SDI), 168,
    495, 496
SAP HANA smart data quality (SDQ),
    495, 496

SAP HANA smart data streaming (SDS), 168,
    497, 498, 517
    *benefits*, 499
SAP HANA SPS 10, 322
SAP HANA SPS 11, 283, 295, 319, 455
SAP HANA SQLScript Reference, 40
SAP HANA studio, 149, 150, 151, 175,
    445, 514
    *Administration Console*, 163
    *Backup*, 154
    *Catalog*, 155
    *Content*, 155, 159
    *create calculation view*, 187
    *data preview*, 534
    *development object*, 167
    *installation*, 52
    *main workspace*, 154
    *perspectives*, 152
    *Provisioning*, 155
    *Quick View tab*, 152
    *screen*, 152
    *security*, 156
    *session client*, 152, 168
    *SQL Console*, 162
    *systems view*, 154
    *working areas*, 152
    *XS project*, 166
SAP HANA Text Analysis XS JavaScript
    API, 322
SAP HANA Troubleshooting and Performance
    Analysis Guide, 40
SAP HANA web-based development
    workbench, 52, 150, 170, 175, 414, 445
    *editor*, 171
    *performance analysis mode*, 174
    *table data*, 172
SAP HANA XS, 85, 86, 179, 291, 317,
    535, 541
    *application privileges*, 457, 460
    *project*, 166
SAP HANA XS DB Utilities JavaScript API
    Reference, 41
SAP HANA XS JavaScript API Reference, 41
SAP HANA XS JavaScript Reference, 40
SAP HANA XSUnit JavaScript API
    Reference, 41
SAP Help, 39

SAP Hybris, 88
SAP InfiniteInsight, 530
SAP landscape, 375
SAP Learning Hub, 37
SAP LT Replication Server (SLT), 409, 478
  *benefits*, 483
  *configuration*, 482
  *features*, 481
  *replication process*, 480
  *trigger-based replication*, 480
SAP Lumira, 54, 421, 519, 521, 529, 531, 540
  *charts*, 530
  *information*, 529
  *storyboard*, 531
SAP NetWeaver
  *old architecture*, 65
SAP Predictive Analytics, 529, 530, 540
SAP Replication Server (SRS), 484
  *benefits*, 485
  *log-based replication*, 484
SAP resources, 39
SAP S/4HANA, 72, 80, 86, 97, 464
SAP Solution Manager, 376
SAP Store, 53
SAP SuccessFactors, 88
SAP Support Mode, 377, 391
SAPUI5, 25, 38, 41, 85, 86
  *Developer Guide for SAP HANA*, 41
  *views*, 535
Savepoint, 76, 78, 99
Scalable Vector Graphic (SVG), 326
Scalar functions, 269, 283, 285
Scale-out architecture, 75
Schema, 156, 162, 394, 396
  *mapping*, 367, 368, 380, 393
  *tables*, 156
SCORE() function, 317
Scripted calculation views
  *migrate*, 297
Search, 314
Seasonal patterns, 327
Secondary storage, 76
Security, 282, 359, 433, 438
  *concepts*, 435, 437
  *SAP HANA studio*, 156

Security (Cont.)
  *SAP HANA web-based development workbench*, 171
  *testing*, 458
  *usage*, 438
Segmentation, 328
SELECT *, 301, 306
SELECT statement, 276
Self-joins, 110, 135
Self-service, 520, 523, 534
Semantics node, 202, 208, 214, 215
  *Column tab*, 202
  *hide fields*, 203
  *hierarchies*, 254
  *input parameters*, 242
  *renaming fields*, 202
  *session client*, 204
  *top node*, 189
  *variables*, 239
  *View Properties tab*, 203
Sentiment analysis, 320, 334
Separate statements, 279
Sequential execution, 289
Servers, 75
Session client, 152, 168, 440
  *settings*, 169
Set-oriented, 272, 300
Shared hardware, 79
SHINE, 53, 118, 160, 161, 287, 326, 347
  *datasets*, 54
Show Line Numbers, 162
Sidecar deployment, 80
  *advantages*, 81
  *blank system*, 82
SINA, 318, 333
Single sign-on, 441, 462
Single value, 239, 258
Slow disk, 67
Social network analysis algorithms, 329
Software, 51
Software as a Service (SaaS), 88
Spatial
  *data*, 323
  *data types*, 278, 300
  *functions*, 326
  *import data*, 325
  *join*, 115, 135, 194, 209, 220, 323, 324

Spatial (Cont.)
  *join type*, 278
  *processing*, 311, 323, 333
  *properties*, 324
SQL, 85, 269, 272, 341
  *analytic privileges*, 204, 452, 455, 462,
    463, 465
  *button*, 162
  *conditional statements*, 278
  *creating calculated columns*, 276
  *creating projections*, 276
  *creating tables*, 275
  *creating unions*, 277
  *Data Definition Language*, 273
  *Data Manipulation Language*, 273
  *dynamic*, 282, 302, 307
  *engine*, 204, 346, 413, 422, 425
  *Expression Editor*, 228
  *filter data*, 276
  *guidelines*, 359
  *language*, 272
  *reading data*, 276
  *security*, 284, 289
  *set-oriented*, 272
  *statements*, 162
  *Structured Query Language*, 271, 299
  *views*, 105, 184, 213
SQL Console, 152, 162, 290, 347, 353
  *schemas*, 162
  *text editors*, 162
SQL Editor, 454
SQL Plan Cache, 365
SQLScript, 85, 269, 272, 278, 292, 307, 331,
  341, 359, 362, 384
  *compiler*, 279
  *decision tables*, 253
  *declarative logic*, 281
  *dynamic SQL*, 282
  *for loop*, 281
  *multilevel aggregation*, 292
  *optimizer*, 279
  *procedures*, 288
  *security*, 282, 283
  *separate statements*, 279
  *while loop*, 281
Standard
  *deviation*, 129

Standard (Cont.)
  *union*, 200
Star join node, 209, 213, 215, 217, 219
  *calculated columns*, 226
  *data foundation*, 199
  *restricted columns*, 232
Star join views, 123, 126, 136
  *analytic views*, 123
  *calculation view of type cube with
    star join*, 123
Star joins, 122
  *referential joins*, 122
Statements, 274
Static List input parameter, 243, 259
Statistics algorithms, 329
Stored procedures, 70, 97, 288
Structured Query Language, 271, 299
Subtype, 188
Sum, 129
Supervised learning, 328, 336
Synchronous, 99
  *replication*, 79
_SYS_REPO, 284, 440, 454, 459, 461
SYSTEM, 439, 458, 459
System administrator, 369
System identity (SID), 156
System privileges, 447
  *types*, 447
Systems tab, 438
Systems view, 154, 162, 177
  *folders*, 154

**T**

Tables, 103
  *context menu*, 176
  *create*, 275
  *data preview*, 157
  *data source*, 184, 213
  *definitions*, 156
  *export data*, 378
  *functions*, 251, 269, 283, 286
  *join*, 345
  *left and right*, 107
  *link*, 104
  *partitioned*, 75
  *recursive*, 110

Tables (Cont.)
  *select*, 104
  *table definitions*, 156
  *types*, 251, 275
Technical performance tuning experts, 25
Template roles, 443
  *modeling role*, 444, 460
  *monitoring role*, 444, 460
Temporal join, 110, 113, 114, 135, 137, 144, 220
Tenant, 86
Text, 311, 314
  *analysis*, 333
  *editors*, 162
  *index*, 314
  *mining*, 333
Text analysis, 311, 314
  *results*, 321
  *usage*, 320
Text join, 110, 112, 113, 135, 138, 144, 145, 194, 369
  *left outer join*, 113
Text mining, 311, 313, 314, 315, 322
  *capabilities*, 322, 333
Threshold value, 356
Time dimensions, 188
Time series, 328
Time-based calculation views, 189, 215
Time-dependent hierarchies, 207, 256
  *value help*, 257
Timeline view, 351
Trace configuration, 354
Traces, 171
  *SAP Web-based Development Workbench*, 171
Training courses, 26, 37, 38
  *BW362*, 29, 38
  *HA100*, 27, 32, 37
  *HA200*, 27
  *HA215*, 38
  *HA300*, 27, 32, 38
  *HA360*, 32, 38
  *HA400*, 29, 38
  *HA450*, 38
  *HA900*, 32, 38
  *SAPX05*, 38
Transaction Control Language (TCL), 273

Transaction manager, 77, 99
Transactional data, 135
Transact-SQL (T-SQL), 272
Transform, 471
Transient Provider, 537, 539
Translate, 367, 389
  *labels*, 389
  *Repository Translation Tool (RTT)*, 389
Transport, 374, 378, 393, 395
  *delivery unit*, 378
  *export and import*, 376
  *information models*, 368
TREAT expression, 324
Trigger, 479
Trusted data, 521, 534

**U**

UDF, 283, 284, 288, 300, 302
  *characteristics*, 294
Undelimited identifier, 274
Unicode, 274, 481
Union node, 200, 214
  *pruning configuration table*, 201
Union with constant values, 200
Unions, 104, 126, 129, 130, 136, 154, 345, 361
  *all*, 130
  *creating*, 277
  *pruning*, 362
  *with constant values*, 130
Universe, 534
User, 433, 437, 439
  *_SYS_REPO user*, 440
  *create*, 440
  *new*, 440
  *SYSTEM*, 439

**V**

Validation rules, 357, 369, 370, 390, 393
  *errors*, 371, 394
  *examples*, 369
Value help, 233
  *hierarchies*, 257
  *views*, 411, 424

Variables,  223, 238, 258, 261, 262, 279
   create,  239, 240
   modeling,  239
   types,  239, 258
Variance,  129
VDA,  405
View Editor,  355
Views,  101, 102, 103, 135, 136, 293, 449
   disappear,  105
   save,  105
Virtual classrooms,  36
Virtual data model (VDM),  403, 410
Virtual machines,  94
Virtual tables,  156, 184, 213, 251, 488,
   489, 495
   add,  491
   using,  492
   vs native tables,  489
Visualize Plan,  343, 348, 360, 363, 365
Visualize View in PlanViz Editor,  355

VMware,  52
VMware vSphere,  87, 94, 98

# W

Warm data,  79, 495
Web
   applications,  534
   services,  85, 502
Web-based development tool,  175
Weighted score tables,  329
Well-Known Binary (WKB),  325
Well-Known Text (WKT),  325
Where-Used,  385, 395
While loop,  281
With results view,  289
Workspace root,  165

# X

XML-based analytic privileges,  452